Obedience from First to Last

Princeton Theological Monograph Series
K. C. Hanson, Charles M. Collier, D. Christopher Spinks,
and Robin A. Parry, Series Editors

Recent volumes in the series:

Steven C. van den Heuvel
*Bonhoeffer's Christocentric Theology and Fundamental
Debates in Environmental Ethics*

Andrew R. Hay
God's Shining Forth: A Trinitarian Theology of Divine Light

Peter Schmiechen
*Gift and Promise:
An Evangelical Theology of the Lord's Supper*

Hank Voss
*The Priesthood of All Believers and the Missio Dei:
A Canonical, Catholic, and Contextual Perspective*

Alexandra S. Radcliff
*The Claim of Humanity in Christ: Salvation and
Sanctification in the Theology of T. F. and J. B. Torrance*

Yaroslav Viazovski
*Image and Hope:
John Calvin and Karl Barth on Body, Soul, and Life Everlasting*

Anna C. Miller
*Corinthian Democracy:
Democratic Discourse in 1 Corinthians*

Thomas Christian Currie
*The Only Sacrament Left to Us: The Threefold
Word of God in the Theology and Ecclesiology of Karl Barth*

Obedience from First to Last
The Obedience of Jesus Christ in Karl Barth's Doctrine of Reconciliation

EDMUND FONG

FOREWORD BY
MURRAY A. RAE

☙PICKWICK *Publications* • Eugene, Oregon

OBEDIENCE FROM FIRST TO LAST
The Obedience of Jesus Christ in Karl Barth's Doctrine of Reconciliation

Princeton Theological Monograph Series 242

Copyright © 2020 Edmund Fong. All rights reserved. Except for brief quotations in critical publications or reviews, no part of this book may be reproduced in any manner without prior written permission from the publisher. Write: Permissions, Wipf and Stock Publishers, 199 W. 8th Ave., Suite 3, Eugene, OR 97401.

Pickwick Publications
An Imprint of Wipf and Stock Publishers
199 W. 8th Ave., Suite 3
Eugene, OR 97401

www.wipfandstock.com

PAPERBACK ISBN: 978-1-5326-8302-2
HARDCOVER ISBN: 978-1-5326-8303-9
EBOOK ISBN: 978-1-5326-8304-6

Cataloguing-in-Publication data:

Names: Fong, Edmund, author. | Rae, Murray, foreword.

Title: Obedience from first to last : the obedience of Jesus Christ in Karl Barth's doctrine of reconciliation / by Edmund Fong ; foreword by Murray A. Rae

Description: Eugene, OR : Pickwick Publications, 2020 | Princeton Theological Monograph Series 242 | Includes bibliographical references and index.

Identifiers: ISBN 978-1-5326-8302-2 (paperback) | ISBN 978-1-5326-8303-9 (hardcover) | ISBN 978-1-5326-8304-6 (ebook)

Subjects: LCSH: Barth Karl—1886–1968. | Jesus Christ—Crucifixion—History of doctrines—20th century. | Jesus Christ—Resurrection—History of doctrines—20th century. | Reconciliation—Religious aspects—Christianity.

Classification: BX4827.B3 F65 2020 (print) | BX4827.B3 F65 (ebook)

Journal of Theological Interpretation 12, no. 1 (2018): 127–46. "'The One and the Many': Pondering the Hermeneutics of the Doctrine of the Atonement from the 'Reception of Doctrine' Approach." Edmund Fong. Copyright © 2018 by The Pennsylvania State University. This article is used by permission of The Pennsylvania State University Press.

All Scripture quotations, unless otherwise indicated, are taken from the HOLY BIBLE, NEW INTERNATIONAL VERSION. Copyright © 1973, 1978, 1984 by International Bible Society. Used by permission of Hodder & Stoughton Ltd, a member of the Hodder Headline Group. All rights reserved. "NIV" is a registered trademark of International Bible Society. UK trademark number 1448790.

Manufactured in the U.S.A. 03/11/20

To
Mei
Bone of my bones; Flesh of my flesh,
Sacrificial Mother,
Constant Companion,
Enduring Friend

Although he was a son, he learned obedience from what he suffered . . .

—Hebrews 5:8

Contents

Foreword by Murray A. Rae | ix

Acknowledgments | xi

List of Abbreviations | xiii

Introduction | 1

Part I: The "Backward" Movement of the Obedience of Jesus Christ

1. The Divine Obedience of the Eternal Son in the Theology of Karl Barth | 11

2. Divine Obedience and Trinitarian Ontology: Reading Karl Barth's Actualistic Ontology in the Light of the Obedience of the Eternal Son | 38

Part II: The Present Orientation of the Obedience of Jesus Christ as It Is in the Incarnation

3. The Obedience of Jesus Christ in Karl Barth's Christology in the *Church Dogmatics* | 87

4. Karl Barth's Reading of the Metaphysics of the Obedience of Jesus Christ | 126

5. The Spirit in Relation to the Son's Incarnate and Intra-Trinitarian Obedience to the Father | 156

6. The Obedience of Jesus Christ in Barth's Doctrine of the Atonement | 182

Part III: The "Forward" Movement of the Obedience of Jesus Christ

7   "The Obedient One, Obedient in Our Place": An Alternate Account of Barth's Doctrine of the Atonement | 231

8   "Freedom to Obey": Relating Divine Freedom and Divine Obedience, and Human Freedom and Human Obedience | 273

Conclusion | 315

Bibliography | 323
Index | 339

Foreword

THE OBEDIENCE OF JESUS Christ to the will of the Father is an explicit theme in Scripture that is frequently mentioned but rarely probed in depth. It is also a prominent feature of the doctrine of reconciliation that is central to Karl Barth's *Church Dogmatics*. Yet in this case too Barth's detailed consideration of the obedience of the divine Son has not occasioned much discussion in the extensive scholarly literature on Barth's theology. It has not been ignored, but neither has it been studied in any depth. What warrant might there be for a monograph such as this focused especially on Barth's account of Jesus' obedience to the Father? The first and obvious point to be made is that Barth himself considers it to be a matter of sufficient importance to warrant a full section of the *Church Dogmatics*. Section 59, accordingly, is titled "The Obedience of the Son of God" and extends for a full two hundred pages. Barth's extensive treatment of the matter provides its own justification for a careful and detailed study.

But we might put the matter another way. Suppose we compare the *Church Dogmatics* to a vast theological landscape. There are numerous features of the landscape that stand out and draw our attention and that have indeed been the focus of extensive study. But as with any landscape, if we shift our viewing angle and survey the scene from a less frequently visited vantage point, it is likely that new vistas will be opened up and at least some of the landscape's most prominent features will be viewed in a different light. So it is with this volume that Edmund Fong has delivered into our hands. To speak of the obedience of the divine Son, for example, and to project that obedience back into the intra-triune life of the Godhead, as Barth does, raises difficulties that can only be resolved, Fong argues, if we accept the actualistic ontology said to have been adopted by Barth and over which there has been much debate in recent years. Readers may not be persuaded by the conclusion that Fong draws, but attending to the matter through the lens of Christ's obedience to the Father adds fresh insight to the debate. New insights are offered too into the question of whether Jesus assumed fallen human nature, and, as might be expected in a study of Christ's obedience, into the question of whether the two natures of Christ entails that there is both a human and a divine will.

The volume as a whole, however, is concerned especially with how the obedience of the divine Son functions in Barth's understanding of the atonement. Christ the obedient Son is counted among the disobedient, takes the place of disobedient humanity, and yet precisely in doing so, he exercises the true obedience to which humanity is called. This takes us to the heart of the Gospel, to the drama of God's reconciling love in action. From this new vantage point, that of the Son's obedience, the saving work of God may be viewed afresh. The trajectory of the argument takes us back to Gethsemane where the obedience of the Son takes the form of prayer. That is fitting, of course, for the meaning of the Hebrew word *obed*, from which the English word obedience is derived, simply means "one who worships." Obedience is properly understood as the freedom to worship and to pray, to enter, that is, into that intimate communion with the Father which characterizes the life of the Son. That Christ is obedient in our place means, in the end, that such freedom is given also to us.

Edmund Fong offers us in this volume a sophisticated and searching examination of Barth's employment of the motif of the Son's obedience and offers us new insight not only into the intricacies of Barth's theology, but also into the work that Christ does for us.

Murray A. Rae

Acknowledgments

THIS VOLUME IN YOUR hands is an expanded version of a doctoral dissertation completed in 2017 at the University of Otago, Dunedin, New Zealand. As is the experience of all who have successfully undertaken doctoral studies, I remain in a debt of gratitude to the following, all of whom in one way or another contributed to this book coming to fruition:

My primary supervisor, Prof. Murray Rae, for his clear-minded and patient supervision. Murray's preference for concise and lucid prose has pushed my writing towards a clarity that I otherwise would not have achieved. His penetrating comments at various points served to clarify and strengthen the overall argument. All existing errors remain my own. I would also like to thank Murray for his commitment to the doctoral supervision. He generously granted me his time whenever I was in Dunedin. Throughout our interaction, Murray displayed a genuine care in my well-being that extended beyond the progress of the research.

My second supervisor, Prof. Roland Chia of Trinity Theological College (TTC), Singapore, for his warm friendship and encouraging supervision. I will always remember with fondness the times spent in his office talking about Barth, the thesis, and all things theological. It is with a great sense of excitement and privilege that I have come to serve alongside Roland as his fellow colleague, continuing to benefit from his guidance and knowledge.

My examiners, Prof. Oliver Crisp, Assoc. Prof. Paul D. Jones, and Rev. Assoc. Prof. Christopher Holmes, for their insightful comments and suggestions, all of which have led to the betterment of the original dissertation.

The team at Pickwick Publications—Matt Wimer, Charlie Collier, Jacob Martin and Calvin Jaffarian—for ensuring a smooth process in seeing the publication of this book to its very end.

Dr. Michael Mukunthan, Librarian at TTC, for kindly finding for me a dedicated workspace within the library during the period of research.

My friends, Daryl Ooi and Chin Gay Koh, who sacrificially took time from their busy schedules to read an earlier draft of the dissertation. Their comments are appreciated and it is my hope that they have found their time well spent in being introduced to the theology of Karl Barth.

The leaders of Adam Road Presbyterian Church (ARPC). The doctoral studies would not have been possible without the financial support of ARPC and their willingness to recalibrate my pastoral ministry involvement so that adequate time could be devoted to the research. I remain thankful to the leaders for their unprecedented generosity in continuing my financial support even as I have moved on to lecturing responsibilities at TTC.

My parents, Loon Siong and Louise, for their unfailing love and support. They have helped in more ways than one, from rendering practical support to their unceasing prayers for their children and grandchildren. Dad and mum, you have displayed in your life what Barth held dearly onto, that is, the best expression of our obedience to our Heavenly Father is revealed in the exercise of prayer.

Finally, I dedicate this work to my wonderful God-given wife, Mei. You are my cherished companion and soulmate, and I enjoy every moment that I have with you. I am mindful of how you sacrifice your personal interests for the family, and I thank you for your unwavering support towards my academic pursuits. Together with our beautiful children—Phoebe, Chloe, and Jonathan—you constantly serve as a reminder that the simple joy of life is to be found in the dear relationships that God has bestowed upon us.

Abbreviations

Works by Karl Barth

CD	*Church Dogmatics*
ChrL	*The Christian Life*: *Church Dogmatics, Volume IV, Part 4*
DO	*Dogmatics in Outline*
DG	*Dogmatik im Grundriss*
ET	*Evangelical Theology*
KD	*Die Kirchliche Dogmatik*

Other Works

I. *Sent.*	Thomas Aquinas, *Scriptum super libros Sententiarum, Book I*
AH	Irenaeus, *Against Heresies*
BTDB	*Baker Theological Dictionary of the Bible*
De potentia	Thomas Aquinas, *On the Power of God, Third Book: Questions VII–X*
Dem	Irenaeus, *Proof of the Apostolic Preaching*
Disputatio	Maximus the Confessor, *Disputations with Pyrrhus*
DLGTT	*Dictionary of Latin and Greek Theological Terms*
EDB	*Eerdmans Dictionary of the Bible*
Inst.	John Calvin, *Institutes of the Christian Religion*
NPNF	*Nicene and Post-Nicene Fathers*
Opusc.	Maximus the Confessor, *Opuscula theologica et polemica*
PDTT	*Pocket Dictionary of Theological Terms*
ST	Thomas Aquinas, *Summa Theologica*

Introduction

THE CLAIM COULD BE made that Swiss theologian Karl Barth (1886–1968) stands as one of the most prominent theologians of all time. His *magnum opus*, the *Church Dogmatics*, possesses a commanding presence that is hard to ignore. While it is difficult to pinpoint a single definitive center to the *Dogmatics*, most of Barth scholarship is agreed that Barth's conception of divine action provides an overall unity. Specifically, this divine action consists in God's act of "self-determination" within the divine election to be the God who is for humankind in Christ Jesus.[1] Given further that it is rebellious humanity in view, the theme of reconciliation is intrinsic to the very idea of God *pro nobis*. In this way, Barth's doctrine of reconciliation could be argued to form a unifying center for his theology. As Colin Gunton said, Barth's theology is "one directed to the articulation of God's purposes for . . . [the] realizing of salvation."[2]

Considering the centrality of the doctrine of reconciliation in Barth's theology, this volume aims to demonstrate the important function played by the motif of the obedience of Jesus Christ in his doctrine of reconciliation within the *Dogmatics*. Despite receiving a direct mention in the heading of Barth's substantial treatment of reconciliation—*CD* IV/1 §59 "The Obedience of the Son of God"—Barth's appropriation of the motif of Jesus' obedience has yet to be given the sustained and careful treatment it deserves.[3] The silence is curious indeed, and my intention of filling the lacuna serves as the major impetus for this volume.

Two preambles that guide our discussion deserve mentioning at this point. First, the scope of the study will be focused on the *CD*. Barth's *magnum opus*, by itself, presents more than sufficient material to work with. Second, the manner the study will be conducted follows more the lines of a

---

1. *CD* II/2, 3, 14.
2. Gunton, "Salvation," 143–58 (the quote is from p. 143).
3. To date, as far as to my knowledge, there has only been one unpublished monograph devoted to this topic: Martin, "Freedom to Obey," although the topic has certainly been discussed in other monographs and essays.

dogmatic than a chronological inquiry. Rather than sequentially considering the portions where Barth treats Jesus' obedience within the *CD*, our discussion is driven and shaped by doctrinal or theological issues related to Jesus' obedience arising from Barth's handling of the subject matter. The relevant theological issues to be raised, in turn, are organized and presented according to three broad sections that shape the thesis. All three sections deal with the three-dimensional orientation of Barth's treatment of the obedience of Jesus Christ. There is i) a "backward" direction in the unprecedented sense of drawing the incarnate obedience of Jesus back into the Godhead ii) a present orientation considering the nature of Jesus' obedience "as it is" in the incarnation, and iii) a "forward" direction showing how the obedience of Christ leads to the obedience of those who are reconciled. It will be seen that Barth's consideration of Christ's obedience intersects with other loci of his theology, namely, his Trinitarian doctrine, Christology, doctrine of the atonement, and theological ethics. The remainder of this introduction presents an overview of the chapters to follow.

Part I of the book consisting of the first two chapters focuses on Barth's unprecedented move in drawing the obedience of Jesus Christ "backwards" into the triune Godhead to relate it to the divine obedience shown by the eternal Son. A major consideration is to elucidate the implications such a move has on Barth's construal of Trinitarian ontology.

Chapter 1 highlights the two key points where Barth posits the Son's divine obedience to the Father in eternity: *CD* II/2 where Barth speaks of election, and the first section of *CD* IV/1 §59 "The Way of the Son of God into the Far Country." I contend that Barth faces an immense difficulty in positing an intra-Trinitarian obedience. Given that an act of obedience presupposes the submission of one will to another, Barth, with his notion of an intra-Trinitarian obedience, risks contravening his basic rubric of the Trinity as "one divine subject in three modes of being" possessing one will and one volition. Consequently, I maintain that the only way divine obedience within the triune Godhead can be upheld is by drawing upon what scholars have termed *a posteriori* as Barth's "actualistic ontology." In essence, actualistic ontology states that God being the triune God (i.e., the divine processions) is at one and the same instance his self-election to be the God who is for us in Christ Jesus (i.e., the divine missions). This reading allows the second mode of being of the triune God, the Son of God, to be conceived as eternally begotten by the Father who in the "moment" of eternal generation—if we can speak of a "moment" as such—is already immediately identified as the "pre-existent" God-man Jesus Christ. On this proleptic and actualistic account, the obedience rendered by the incarnate Lord *in time* is counted as that rendered by the Son *in eternity*, thus providing Barth legitimate leeway to posit the notion of the obedience of the eternal Son.

The above manner of speaking of divine obedience and actualistic ontology already draws into discussion the Trinity-election debate that has surrounded Barth studies over the past two decades.[4] In chapter 2, I weigh in on the debate. On the one hand, Barth's notion of the divine obedience of the eternal Son coheres and is consistent with his Trinitarian doctrine only if some form of an actualistic ontology framework is appropriated. On the other hand, I seek to faithfully represent what I deem to be Barth's thoughts on the matter, even as he withheld his definitive view, leaving instead throughout the *Dogmatics* a sizeable number of intermittent statements that could favor proponents on either side of the debate. Incorporating findings from four otherwise discrete areas—i) Aquinas' reading of the relation between the divine processions and the divine missions; ii) Barth's specification of the divine freedom, the divine knowing and willing; iii) Eberhard Jüngel's reading of divine ontology in engagement with Barth, and iv) Barth's view of time and eternity—I proffer the view that for Barth, the divine act of self-determination expressed in the divine election is ontologically and chronologically coincident and coterminous with God being the triune God. That is to say, Barth sees triunity and election as equally present to God. But in terms of logical priority, the evidence suggests that triunity takes precedence over election. I contend for this particular reading of Barth's actualistic ontology in chapter 2, and propose this reading as the framework within which Jesus' incarnate obedience is situated for the rest of our exploration.

Part II, consisting of chapters 3–6, considers the present orientation of the obedience of Jesus Christ "as it is" in the incarnation.

Chapter 3 looks at the function played by Jesus' incarnate obedience in Barth's Christology. Four culminating moments of Barth's Christology within *CD* are examined—*CD* I/2 §15 "Jesus Christ as *vere Deus, vere homo*"; *CD* II/2 §33 "Jesus Christ as electing God, elected man, and the electing man who elects God"; *CD* IV/1 "Jesus Christ, the Lord as Servant," and *CD* IV/2 "Jesus Christ, the Servant as Lord." In all four sections, Barth not only affirms Jesus' incarnate obedience as an authentic and genuine human act, but Jesus' obedience is found to underpin Barth's major Christological descriptions. The incarnate obedience of Jesus also corroborates the reading of actualistic ontology advanced earlier. This is seen especially under Barth's specification of the *communicatio operationum* in *CD* IV/2

---

4. For a good overview of the issues at hand that characterize the Trinity-election debate, see the collection of essays: Dempsey, *Trinity and Election*.

where the human obedience of Jesus Christ plays a co-participatory role—albeit one that is secondary and derived—in the "common actualization of the human and divine essences." This, Barth reminds us, is a determination undertaken not just at the point of the incarnation but in the eternal election of Jesus Christ. The operation of the "common actualization" gives the motif of the obedience of Jesus Christ a maximal function and role, one that stretches it even to God's self-determination of his divine being in the primordial act of divine election.

Chapter 4 continues the exploration of Jesus' obedience "as it is" in the incarnation by drawing into discussion three questions that have significant implications for how we conceive Jesus' obedience. They are: first, did Jesus assume a "fallen" or "unfallen" human nature in the incarnation? If the former, how does Barth absolve Jesus of (original) sin, considering the strong pedigree within the tradition of associating fallenness with sin? If the latter, how would that bear on the idea of Jesus' complete and total identification with those he came to save? Second, how did Jesus remain without sin? Was he, to express it in the common scholastic idiom, *posse peccare et non pecarre* (able to sin but did not sin) or was he *non posse peccare* (not able to sin)? Third, bearing in mind that Jesus was truly God and truly man, was it a case of Jesus submitting his single will to the Father, or Jesus subjecting his human will to conformity with his divine will? That is to say, did Barth espouse a monothelite or dyothelite position? And how would the position adopted affect the way we conceive Jesus' obedience? Naturally, the views of Maximus the Confessor will be engaged in discussing this topic of dyothelitism.

Chapter 5 picks up another crucial topic—Barth's pneumatology—and addresses the question, "What is the Spirit's role in Jesus' obedience?" The chapter explores the Spirit's activity at two levels: first, the incarnate obedience displayed by the Son in his life and ministry, and second, the intra-Trinitarian obedience of the Son to the Father in eternity. The chapter concludes with a constructive suggestion concerning the way the inner-triune relationships are conceived within the Western (Latin) model that Barth inherited. This suggestion complements and supports the actualistic ontology advanced within this study that frames the obedience of Jesus.

In chapter 6, the focal point narrows to the function Jesus' obedience has in relation to the atonement. I contend in chapter 6 that a proper reading of Barth's doctrine of the atonement must resist the impulse to begin straightaway at Barth's notable judicial account "The Judge judged in our place." Instead, one should begin where Barth himself located the atonement: as an event in God's triune being via his doctrine of election. I submit that inherent within Barth's doctrine of election is a substitutionary "pattern of exchange." This "pattern of exchange" already contains the actuality of the atonement, and Barth's formal doctrine of the atonement is but the vehicle of expression to convey this deeper actuality at play. It is just that Barth chooses the judicial framework. A side argument that arises at this point concerns Barth's openness to other frameworks or approaches that equally express this "pattern of exchange" in language other than that of the judicial. Seen in this light, the obedience of Jesus Christ is that which renders effective this substitutionary "pattern of exchange" in eternity within the decisive act of God's self-determination to be the triune God *pro nobis*. Chapter 6 also considers the criticisms that have been leveled against Barth, especially those pertaining to his doctrine of the atonement and the wider actualistic ontology it presupposes.

Part III of the book consisting of the last two chapters move the discussion "forward" by addressing how the motif of the obedience of Jesus Christ—under Barth's theological specification—can further discussion in two areas, that of the doctrine of the atonement and the issue of how Jesus' obedience relates to the notion of freedom.

Picking up a suggestion from the previous chapter, chapter 7 advances an alternative account of the doctrine of the atonement that centers on the motif of obedience as providing material content. That is, I specify an account of the atonement that goes under the rubric "Jesus Christ, the obedient one, obedient in our place." Following the same fourfold "for us" pattern that governed Barth's judicial account, I demonstrate how Jesus Christ can be conceived as i) the truly obedient one ii) the one counted as the disobedient one iii) the obedient and (counted as) disobedient one *in our place*, and iv) the one who acted in true obedience. The utility of this alternate approach to Barth's doctrine of the atonement is seen in the following two ways. First, this approach corroborates what I term a "narrative of obedience." Simply put, a narrative of obedience is a framework of understanding that capitalizes on the notion of obedience to offer an explanation as to what God is doing and intending with the divine economy of creation and salvation. At its core, this narrative specifies that God allows time to his most beloved part of creation, humankind, to nurture and develop to perfection the trait of obedience. I will expound in greater detail this narrative of obedience via one of its earliest proponents, Irenaeus of Lyons. Despite undeniable differences between Barth and Irenaeus, I seek to show that the alternative account of Barth's atonement doctrine centering on obedience supports and corroborates the basic form of this narrative of obedience. The second utility that the alternative account of Barth's atonement doctrine brings is that it provides a concrete picture for us to envisage how Jesus' obedience translates to our own obedience. This translation is seen especially under our consideration of the fourth aspect of Barth's fourfold pattern—Jesus Christ is the one who acted in true obedience. In exploring Barth's reading of the struggle that Jesus faced in seeking to obey God in the Garden of Gethsemane (*CD* IV/1, 259–73), our consideration reveals the novel turn that Barth takes in locating the source of Jesus' struggle, in the process accentuating even more Jesus' obedience.

In chapter 8, I turn to focus on a parallel concept that surfaces whenever obedience is mentioned, that is, freedom. My aim is to depict the relationship as Barth conceives between, on the one hand, divine freedom and divine obedience and, on the one hand, human freedom and human obedience. The progression of the argument is as follows: I begin by outlining specifications of the freedom-obedience relation as spelt out in philosophical discussions and show how the two notions are often conceived as antithetical. I then summarize what has been presented in chapter 2 earlier on Barth's understanding of divine freedom; this being a freedom-in-Godself that is simultaneously a freedom-for-creation-and-redemption-in-election. I further the train of thought by showing how such a specification of divine freedom already draws divine obedience into a complementary relation to divine freedom in such a way so as to say that divine freedom is fully and perfectly expressed in divine obedience. The third section of the chapter advances the overall argument by focusing on Barth's coordination of divine and human action. Here, I draw upon Barth's presentation of the theological basis for ethics as grounded in the divine election (*CD* II/2 §36) and his treatment of the *concursus Dei* (*CD* III/3). The key connection, once again, is Barth's actualistic equation of divine obedience with Jesus' incarnate obedience. If the divine election of Jesus Christ takes place so that we might be elected to respond in true human action and freedom *to* this electing God, and if the *concursus Dei* concerns the coordination of divine lordship with free and autonomous creaturely activity, then the center point from which we comprehend these two theological truths is the obedience of Jesus Christ in the divine election. The fourth stage of the argument reveals that Barth's key specification of obedience serving as a perfect expression of freedom rests upon his doctrine of the *analogia relationis*: as it is with the relation between divine freedom and divine obedience seen in Jesus Christ, so it is with the relation between human freedom and human obedience. That there is an *analogia relationis* in the first place is due to the fact that, for Barth, the determination of the human being occurs primally in the divine election of Jesus Christ. The final stage of the argument returns us to Gethsemane, where we see Barth upholding the notion that the chief expression of one's obedience and freedom is prayer, seen most clearly, once again in Jesus Christ. "[I]n this prayer of Jesus there took place quite simply the completion of the penitence and obedience which He had begun to render at Jordan and which He had maintained in the wilderness," Barth states.[5] To be the obedient one is to be the one deep in the exercise of prayer.

A conclusion provides a summative and definitive statement on Barth's unique contribution to our dogmatic understanding of Christ's obedience. In all, Barth himself highlighted the importance of the doctrine of reconciliation, saying: "To fail here is to fail everywhere. To be on the right track here makes it impossible to be completely mistaken in the whole."[6] This thesis seeks to show the pivotal role the obedience of Jesus Christ plays in guiding Barth along that track.

---

5. *CD* IV/1, 272.
6. *CD* IV/1, ix.

Part I

The "Backward" Movement of the Obedience of Jesus Christ

The Divine Obedience of the Eternal Son in the Theology of Karl Barth

> If the humility of Christ is not simply an attitude of the man Jesus of Nazareth, if it is the attitude of this man because . . . there is a humility grounded in the being of God, then something else is grounded in the being of God Himself. For, according to the New Testament, it is the case that the humility of this man is an act of obedience . . . . If, then, God is in Christ, if what the man Jesus does is God's own work, this aspect of the self-emptying and self-humbling of Jesus Christ as an act of obedience cannot be alien to God. But in this case we have to see here the other and inner side of the mystery of the divine nature of Christ and therefore of *the nature of the one true God—that He Himself is also able and free to render obedience*.[1]

WITH THESE WORDS, KARL Barth takes the humility and obedience of Jesus Christ and draws it "backwards" into the triune life of God, such that humility and obedience is said to belong to the very essence and being of God himself. That Jesus Christ is humble and obedient as the *Logos incarnatus* (the Word incarnated) is a fact that most, if not all, orthodox theologians are willing to assert. Fewer, however, are willing to follow Barth in intimating the unprecedented move that this humility and obedience is to be extended likewise to the eternal Son himself; understood within Barth's Trinitarian theology, to the one divine subject that the triune God is.[2] Some, in fact, see this particular move of Barth as uncalled for. G. C. Berkouwer, for example, deemed Barth's move to be "an unacceptable conclusion" and one that "can only be characterized as speculation."[3] Rowan Williams labelled Barth's climactic description of this intra-Trinitarian obedience in *CD* IV/1 as "one of the most unhelpful bits

---

1. *CD* IV/1, 193 (added emphasis).
2. Swain and Allen, "Obedience of the Eternal Son," 114, attribute the origination of this idea to Barth.
3. Berkouwer, *Triumph of Grace*, 304.

of hermetic mystification in the whole of the Dogmatics."[4] Kevin Giles called it "one of [Barth's] most colourful pieces of abstruse rhetoric in his *Church Dogmatics*."[5] Colin Gunton admits that the notion of God being obedient to God is a paradoxical and counter-intuitive concept, and views that Barth is "pushing the paradox as far as it will go."[6] Often, the disapproval flows from a perception that intra-Trinitarian obedience is inevitably entangled in some form of subordinationism—the ancient heresy.[7]

On the other hand, there has been a wave of Barth scholars in the recent two decades, led by Bruce McCormack, who have advanced the notion that from *CD* II/2 onwards and certainly by the time he reaches *CD* IV/1, Barth has revised his doctrine of the Trinity. Retaining the core center but modifying the edges, Barth allowed his doctrine of election to bear more significantly and directly on the being of the triune God. On their view, Barth's positing of an intra-Trinitarian obedience actually seals the argument. As McCormack argues, to say that obedience is essential to God is to take a willed act of self-determination "precisely as a determination of the divine essence."[8]

Clearly, why and how Barth develops the idea of divine intra-Trinitarian obedience, and whether he can finally maintain this idea in the context of his wider theology forms a pertinent topic in relation to the obedience of Jesus Christ. Our attention will be directed towards this task in the first two chapters of this volume. This chapter will expound on the idea of intra-Trinitarian obedience as it appears at two key junctures in *CD*: i) Barth's first discussion of the motif in *CD* II/2 where he considers election, and ii) his fully blossomed treatment in *CD* IV/1 §59 under his doctrine of reconciliation. Along the way, Barth's Trinitarianism, his doctrine of election, and the question of subordinationism will also be considered.

The argument advanced in this largely descriptive chapter is that Barth's positing of a divine obedience between the Father and the Son in the triune relationship makes good sense only when it is located against the backdrop of what Barth scholars have *a posterior* labelled as Barth's "actualistic ontology" that follows from his doctrine of election. Undoubtedly, the term calls for further explanation. Briefly stated, actualistic ontology

---

4. Williams, "Triune God," 129.
5. Giles, "Barth and Subordinationism," 345.
6. Gunton, *The Barth Lectures*, 164.
7. So for example, Jowers, "Reproach of Modalism," 246, states: "We object to Barth's idea of an eternal obedience rendered to the Father by the Son, a hypothesis introduced in *CD* IV/1 which undermines Barth's case against subordinationism set forth in volume I."
8. McCormack, "Trinity after Barth," 110.

is the conception of divine ontology that results when the divine act of God electing himself to be God for humanity in Christ Jesus is allowed to exert "ontological pressure" on the being of God. The pressure exerted, in turn, is seen to range across a spectrum. *Minimally* speaking, the divine act of election and the triune being of God are both equally primordial and "basic" to him. *Maximally* speaking, God so determines his own triune being in and through the course of the divine act of election.[9] The steps in Barth's thoughts leading to his full exposition of divine obedience and whether he can justifiably speak of this obedience will be treated in this chapter, while the ontological implications on the doctrine of the Trinity await the following chapter.

One final clarification on methodological procedure is in order. It might rightly be asked if a consideration of the obedience of the Son in his incarnation should precede that of the obedience of the eternal Son, that is, if part two of this volume should come before this present part. While acknowledging that such an approach would be closer and more faithful to Barth's "order of knowing"—the economic Trinity always reveals the immanent Trinity—I have reversed the order, beginning with the "order of being" and the immanent Trinity first. My reason for doing so is because Barth's actualistic ontology frames both discussions of obedience such that not only is the consideration of obedience in the eternal Son coherent only within that actualistic framework, the same could be said of Jesus' incarnate obedience. As we shall see in chapter 3, much of what Barth has to say about Jesus' incarnate obedience flows from this actualistic ontology. For the sake of pedagogical clarity and simplicity, I have chosen to begin with the obedience of the eternal Son first by way of leading us into a deliberation over Barth's actualistic ontology. In doing so, our consideration in the second major part of this thesis can focus on showing how Barth's actualistic ontology plays out in his explication of Jesus' incarnate obedience. That said, the methodological reversal is purely a pedagogical move and should not be misconstrued as a disagreement with Barth's own "order of knowing."

The Divine Obedience of the Son in CD II/2 §33 under the Doctrine of Election

It is in *CD* II/2 §33 where Barth asserts the claim of Jesus Christ being the electing God that we find his first explicit mention of an intra-Trinitarian

---

9. For a good summary of Barth's actualistic ontology and how it bears on his basic framework for theological ethics, see Nimmo, *Being in Action*, 4–12. Nimmo himself leans towards a maximal reading of Barth's actualistic ontology.

obedience.[10] I reproduce the following lengthy but consequential quote for our consideration:

> In the beginning, before time and space as we know them, before creation, before there was any reality distinct from God which could be the object of the love of God or the setting for His acts of freedom, God anticipated and determined within Himself (in the power of His love and freedom, of His knowing and willing) that the goal and meaning of all His dealings with the as yet non-existent universe should be the fact that in His Son He would be gracious towards man, uniting Himself with him. In the beginning it was the choice of the Father Himself to establish this covenant with man by giving up His Son for him, that He Himself might become man in the fulfilment of His grace. *In the beginning it was the choice of the Son to be obedient to grace*, and therefore to offer up Himself and to become man in order that this covenant might be made a reality. In the beginning it was the resolve of the Holy Spirit that the unity of God, of Father and Son should not be disturbed or rent by this covenant with man, but that it should be made the more glorious . . . . This choice was in the beginning. *As the subject and object of this choice, Jesus Christ was at the beginning.* He was not at the beginning of God, for God has indeed no beginning. But *He was at the beginning of all things, at the beginning of God's dealings with the reality which is distinct from Himself.* Jesus Christ was the choice or election of God in respect of this reality. He was the election of God's grace as directed towards man. He was the election of God's covenant with man.[11]

At first glance, the mention of "Son," "obedience" and "covenant" might lead one to conclude that Barth here envisages some form of an intra-Trinitarian *Pactum Salutis* ("covenant of redemption") located under the wider scheme of Covenant Theology. Allowing that Covenant Theology is not a monolithic scheme of thinking, there is nevertheless a commonality traced across the various strands, succinctly expressed in the following passage from Turretin:

> The pact between the Father and the Son contains the will of the Father giving his Son as *hypotroten* (Redeemer and head of his mystical body) and the will of the Son offering himself as a

---

10. It could be argued, however, that the grounds for Barth speaking of the divine obedience of the eternal Son have already been prepared under Barth's explication of the divine perfection of God's constancy in *CD* II/1, 490 onwards.

11. *CD* II/2, 101–2 (added emphasis).

sponsor for his members to work out that redemption (*apolytrosin*). For this the Scriptures represent to us the Father in the economy of salvation as stipulating the obedience of his Son even unto death, and for it promising in return a name above every name that he might be the head of the elect in glory; the Son as offering himself to do the Father's will, promising a faithful and complete performance of the duty required of him and restipulating the kingdom and glory promised to him.[12]

While there is a temptation to deduce that Barth is referring to the notion of a *Pactum Salutis*, a recollection of the basic contours of Barth's Trinitarianism and his own misgivings about Covenant Theology (articulated later in *CD* IV/1) will restrain such a preliminary conclusion. Barth's famous dictum that God *is* in his threefold repetition the one Subject three times—"not of three divine I's, but thrice of the one divine I"—[13] points to a clear and irrefutable understanding on Barth's part of the triune God as the one single subject in three modes of being (*seinsweisen*).[14] For Barth, it is paramount that with the one divine subject that the triune God is, there can only be one "personality" or "self-consciousness," rather than three individual "personalities" or centers of consciousness seated in each mode of being.[15] The one mind, one will and one energy of operation is "passed" in its entirety from the Father, through the Son, to the Holy Spirit so that it is equally shared by all three.

---

12. Turretin, *Institutes Vol. 2*, XII.ii.13, 177, quoted in Webster, "'Will of the Lord,'" 28–29.

13. *CD* I/1, 351.

14. *CD* I/1, 359. Barth's rejection of the traditional term "persons" in favour of "modes of being" is not without its own debate, with the issue centering on whether Barth's usage of *seinsweisen* leans him towards the ancient heresy of modalism. The following authors think not, although some question the appropriateness of Barth's usage of the term: Bromiley, *Introduction to the Theology of Karl Barth*, 16; Hunsinger, "*Mysterium Trinitatis*," 191n7, and "Karl Barth's Doctrine of the Trinity," 301; Torrance, "The Trinity," 72–89; Taylor, "In Defence," 33–46; and Jowers, "Reproach of Modalism." Letham, *Holy Trinity*, 289, defends Barth against charges of modalism, yet concludes: "There is this persistent ambiguity at the heart of Barth's trinitarianism that does not change. If he is not modalistic, he will escape from the charge of unipersonality only with the greatest difficulty." On the other hand, Ovey, "Private Love?," 198–231, argues that Barth's usage of the term does not free him from modalism as defined from patristic notions of the heresy.

15. It must be emphasized that in using the word "personality," Barth did not intend any relation to the word "person" (ὑπόστασις) as used in the church doctrine of the Trinity (*CD* I/1, 351). Instead, Barth sees embedded in the word "personality" the idea of self-consciousness (*CD* I/1, 357–58; *CD* IV/1, 205).

Defined this way, the difficulty of using the language of "obedience" to describe the relationship between the Father and the Son within the *Pactum Salutis* surfaces. The root of the difficulty has to do with terminology. The notion of obedience in itself calls for two distinct sets of consciousness, two rationally or intellectually operating appetites and wills, and obedience is realized only when there is freely willed activity on the part of one party to the other.[16] Take for example, when I ask my twelve-year old daughter to clean up the mess in her room: as an individual distinct from me, she needs to be conscious of what I am asking, to rationally process the command, and finally to will herself to do it (if only it was that simple!). Only under such conditions of a distinct and separately operating center of consciousness is obedience realized.[17]

Read in the above manner, the notion of an intra-Trinitarian *Pactum Salutis* is highly susceptible to portraying the relations as an encounter of wills, leading to a conception of the Father and Son as distinct centers of willing.[18] Certainly, this would run counter to Barth's underlying Trinitarianism. He himself deemed that the *Pactum Salutis* would inevitably push the understanding of the modes of being of Father and Son toward their being subjects in their own right with their individual distinct centers of willing—an idea he clearly rejected.[19] As Barth asserted in *CD* IV/1: "When the covenant of grace was based on a pact between two divine persons, a wider dualism was introduced into the Godhead . . . making it doubtful whether *in the revelation of this covenant we really had to do with the one will of the one God*."[20]

---

16. I am assisted in my definition of obedience by Mansini, "Humility and Obedience," 91–92.

17. Even in cases of "blind obedience" where there might not be a pronounced intellectual comprehension, there is still the distinct willing of another will.

18. Webster, "'Will of the Lord,'" 29, makes this comment while generally endorsing the concept of a "covenant of redemption."

19. Barth states in *CD* IV/1, 205 that the usage of the word "persons" in the doctrine of the Trinity "was never intended to imply . . . that there are in God three different personalities, three self-existent individuals with their own special self-consciousness, cognition, *volition*, activity, effects, revelation and name" (added emphasis). A conceptualization of the Trinity whereby Father, Son and Spirit each have their own centers of volition would gravitate heavily towards Social Trinitarianism. See Leftow, "Anti Social Trinitarianism," 204–5, where he states: "In most versions of [Social Trinitarianism], each Person has his own discrete mind and will, and 'the will of God' and 'the mind of God' are either ambiguous or refer to the vector sum of the Persons' thoughts and wills." Leftow further contends that Social Trinitarianism is unable to provide a satisfactory account of monotheism.

20. *CD* IV/1, 65 (added emphasis). For a fuller treatment of Barth's critique to Covenant Theology and a response, see McGowan, "Karl Barth and Covenant Theology," 113–35.

Inasmuch as the foregoing discussion clarifies that Barth was unlikely to be referring to any form of a *Pactum Salutis* between the Father and the Son, it does not alleviate the difficulties connoted in Barth's employment of the term "obedience." In fact, it heightens it. The critical question now surfaces clearly for Barth: if his reservation towards Covenant Theology flows from his concern about the persons of the Trinity being portrayed as separate centers of consciousness and willing, would not Barth in his usage of the term "obedience" to describe the relationship of the Son to the Father expose himself all the more to that very risk? Especially when it is has been shown that the act of obedience requires an operation of a distinct will? Clearly, in order to progress in this conundrum, we have to focus on *how* and *in what way* Barth attributes obedience to the Son without conflicting with his underlying Trinitarianism. But herein lies the difficulty. Nowhere in *CD* or in his wider writings does Barth explicate *how* the eternal Son can be obedient. Instead, he simply assumes and applies the axiom. Furthermore, Barth nowhere discusses the implications of predicating obedience to the eternal relations between the Father and Son for his doctrine of the Trinity.

Now, it could be said by means of a rejoinder that Barth might have found the question irrelevant or maybe even impertinent in the first place. In maintaining his methodological-epistemological axiom "There is no God behind the back of Jesus Christ," Barth would have consistently read what he sees in the economic Trinity—in this case the obedience of the incarnate Christ—back into the immanent Trinity, without deeming it necessary to further justify or defend his reading. While acknowledging this possibility, the notion of an intra-Trinitarian obedience does pose what I perceive to be a genuine difficulty and a legitimate question, especially given Barth's doctrine of the Trinity with its emphatic stress on a singular center of volition within the Godhead. It is left to his followers—and such is this volume's partial purpose—to reconstruct how Barth could have possibly envisaged the obedience of the eternal Son and the consequences ensuing from such a reading.[21]

The first possible reconstruction would involve challenging a key assumption I have made and to suggest that Barth did not see obedience as requiring another distinct seat of consciousness or volition. Hence, Barth felt free to employ the concept without thinking he was doing any violence

---

21. It is appropriate at this juncture to mention another work investigating the same theme of the eternal Son's obedience—Martin, "Freedom to Obey." Martin's main thesis is that Barth presents the obedience of Jesus Christ as correspondent and reflective of the obedience of the eternal Son within the triune relationships in the Godhead, a thesis I do not disagree with. But my main reservation is that she nowhere explores how the eternal Son can be described as obedient in the first place.

to his doctrine of the Trinity. So, under this view, when Barth speaks of the obedience of the eternal Son, he is merely using the term "obedience" as another way of describing what God as a single divine subject had decided to do in his singular volition, despite obedience being clearly portrayed here as rendered from one to another, presupposing the exercise of a separate volition in the process. One cannot deny that such a usage of the term "obedience" circumvents the conventional application of the word. That Barth was traveling in this particular direction is unlikely, and even if Barth were doing so, his usage of the term would have unfortunately been ill-suited and confusing, given how the term is conventionally perceived. I believe that Barth, being the brilliant theologian he was, would have avoided such carelessness, or at the very least, highlight that he was making such a move if he was indeed doing so.[22]

The second possible reconstruction would be to grant that Barth, in using the term "obedience," had full cognizance that it would imply a duality of volition and will. Yet he went ahead, confident that it would not bring about any detriment to his doctrine of the Trinity. This possibility requires us to turn our attention to two related questions of critical significance: what is the *context* under which Barth speaks of the Son rendering obedience? And *who* is this eternal Son who renders obedience to the Father? I suggest it is in answering these two questions that the conundrum of *how* Barth could attribute obedience to the eternal Son begins to be resolved.

Karl Barth's Doctrine of Election

As seen earlier, Barth's mention of the obedience of the Son occurs within his exposition of the doctrine of election as part of his doctrine of God, specifically with reference to Barth's adage that "Jesus Christ is both the electing God and the elected man."[23] A full demonstration of Barth's exposition of the doctrine of election is impossible within the short compass of this chapter, and we will return to this key doctrine in further chapters. What follows

---

22. This is the argument employed, although in part, by Sumner, "Obedience and Subordination," 130–46. Sumner considers that God's differentiation of an I and a Thou within the one divine life means that God has it within himself to "command" and to "obey" within the structure of that relation, without the necessary predication of two willing or volitional agents at work (141). Jones, *Humanity of Christ*, 212, also hints at this possibility. He reckons that Barth, in predicating divine obedience to the eternal Son as he relates to the Father, is intensifying and "sharpening" God's triune self-differentiation, moving beyond the category of "appropriation" and reconstituting the way in which God interrelates, while "not embracing anything like the idea of three 'centres' of consciousness."

23. *CD* II/2, 94 onwards.

instead is a listing of several related key insights intended to clarify *who* the eternal Son that renders obedience to the Father is.

First, the particular location of the doctrine of election within the *CD* indicates the central and pivotal role played by the doctrine in Barth's thinking. John Webster aptly described Barth's doctrine of election as the centerpiece of the doctrine of God and one of the most crucial chapters in *CD* as a whole. The doctrine sums up much of what Barth has said thus far and points forward to essential features of the doctrine of creation and reconciliation.[24] Barth himself acknowledged that he was the first theologian—as far as he was aware—to locate the doctrine of election in the doctrine of God.[25] In doing so, Barth instructs us in the right way to understand the subject matter of election from two converse perspectives, well-captured and expressed by Colin Gunton. First, any talk about the doctrine of election is really talk about who God is, and second, any talk about what the Christian means by God is to talk about the electing God. That is to say, the Christian God is one who elects.[26] Insofar that one agrees with the foregoing statement, one resonates with the reason that Barth described the election of grace as "the whole of the Gospel, the Gospel *in nuce*."[27]

Second, then, election for Barth is primarily not about something God *does*, as in issuing a decree, but concerns first and foremost *who* God *is* as He is turned to us in Jesus Christ.[28] Here, we see most clearly Barth's departure from his Reformed predecessors, who largely associated election with the *decretum absolutum*. This means that for Barth, election is, even before being about the election of man, something that God does *in*, *with* and *to* himself.[29] It is God's "self-ordaining of Himself,"[30] his "self-determination" identical with the decree of His movement towards man,[31] and his "self-giving."[32] Election is a movement bound within the realm of the grace of God and flowing from the very being of God Himself, who is—as Barth was fond of stating—the God who loves in freedom. For Barth, "the election of God consists in the fact that from all eternity, in an act of unconditional

---

24. Webster, *Barth*, 88.

25. *CD* II/2, 76. Barth goes on in the sub-section to examine and critique six other historical arrangements in terms of their placement of the doctrine of election (pp. 76–94).

26. Gunton, "Karl Barth's Doctrine of Election," 91.

27. *CD* II/2, 14.

28. Gibson, *Reading the Decree*, 30.

29. Gunton, "Karl Barth's Doctrine of Election," 92.

30. *CD* II/2, 89.

31. *CD* II/2, 91–92.

32. *CD* II/2, 121.

self-determination, He has ordained Himself the bearer of this name."[33] And that is the name Jesus Christ.

Third, this means election is fundamentally, according to Barth, an eternal, "primal and basic decision" (*Ur- und Grundentscheidung*) of God in which "He wills to be and actually is God,"[34] a decision occurring in the "beginning." Barth defines this "beginning" carefully as the "beginning of God before which there is no other beginning apart from that of God within Himself,"[35] a "beginning of God over against the reality which is distinct from Himself," and by which "time is founded and governed."[36] It is apparent that Barth views election as the eternal decision that leads to the founding of time and hence the beginning of God's dealings with a reality distinct from Himself. Election therefore can be described as the first of God's works *ad extra*, as an *opus internum ad extra* of the Trinitarian God (an internal work directed outside of himself).[37] More than that, Barth's doctrine of election reveals his underlying "actualistic ontology."[38] George Hunsinger in his seminal work *How to Read Karl Barth* defines "actualism" as referring to Barth's preference to speak of God in terms of the language of occurrence, happenings, events, decisions, history and act, rather than in the terms of metaphysical "substance" language.[39] While acknowledging Hunsinger's definition, I agree with Paul Nimmo that Barth's actualistic ontology goes much deeper and that "the true profundity of [Barth's] actualistic ontology lies in the statement that God in Godself is 'not another than He is in his works.'"[40] Understood this way, election is not just God's "self-determining" towards humanity, but is at one and the same time God's own "self-determining," so that, as Barth states, "the determination (*Bestimmtheit*) belongs no less to Him than all that He is in and for Himself."[41] In short, the essence of Barth's actualistic ontology can be summarized in

---

33. *CD* II/2, 100.
34. *CD* II/2, 76.
35. *CD* II/2, 94.
36. *CD* II/2, 99.
37. *CD* II/2, 25.

38. It must be stated at the outset that Barth nowhere uses the term "actualistic ontology" in *CD*. Rather, it is a term that later Barth scholars have derived and applied *a posteriori* to Barth to describe the particular ontology Barth adopts in his writing. See the following chapter for a deeper discussion.

39. Hunsinger, *How to Read*, 30–32. For reasons that we shall come to see later, Hunsinger prefers the term "actualism" to "actualistic ontology."

40. Nimmo, *Being in Action*, 7, quoting *CD* II/1, 260.

41. *CD* II/2, 7.

the following pithy statement of Barth's: "God *is* who He is in His works."⁴²
That much is true, but as we shall see in the following chapter, the on-going debate within Barth scholarship centers on how the "is" should be read: whether in a *constitutive* sense—God's works actually constitute who he is—or rather in the sense of *specification*—God's works reveal truly and in a consistent manner who he is.

Fourth, it follows consequently from the earlier three points that Jesus Christ is right at the "eternal beginning" of God and at the beginning of all things. Barth grounds this particular point via an excursus in which he exegetes John 1:1-2, contending that "the Word" (ὁ λόγος) is none other than Jesus Christ.⁴³ Barth concludes his excursus in the following manner:

> [I]n the name and person of Jesus Christ we are called upon to ... recognise the beginning of the Word and decree and election of God . . . . If this is so, then there is no higher place at which our thinking and speaking of the works of God can begin than this name. We are not thinking or speaking rightly of God Himself if we do not take as our starting-point the fact . . . that from all eternity God elected to bear this name. Over against all that is really outside God, *Jesus Christ is the eternal will of God, the eternal decree of God and the eternal beginning of God.*⁴⁴

The above four insights converge to lead to the key question under consideration: "Who is this eternal Son who renders obedience?" The logic of Barth's doctrine of election and the actualistic ontological framework flowing from it leads to the ineluctable answer—the eternal Son who renders obedience is the one mediator, the God-man Jesus Christ. Read this way, one could proceed to argue that in all of Barth's references to the "eternal Son," he is not envisaging an abstract, unknown eternal Son who is as-he-is, but rather the eternal Son who is as-he-is-in-view-of-his-incarnation. Stated differently: Barth is not conceiving an abstract, unknown, and unidentified *Logos asarkos*, but he is thinking of the *Logos asarkos* who is always the *Logos incarnandus* at the same time. That Barth follows this path becomes unmistakably clear when he states later in *CD* IV/1: "In this free act of the election of grace *the Son of the Father is no longer just the eternal Logos, but as such, as very God from all eternity He is also the very God and very man He will become in time.*"⁴⁵

---

42. *CD* II/1, 260 (added emphasis).
43. *CD* II/2, 95-99.
44. *CD* II/2, 99 (added emphasis).
45. *CD* IV/1, 66 (added emphasis).

The further implication, as John Thompson reminds us, is that for Barth, the Son of Man in his union with the Son of God existed in the divine counsel,[46] and that God purposed and willed from all eternity before the beginning of all creation and time as we know it to have the true humanity of Jesus Christ as the primary content of his eternal election of grace.[47] To press the point home: the true man Jesus was in the beginning with God, even prior to the dawn of his own time. It is in this sense that Barth speaks of the "pre-existing God-man."[48] As Eberhard Jüngel stated in his monograph *Gottes Sein ist im Werden*,[49] "The man Jesus, too, is already with God in the beginning in the primal history of the eternal covenant."[50]

A precaution, however, must be sounded at this point. The pre-existence of the God-man Jesus Christ in the beginning with God should not be conceived as implying the eternal existence of a "heavenly" man, or as Jüngel stated, a "projection of a temporal existence unto eternity."[51] Thompson shows us such a notion would contain a double error: i) implying creation was eternal along with this eternal man—an idea Barth repeatedly disavowed, and ii) saying the Son of God was united in the incarnation with an already existent man—an idea contrary to what has always been regarded as the traditional understanding of the hypostatic union.[52] Instead, the key as Jüngel propounds is to appropriate the doctrine of the *enhypostasis* and *anhypostasis* of the human nature of Jesus Christ.[53] Speaking of the temporal existence of Jesus in the sense of the *anhypostasis* would mean that "Jesus' existence would not be what it is if it were not *already* in the

---

46. Thompson, "Humanity of God," 255.

47. *CD* IV/2, 31; *CD* II/2, 116.

48. *CD* II/2, 110. The statement occurs in the context of Barth's agreement with Athanasius where Athanasius ascribed to the eternal Son of God a determination towards the elected man Jesus. Barth states: "The Subject of this decision is the triune God—the Son of God no less than the Father and the Holy Spirit. And the specific object of it is the Son of God in His determination as the Son of Man, the God-Man, Jesus Christ, who is as such the eternal basis of the whole divine election." It is interesting to note that the original German reads, "*der praeexistierende Gottmensch Jesus Christus*" (*KD* II/2, 118) and that the word "pre-existing" is interestingly missing in the English translation.

49. Jüngel, *Gottes Sein Ist Im Werden*; *ET* idem., *God's Being*. Future references will be to the *ET*.

50. Jüngel, *God's Being*, 95.

51. Jüngel, *God's Being*, 96.

52. Thompson, "Humanity of God," 257.

53. Jüngel, *God's Being*, 96. Webster, in his translation, defines *enhypostasis* as signifying that the human nature of Jesus subsists in the divine Word, while *anhypostasis* signifies that Jesus' human nature is not self-subsistent (see n. 88).

'eternal decision of God by which time is founded and governed.'"[54] And speaking of the temporal existence of Jesus in the sense of the *enhypostasis* would mean that "this existence really is temporal existence."[55] Jüngel here draws the doctrine of the *en-*and-*anhypostasis* of Jesus' human nature from how it is commonly understood and employed—in the incarnation of Jesus Christ in "the fullness of time" (cf. Gal 4:4)—and extends it retrospectively to the inner life of the triune God. The fact that God elects himself in eternity to be the God who is turned to us in Christ Jesus provides the basis for Jüngel to undertake this "retrospective" appropriation of the *en-*and-*anhypostasis* doctrine into the inner life of God. Although Barth himself nowhere explicitly employs the doctrine in this manner, his own discussion on the *en-*and-*anhypostasis* of Jesus' human nature indicates that the move suggested by Jüngel is neither inconsistent nor impossible within the terms of Barth's doctrine of God.[56]

The upshot of the above discussion pivotal to our central idea is this: the eternal Son who renders obedience is none other than the one mediator, the perfect God-man Jesus Christ. Specifically, *the obedience rendered is by the God-man Jesus Christ*. In the incarnation, the eternal Son comes to have a (human) volition and willing distinct from the one volition and willing common to all three modes of being of the Triune God. In virtue of the assumed human nature, the God-man Jesus Christ is now able to render obedience to the Father by aligning his human will to the divine will. This is a view taken to be orthodox and undisputed.[57] As seen from the preceding discussion, Barth's stress lies on an incarnation that can be described as "actualistically foreseen." First, "foreseen" in that the incarnation is viewed in an "anticipatory" sense prior to and thereafter in a "fulfilment" sense posterior to its actual occurrence in time and history. And second, "actualistic" in that this foreseeing is not in a "gnoseological" or "ideal" sense (i.e., only in the "mind of God"),[58] but that the very thing "foreseen" comes to implicate the being of the second person of the Trinity. The identity of God qua Son is now no longer without, but ontologically includes *the concrete life of Jesus Christ shown specifically in his obedience*

---

54. Jüngel, *God's Being*, 96. Jüngel quotes *CD* II/2, 99 (original emphasis).

55. Jüngel, *God's Being*, 96.

56. Barth's discussion on the *en-*and-*anhypostasis* is found in *CD* I/2, 163–65. We will further explore his treatment in chapter 3.

57. Mansini, "Humility and Obedience," 92, 95.

58. Jüngel, *God's Being*, 96.

unto suffering and death. In election and God's self-determination, the Son freely takes on an identity bound to his incarnate existence.[59]

Thus, in view of the above discussion, it can be safely read that when Barth speaks of the obedience of the Son as both the electing and elected one in *CD* II/2,[60] he is speaking of the obedience that the God-man Jesus Christ renders. This is an obedience that is foreseen and counted in a proleptic manner as concrete and actual, consistent with the actualistic ontological framework ensuing from Barth's doctrine of election. Insofar that Barth conceives the eternal Son as the God-man Jesus Christ, Barth speaks of the obedience offered by Jesus Christ as the Son's own *electing* and *decision* to be *the elected one*. As Barth himself states, the Son elects himself "to be man, and as man, to do the will of God."[61] It is in this sense that Jones affirms: "*Gehorsam* reaffirms an axiomatic claim: that Jesus Christ as 'electing God' is none other than the divine Son of the Father."[62]

This is what Barth does in *CD* II/2. If Barth had simply stopped here, his account of the obedience of the eternal Son would have been congruous with his wider theology, and it would not pose any significant challenges. But Barth carries on in *CD* IV/1 to take the melody of the eternal Son's obedience and transpose it to an even higher key, linking the obedience to the eternal generation of the Son within the immanent relations in the triune Godhead. It is to this notion that we must now turn our attention.

The Divine Obedience of the Son in CD IV/1 §59 under the Doctrine of Reconciliation

With *CD* IV/1–3, we arrive at Barth's doctrine of reconciliation. That what has been termed "Barth's mature Christology" is integrated at this point with his doctrine of reconciliation is no mere happenstance. Rather, such a deliberate move speaks pointedly against accounts that frequently separate the person of Christ and his work. On Barth's account, "the person of Christ *is* his saving work, so that an adequately articulated Christology will also be a theology of salvation," as Gunton states.[63] In fact, Barth's integration of topics extends beyond that of Christology and soteriology to include

---

59. Jones, *Humanity of Christ*, 207.
60. *CD* II/2, 101–2, 105.
61. *CD* II/2, 105.
62. Jones, *Humanity of Christ*, 206.
63. Gunton, "Salvation," 144. Webster, *Barth*, 116, states that Barth's treatise seeks to defy "christological or soteriological abstraction." See also Holmes, "Person and Work of Christ," 37–55, for a discussion and evaluation of Barth's move.

hamartiology, pneumatology, ecclesiology and a theology of the Christian life. The integration is woven into his presentation of the material, with the result that the entire volume forms nothing less than a beautiful architectonic presentation of the person and work of Christ.[64]

It is within the context of Barth's doctrine of reconciliation and his mature Christology that we find Barth's climactic description of the obedience of the eternal Son, under the first sub-section of §59 entitled "The way of the son of God into the far country."[65] The allusion to the parable of the prodigal son in the title is obvious (Luke 15:11-32), but it is not until the following part-volume that Barth makes his reference to the parable explicit.[66] Barth clarifies that if the focal point of *CD* IV/2 is on the homecoming and exaltation of the Son, then the focus of *CD* IV/1, in particular §59, is on the humiliation of the Son of God expressed appositely in his (eternal) obedience.

The theme of humility and obedience hence dominates the first sub-section of §59. Barth begins with a reminder that the atonement is the "very special history of God with man . . . [and] of man with God."[67] In considering this history, Barth locates the first aspect under the condescension of God, where he affirms the following four points of logical progression.[68]

First, Barth presents the one whom the New Testament calls "Lord" as none other than the man Jesus who, as the Son of God, is obedient to the will of the Father. At this point, Barth indicates an early stirring of an idea he will develop more fully: "The true God—if the man Jesus is the true God—is obedient. We have to keep before us the difficulty of this equation if we are to be clear what we have to understand and to accept or reject as the content of the New Testament witness to Christ."[69] Second, Jesus' obedience as the Son of God must be understood in the context and fulfilment of Israel as the son of God and the obedience concomitant with Israel's sonship.[70] Yet, Barth acknowledges Jesus' sonship as of a higher divine order, and proceeds to describe God in terms of a command-obedience relation: "He is not only the One who commands, but the One who is called and pledged to obedience."[71]

---

64. A helpful schematic diagram of the order of presentation of *CD* IV/1-3 can be found in Jüngel, *Karl Barth*, 48-49.

65. *CD* IV/1, 157.

66. *CD* IV/2, 21-25.

67. *CD* IV/1, 157.

68. *CD* IV/1, 158.

69. *CD* IV/1, 164.

70. *CD* IV/1, 166-70.

71. *CD* IV/1, 170.

Third, Jesus as the Son of God in obedience to the Father and in fulfilment of his Israelite vocation exists in solidarity with sinful Israel, going to the extent of being negated by God, and standing under the wrath and judgment of God.[72] Fourth, the history of Jesus is also the history of God. That is to say, what Jesus the God-man experiences, God experiences.

The foregoing discussion culminates in Barth's resolute principle that governs his understanding of God's work of reconciliation and revelation: "Who the one true God is, and what He is, i.e., what is His being as God, and therefore His deity, His 'divine nature,' . . . all this we have to discover from the fact that as such He is very man and a partaker of human nature, from His becoming man, from His incarnation and from what He has done and suffered in the flesh."[73]

From this point, Barth moves to consider what he deems to be the two movements which encompass the Son's obedience of suffering: an "outer" movement seen in his self-humiliation and his way into "the far country" terminating in his death on the cross, and an "inner" movement whereby the Son renders obedience to the Father.[74] Barth's point is that *the outer movement is predicated upon the inner movement*; hence he deals with the second and "outer" movement first. In his treatment, Barth is guided by his leading question, "*Quo iure Deus homo* (How is it that God became man)?"[75] Barth emphasizes that the incarnation does not contradict God's divine nature; in fact, it corresponds to that nature which is to love in freedom. God's divine constancy or immutability does not occlude this possibility.[76] Barth contrasts our difficulty to grasp this concept with his own *modus operandi*:

> If we think that this is impossible it is because our concept of God is too narrow, too arbitrary, too human—far too human. Who God is and what it is to be divine is something we have to learn where God has revealed Himself and His nature, the essence of the divine. And if He has revealed Himself in Jesus Christ as the God who does this, it is not for us to be wiser than He and to say that it is in contradiction with the divine essence.[77]

---

72. *CD* IV/1, 172–75.
73. *CD* IV/1, 177.
74. *CD* IV/1, 177.
75. *CD* IV/1, 184.
76. *CD* IV/1, 187.
77. *CD* IV/1, 186.

In summary, the essence of what Barth is saying is captured in the following succinct but memorable expression of his: "God gives Himself, but He does not give Himself away."[78]

Having treated the "outer" movement of the Son's obedience, Barth continues with the "inner" movement, which forms the focus for our discussion in this chapter.[79] The preceding discussion has laid the foundation for Barth to flow seamlessly to his bold assertion captured in the opening quote of this present chapter—if Jesus is obedient, and if it is only in Jesus Christ that we come to understand the divine nature, then God in his eternal divine nature must also be able to render obedience.[80] Barth immediately acknowledges the difficulty and even the elusiveness of speaking of an obedience that takes place within God:

> Obedience implies an above and a below, a *prius* (before) and a *posterius* (after), a superior and a junior and subordinate. Obedience as a possibility and actuality in God Himself seems at once to compromise the *unity* and then logically the *equality* of the divine being. Can the one God command and obey? Can the one God be above and below, the superior and the subordinate? If we speak of an obedience which takes place in God, do we not have to speak necessarily of two divine beings, and then of two beings who are not equally divine, the first and commanding properly divine, the second and obeying only divine in an improper sense?[81]

Barth recognizes that the difficulty stated above has led to an alternate way of speaking of obedience within God, but one that he considers erroneous. That is, the whole sphere by which obedience occurs is relegated to, as Barth states, "a kind of forecourt of the divine being," to a dispensation or economy which is only in relation to the world and having nothing to do with the true and proper being of God.[82] Barth labels the first error of speaking of two divine beings that are unequal in their divinity as "subordinationism," and the second error of not allowing obedience to be a true attribute of the divine being as "modalism."[83]

---

78. *CD* IV/1, 185. Barth's treatment of the "outer" movement of the Son's obedience includes a fine discussion on other topics of minor relation, for example, the *Extra Calvinisticum* (180–81), theories of *kenosis* (181–83) and the implications of Jesus' humility and obedience on New Testament ethics (188–92).

79. *CD* IV/1, 192.

80. *CD* IV/1, 193.

81. *CD* IV/1, 195 (added emphasis).

82. *CD* IV/1, 196.

83. A working definition of "subordinationism" and "modalism" especially as Barth

In confronting these two errors, Barth appeals to three presuppositions following from his earlier findings. First, *God himself* must be the acting subject in the work of reconciliation between the world and himself. Second, God's activity of reconciliation must be the most proper, direct and immediate *presence* and *action of God himself* in the sphere of human and world history. And third, God's presence and action as reconciler *is* the existence of the humiliated and lowly and obedient man Jesus of Nazareth.[84] The first presupposition rules out subordinationism, the second modalism, and the third further bolsters Barth's case. The logical weight of the three presuppositions presses Barth to say further: "We have not only not to deny but actually to affirm and understand as *essential* to the being of God the offensive fact that there is in God Himself an above and a below, a *prius* and a *posterius*, a superiority and a subordination."[85] The key word stressed is "essential"—Barth sees the obedience that takes place within the eternal Godhead as essential to who God is, and not just accidental. This explains why Barth stated earlier that the obedience of Christ is the "dominating moment in our conception of God."[86]

Because Barth is cognizant that any talk of obedience within the triune God risks compromising the unity of the Godhead, he pushes on in his argument to advance the notion that divine unity, far from prohibiting a relation of obedience, consists actually in the fact that "in Himself [God] is both One who is obeyed and Another who obeys."[87] The key to grasping this seeming paradox lies in freeing ourselves from two unfortunate ways of thinking about unity. The first has to do with the thinking that associates unity simplistically with "being in and for oneself," with the notion of "singleness and solitariness" and hence the inability to accommodate another.[88] Barth asserts that such is not the divine unity. Rather, the divine unity "is a unity which is open and free and active in itself—a unity in more than one mode of being, a unity of the One with Another, of a first with a second,

---

understands them is necessary at this point. According to Giles, "Barth and Subordinationism," 328, "subordinationism" involves the error of the "eternal dividing and separating of the divine three [persons] in being/essence *and* power/authority, thereby creating a hierarchical model of the Trinity." The significant point is that the second divine being is of *lesser* divinity. "Modalism" on the other hand, as used by Barth here, involves regarding the deity of the humiliated and lowly Christ merely as a mode of *appearance* or activity of the one true Godhead whose true being is otherwise unknown (*CD* IV/1, 196).

84. *CD* IV/1, 197–99.
85. *CD* IV/1, 200–201 (added emphasis).
86. *CD* IV/1, 199.
87. *CD* IV/1, 201.
88. *CD* IV/1, 202.

an above with a below, an origin and its consequences."[89] Barth questions whether within this understanding of unity the concept of subordination necessarily involves inferiority and therefore deprivation and lack—that would be more of "subordinationism." Instead, Barth submits that subordination within the unity of the Godhead involves an "inner order" whereby there exists a downward direction possessing its own similar dignity and significance.[90] The upshot of Barth's discussion is that he repudiates "subordinationism" while endorsing "subordination."[91]

With this definition of divine unity in mind, Barth carries on to write one of his most eminent paragraphs expressing the dynamics of an eternal obedience existing within the oneness of the triune Godhead:

> As we look at Jesus Christ we cannot avoid the astounding conclusion of a divine obedience. Therefore we have to draw the no less astounding deduction that in equal Godhead the one God is, in fact, the One and also Another, that He is indeed a First and a Second, One who rules and commands in majesty and One who obeys in humility. The one God is both the one and the other. And, we continue, He is the one and the other without any cleft or differentiation but in perfect unity and equality because in the same perfect unity and equality He is also a Third, the One who affirms the one and equal Godhead through and by and in the two modes of being, the One who makes possible and maintains His fellowship with Himself as the one and the other. In virtue of this third mode of being He is in the other two without division or contradiction, the whole God in each. But again in virtue of this third mode of being He is in neither for itself and apart from the other, but in each in its relationship

---

89. *CD* IV/1, 202.

90. *CD* IV/1, 202.

91. Others like Letham, *Holy Trinity*, 400, take it a step further, preferring to use the word τάξις (order) instead of subordination. See also Tolliday, "Obedience and Subordination," 138–60, who argues that Barth was more willing to posit a subordination (though not subordinationism) of the Son to the Father following his doctrine of election than he was in his earlier Trinitarian doctrine in *CD* I/1. It is equally important at this point to mention that Barth's understanding of "subordination" within the triune Godhead differs widely from that of the on-going theological movement of "the eternal subordination of the Son" advocated by the likes of Ware, *Father, Son, and Holy Spirit*. McCormack, "God Who Graciously Elects," highlights that the model of Trinitarianism assumed by those who support the eternal subordination of the Son veers towards that of Social Trinitarianism, which clearly is at odds with Barth's own Trinitarian rubric. Darren Sumner's comment in this regard is notable: "When Barth speaks of God the Son's obedience to the Father even in the inner life of God, Barth means something *completely different* by it" (Sumner, "Some Observations").

to the other, and therefore, in fact, in the totality, the connexion, the interplay, the history of these relationships.[92]

To take stock for a moment, an isolated reading of CD IV/1 might leave one with a similar chief question from CD II/2: *how* can Barth attribute obedience to the Godhead *ad intra*, even if it is from one mode of being to another, without doing violence to his doctrine of the Trinity? Here, I emphasize the point that Barth's positing of divine unity as being able to accommodate another—even allowing for a notion of subordination within that unity—will not be sufficient to dispel the difficulty flowing from the above question.

In reply, the above question proves once again the importance of reading Barth within his complete oeuvre, or at least, to allow the different part-volumes of the *Dogmatics* to illuminate each other. When Barth's treatment of the eternal obedience of the Son in his election in CD II/2 bears on his account here in CD IV/1, a plausible answer is provided to the pressing question above. The eternal Son—the main protagonist in the "drama of obedience"—is not the abstract, unknown, eternal Son. But, because of God's self-ordaining and self-determining in his divine election, he is already from all eternity "the very God and very man He will become in time."[93] In line with Barth's actualistic way of thinking, the human obedience rendered by this very God-man is already "foreseen" and adjudged to be concrete and actual in eternity before the dawn of its time, and counted as "divine obedience."

Now, had Barth stopped here, he would have produced a compelling account of eternal obedience within the divine Godhead, although not above criticism. However, Barth does not end here, but in his move to ground the obedience of the incarnate Son in the being of God himself, Barth lifts the notion of eternal obedience to its climactic high point and *links the obedience to the eternal generation of the Son by the Father*. Barth's move in effect instates obedience as something that characterizes the eternal relation between the Father and the Son in both its distinctness and its reciprocity. The immediate mentioned notion is captured in the critical passage reproduced below:

> The One who in this obedience is the perfect image of the ruling God is Himself . . . God by nature, God in His relationship to Himself, i.e., God in His mode of being as the Son in relation to God in His mode of being as the Father, One with the Father and of one essence. In His mode of being as the Son He fulfils

92. CD IV/1, 202–3.
93. CD IV/1, 66.

> the divine subordination, just as the Father in His mode of being as the Father fulfils the divine superiority. *In humility as the Son who complies, He is the same as is the Father in majesty as the Father who disposes. He is the same in consequence (and obedience) as the Son as is the Father in origin. He is the same as the Son, i.e., as the self-posited God (the eternally begotten of the Father as the dogma has it) as is the Father as the self-positing God (the Father who eternally begets).* Moreover in His humility and compliance as the Son He has a supreme part in the majesty and disposing of the Father. The Father as the origin is never apart from Him as the consequence, the obedient One. The self-positing God is never apart from Him as the One who is posited as God by God. The One who eternally begets is never apart from the One who is eternally begotten. Nor is the latter apart from the former. The Father is not the Father and the Son is not the Son without a mutual affirmation and love in the Holy Spirit. The Son is therefore the One who in His obedience, as *a divine and not a human work*, shows and affirms and activates and reveals Himself—shows Himself to be the One He is—not another, a second God, but the Son of God, the one God in His mode of being as the Son.[94]

Barth clearly raises the stakes in the above passage by siting the obedience of the Son in his being eternally begotten by the Father, or in what is otherwise classically termed "the divine processions." Furthermore, the difficulty is intensified with Barth's identification of this obedience as a "divine and not a human work."

A person who takes issue with this particular move is Roman Catholic theologian Thomas Joseph White, OP.[95] White argues that the coupling of the notion of obedience to the eternal generation of the Son, such that obedience comes to characterize the divine procession of the Son from the Father, inevitably obfuscates the unity of, first, the divine will and, second, the power of God. For White, this undermines and renders problematic Barth's assertion of the incarnate Son sharing in the same deity as the Father.[96] The following briefly delineates White's argument.

Because the one divine nature subsists *hypostatically* in the three Trinitarian persons or modes of being, the divine persons or modes of being

---

94. *CD* IV/1, 208–9 (added emphasis).

95. White, "Intra-Trinitarian Obedience," 377–402, reprinted in *The Incarnate Lord*, 277–307.

96. White, *The Incarnate Lord*, 280.

can only be distinguished by their relations of origin.[97] It follows then that whatever "founds" the relations of origin in God can serve as the principle to distinguish the modes of being in God. The fact that Barth posits obedience as "founding" the relations of origin between the Son and the Father and hence the way of distinguishing the modes of being in God eternally means that, for Barth and according to White, "the relationship of commanding and subordinate obedience is . . . constitutive of the divine nature and 'deity' of God as triune."[98]

Herein lies the difficulty for White: if the Son is characterized in all that he is—in his constitution as a mode of being—by obedience, such that "[t]here is nothing in him that is not consent of will to another," how then can the Son simultaneously possess in himself eternally the unique omnipotent will of God?[99] In this case, the consent of the will of the Son to the Father becomes the defining key in distinguishing the modes of being and hence the nature of the Godhead. The will to be *received in* and *consented to* by the Son forms the foundation for the Son's procession and differentiation from the Father as Son and Word.[100] In other words, the issue at hand has to do with the question of the unity of God's will, which as White sees it, leads to a compromise of the Son's omnipotence. If obedience characterizes the very procession of the Son from the Father, it would mean that the Son is not able to possess the will of the Father in a plenary fashion. But conversely, if the Son is omnipotent, there would be no need for the Son, in his procession from the Father and in his entire mode of being, to be characterized by consent to another's will, which lies at the center of the notion of obedience. This leads White to state: "We must rethink the claim to eternal obedience in the Son, or else qualify in important ways any affirmation of his omnipotence."[101] Other scholars have joined in the chorus of voices

---

97. White, *The Incarnate Lord*, 290. In fact, White further reminds us via Thomas Aquinas that these same "subsistent relations" of the persons of God themselves constitute the inner life of God, and in that sense, they are the divine nature itself (otherwise one would end up with the divine nature being a fourth hypostasis!)

98. White, *The Incarnate Lord*, 291.

99. White, *The Incarnate Lord*, 296.

100. White, *The Incarnate Lord*, 297.

101. White, *The Incarnate Lord*, 298. White does allow for another possibility as to how Barth can predicate obedience eternally to the divine Godhead. Suppose that God, who is omnipotent in the mode of being as Father, chooses to "void" himself of the attribute of omnipotence as a condition for being in the mode of being of the Son. This would, however, involve a theory of voluntary kenosis and drawing it back to eternity, leading to a Trinitarian antinomy in Barth's thinking and further complications. In any case, in this route, one would have simply taken a "nineteenth-century kenosis theory" and "displaced [it] from time into eternity" (297–98; 300).

expressing concern over Barth's move of tethering the divine obedience of the Son to his eternal generation, in particular the implications it holds for his doctrine of the Trinity.[102]

By way of review, I empathize with White's concern that an intra-Trinitarian obedience attached to the Son's eternal generation threatens the unity of the one divine will within the three modes of being of the triune God. In fact, it is this concern that I have largely sought to address in seeing how Barth could coherently posit an intra-Trinitarian obedience. However, I fail to see as White does how a will received from the Father and consented to by the Son compromises the Son's omnipotence. Furthermore, I surmise that Barth likewise would not agree with White on this particular point.

The ingenuity that Barth brings to discussions on the doctrine of God via his actualistic ontological thought lies in the fact that God's being and essence—who God is and what He is like—is determined in his act, specifically, the act of becoming incarnate in the God-man Christ Jesus. Omnipotence then, for Barth, is not defined metaphysically in "substance" language *a priori*. Rather, omnipotence is defined by the one divine eternal act of election whereby God self-elects himself to be the God turned toward us in Christ Jesus. This is why Barth can say:

> God was always the One whose condescension showed itself to be unlimited in the suffering and death of the man Jesus . . . . *The Almighty exists and acts and speaks here in the form of One who is weak and impotent*, the eternal as One who is temporal and perishing, the Most High in the deepest humility. The Holy One stands in the place and under the accusation of a sinner with other sinners. The glorious One is covered with shame. The One who lives forever has fallen a prey to death. The Creator is subjected to and overcome by the onslaught of that which is not. In short, the Lord is a servant, a slave.[103]

102. Giles, "Barth and Subordinationism," 344, similarly struggles over this point of *CD* IV/1 and questions if subordinationism is ultimately introduced into Barth's thinking. He concludes that Barth's understanding of the triune God as high and humble and of the Son as subordinated, obedient and suffering "reaches breaking point," opening up "profound tensions for his doctrine of the Trinity." In the last resort, Barth "resorts to convoluted, poetic language in which he speaks of "a subordination in God himself," which has led some to think he is actually endorsing the eternal subordination and obedience of the Son," but Giles demurs, basing his conjecture on Barth's earlier doctrine of God (346). Williams, "Triune God," 129, allows for Barth's trinitarianism in *CD* IV/1 to move towards a much more "pluralist" conception of the Trinity than was the case in *CD* I/1. Jones, *Humanity of Christ*, 208, states that Barth, in this particular move, is radicalizing the "immanent" distinctions between God's first, second and third ways of being, and at the very least, redefining his doctrine of God.

103. *CD* IV/1, 176 (added emphasis).

In Barth's mind, far from obedience compromising God's omnipotence, the reverse seems to be the case: it is through the Son's obedience that he exercises the divine omnipotence.

Nonetheless, White's basic concern of intra-Trinitarian obedience compromising the unity of the one will and volition in the triune Godhead is one that I fully share with him. I would like to suggest, however, that Barth's actualistic ontology does create the (logical) space for him to maneuver and to maintain *to a certain point* the idea of an eternal obedience in the Son, *even when this obedience is tethered to his eternal generation from the Father*. Such a maneuver, however, would require Barth to grant unconditionally that in the eternal divine processions characterizing the triune God, *the Father already begets the Son from all eternity and primordially as the "pre-existent" God-man Jesus Christ*. In line with Barth's actualistic ontology, this eternally begotten Son, with his (proleptic *an-*and-*enhypostatic*) human volition, is seen to render obedience to the Father from eternity.[104] Clearly, this position takes us to the farthest edge of Barth's actualistic ontology possible, stretching his manner of speaking of intra-Trinitarian obedience to its limit. But I maintain that it is still a legitimate assertion that can be contained within the framework of Barth's actualistic ontology.

Without resorting to Barth's actualistic ontology, is there another way of accounting for an intra-Trinitarian obedience that takes place within the divine Godhead? White contends there is, and offers what he terms "a more benign (re)interpretation."[105] If Barth's impetus in positing eternal obedience is to anchor Jesus' incarnate economic obedience to some "ground"[106] or "ontological presupposition"[107] within the pre-temporal being of Godself, then one possibility as White states,

> is to consider the Son's origination from the Father *alone* as *a sufficient condition* for the filial character of his economic mission. In this case, God the Son receives and possesses from the Father the unique divine nature, power, and will of God from all eternity. This divine receptivity in turn acts as the transcendent ontological foundation for the temporal mission of Christ.[108]

In the above interpretation of divine obedience, the obedience of Christ is "segregated" and pertains to his human nature only, hence not

---

104. I think White himself recognizes the possibility of this potential resolution. See White, *The Incarnate Lord*, 298n44.

105. White, *The Incarnate Lord*, 280.

106. *CD* IV/1, 193.

107. White, *The Incarnate Lord*, 280.

108. White, *The Incarnate Lord*, 301 (original emphasis).

characterizing the eternal life of the Son as deity. As such, it does not stand at the origin of the Son's being eternally begotten by the Father. Rather, the divine procession of the Son from the Father results in and is characterized by an eternal relativity expressed in a *filial receptivity* whereby the Son receives from the Father the one divine life, power, and will. It is this *filial receptivity*, this *receptive character* of the mode of being of the Son with respect to the mode of being of the Father that provides the basis and ontological presupposition for the Son's obedience in his temporal mission. The upshot of this interpretation is that in his eternal mode of being, the Son's actions of obedience transpire *only* historically in his incarnation, and can *only* do so because of his human agency.[109] Yet, these human actions always work in a theandric manner to reveal Jesus' filial relation to the Father, and the presence in him of a divine will received from the Father. In short, White's benign (re)interpretation of Jesus' obedience locates the (eternal) ground and basis of that obedience *not in an obedience-command relation* but in *a filial-paternal receptivity* that characterizes the divine procession of the Son from the Father within the triune life of God.[110]

In certain respects, White's (re)interpretation is accurate. Barth's actualistic ontology enables him legitimately to speak of the incarnate obedience of the Son as identifiable and equivalent to *the eternal obedience rendered by the Son to the Father in the triune life*, given that following Barth's scheme the eternal Son is eternally begotten from the Father as already the "preexistent" God-man Jesus Christ.[111]

---

109. White, *The Incarnate Lord*, 304. This statement reveals that White likewise sees the action of obedience as requiring a distinct volition.

110. I draw our attention at this juncture to Swain and Allen, "Obedience of the Eternal Son," another essay exploring the notion of divine obedience in the eternal Son according to "classical trinitarian metaphysics" (115). The basic idea proposed is similar to White's—the mode of acting (*modus agenda*) of the Son in his economic obedience follows from his mode of being (*modus essendi*) as the eternally begotten Son. The major difference, however, is that Swain and Allen see no difficulty in describing the relation of "receptive filiation" the Son has with the Father as that of divine obedience (124). They see the eternal Son's obedience to the Father in the work of salvation, as "not indicative of a *second will* alongside that of the Father but of *the proper mode whereby Jesus shares the Father's will as the only-begotten Son of the Father*" (emphasis theirs). Along with White, I agree that *one cannot directly equate a relation of filial receptivity to that of obedience*, mainly because obedience requires reciprocity of wills and a distinct act of volition, whereas filial receptivity does not. I am not altogether confident that Swain and Allen can attribute obedience to the relation of filial receptivity without positing the presence and exercising of two wills.

111. White, as a result of his (re)interpretation, states that ultimately "the obedience of the eternal Son" can at best be understood in a figurative or metaphorical sense (*Incarnate Lord*, 281). I contend, however, that this is where Barth's actualistic ontology allows us to think of the obedience of the eternal Son in a literal sense.

However, I contend that Barth's actualistic ontology is conceptually and logically unable to support the idea of an "antecedent obedience" found within the perfection of the triune life that serves as the eternal ground or basis from which the subsequent temporal obedience of Christ is engendered. The flow of the logic of thought, unfortunately, is unidirectional. If anything, this antecedent ontological ground must be found elsewhere, and White is to be commended for locating it in the filial-paternity relation arising naturally from the divine processions of begetting and being begotten between the Father and Son, without in any way positing that filial-paternity relation as an antecedent obedience.[112] Neither, I emphasize, is a framework of actualistic ontology capable of supporting what seems to be Barth's way of envisaging the divine obedience of the Son as a distinct and separate "*divine and not a human* work."[113] This particular statement of Barth remains a perplexing point. If Barth intends by the statement a divine obedience rendered by the second mode of being of the triune God independent from and devoid of any consideration of him being the "pre-existent" God-man, I concede that Barth would have run counter against his underlying Trinitarian rubric of the one divine subject with one will and one volition. In doing so, he would have—regrettably—raised for himself an unresolvable tension, and finally, an aporia in his doctrine of the Trinity.[114]

---

112. See also White, "Divine Simplicity and Holy Trinity," 66–93, where he basically rehearses his argument again, but this time under the overarching rubric of the doctrine of divine simplicity.

113. *CD* IV/1, 209 (added emphasis).

114. Neder, "History in Harmony," 148–76, shows awareness of the difficulty involved. On the one hand, Neder posits that Barth identifies the hypostatic union with the dynamic of divine lordship and human obedience in the one history of Jesus Christ. On the other hand, Barth asserts the divine obedience of God the Son in addition to this human obedience. The central question is how does the divine Son obey and how is this divine action of obedience related to the human action of obedience? According to Neder, since Barth's conception of the hypostatic union calls for a unity but yet clear distinction of the divine and human action, "the question cannot be resolved by identifying Jesus Christ's divine obedience and his human obedience. For in that case, there could be no two natures doctrine at all" (175–76, with the quotation being from p. 176). Yet, Neder is equally aware of the difficulty of positing an "independent" divine obedience. Ultimately, Neder leaves the question unanswered, stating that this is a "major conceptual problem" that remains for Barth's specification of the hypostatic union (176). The only way out of this dilemma, as I see it, is to identify the divine obedience of the Son as the human obedience of Jesus, and not attempt to posit another distinct divine obedience separate from the human obedience of Jesus.

Conclusion

A long and difficult argument of theology lies behind us. Nonetheless, I hope the central contention has been sufficiently argued. That is, Barth's novel notion of the intra-Trinitarian obedience of the eternal Son is coherent only when read through the category of his actualistic ontology, which in itself is consequent on Barth's doctrine of election. That the eternal Son is not an abstract, unknown *Logos asarkos*-and-*aincarnandus* but the *Logos asarkos*-who-is-at-the-same-time-*incarnandus* means that the God-man Jesus Christ's actions of obedience were already "actualistically" foreseen and counted as such from the beginning in eternity. If Barth is not to subvert his emphasis on a unity of will and volition in the Trinity, and assuming that Barth is employing the term "obedience" within its conventional meaning involving an exercise of two separate wills, then the "pre-existent" God-man Jesus Christ as the eternal Son who renders obedience to the Father forms the most felicitous reading of Barth's notion of an intra-Trinitarian divine obedience. Even if there are difficulties with such a reading of Barth, it is granted that these difficulties arise from questions addressed towards Barth's actualistic ontology, not from how obedience fits within that actualistic ontology. This chapter has also presented Barth, in *CD* IV/1, as grounding the divine obedience in the eternal relations within the immanent Trinity, specifically, in the divine processions expressed as the eternal begetting of the Father and the eternal begotten-ness of the Son. In this way, Barth gives the notion of divine obedience, as understood within his actualistic ontology, its most precise description. In the immanent life of the Trinity, *the Father already begets the eternal Son as the "pre-existent" God-man Jesus Christ.*

Clearly, the immediately preceding statement carries with it massive implications for an understanding of the being of the triune God, especially as it pertains to the divine processions (the intra-God relation) and the divine missions (the God-creation relation). Our understanding of Trinitarian ontology is also inevitably implicated. Stated another way: there is two-way traffic happening here. So, while the notion of an intra-Trinitarian obedience is best understood within Barth's actualistic ontology, Barth's grounding of that intra-Trinitarian obedience in the divine processions also raises interesting and challenging questions for how that actualistic framework is to be conceived, especially as it bears on a Trinitarian ontology. It is to this central enquiry that I turn in the following chapter.

2

Divine Obedience and Trinitarian Ontology

Reading Karl Barth's Actualistic Ontology in the Light of the Obedience of the Eternal Son

THE DISTINCTIVE MOVE THAT Karl Barth made in taking the obedience of Jesus Christ and extending it "backwards" into the Trinitarian life of God was explored in the previous chapter. The chapter concluded that the intra-Trinitarian obedience of the eternal Son makes sense and coheres with Barth's doctrine of the Trinity only when read against the backdrop of his actualistic ontology. Because the eternal Son is presented and identified as the *praeexistierende* God-man Jesus Christ, the obedience displayed by Jesus Christ in his incarnation is "actualistically" foreseen and counted as that rendered by the eternal Son to the Father.

While the above is true, Barth's conjoining of the intra-Trinitarian obedience to the eternal Son's being begotten by the Father certainly challenges the way we think about the being of the triune God, especially as it pertains to the relationship between the immanent and the economic Trinity, or the divine processions and the divine missions. Undoubtedly, Barth's pinning of the command-obedience relation to the divine processions between the Father and the Son bears on our understanding of Trinitarian ontology, and raises the pertinent question of how "thick" and "deep" one should go with a reading of Barth's actualistic ontology.

This present chapter is devoted toward answering that central question. What distinguishes this chapter from the previous one is that while the former chapter demonstrated how one can sustain Barth's notion of the obedience of the eternal Son by appealing to his actualistic ontology, this chapter seeks to establish how far and wide the perimeters of that actualistic ontology should extend. This will set the stage for our discussion of Jesus' incarnate obedience in the following chapter.

The argument takes the following shape. First, I will outline three main responses that have arisen among Barth scholars to Barth's move of pegging divine command-obedience to the divine processions. The upshot of the discussion is that majority of scholars who affirm Barth's move do so on the basis of Barth working with some version of an actualistic ontology. Aligning myself broadly with this group, I proceed in the second section to establish the key contours and parametric boundaries of what I consider to be a faithful reading of Barth's actualistic ontology. I will do this by exploring four strands of thought that help to clarify the matter at hand: i) a "traditional" reading of the relation between the divine processions and the divine missions via Thomas Aquinas ii) the "actualistic" nature of God's freedom and his knowing and willing under Barth's treatment of the divine perfections iii) Eberhard Jüngel's reading of Barth's actualistic ontology, and iv) Barth's view of time and eternity. The third relatively brief section will validate my specific reading of Barth's actualistic ontology with what I see as the crucial question: "*Where*, and if so, *how* does the concept of a *Logos asarkos* 'in-himself-and-as-such' (as I term it) fit within the actualistic ontological framework proposed?" In all of this, I hope the particular reading of Barth's actualistic ontology propounded accords with and respects Barth's central yardstick for how he envisaged the triune being of God: as the one who truly loves in freedom.[1]

Responses within Barth Scholarship to Barth's Notion of the Obedience of the Eternal Son

Responses to Barth's insistence upon the intra-Trinitarian obedience of the eternal Son can be grouped in three broad camps. The following section will list the main proponents of each view alongside their estimations of whether Barth essentially espoused some version of an actualistic ontology.

Paul Molnar: Barth's Positing of Divine Intra-Trinitarian Obedience as Misguided

I begin with Paul Molnar. In his essay "The Obedience of the Son in the Theology of Karl Barth and of Thomas F. Torrance,"[2] Molnar views that Barth illegitimately read back elements of the economy into the immanent Trinity when he posited the intra-Trinitarian obedience of the eternal Son in *CD* IV/1. He believes that Barth's move is basically misguided and "places his thinking in conflict with itself."[3] Molnar affirms: "While the

---

1. The title of *CD* II/1 §28 "The Being of God as the One Who Loves in Freedom."
2. Molnar, "Obedience of the Son," 50–69.
3. Molnar, "Obedience of the Son," 59.

incarnate Son subordinates himself to the Father *for us* in obedience, one cannot read this back indiscriminately into the immanent Trinity without causing problems."[4] The problems are: first, Barth blurs the distinction between the divine processions and missions; second, Barth's move fails to sustain his own wish to distinguish (without separating) the immanent and economic Trinity; third, Barth employs a problematic analogy to explain subordination within God's being (that of the husband-wife relation), and fourth, Barth introduces hierarchy into the immanent Trinity.[5] Ultimately, Molnar sees Barth's error as one of confusing the order of the persons of the Trinity with their being, an error that opens the door to "subordinationism and to modalism" or even to "monism, dualism or tritheism."[6] The essay evidently displays Molnar's preference for Torrance's manner of ascertaining the obedience of the Son. Torrance affirms that obedience falls "within the life of God,"[7] while not undertaking any of the moves and committing the same mistakes that Barth made.

Molnar's response is unsurprising. From the beginning of his critical engagement with Barth, Molnar has always maintained a crucial place for the *Logos asarkos* (in-himself-and-as-such).[8] A failure to do so, Molnar contends, "compromise[s] God's freedom with the implication that the economy, rather than God himself, defines his eternal being."[9] This means that Molnar is inclined, from the outset, toward resisting any version of an actualistic ontology being "imposed" on Barth.[10] Molnar's reservation is clearly displayed in the following statement: "It is here that one must make a choice. One may either adopt an actualistic ontology of personhood that allows events in history to determine who God is in eternity and thus who Christ is as the second person of the Trinity. Or one may recognize God's

---

4. Molnar, "Obedience of the Son," 64 (original emphasis).
5. Molnar, "Obedience of the Son," 64–65.
6. Molnar, "Obedience of the Son," 65–66.
7. Molnar, "Obedience of the Son," 64. Molnar quotes from Torrance, *Christian Doctrine of God*, 264, 144.
8. Molnar, *Divine Freedom*.
9. Molnar, *Divine Freedom*, 58. This reveals Molnar's basic conception of God's freedom as primarily sourced in the fact that God has his existence from himself alone, and shows his desideratum to separate and maintain the dialectic tension between "God's freedom *from* the world" and "God's freedom *for* the world." Standing in contrast to Molnar's conception of freedom is someone like Kevin Hector, who describes God's freedom as follows: "God is free-*from* the world in order to be free-*for* it." See Hector, "God's Triunity," 256, and Molnar, "The Trinity, Election and God's Freedom," 294–306.
10. See the following essays by Molnar: "Can the Electing God Be God without Us?," 199–222; "Can Jesus' Divinity?," 40–81, and "Perils of Embracing," 454–80. The essays have reappeared (with others) in a new volume: *Faith, Freedom and the Spirit*.

grace in faith and thus refrain from constructing an ontology that demands that something must happen *to* the Logos by virtue of the incarnation."[11] It is clear on which side Molnar takes his stand.[12]

George Hunsinger: The Intra-Trinitarian Obedience of the Eternal Son Based on the Doctrine of Antecedence

In his recent work, *Reading Barth with Charity: A Hermeneutical Proposal*,[13] renowned Barth scholar George Hunsinger expounds the key section of *CD* IV/1, pp. 192–210, where the idea of the eternal Son's obedience receives its climactic expression.[14] Hunsinger lays out clearly the main principle governing the *modus operandi* of his exposition: "The argument is an exercise in Barth's *doctrine of antecedence*. After considering the Son's obedience on earth, Barth asks about the condition for its possibility. What can be said about its antecedent ground?"[15] It is this doctrine of antecedence that Hunsinger appropriates to justify Barth's positing of the obedience of the eternal Son. Highlighting obedience as that which distinguishes God's Son in his humanity from all other humanity, Hunsinger locates that obedience antecedently in the Son's being in eternity. He states: "Obedience is not just something the Son does. It is something that he is. His whole raison d'être is to be obedient, *first in eternity and then (on that basis) also in time*."[16] Hunsinger closes with an unambiguous invocation of the doctrine of antecedence that has so clearly guided his train of thought throughout his exposition:

> The Son is constituted by being eternally begotten of the Father and "determined" for obedience to him within the eternal Godhead. This obedience, perfectly rendered, is what expresses the "ceaseless unity" of the Father and the Son and their perfect agreement in all that they will and do. *It is an obedience,*

---

11. Molnar, "Can Jesus' Divinity?," 59 (original emphasis).

12. This is not to say that Molnar does not recognize the actualistic tenor of Barth's theology. Rather, he resists allowing this actualistic impulse to be pressed into the domain of divine Trinitarian ontology.

13. Hunsinger, *Reading Barth*.

14. Hunsinger, *Reading Barth*, 88–113.

15. Hunsinger, *Reading Barth*, 89 (added emphasis). Hunsinger's emphasis on the doctrine of antecedence reiterates itself throughout his exposition, governing the way he reads key terms and concepts such as "history" (*Geschichte*) (97), time and eternality in Barth's thought (98–99), and what it means to speak of Jesus Christ as the Son of God (109).

16. Hunsinger, *Reading Barth*, 110 (added emphasis).

> *agreement, and oneness antecedent to all God's ways and works with the world.* This antecedent obedience, agreement and oneness is what Barth had previously described . . . as God's "history" in and for himself.[17]

Hunsinger is certainly to be lauded for his constant appeal and consistent application of the doctrine of antecedence, a doctrine that I believe Barth upheld throughout the period of his writing. However, in my opinion, what needs further clarification even as Hunsinger appeals to the doctrine of antecedence is precisely how such an antecedent intra-Trinitarian obedience can be maintained without contravening Barth's Trinitarianism with its insistence on a single divine subject (in three modes of being) with one mind, will and volition. Granted that Barth himself failed to explain this crucial move, credit must go to Hunsinger who attempts an explanation.[18]

Hunsinger's explanation begins with him acknowledging the difficulties posed by the attribution of obedience to the eternal Son. He ponders the wisdom of this move, asking if it would have been better if Barth had simply located the eternal basis and ground of all that God does in time, in God's being as the One who loves in freedom.[19] Harking back to a move Barth made in *CD* II/1, pp. 354–58, where Barth likewise read grace antecedently back into the eternal being of God without offering an explanation for doing so, Hunsinger similarly applies Barth's explanation there and then to the antecedent intra-Trinitarian obedience. Hunsinger states: "There is no scope in eternity for the specific form assumed by the Son's obedience in the economy . . . . The Son's antecedent obedience must occur, if at all, in a very different form—a form that is 'hidden from us and incomprehensible to us' (II/1, 357). *The eternal obedience of the Son must differ from any obedience that we know*."[20]

That said, however, Hunsinger interestingly carries on to connect the Son's eternal (though functional) "subordination" to the Father and his incarnate obedience on earth. In this case, "the Son's free obedience in time would mirror his eternal relationship of perfect submission to his Father."[21] In turn, the Son's perfect relationship of submission to the Father is expressed in the Son being all that he is and all that he has only "through the renunciation of his own will," first in eternity but then also in time.[22]

---

17. Hunsinger, *Reading Barth*, 112–13 (added emphasis).
18. Hunsinger, *Reading Barth*, 115–19.
19. Hunsinger, *Reading Barth*, 115–16.
20. Hunsinger, *Reading Barth*, 118 (added emphasis).
21. Hunsinger, *Reading Barth*, 119.
22. Hunsinger, *Reading Barth*, 119.

Hunsinger is convinced that, on this interpretation, there would be no positing of a duality of wills between the Father and the Son. The Son would share in the one divine will by "subjecting himself perfectly to the [Father's will]" and by receiving that will "from the Father in the mode of perfect and eternal submission." Hunsinger concludes: "There would therefore be no 'irresolvable aporiae' of two opposing or dichotomous divine wills in Barth's doctrine of the eternal Trinity."[23]

I appreciate Hunsinger's attempts to tie back his explanation with the doctrine of antecedence that he so emphasizes. However, I am less clear about his reference to the Son's submission to the Father in eternity within his attempt to locate an antecedent obedience within the triune life. If Hunsinger is merely stating the perfect submission of the Son to the Father as the *ground* or the *basis* of the Son's incarnate obedience (in time), then all would be fine, and Hunsinger's argument would resound very similarly to White's alternative interpretation that we came across in the previous chapter.[24] But if Hunsinger is *equating* or *identifying* the antecedent obedience with the perfect submission of the Son to the Father (in eternity), then, in my opinion, the explanation is not as straightforward and ultimately strains at tenability.

As we have seen, in order for an antecedent obedience to be located in the Son's perfect relationship of submission to the Father, it would require the exercise of a distinct center of volition. Yet, any distinct and separate act of volition within the triune Godhead has to be intricately defined—if possible at all—so as not to violate the basic rubric of Barth's doctrine of the Trinity. This, Hunsinger attempts to do by locating the distinct act of willing called for by the idea of "obedience" in the act of the Son's "renunciation of his own will" and his "subjecting himself perfectly to the [Father's will],"[25] while maintaining the unity of the one divine will within the triune Godhead. That Hunsinger heads in this direction is revealed in a footnote where he reveals his preference to conceive of the one divine will as "one indivisible divine will *in different hypostatic forms*" as opposed to "one undifferentiated divine will."[26] Even with such precise and nuanced qualifications, the basic shape of Barth's doctrine of the Trinity—restated again in *CD* IV/1—speaks of one "personality" (*Persönlichkeit*), one speaking and acting divine subject, rather than "three different personalities, three self-existent individuals with their own special self-consciousness, cognition,

---

23. Hunsinger, *Reading Barth*, 119.
24. White, *The Incarnate Lord*, 301 onwards.
25. Hunsinger, *Reading Barth*, 119.
26. Hunsinger, *Reading Barth*, 119n5 (added emphasis).

volition, activity, effects, revelation and name."[27] As I see it, Hunsinger's argument runs into difficulties at this point. He either has to resist equating or identifying the antecedent obedience of the Son with his submission to the Father in eternity, or modify some aspect of Barth's underlying doctrine of the Trinity to allow for more than one center of volitional activity within the one divine subject the triune God is. In the final analysis, if Hunsinger is to insist on the doctrine of antecedence, I maintain that his initial explanation of the ineffable form of *that* antecedent obedience would be the most he could appeal to and the best he could proffer.

An alternate recourse is available, however, and it consists in Hunsinger turning to an earlier explanation he gave in articulating how it is that Jesus Christ can be the subject of the divine act of election. Drawing on his concept of Barth's view of eternality and time, Hunsinger sums up his argument:

> Note especially that the idea here in Barth is *prolepsis*, not *incarnandus*. The claim at this point is . . . the more radical one that in the mind of God the earthly Jesus is already present as such to the eternal Son and assumed into hypostatic union with him in pretemporal eternity . . . . His election . . . enjoys a double temporal location: it occurs before time as well as in time (though in different respects) (II/2, 184). It occurs in both simultaneity and sequence . . . . In the eyes of God, the whole God-Man Jesus Christ already exists concretely before the foundation of the world (III/1, 51).[28]

I read the above statement as an advance in Hunsinger's thinking on this matter of Jesus Christ as the subject of election.[29] Furthermore, from this point, it takes just one further step to apply the *prolepsis* motif to the intra-Trinitarian obedience of the eternal Son. That is, if, in the eyes of God and in pre-temporal eternity, the eternal Son is already seen to be hypostatically united to his human nature, I see no further restraint that prevents

27. *CD* IV/1, 205 (added emphasis).
28. Hunsinger, *Reading Barth*, 62–63.
29. I say "advance" because Hunsinger resorted to a slightly different argument in an earlier essay. In Hunsinger, "Election and the Trinity," 179–98, Hunsinger maintained that strictly speaking, it is the eternal Son and not the Son *incarnatus*, nor even the Son *incarnandus*, who is the subject of election. Nevertheless, as Hunsinger said: "Because the eternal Son is not only eternal but also *incarnandus*, and because the Son *incarnandus* is numerically identical with the Son *incarnatus*, it is not illegitimate to say that in a certain respect (*secundum quid*) it is the Son *incarnatus*, or Jesus Christ, who is the subject of this decision" (183). Here in *Reading Barth*, one can sense via the *prolepsis* motif a greater receptivity and less restraint on Hunsinger's part in directly affirming Jesus Christ as the subject of election.

Hunsinger from conceiving the obedience of the eternal Son as—*proleptically*—the obedience of the God-man Jesus Christ. As evident from the previous chapter, that is the course I have taken.

Notwithstanding the above, I understand why Hunsinger might refrain from making this move. The *prolepsis* motif shares much commonality with a framework of actualistic ontology, with the key difference being that the latter penetrates "deeper" to bear on the ontological identity of the second mode of being of the triune God himself, as compared to *prolepsis* which basically leaves that ontological identity "untouched" (a differentiation I will return to in a moment). Given Hunsinger's aversion to the idea of actualistic ontology, he would have preferred to uphold the doctrine of antecedence in arguing for the intra-Trinitarian obedience of the eternal Son. But—to repeat an earlier conclusion—in so doing, the best explanation Hunsinger can offer is to appeal to the ineffable and unspecifiable nature of that antecedent obedience.

Darren Sumner, Paul Jones, Bruce McCormack, and Paul Nimmo: The Intra-Trinitarian Obedience of the Eternal Son as Affirmation of Barth's Actualistic Ontology

Proponents in the third broad camp of responses, far from seeing Barth's notion of the divine obedience of the eternal Son as misguided, argue for the opposite case, viewing Barth's move as a stroke of his genius and a definitive indication of his underlying actualistic ontology. While the term begs for a more precise definition—a task I will carry out in the second section of this chapter—the preliminary definition provided in the previous chapter suffices for now. At its core, an actualistic ontology involves the view that God has allowed the divine act of election wherein he elects himself to be the God for us in Jesus Christ to "condition" or "qualify" his own being as the triune God. The proponents I list in this section all agree with this basic definition; where they differ is the extent to which God's electing act is allowed to bear on his triune being. I will feature the proponents in increasing order of what I perceive as a "minimal" to a "maximal" contention of Barth's actualistic ontology.

Darren Sumner

I begin with Darren Sumner. In his essay "Obedience and Subordination in Karl Barth's Trinitarian Theology,"[30] Sumner considers the weightiest critique levelled against Barth's notion of divine obedience to be that of a postulation of two divine wills within the Trinity, thereby implying some version of Social Trinitarianism.[31] Sumner defends Barth against this charge by making the following moves. First, he endorses Barth's theological ontology as actualistic in nature, stating in clear terms the following: "Barth rejected the division between God's being and act. His ontology is actualistic, suggesting that God's being is in his eternal decision, actualized in the history that God has elected for himself."[32] The actualistic nature of Barth's ontology extends to the way eternity is to be conceived. He continues: "Thus, 'eternity' does not describe God's being *apart from* the history that God is, since there is no moment at which God is not the Son who obeys and the Father who is obeyed."[33] Second, Sumner affirms dyothelitism and utilizes Barth's doctrine of the common actualization of the human and divine essences to contend that "[w]hile there is one divine will, in God's second way of being that will is in relation to a particular human will as well."[34] The will of the Son may hence be differentiated from the will of the Father. Consequently, the obedience of the divine Son is also a human obedience.[35] Bringing together these two moves, Sumner presses home his argument that God the Son can obey the Father because he is eternally the God-human, with two natures and two wills. Articulated in *proleptic* language, the fact that the Son has never been without his humanity means that the relation of obedience can be extended from the Son's temporal mission into eternity.[36] Sumner concludes his argument with the following words: "[A]n actualistic ontology means that Barth need not predicate obedience to the pre-incarnate Son in a strictly figurative sense—for here it has become proper to God the Son."[37]

---

30. Sumner, "Obedience and Subordination."
31. Sumner, "Obedience and Subordination," 133.
32. Sumner, "Obedience and Subordination," 138.
33. Sumner, "Obedience and Subordination," 138 (original emphasis).
34. Sumner, "Obedience and Subordination," 142.
35. Sumner, "Obedience and Subordination," 142.
36. Sumner, "Obedience and Subordination," 143.
37. Sumner, "Obedience and Subordination," 144.

Paul Dafydd Jones

Paul Dafydd Jones draws on similar lines of thought in his own consideration of the eternal Son's obedience. Jones suggests that Barth's positing of divine obedience within the triune Godhead raises a subtle revision to the tradition. On the one hand, it challenges us to associate obedience and humility not only with Christ's humanity, but also his divinity.[38] On the other hand, it maximizes the way we think about the divine processions. The Father's eternal begetting of the Son is complemented by the Son's begottenness and his act of obedience.[39] But of paramount significance is Jones' contention that with the term "obedience," Barth intends that within the triune God there is "a history of 'being' and 'becoming' such that the identity of God qua Son becomes unthinkable in isolation from, and is in fact ontologically inclusive of, the concrete life of Jesus Christ."[40] In other words, the Son's obedience in the economy of salvation has ontological consequences for God's own triune being.

Jones conceives the event of God's self-determination in relation to the Son's life bearing on God's being as a "narrative" consisting of a "beginning," a "middle," and an "end."[41] "The beginning of the narrative is God's immanent life as it happens 'apart from' and 'before' the concrete reality of God's elected creature," Jones states.[42] He concedes that it is here at the "beginning" that Barth gives a place to the *Logos asarkos* "in-himself-and-as-such," albeit a place that is highly limited and circumscribed. The "middle" is where the divine Son in obedience exercises God's love and stoops down to an existence under the conditions of finitude, committing himself wholeheartedly to a history in which he bears God's rejection of sin. And the "end" of the Son's history is where the incredible—in fact audacious—disclosure is made that God has unconditionally and freely decreed that what happens economically in the incarnation of the Son is to have relevance for who God is in himself.[43] As Jones asserts: "God makes the 'middle' of the Son's life—his being the concrete person of Jesus Christ—the 'end' of the Son's life to such an extent that it has relevance for God's own being."[44]

---

38. Jones, "Obedience, Trinity, and Election," 143.
39. Jones, "Obedience, Trinity and Election," 141.
40. Jones, "Obedience, Trinity and Election," 145.
41. Jones, "Obedience, Trinity and Election," 146.
42. Jones, "Obedience, Trinity and Election," 147.
43. Jones, "Obedience, Trinity and Election," 148–49.
44. Jones, "Obedience, Trinity and Election," 150.

Jones believes that his particular conception of Barth's actualistic ontology maintains the delicate and difficult balance between, on the one hand, preserving the freedom and perfection of the immanent triune life, and on the other hand, taking seriously the actualistic impulse of Barth's doctrine of election as an ontologically significant event of divine self-determining proportions. The balance that Jones strives for is seen in the following extended quotation:

> Barth develops a theological ontology in which God's triune being and God's elective activity converge—so much so that God "opens" Godself as Son, and qualifies God's being in terms of the actual life, death, and resurrection of Jesus Christ. This does not mean that God is less than fully actualized "prior" to the incarnation, or that God's being depends on . . . the concrete life of Jesus Christ. Nor does it mean that the identity of the Son is . . . rendered crudely equivalent to . . . the mission definitive of the person who is the *Logos ensarkos*. What it means is that Barth has reconceived the immanent Trinity in a way fitted to his own post-metaphysical theology . . . . God's triunity is distinguished, reaffirmed—perhaps even *intensified*—given the Son's self-determination to become and be the "electing God" and "elected human."[45]

The effect is, as Jones states in his earlier work, to "underscore that God's decision to be incarnate is coincident and coordinate with, and therefore has equivalent dogmatic importance to, God's decision to exist as Father, Son and Holy Spirit."[46] Under Jones' conception of Barth's actualistic ontology, there is no need to prioritize between the Trinity and election. Rather, God's elective self-determination and God's Trinitarian self-definition are both equally basic for God.[47]

Bruce McCormack

In turning to Bruce McCormack, one is looking at the principal theologian to have introduced to the English-speaking guild of Barth scholarship the concept of extending Barth's actualistic motif into the realm of Trinitarian ontology.[48] McCormack's argument has been well-documented and

45. Jones, "Obedience, Trinity and Election," 153–54 (original emphasis).
46. Jones, *Humanity of Christ*, 81.
47. Jones, *Humanity of Christ*, 81n51.
48. McCormack, "Election and Trinity: Theses," 204, highlights a list of German theologians who had gone before him in advancing a similar notion. In a subsequent

vehemently argued since his manifesto essay "Grace and Being: The Role of God's Gracious Election in Karl Barth's Theological Ontology,"[49] and in many subsequent essays on the matter.[50] McCormack's presentation of Barth's actualistic ontology can be seen in three complementary approaches. First, McCormack's presentation of Barth's actualistic ontology flows from his discussion of Barth's dictum "Jesus Christ is the subject of election."[51] A second approach proceeds by means of a discussion on the topic of the impassibility and immutability of God.[52] A third approach can be seen in McCormack's wider discussion of the obedience of Christ Jesus and how it relates to the obedience of the eternal Son. Since this third approach is germane to our theme, I will explore its argument in detail.

McCormack rightly contends that from the beginning of CD IV/1 §59, Barth identifies the man Jesus of Nazareth with God Himself, and in this way, Barth is preoccupied with Jesus' *history* of obedience that is equated directly with the history of God.[53] Yet, how does one posit a divine obedience within Godself, specifically in the second mode of being of the eternal Son? McCormack here draws on what he terms "Reformed Kenoticism," which is to be distinguished from kenotic theories of the nineteenth century.[54] For Barth, the element of *kenosis* does not happen through the divestment of anything proper to deity.[55] Instead, McCormack's central contention is that the *kenosis* happens through *a certain willed restraint on the part of the eternal Son not to use his divine attributes upon the human nature, but instead to be totally receptive and "open" to the experiences the human nature might bring*. In other

---

essay a year later, "Karl Barth's Version," 88–144, McCormack details the development of the notion within the German-speaking guild of Barth scholarship. He begins with what he views as the pioneering work of Jüngel, *God's Being*, outlines and comments on the alternate model of Trinitarian ontology as provided by Härle, *Sein Und Gnade*, before turning to the determinative article, Goebel, "*Trinitätslehre Und Erwählungslehre Bei Karl Barth,*" 147–66.

49. McCormack, "Grace and Being," 92–110.

50. To name a few, see McCormack, "Seek God," 62–79; "Foreword," 291–304, and "Let's Speak Plainly," 57–65.

51. This is the approach taken in McCormack, "Grace and Being," and "Seek God."

52. The key essays for this approach are McCormack, "Historicized Christology," 201–34, and "Divine Impassibility," 150–86, though the seed of the argument was presented early in "Ontological Presuppositions," 346–66.

53. McCormack, "Divine Impassibility," 161.

54. McCormack, "Reformed Kenoticism," 243–51.

55. This is in contrast to the kenotic accounts of one like Gottfried Thomasius, who maintained that the eternal Son of God divested himself of the "relative" divine attributes such as omnipotence, omniscience and omnipresence in order for the incarnation to happen.

words, the second mode of being of the triune God, in relation to the human nature he will assume in the incarnation, is marked by a posture of receptivity. And behind that receptivity, the Logos is characterized by a further humility on his part.[56] Yet, if the incarnation is not to result in any change on the part of the Logos (McCormack hereby preserves God's immutability), then that receptivity and humility must in turn be *eternally* characteristic of the eternal Son. McCormack underscores the *eternal* receptivity and humility by propounding that "the *only* act of the [eternal] Son of God in relation to his humanity is the act in which he gives it existence in his own being and existence. All subsequent acts of the God-man made possible by *this singular act* are acts performed by the man Jesus."[57]

Not simply stopping at humility, however, McCormack, in following Barth, carries on to link humility with obedience. He differentiates between humility and obedience, citing the former as representing a posture or attitude and the latter a freely willed activity in the presence of a command and with a definite goal in view.[58] Based on this distinction, McCormack contends that for Barth to make obedience *essential* to God is for God himself—in the eternal receptivity that characterizes him—to take the freely willed activity of the Son of God, *specifically the freely willed activity vis-à-vis that carried out by the man Jesus Christ*, into his very being, so much so that *the divine essence is determined in Jesus Christ*.[59] Obedience, for McCormack, forms the "personal property" of the Son (as contrasted with the "common properties" shared by all members of the Godhead) in that it is what makes him to be the Son.[60] He states: "We can say with confidence that Barth . . . believes obedience is *essential* to God. That is to say: a willed activity whose purposive character can have to do only with the covenant of grace is essential to God."[61] Here, we arrive at the actualistic nerve of McCormack's proposal: to bring the notion of obedience into the triune Godhead is to consider the concrete life of Jesus Christ with such seriousness that God qualifies or determines his own being in terms of Jesus Christ.

A proposal as weighty as this generates ontological implications of equal proportion. First, if obedience is the "personal property" of the Son, if it is what makes the Son to be the *Son*, then it means that *there never was a*

---

56. McCormack, "'With Loud Cries and Tears,'" 50.
57. McCormack, "Divine Impassibility," 177 (original emphasis).
58. See McCormack, "Karl Barth's Version," 140–41.
59. McCormack, "Trinity after Barth," 109–10. McCormack refers to CD IV/2, 84.
60. McCormack, "Trinity after Barth," 110. In this way, McCormack revises the Traditional account that views the personal property of the Son as filiation.
61. McCormack, "Election and Trinity: Theses," 212 (original emphasis).

"moment" in the eternal Son's mode of existence whereby he was not in a position of humility and receptivity to what the obedience of the man Jesus would mean for his being. This leads in turn to only one conclusion. And that is, the being and personal identity of the eternal Son has always been anticipated and counted concretely as such by what he will become in time through his assumption of a human nature.[62] Other than that, the second mode of being of God has no separate independent mode of existence; there is no Logos *asarkos* that is not at one-and-the-same-time the Logos *incarnandus*. "The second 'person' of the Trinity has a name and His name is Jesus Christ," thus states a popular catchphrase of McCormack's.[63]

Second, McCormack contends that to treat obedience as the "personal property" of the Eternal Son is to (re)read, as Barth does, the entire intra-Trinitarian relations in view of this dynamic of obedience. As seen in the previous chapter, for Barth, reckoning with divine obedience means that the intra-Trinitarian relation within God in his three modes of being can now also be legitimately described under the rubric of a command-obedience structure. Expressed most strikingly in *CD* IV/1 §59, the language of "self-*positing*" and "self-*positedness*" replaces the traditional language of "eternal generation."[64] It is the Father's command that "posits" the Son—and in doing so it makes the Father to be *Father*. Likewise, it is the Son's eternal receptivity arising from his humility and his obedience as the God-man Jesus Christ to what He will do in time that lends itself to the Son's "posited-ness"—and once again, it makes the Son to be *Son*. McCormack further asserts that this language of "self-*positing*" and "self-*posited-ness*" strongly suggests that *the eternal "generation" of the Son (and along with that, the eternal "spiration" of the Spirit) is of a willed and purposive nature, directed towards God's becoming-for-us in the incarnation of the Son.* He states: "There are not two divine acts 'in' eternity, one in which God constitutes himself as triune and one in which he freely elects to be God for 'us'. There is only one divine act in eternity in which both of these things take place."[65] By assimilating "eternal generation to the command-obedience structure of the covenant of grace,"[66] McCormack contends that "the [divine] processions contain the [divine] missions and cannot be rightly construed apart from them."[67]

---

62. McCormack, "Trinity after Barth," 111.
63. McCormack, "Grace and Being," 100.
64. McCormack, "Divine Impassibility," 172.
65. McCormack, "Divine Impassibility," 172.
66. McCormack, "Trinity after Barth," 110.
67. McCormack, "Processions and Missions," 116. See also "Election and Trinity: Theses," 215–16.

From this point, it is not difficult to follow how McCormack proceeds to the most controversial and debated aspect of his proposal—his assertion that election (logically) precedes triunity. McCormack limits the boundary of his assertion to the "logical" realm, for he recognizes that election is an eternal decision that defies any attempts to temporalize it. That is, we cannot think of election in such a way that a "before" and "after" is introduced into the being of God in pre-temporal eternity.[68] Granted this limitation, McCormack's proposal is nonetheless still controversial enough to ruffle some feathers. That God's triune being should be *"given in"* the eternal act of election, or that the "works of God *ad intra* (the Trinitarian processions) find their ground in the *first* of the works of God *ad extra* (viz. election),"[69] are claims destined to meet with resistance. Yet, McCormack deems this to be an inevitable conclusion dictated by Barth's twofold dictum that "Jesus Christ is the subject of election" and that humility and obedience are *essential* to the being of God.

To recapitulate: the obedience of the eternal Son provides the occasion for McCormack to present his particular reading of Barth's actualistic ontology. To predicate divine obedience to God the Son is to say that the being of God is determined via an "actualistic anticipation" in the "becoming" of the Son in his incarnation, in his act of obedience, and that there is *no pre-determined essence of God apart from his divine decision of election*. The consequence naturally follows for McCormack that, if this is so, *election logically precedes triunity*.

One last comment deserves mention. In recent years, McCormack has argued on more than one occasion that the command-obedience relation is, in the final analysis, metaphorical in nature. In the 2011 Kantzer Lectures, he said:

> When in later volumes of *CD*, Barth posits an eternal humility or obedience which he states is constitutive of the being of the Son . . . *he is really talking about the act of a single subject in his second mode of being*. The command-obedience structure . . . is *metaphorically intended*. It can only be that because the names "Father" and "Son" are themselves employed analogically. . . . What we have in Barth's case is an eternal act of self-repetition in the being of one divine subject... That there is the thinking of eternal subordination in Barth is quite true, but it is not the subordination of one divine subject to another . . .[70]

---

68. McCormack, "Grace and Being," 101.

69. McCormack, "Grace and Being," 103 (original emphasis).

70. McCormack, "God Who Graciously Elects" (approx. 45 mins., 15 secs. into Lecture 1; my paraphrase and emphasis).

The above comment need not be read as a detraction of McCormack's earlier affirmations. As seen, the unique feature of an actualistic ontology is that it is able to predicate—literally and not just figuratively—obedience to the eternal Son, since the obedience of the God-man Jesus Christ is actualistically and proleptically counted as that of the eternal Son. However, in the rendering of that (literal) obedience from the eternal *Son* to the *Father*, McCormack is right to say that it has to be metaphorical in the final intent, for the Son and the Father are not two different divine subjects, but two different modes of being of the one divine subject.

Paul Nimmo

We move finally to Paul Nimmo. Among the four interlocutors who affirm Barth's actualistic ontology, I have placed Nimmo the last in terms of a sequence of increasing intensity relating to the way Barth's actualistic ontology is argued and applied. Not only is Nimmo in full agreement with what he calls a "strong" reading of Barth's conceptualization of the relation between the Trinity and election, he constructively extends the implications of Barth's actualistic ontology beyond the being of the eternal Son to include that of the eternal Spirit as well.[71] Nimmo's endorsement of Barth's actualistic ontology arising from the notion of obedience in the eternal Son is seen in the following quotation:

> [O]nce obedience in a second mode of being of God is seen as being both the fulfilment of a decree and essential to the being of God, then *the being of God itself in its Trinitarian modes of being is posited as being determined by the decree of election* in which it is determined what God will be in time. In other words, election logically precedes the Trinity: the eternal act of election as an act of self-determination is primal and there is no triunity behind or without it.[72]

From the above statement, it is unsurprising that Nimmo draws the same conclusion as McCormack. But Nimmo takes a further step in extending the application of Barth's actualistic ontology to predicate the same of the Holy Spirit. Insofar as the determination of the eternal being of the Son coincides with his eternal determination to be incarnate, so the determination of the eternal being of the Spirit coincides with his mediating activity

---

71. The main essay capturing this move is Nimmo, "Barth and Election-Trinity," 162–81.

72. Nimmo, "Barth and Election-Trinity," 173 (added emphasis).

in time between Jesus Christ and the community of God.[73] In other words, the Spirit in eternity is never the *pneuma anecclesion in abstracto* (the Spirit without the community of God, a third person of the Trinity "as such"), but is the Spirit only while simultaneously being the *pneuma inecclesiandus* (the Spirit destined to be "enchurched").[74]

By way of summary, in the first major section of this chapter, I have surveyed the responses of several scholars to Barth's attachment of the command-obedience structure of relation between the Father and the Son to the divine processions within the immanent Trinity. Three main responses have been noted: i) his move is seen as misguided and erroneous; ii) it is affirmed on the basis of his principle of antecedence (rather than his actualistic sensibilities), or iii) it is seen as decisive for Barth's actualistic ontology. Even within the last response we find a spectrum of ways to read Barth's actualistic ontology. That said, the proponents of the last response all agree that it is Barth's actualistic ontology that enables the obedience of the God-man Jesus Christ to be read proleptically and actualistically as that rendered by the eternal Son. After all, the eternal Son *is* Jesus Christ (when read within an actualistic framework). The points of divergence among those aligned with the third response arise mainly from *the degree* that the Son's self-determination for incarnation is allowed to bear on his immanent being. That is to say: which should have priority when we think of God—triunity or election?

An Account of Barth's Actualistic Ontology

It is evident by now that my own persuasion lies with the third set of responses. My concern in this present section is to explore the degree and depth to which this actualistic ontology ought to be read. Should Barth's actualistic ontology be read in a way that gives priority to triunity, or election?

Those familiar with Barth's theology, however, will be aware of the difficulties of this particular task, for Barth nowhere in the *Dogmatics* (or in his writings elsewhere) expounded what could serve as his definitive view on this issue, and instead throughout the *Dogmatics* we find statements that could indicate either position! While acknowledging the richness and expansiveness, and even at times the verbosity, of Barth's rhetoric, one agrees with Paul Jones who states that this is surely one area where we wish Barth had said *more!*[75] That Barth's work displays breadth,

---

73. Nimmo, "Barth and Election-Trinity," 174–75.
74. Nimmo, "Barth and Election-Trinity," 178.
75. Jones, *Humanity of Christ*, 90.

complexity, and even dialectic undercurrents should, however, caution the reader against the strategy of merely hurling out quotes from the *Dogmatics* to assert one's position. Instead, the polyphony of voices regarding this topic must be allowed to confront us in all their fullness, and the final reading of Barth's actualistic ontology advocated must deal seriously with these different perspectives. More importantly, one will need to draw from the nearby vicinity of Barth's theology other areas and considerations that will illuminate our reading. To that end and in this section, I will incorporate findings from four otherwise discrete areas to present what I hope is a faithful reading of Barth's actualistic ontology.

Before I begin, however, the underlying premise that Barth operates with an actualistic ontology needs to be brought out into the open and briefly addressed. We must ask whether it is right in the first place to say that Barth espoused an "actualistic ontology." Hunsinger, for one, has distinguished between two understandings of "ontology." The first, which he defines as the "proper" sense of the term and which he labels "ontology^1," refers to that "branch of metaphysics that deals comprehensively with the nature of being and of beings." The second, which Hunsinger uses in an "extended" sense and which he labels "ontology^2," has a "looser" tenor about it, and refers "to a general area of action, inquiry, or interest" and is "descriptive with no claims of being systematic or explanatory."[76] On Hunsinger's reading, Barth disavowed ontology^1, mainly because it was indebted and beholden to metaphysical philosophical concepts and because of its tendency to act as a controlling system. If anything, Barth upheld more of an ontology^2, maintaining an eclectic approach in which he used philosophical concepts in an ad hoc and non-systematic way, and only when necessary, to bolster his ontological claims. Hunsinger goes on to allege that the "revisionists" (in the Trinity-election debate) have spoken in ontology^1 terms under the pretext of speaking of ontology^2. Clearly, these statements reveal Hunsinger's proclivity to view all discussions of an actualistic ontology as falling under the category of ontology^1.

In my opinion, Hunsinger is right to remind us of Barth's rejection of an ontology^1, but I remain unpersuaded that all claims of Barth espousing an actualistic ontology entail that Barth upheld ontology^1. It is essential to clarify what we mean by the term "actualistic ontology." Very few readers of Barth will deny that, while Barth increasingly eschewed a metaphysical approach to theology, his statements and claims have ontological implications, even implications pertaining to a Trinitarian ontology.[77] It is my view that

76. Hunsinger, *Reading Barth*, 2.

77. I am drawn to the way White, "Introduction," 35, states it: "Barth was deeply interested in ontological structures in reality, read theologically."

those who affirm Barth as upholding an "actualistic ontology" are using the term to encapsulate a series of claims inductively derived from Barth's statements on divine election. In this way, the term "actualistic ontology" is born chiefly out of an *inductive* approach whereby one considers the ontological implications of what has been said and attempts to display them in a cohesive and coherent picture, as opposed to a *deductive* approach where the actualistic ontology acts as a preconceived system derived from metaphysical considerations which dominated as Barth wrote the *Dogmatics*. This, at least, is my own intent in using the term "actualistic ontology."

A Traditional or Classical Reading of the Divine Processions and the Divine Missions via Thomas Aquinas

Since a major part of the discussion revolves around the correctness of Barth's pinning of divine obedience to the divine processions, it would be appropriate to explore in closer detail a traditional or classical reading of the relation between the divine processions and the divine missions. In this way, one gains a better picture of Barth's standing in relation to the tradition. This we will do by turning to the thirteenth-century theological giant, Thomas Aquinas.

The portion of Aquinas' *Summa Theologica* which treats the doctrine of God consists of three parts. They pertain to, first, the divine essence of God, second, the distinction of persons, and third, the procession of creatures from him.[78] That Aquinas includes a discussion of the economy of creation and salvation under his doctrine of God and that he speaks of this using the language of "procession" signifies his move to originate the economy in the Trinitarian nature of the divine persons, specifically in their divine processions. As Gilles Emery, OP, states in his commentary on Aquinas' Trinitarian theology:

> Since *it is in knowing himself that God knows the creatures of which he is the exemplar and Creator*, and since *it is in loving*

---

78. ST I, q. 2, prologue. Aquinas' beginning with a consideration of the divine essence should not be misconstrued as him taking a "Latin" approach which starts from the unity of the divine essence versus a "Greek" approach which starts from a consideration of the divine persons. This view of seeing the two approaches as diametrically opposed—with the former originating in Augustine and the latter in the Cappadocian Fathers—belongs to an older historiography in relation to the study of the doctrine of the Trinity. Rather, as Emery ("Essentialism or Personalism," 528, 534) highlights, one must always bear in mind the "redoublement" of Trinitarian language appropriated by Aquinas, which concurrently accounts for the double perspective of the common nature and the Trinitarian relations, whenever we explore Aquinas' Trinitarianism.

himself that God wills and loves his creatures, we cannot study creation until we have considered God's immanent actions. For the same reason, the investigation of the Trinity's action in the world must be preceded by the study of the processions of Word and Love in God's eternity: *the generation of the Word and the procession of Love are the source of God's works in the world.*[79]

The above statement pinpoints the specific way the divine processions connect with creation and creatures, and highlights the priority, for Aquinas, in beginning with the processions. For Aquinas, the divine processions within the triune Godhead consist in an "immanent" rather than a "transitive" action. With the former, the action remains within the acting subject, while with the latter, it passes over to a reality external to itself.[80] Aquinas proceeds to identify the first and most obvious "immanent" action as being located in the intellect, whereby in the action of knowing, what is known remains in the intellectual agent, and what immanently proceeds from this action of knowing is the word.[81] The second of the "immanent" actions, Aquinas locates in the will. In willing, another procession takes place, that of love. Just as it is for the word, whereby the object spoken or understood remains in the intelligent agent, so it is for love, whereby the object loved remains in the lover.[82] It is from the immanent processions of the word and love, arising in turn from the immanent actions of knowing and willing, that we find the divine processions of the eternal generation of the Son and the spiration of the Spirit.[83] Aquinas further concludes that other than the procession of the Word (the Son) and of Love (the Spirit), no other procession is possible in God.[84]

Here is the point of significance not to be missed. For Aquinas, the immanent processions of word and of love immediately establish a connection between God's actions in the world and the divine processions. Specifically, *the intra-Trinitarian processions already include God's principles of creative and salvific action*. God knows all things through the begotten Word (the Son) and God loves all beings through the Love (the Spirit), both of whom proceed

---

79. Emery, *Trinitarian Theology*, 42 (added emphasis).

80. ST I, q. 27, a. 1. The mistake of Arianism was that it misread the divine processions as an instance of a "transitive" action.

81. ST I, q. 27, a. 1.

82. ST I, q. 27, a. 3.

83. In ST I, q. 27, a. 2, Aquinas explains why it is appropriate to call the procession of the Word as "generation" while in ST I., q. 27, a. 4, he explains why it is not appropriate to call the procession of the Spirit as "generation."

84. ST I, q. 27, a. 5.

from him.⁸⁵ In this way, the eternal processions serve as the cause and rationale (*causa* et *ratio*) of the making of creatures,⁸⁶ and the coming forth of the divine Persons serve as patterns of the coming forth of creatures.⁸⁷

Aquinas, however, is very careful with the way he draws his connections, stating that the divine persons (Father, Son, and Holy Spirit) are related to creatures *not through the relations of origins that they enjoy within the eternal Trinity*, but through the divine essence wherein is "included" the divine persons, since the relations of the persons is the divine essence, on Aquinas' account. To clarify: Aquinas is keen to establish the point of connection between the divine persons and creatures as deriving *not* from the divine persons' personal relations (of origin) but from the divine essence which they are. This is a fine distinction and nuance worth guarding, because, as Emery states:

> Each divine person is distinguished and constituted through the relation he has with the other divine persons; it is not the relationship to creatures which distinguishes and constitutes the divine person. If one brings the relationship to creatures into this region, it will lead one back into thinking that the Trinity's very existence as three distinct persons, depends on how God acts in the world, as if the world could fashion a divine person's being.⁸⁸

---

85. Emery, *Trinitarian Theology*, 74.
86. I *Sent.* d. 14, q. 1, a. 1, quoted in Emery, *Trinitarian Theology*, 343.
87. ST I, q. 45, a. 6.
88. Emery, *Trinitarian Theology*, 341. The argument is more complex than that presented above, and it involves Aquinas' understanding of the notion of relation and person. In short, for Aquinas, the category of relation carries a double aspect: there is the aspect of the pure relation and the aspect that this relation inheres in a subject. Within God, the first aspect consists in the pure person-to-person relations of origin (paternity, filiation, spiration, and procession). For the second aspect, the relation does not exist accidentally in God as it does for the creature, but it exists substantially in God. It is in this sense that the divine relation is identical to the very being of the divine essence (see ST I, q. 28, a. 2; q. 39, a. 1). By bringing these two aspects into each other, Aquinas conceives the divine person as a relation who subsists. Aquinas proceeds further to see the relationship the divine person has with creatures as finding its point of "entry" in the second aspect of the divine relation, that is, the aspect where the relation "includes" the divine essence and is held in connection with the divine essence. Because God creates through his essence (or his nature)—specifically in the wisdom and will and power that he is—his creating act gives creatures a participation in the attributes that God possesses "essentially" in himself and to their fullest degree. It is in this sense that creatures are said to "pre-exist" in the divine nature, and that the divine nature likewise serves as the cause and the source of all created things. See Emery, *Trinitarian Theology*, 340–42, and "Essentialism or Personalism," 535.

While bringing the relationship between the divine processions and God's work of creation as close together as possible—to the point of saying that the divine processions are inherently followed by a "procession toward external nature"[89]—Aquinas maintains that creation in no way adds to the "circle" of the divine processions.

Aquinas' discussion on the divine missions is a natural and further extension of his discussion on the relation between the divine processions and the work of creation. The processions of the divine persons underpin not only the coming forth of creatures from God but also their return to him, albeit a return not to a pre-existent state, but to a glorified state that flows from, as Aquinas himself states, a "supernatural participation of Divine goodness" enabled by the missions of the Son and the Spirit.[90] That Aquinas' enquiry into the divine missions occurs as a fitting conclusion to his treatise on the doctrine of God is to reemphasize the point that to think about the divine missions is still to consider the divine persons in their relationships, being, and properties. At the same time, it reinforces the message that their immanent divine life is not separated from the Trinitarian economy.[91] In fact, the concept of immanent processions and Trinitarian relations of origin includes the notion of missions, because, as Aquinas states, a divine mission has as its underpinning an eternal procession. "Added" to this eternal procession is the "temporal" procession wherein the divine person renders himself in an innovative way and in a new mode of presence where he had not previously.[92]

Yet again, here is a point not be missed: sufficient evidence indicates that *Aquinas did not envisage the divine missions as a second procession or a second divine act.* He states: "[M]ission . . . includes the eternal procession, with the addition of a temporal effect . . . . Hence the procession may be called *a twin procession*, eternal and temporal, not that there is a double relation to the principle, but *a double term, temporal* and *eternal.*"[93] Contemporary Thomist scholars have further reinforced this notion. As Emery states: "There are not two different processions, one eternal and one temporal. The phrase *temporal procession* means the eternal procession *joining itself* to the effect through which the divine person makes himself newly

---

89. *De potentia*, q. 9, a. 9, quoted in Emery, *Trinitarian Theology*, 73.

90. ST II–II, q. 2, a. 3.

91. Emery, *Trinitarian Theology*, 362.

92. ST I, q. 43, a. 1: "[T]he mission of a divine person . . . [means] in one way the procession of origin from the sender, and . . . [means] a new way of existing in another; thus the Son is said to be sent by the Father into the world, inasmuch as He began to exist visibly in the world by taking our nature."

93. ST I, q. 43, a. 2, ad. 3 (added emphasis).

present in the world."[94] Or as White expresses: "The missions of the Son and Spirit . . . *are the processions themselves* rendered present to spiritual creatures by sanctifying grace."[95]

From the above brief survey, one uncovers a substantial degree of overlap and congruence between Thomas Aquinas and Karl Barth when it comes to the topic of the relation between the divine processions and the divine missions. That is, it would be right to say that neither conceived of the divine processions and the divine missions as two acts in pre-temporal eternity, but rather, that *the divine missions were already contained in the processions*.[96] In other words, although the divine missions are distinguishable from the divine processions, they are inseparable. This is the basic point forming McCormack's central contention.[97] Challenging the common viewpoint that the divine processions and the divine missions are two *separate* acts—often with the added corollary that the former act is viewed as "necessary" while the latter is viewed as "free"—McCormack states:

> To say that Jesus Christ is the subject of election and to mean it as Barth means it requires, at a minimum, that the event of God's self-constitution as triune (i.e., the processions) and the event of his turning toward the human race in the covenant of grace (i.e., the missions) be one and the same event—albeit *one event with two terms*.[98]

The above statement identifies the very nerve of Barth's actualistic ontology. McCormack's discernment and underscoring of this point, coupled with his garnering of support from Thomas Aquinas, is to be lauded. I submit that this forms the core substance and the primary signification of what it means to say that Barth espoused an actualistic ontology: *triunity and election are equally primordial and basic to who God is*. In other words, when we conceive of God's being from his revelation, we cannot think of God being the triune God without thinking of him being the electing God at the same time, and vice versa. Anything more than that, such as the further attempt to decipher a priority or precedence between the two, should be secondary. Even then, the

---

94. Emery, *Trinitarian Theology*, 368.

95. White, "Introduction," 25–26 (added emphasis).

96. I am trying to be as precise as I can in my usage of terms here. I would not even say that the divine missions is *anticipated* in the divine processions, because "anticipation" leans towards seeing the divine missions as a second divine act.

97. McCormack, "Processions and Missions." McCormack acknowledges the work of Levering, "Christ, Trinity, and Predestination," 244–73, as providing the impetus for his essay.

98. McCormack, "Processions and Missions," 114–15 (original emphasis).

basic contention of an actualistic ontology requires that the priority or precedence under consideration be limited to the logical and not the chronological or temporal realm. The reason is evident: if God's self-determination to be the triune God and his self-election to be the God for us in Christ Jesus occurs in one and the same (divine) event in eternity, then there can be no temporal "before" or "after" to triunity and election. In this case, what remains is the logical question: "What ought humans to think of first in their efforts to think about the eternal being of God responsibly?"[99]

In relation to the above question, McCormack acknowledges the fundamental difference between Aquinas and Barth. That Aquinas begins in the *Summa Theologica* with an approach whereby the divine essence of God is discussed with the considerable aid of metaphysical distinctions and tools means that Aquinas would be inclined toward giving the logical priority to triunity. On the other hand, Barth's approach that works exclusively from the economy to the immanent Trinity suggests, according to McCormack, that he would have been open to placing the logical priority on election.[100] This difference aside, McCormack contends that Aquinas could be read "down" into Barth (since Aquinas begins with the divine processions) and Barth read "up" into Aquinas (since Barth begins with the divine missions) such that the two great theologians meet in the middle, their point of convergence being the shared affirmation of a single eternal act in which both the processions and the missions take place.[101]

Overall, it is important not to misread my purpose for drawing Thomas Aquinas into the discussion. I am nowhere advocating that Aquinas spoke or even approved of speech like that of Barth's that specifies command and obedience as the personal properties of the Father and Son respectively. It is clear for Aquinas that the divine persons arise from the divine relations which in turn derive from the divine processions.[102] As such, the only personal properties that Aquinas would allow for would be that of paternity for the Father and filiation for the Son, with both properties arising from the divine procession of begetting and being begotten respectively. Rather, my purpose for engaging Thomas Aquinas is to highlight the point that the basic assertion of Barth's actualistic ontological framework, which sees triunity and election as equally primordial and basic to who God is, is coherent with

---

99. McCormack, "Election and Trinity: Theses," 208.

100. McCormack, "Processions and Missions," 101–2, 115.

101. McCormack, "Processions and Missions," 115.

102. Aquinas takes extra care to ensure in his treatise that the divine persons are not seen to be derived from the essence, for that would mean dividing the essence among the three persons (Emery, "Essentialism or Personalism," 546–47).

Aquinas' "actualistic" notion that the divine missions is already contained in the divine processions within one and same divine event.

Barth's Actualistic Reading of God's Freedom, God's Knowing, and God's Willing

The second area draws upon what Barth had to say about God's freedom and his knowing and willing under the doctrine of the perfections of God in *CD* II/1. It presents at its most basic consideration the case that Barth's account of divine freedom and the divine knowing and willing remain generously open to the core contention of the actualistic ontology outlined above, namely, that triunity and election are both equally basic and primordial to who God is. Rendered slightly differently: God's decision of election bears on who he is essentially.

First, however, we have to answer the prior and fundamental question that surfaces whenever the topic of Barth's doctrine of the perfections of God is brought into relation with his actualistic ontology. That is, should Barth's basic description of God's being as a being-in-act be read in the conventional sense of *specification*, or does it consists in the more provocative notion of *constitution*? So, for example, when Barth states: "God is who He is in His works,"[103] or "God is who He is in the act of His revelation,"[104] does the term "God is" in the above two quotations signify that God in his innermost being is not different from who he specifies himself to be in his act of revelation? Or does the actualism run deeper to signify that God's very own being is determined or even somehow "constituted" in the eternal decision whereby God in Christ Jesus elects to be God *pro nobis*?

Far from being pedantic, the answer to the above question is the determining key to how one conceives Barth's actualistic ontology. On the one hand, a reading of God's being-in-act as primarily an act of specification implies the *prior existence* of the subject whose being is being specified, naturally gravitating the whole discussion toward a scenario where *being precedes act*. On the other hand, a reading of God's being-in-act in a constitutive sense aligns one closer to the actualistic notion whereby *being and act coincide and "happen" together at the same moment*. The latter view, I propose, is the minimum ontological thinking required to support the actualistic ontology advocated in this volume where triunity and election are equally "present" to God.

---

103. *CD* II/1, 260.
104. *CD* II/1, 262.

A cursory reading of the introductory section of *CD* II/1 §28 indicates, however, that answering the above question is not as straightforward as one might imagine. The section contains numerous pithy statements and claims of Barth that, on a surface reading, could pull Barth in either direction.[105] While this complicates matters, it is to be expected. According to McCormack, the roots of Barth's actualistic ontology can be traced to the breakthrough he achieved with his doctrine of election. If so, and Barth started on the significant re-working of his doctrine of election from the *Göttingen Dogmatics* following the lead from Pierre Maury's lecture in 1936,[106] then *KD* II/1 published in 1939 would capture the burgeoning phase of Barth's actualistic ontology before its full maturation in *KD* II/2 published three years later. Subscribing to McCormack's plausible account of Barth's intellectual thought development would mean that the ontological statements in *CD* II/1 should not be read on its own, but in tandem and in anticipation of what Barth would come to say more fully in *CD* II/2 and onwards. In other words, bearing in mind the particular stage of development in Barth's thought, the ontological statements on God's being as a being-in-act in *CD* II/1 should at least be interpreted as displaying an openness to the particular reading of Barth's actualistic ontology advocated in this chapter.

A fine example of an ontological statement would be the following noteworthy assertion from Barth in *CD* II/1: "The fact that God's being is event, the event of God's act . . . means that it is His own conscious, willed and executed decision [*bewußte, gewollte und vollbrachte Entscheidung*] . . . . No other being *exists absolutely* [*ist schlechterdings*] in its act. *No other being is absolutely its own, conscious, willed and executed decision.*"[107] Although some have argued for the statement to be read with a sense of specification, I maintain that the constitutive meaning of the statement is more plausible.[108]

105. So for example the earlier statement "God is who He is in His works. He is the same even in Himself, even before and after and over His works, and without them" (*CD* II/1, 260) gravitates towards a "specification" reading. Other statements like "God is who He is in the act of His revelation" (*CD* II/1, 262) are neutral, while statements like "What God is as God, the divine individuality and characteristics, the *essentia* or "essence" of God, is something which we shall encounter either at the place where God deals with us as Lord and Saviour, or not at all" (*CD* II/1, 261); "[I]n this very event God is who He is" (*CD* II/1, 262), and "God is also the One who is event, act and life in His own way, as distinct from everything that He is not Himself" (*CD* II/1, 264) suggest a determinative or "constitutive" reading.

106. See McCormack, "Historicized Christology," 213–15; McCormack, "Seek God," 63–65; and Gockel, *Barth and Schleiermacher*, 159–97. Pierre Maury's lecture and his teaching on election has been made available in English in Hattrell, *Election, Barth and French Connection*.

107. *CD* II/1, 271 / *KD* II/1, 304 (added emphasis).

108. Two examples of a "specification" reading would be Price, *Letters of the Divine*

This is especially so when the key term "decision" (*Entscheidung*) is read in anticipation of how it will be employed in *CD* II/2.[109] By the time one reaches *CD* IV/1, we find a Barth who is less restrained in using the language of constitution to describe the self-determining act or event of God.[110]

The idea of interpreting God's being-in-act in a "constitutive" sense rather than with a sense of specification leads, however, to two major difficulties, which need to be addressed before the argument can proceed further. The first difficulty traverses theological lines and goes as follows: if Barth is saying that God's triune being and his divine election are both ontologically basic to who he is, that is, they both happen in the same "event," who then would be the pre-existing subject who elects? A helpful response to this criticism is to consider the divine missions in relation to the divine processions. Just as the Father does not pre-exist the act of begetting the Son in the divine processions, so that there is no Father without the Son, in the same way, the Father does not pre-exist the decision in which he turns toward the human race in the Son and the Spirit (divine missions) at the same time in the same self-determining "event" of triunity and election. The core contention of the actualistic ontology presented here means that just as there is no pre-existent subject behind triunity, there is no pre-existent subject behind election.[111]

The second difficulty arises from philosophical considerations and it concerns "whether it makes [philosophical] sense to talk of any existing entity whose sole determination should be that it is some kind of existing entity," as articulated by Stephen Williams.[112] Williams further identifies a logical gap in Barth's argument in *CD* II/1 where Barth collapses the notion

---

Word, 19, and Stratis, "Speculating about Divinity?," 20–32. Stratis contends that Barth's language of "decision" should be taken in a polemical sense primarily to guard the aseity of God's personhood as "self-moved being" against liberal Protestant perspectives which have defined God's personhood anthropomorphically (26), rather than as a direct explication of his earlier statement that God is *actus purus et singularis* (27). The upshot is that a tight linkage between "decision" and "being" leads inevitably to a reading of *CD* II/2 that prioritizes election over the Trinity, whereas a looser connection between the two terms as Stratis advocates for leads to a different reading of *CD* II/2.

109. See *CD* II/2, 50, for a reading where the "decision" is clearly used in a determinative sense "proper to [God's] own eternal being."

110. Consider the following statement of Barth's in *CD* IV/1, 129 / *KD* IV/1, 141: "Jesus Christ is Himself God as the Son of God the Father and with God the Father the source of the Holy Spirit, united in one essence with the Father by the Holy Spirit. That is how He is God. He is God as He takes part in the event which constitutes [*ausmacht*] the divine being."

111. I agree with McCormack, "Processions and Missions," 121, that in this sense the criticism is a "nonstarter."

112. Williams, "Appendix," 183n17.

of "God as living" into "God is act" without carrying out the necessary analytic work; therefore, there is no compelling reason for one to subscribe to Barth's actualistic understanding of divine ontology.[113] A response to this philosophical objection is to highlight that Barth might deem this objection as an intrusion of philosophy into theology, or worse still, an attempt to philosophize via the *analogia entis*—what is impossible for creaturely/human ontology is held to be so for divine ontology.[114] Barth clearly recognized the uniqueness and exclusivity of divine ontology: "*No other being* exists absolutely in its act. *No other being* is absolutely its own, conscious, willed and executed decision,"[115] and he recognized that his ontological statements in *CD* II/1 were challenging common perceptions of metaphysical thinking like the notion of "essence."[116] In *CD* IV/2, Barth admits of the logical/philosophical difficulty in the strand of his actualistic thinking when it comes to "historicizing" the essences. He states:

> How can a being be interpreted as an act, or an act as a being? How can God, or man, or both in their unity in Jesus Christ, be understood as history? How can humiliation also and at the same time be exaltation? How can it be said of a history which took place once that it takes place to-day, and that, having taken place once and taking place to-day, it will take place again?[117]

Yet, Barth answers that all suspicions and difficulties cannot be regarded as decisive in this matter. "Difficulty or no difficulty," Barth states, "we must attempt to think and state the matter along these [actualistic] lines."[118]

Besides Barth's possible and likely response to this logical/philosophical objection, another possible response could be to turn, once again, to the divine processions. If the divine relations derived from the divine processions are identical to the being of the divine essence, is it not possible to conceive of the being of God as a being-in-act, with the "act" in this instance being the divine (immanent) processions? Either way, I submit that the philosophical objection need not occlude thinking of God's being-in-act in a constitutive sense.

---

113. Williams, "Appendix," 187n25.

114. Williams similarly recognizes this option as a possible response of Barth's (see Williams, "Appendix," 183n17).

115. *CD* II/1, 271 (added emphasis).

116. *CD* II/1, 262.

117. *CD* IV/2, 108.

118. *CD* IV/2, 108.

Divine Freedom

Having established the key premise that Barth's ontological statements in *CD* II/1 do not preclude a determinative or "constitutive" reading of God's being-in-act, I turn now to consider divine freedom, and how the notion as Barth explicates it bears on his actualistic ontology.

First, the entrenched criticism that Barth's actualistic ontology risks compromising the freedom of God needs to be addressed. If God's self-determination as the triune God is coincident and coterminous with God's self-election as the God who is for *us* in Jesus Christ, does that not in some way entail the necessity of creation for the being of God? In reply, it is undeniable that the actualistic ontology advocated herein does call for a revision—more precisely, a subversion—of the way "freedom" and "necessity" are often conceived. The popular conception in the cultural and philosophical milieu of our day is that divine freedom, like human freedom, is defined *via negativa* as freedom from external constraint and conditioning, or internal lack and deficiency. Barth, in his discussion of the perfections of God, certainly considers this particular aspect of freedom, but assigns it a secondary and negative role. Instead, Barth states: "[F]reedom in its positive and proper qualities means to be grounded in one's own being, to be *determined* and *moved by oneself*. This is the freedom of the divine life and love."[119] Barth labels this dimension of God's freedom where God is free in Godself as his "primary" absoluteness, while he labels the aspect whereby God is free in relation to creation, and hence from external limitation, as God's "secondary" absoluteness.[120] It is precisely God's transcendence of external limitation—his secondary absoluteness—that allows him to be immanent to his creatures in a saving manner—his primary absoluteness.[121] The secondary absoluteness serves the primary absoluteness, which constitutes the definition of divine freedom for Barth. Barth proceeds to ground the primary absoluteness of God in the inner-Trinitarian divine life.[122] Yet, it is equally important to note in all the discussion that Barth neither abolishes nor negates the notion of a "secondary" freedom or the "secondary" absoluteness of God.

Based on Barth's definition, God's freedom should hence be conceived first and foremost as a freedom for what I term "*Godself*-determination." That is, our conception of divine freedom should not consist in the mental

---

119. *CD* II/1, 301 (added emphasis).
120. *CD* II/1, 306, 309.
121. Price, *Letters of the Divine Word*, 28.
122. *CD* II/1, 317.

picture of God choosing between alternatives, to exist either this way or another way. But divine freedom is more fundamental than that. It is *the freedom God gives himself to exist in this particular way*—one that is founded upon the singular eternal act of self-determination whereby in a concurrent and coterminous manner God is the triune God and the God who elects in Jesus Christ. This is why God's freedom-in-Godself is simultaneously a freedom-for-creation-and-redemption, a freedom to realize his electing purposes.[123] In fact, to conceive otherwise—the freedom of God as a freedom of choice to exist this way or that—would be to locate the freedom of God in some sort of ontic space "behind" the triunity of God and the eternal decision of election. There is no such space, because, as McCormack states in agreement with Aquinas, "there is in God no unrealized potentiality."[124] Moreover, there is no such ontic space in the first place because, as argued above, there is no such divine subject behind the God who is triune and who is at the same instance the God who elects. Granted that what has just been articulated requires a strenuous effort of rumination and a reversal of the way divine freedom is often conceived, I believe that this revised definition of God's freedom faithfully captures Barth's understanding on this subject matter. Barth again on divine freedom:

> The freedom of God must be recognized as His own freedom and this means—as it consists in God and *as God has exercised it*. But in God *it consists in His Son Jesus Christ*, and it is *in Him that God has exercised it* . . . . [I]n conclusion . . . the freedom of God is the freedom which consists and fulfils itself in His Son Jesus Christ. In Him God has loved Himself from all eternity. In Him He has loved the world. He has done so in Him, in the freedom which renders His life divine, and therefore glorious, triumphant, and strong to save.[125]

Divine Knowing and Willing

The immediate preceding account of divine freedom is concomitant with Barth's account of divine knowing and willing. In fact, Barth brings the two aspects of God's knowing and God's willing together in such a manner that they serve as the key presupposition on which his account of divine freedom is predicated.

---

123. McCormack, "Election and Trinity: Theses," 223, and McCormack, "Processions and Missions," 124.

124. McCormack, "Processions and Missions," 124.

125. *CD* II/1, 320–21 (added emphasis).

Under his wider discussion on the perfection of omnipotence, Barth begins by establishing the claim that in the way God's attributes are his essence, so God's knowledge and will are each his essence. Barth states clearly: "God's knowledge is God Himself, and again God's will is God Himself."[126] God needs neither the existence of objects nor any form of mediation in order to know, but by virtue of the fact that he is God, and that *his being is itself his knowledge*, God already knows (himself) perfectly.[127] The same could be asserted of God's will. Barth makes the following claim that has tremendous import for furthering the notion of God's being-in-act as an act that is determinative or constitutive in nature: "God is His own will, and *He wills His own being*. Thus will and being are equally real in God, but they are not opposed to one another in the sense that the will can or must precede or follow the being or the being the will. Rather, *it is as He wills that He is God*, and *as He is God that he wills*."[128] In Barth's hands, both the divine knowing and willing are tied intricately to God's very own being.

Furthermore, Barth not only links the divine knowing and willing to the being of God, but goes further to conjoin the two in a unity that welds them together in an inseparable and common field of action, while maintaining their distinction and irreducibility. Barth again: "If God's knowledge is God Himself, and again if God's will is God Himself, we cannot avoid the further statement that God's knowledge is His will and God's will His knowledge." He continues: "[This] means, then, that His knowledge is as extensive as His will and His will as His knowledge. *Everything that God knows He also wills*, and *everything that He wills He also knows*. In every way God's knowledge is also His will and His will is a will that knows."[129]

I would like to take the above-mentioned thought pattern of Barth's and apply the common and mutual singular activity of God's knowing and willing to two areas: first, God's knowing and willing of himself and second, of all other things external to Godself. In regard to the latter, God's knowing and willing includes, as Price says of Barth, "the actual, the possible, and even the logically and ontologically impossible, each in its own way."[130] But I posit that in relation to the former, God's knowing and willing of himself involves only actualities, and not possibilities or alternatives. The reason for this is that God knows perfectly who he is, and because his knowing *is* his willing, in knowing himself perfectly, God also (simultaneously) wills

---

126. *CD* II/1, 549.
127. *CD* II/1, 549.
128. *CD* II/1, 550 (added emphasis).
129. *CD* II/1, 551 (added emphasis).
130. Price, *Letters of the Divine Word*, 151 (see also *CD* II/1, 551–52).

himself to be so. In God's innermost being, there is no gap or cleavage between God's knowing and his willing, such that his willing becomes a willing amongst options.

Now, it must be stressed that Barth himself certainly did not separate in such definite terms God's knowing and willing of himself and all other things external to him, but I surmise that the particular move I have just suggested is not too far away from Barth's own thinking.

Three excerpts from Barth support this intuitive hunch. First, Barth recognizes that God "both knows and wills in a way which is true and divine," that "is *proper to Himself* in accordance with His holiness, righteousness and wisdom."[131] What I have attempted to show is *that* "proper" way in which knowing and willing happens within God's being. Second, foreknowledge is predicated of divine knowledge in relation to all its objects—but Barth has a major qualification at this point—"with the exception of God Himself in His knowledge of Himself."[132] Third, Barth attributes to God's will freedom, which forms the corresponding equivalent that divine foreknowledge is to God's knowledge. Yet, in a similar manner to what he does with foreknowledge, Barth stops short of applying this freedom to God's willing of his own being. Barth states: "The freedom of God's will means that it precedes and is superior to all its objects—*with the exception of God Himself*, to the extent that God also and first of all wills Himself."[133] These two exclusions of divine foreknowledge and freedom in willing prove that Barth is keenly aware that God's divine knowing and willing of himself is fundamentally different from all other realities external to him. This is so even though Barth did not explicitly spell out the differences in the way I have attempted here.

More importantly, the specific account of divine knowing and willing presented here coheres with Barth's account of divine freedom that was proffered earlier, and in fact undergirds that account. If the divine knowing *is* the divine willing, then God's perfect knowledge of his being is at the same time his willing to exist and be in that particular way in which he knows himself perfectly. That being the case, the divine knowing will not be a knowledge of alternative states of being, or the divine willing a willing among options. This means that a conception of divine freedom will naturally follow suit where freedom for God too will not be a freedom to choose between different alternatives of existence and being, but rather the freedom of God to be in the particular way defined by the perfect knowing and willing of Godself. That way is: to be the God who is for us in Christ

---

131. *CD* II/1, 551 (added emphasis).
132. *CD* II/1, 558.
133. *CD* II/1, 560.

Jesus. Read this way, Barth's actualistic conception of the perfections of God's freedom and his divine knowing and willing can be seen as en route towards championing the specific model of Barth's actualistic ontology advocated here in this present chapter.[134]

Eberhard Jüngel's Reading of Barth's Actualistic Ontology

In this third area, I turn to an interpretive account of Barth's actualistic ontology as read by one of the foremost interpreters of Barth—Eberhard Jüngel. In my view, Jüngel's reading as presented in his book *Gottes Sein ist im Werden* supports the particular version of Barth's actualistic ontology propounded in this chapter.

The admission must be made at the outset that Jüngel did not set out to address the logical relation between triunity and election, but his work does aid our consideration.[135] At the core of his argument, Jüngel maintains the idea that God's being-for-us, his being *ad extra* revealed in revelation, *corresponds* to his inner-Trinitarian being-in-Godself, his being *ad intra*. In addition, it is the latter that serves as the basis and prototype for the former.[136] Stated another way, God's *relation to us* arises because of God's *self-relation* within his divine being, envisaged in the mutual relations between the three modes of God's being as Father, Son, and Spirit.[137] Employing terminology highly consistent with Barth's actualistic ontology, Jüngel describes this self-relation within God as an *event*, as a "*being-in-becoming*," in that the modes of God's being are "related to each other in

---

134. I say "en route" because Barth's account of divine power does run counter at certain points to what has been proposed here of God's freedom and the divine knowing and willing. Barth states that divine power means that God has "power over everything that He actually wills or could will" (*CD* II/1, 522). McCormack, "The Actuality of God," 235, states that Barth did not need to resort to speaking of a surplus of power that goes beyond what God actually willed to do, and that by speaking of this surplus of power, Barth "trespassed against the very core of his methodological commitments." As mentioned earlier, these inconsistencies could possibly be explained by McCormack's account of the development of Barth's actualistic ontology at the point of writing *CD* II/1. By *CD* II/2, however, we sense a more consistent appeal to God's divine power as defined by and not in abstraction from his electing work in Jesus Christ. There, Barth asks the rhetorical question: "May it not be that it is as the electing God that He is the Almighty, and not *vice versa*?" (*CD* II/2, 45) Barth's last clause—"and not *vice versa*"—suggests that Barth no longer sees election as merely one possibility among others available to God in defining his omnipotence; instead, it forms the definitional key for Barth.

135. A point made by McCormack, "God Is His Decision," 60.

136. Jüngel, *God's Being*, 35–36.

137. Jüngel, *God's Being*, 42.

such a way that each mode of God's being *becomes* what it *is* only *with the two other modes of being.*"[138] Just as important, Jüngel states that this irrevocable determination to be the God whose being is one in becoming lies in the "primal decision" of God. Here is the crucial point not to be missed—*this "primal decision" is at one and the same time a decision of God for man*. I reproduce the crucial statement from Jüngel:

> We have therefore to understand this decision as God's "primal decision" which irrevocably determines God's being-in-act, or rather, as God's primal decision in which *God* determines irrevocably his being-in-act. This self-determination of God is an act of his self-relatedness as Father, Son and Holy Spirit. It is, however, *at the same time*, an attitude and relation of God to man and, indeed, "the attitude and relation in which by virtue of the decision of His free love God wills to be and is God. And this relation cannot be separated from the Christian conception of God as such. The two must go together if this conception is to be truly Christian."[139]

Elsewhere, Jüngel states: "We have to understand God's primal decision as an *event* in the being of God which *differentiates* the modes of God's being."[140]

Embedded in the above discussion is a point of significance not to be missed. Reading Jüngel (as he reads Barth) leads us to deduce the key verity for Barth's actualistic ontology: *being and act are both ontologically "basic" and "present" at the same "moment"* to God. Expressed slightly more complicatedly: God being the triune God and God being the God-who-is-for-us in Jesus Christ is founded in one and the same determinative or constitutive act located simultaneously and in a coterminous manner in the "primal decision" of God. The main consequence stemming from this truth would be, as reinforced by McCormack, that there can be "no being of God that is somehow ontologically prior to this decision."[141] Being cannot (ontologically) precede this self-determining act. If that were to be the case, then the *act* of self-determination would be a determination not in the unqualified

---

138. Jüngel, *God's Being*, 77 (original emphasis). George Hunsinger, "*Mysterium Trinitatis*," 193, helpfully reminds us that this "being-in-becoming" within Godself arises because of the triune nature of God Himself—He is a "unity always becoming one because it is perpetually positing itself as three." Unlike the "becoming" of process theology, it is not due to lack or incompletion, but is the perpetual movement from perfection to perfection.

139. Jüngel, *God's Being*, 85 (original emphasis). The quotation cited by Jüngel is from *CD* II/2, 9.

140. Jüngel, *God's Being*, 86 (original emphasis).

141. McCormack, "God Is His Decision," 60.

sense of *being* something, but only in the qualified sense of *doing* something. Consequently, this would push all talk of God's election and reconciliatory actions towards the direction of a mode of appearance of a divine subject whose *being was already determined prior to and in abstraction from this self-determining act*.[142] Such a notion runs contrary to the actualistic ontology that I believe Barth espoused.

To recap the discussion so far: the virtue of Jüngel's reading of Barth's actualistic ontology is that it encapsulates the central core of Barth's actualistic ontology: the fact that act and being are both equally basic in an ontological way for who God is, and that both coincide in a coterminous manner in the primordial decision of God's self-determination. But Jüngel pushes further. While recognizing the incongruity and the impossibility of speaking of a *chronological* and *ontological* priority and precedence between trinity and election, Jüngel's proposal nonetheless heads in a direction where the *logical* priority and precedence of trinity is asserted over election.[143] Jüngel achieves this through advocating the notion of the "double structure" of the one being of God. In a crucial passage again, he states:

> God's being-in-act was understood to mean that God is his decision. Decision sets in relation, for it is as such a setting-oneself-in-relation. . . . God's setting-himself-in-relation points in both an inward and an outward direction at the same time. This is grounded in Barth's understanding of revelation as the self-interpretation of God in which God is his own "double". . . . We understood *the one being of God in its double structure as a being in correspondence*. And in the statement "God corresponds to himself" we saw the grounding of God's being as the one who loves in freedom. In just this way, the statement defines

---

142. McCormack, "Election and Trinity: Theses," 205–7.

143. In this way, Jüngel differs from McCormack, whom as we have seen, contends for the logical priority and precedence of election over triunity. McCormack himself acknowledges this difference. In McCormack, "Karl Barth's Version," 125, he stated the following: "So, in [Jüngel's] view, the triunity of God has, at most, a *logical* priority over election" (original emphasis). That said, McCormack allows for this possibility. See McCormack, "God Is His Decision," 60, and McCormack, "Election and Trinity: Theses," 206–7, where he stated that "one could continue to speak of a logical priority of Trinity over election but all further talk of an ontological priority would have to be surrendered." This statement reveals the emphatic and the "non-negotiable" core of McCormack's conception of Barth's actualistic ontology. That is, God being the triune God is one and the same time his self-determination whereby he elects himself to be the God for us in Jesus Christ. I believe that anything beyond this core contention, e.g., the logical priority and relationship between election and triunity, would be something which McCormack would allow for a certain degree of flexibility in interpretive differences.

> *the historicality of the being of God* which *reiterates* itself in *the historicality of revelation.*[144]

The above quote reveals the following two key insights. First, the freedom of God even as he loves is one that exists and expresses itself in God's "historicality"—a term Jüngel employs to describe God's being as one that actually demands historical predicates.[145] In other words, God's being is one capable of reiterating itself in revelation via historical predicates. I see the merit of appropriating the notion of "historicality" as a characteristic of the being of God in that it serves as a way of bringing *election as a divine act of God as close as possible in relation to his triunity.*

Second, Jüngel's employment of the "double-structure of God's being," and his commandeering of the terms "reiteration" and "correspondence" to define the relation between the two layers, serves to safeguard the asymmetry of the logical relationship between God's triune being and his being the God who-is-for-us in Christ Jesus. Specifically, God's "being-in-becoming" *in the divine act of election* is predicated upon and sourced in his "being-in-becoming" *within the self-relatedness of the triune God* as Father, Son, and Holy Spirit.[146] God's setting-himself-in-relation in the outward direction is *reiterative* of and *correspondent* to his setting-himself-in-relation in the inward direction. Again: God's "being-already-ours-in-advance" is grounded in his Trinitarian "being-for-himself."[147] Jüngel expresses it well with the following quote:

> [God's *doubly* relational being] means that God can enter into relation (*ad extra*) with another being (and in this very relation his being can exist ontically, *without* thereby being ontologically dependent on this other being), because God's being (*ad intra*) is a being *related to itself*. The doctrine of the Trinity is an attempt to think through the self-relatedness of God's being.[148]

All in all, Jüngel's proposal i) allows us to affirm the economic Trinity as identical to the immanent Trinity while not conflating the two realities, ii) upholds the triune being of God's relation-in-Himself and the triune being of God's relation-in-election-towards-us in the closest relationship possible—both happen in the same singular divine act which I call "God-self-determination"—while maintaining the logical priority and precedence

---

144. Jüngel, *God's Being*, 83 (added emphasis).
145. Jüngel, *God's Being*, 109.
146. Jüngel, *God's Being*, 77.
147. Jüngel, *God's Being*, 91.
148. Jüngel, *God's Being*, 114 (original emphasis).

of the former over the latter, and iii) advances his concepts without capitalizing on the language of "necessity."[149] For these reasons, Jüngel's reading is to be commended as providing firm support for the account of Barth's actualistic ontology contended in this volume.[150]

Barth's View of Time and Eternality

The fourth and final area that I wish to consider is that of Barth's view of time and eternality. Now, I am aware that the topic is one fraught with difficulty. But I am convinced that Barth's view of time and eternality has a direct bearing on the reading of his actualistic ontology. As Aaron Smith has correctly highlighted (in reference to McCormack and Molnar in the protracted Trinity-election debate): "[A]n understanding of time and eternity is integral to each interlocutor's conception of divine being."[151] At the same time, I am under no pretense that the brief discussion to follow does justice to the subject matter. Instead, what I offer are the following two points that I believe suffice for our consideration.[152]

First, that Barth's concept of divine eternality is threefold, in which God's eternity consists in his pre-temporality, supra-temporality, and post-temporality (*Vorzeitlichkeit*, *Überzeitlichkeit*, *Nachzeitlichkeit*), is a well-known facet of Barth's teaching on divine eternality. This means that, as Griswold states, "God is the origin of all time, God accompanies or contains all time, and God is there after time as its goal and hope."[153] Moreover, divine eternity does not consist of pre-, supra-, and post-temporality in the sense

---

149. Jüngel closes his book with the following words: "One final thought remains to be considered. In that we called God's being a being in becoming, we understood that God can reveal himself. But that God does what he can do, that in his revelation he has reiterated himself, *is based on no necessity*" (Jüngel, *God's Being*, 121, added emphasis).

150. It is appropriate to mention here Barth's own endorsement of Jüngel's proposal. In Busch, *Meine Zeit Mit Karl Barth*, 13–15, Busch speaks of a small working group that met at Barth's home to discuss new theological literature, in which Jüngel's *God's Being* was being discussed in the summer of 1965. In that meeting, Busch records: "Barth expressed the highest satisfaction with the book," expressing "no objections to the book, apart from the fact that Jüngel's linguistic style was not always accessible to him." Further in the entry, Busch records that Barth deemed Jüngel's remarks about the doctrine of the Trinity to be "entirely right," although "Barth would have preferred it if [Jüngel] had presented the argument by means of exegetical and historical-theological investigations" (Translation provided by Matthew J. Aragon Bruce, September 3, 2011).

151. Smith, "God's Self-Specification," 20.

152. Two fuller recent volumes which treat Barth's concept of time and eternality that I draw upon are Griswold, *Triune Eternality*, and Langdon, *God the Eternal Contemporary*.

153. Griswold, *Triune Eternality*, 10.

of a sequential agglomeration of these three aspects, but rather is, as Barth states, "the simultaneity of beginning, middle and end, and to that extent it is pure duration."[154] The familiarity of this particular facet of Barth's view on divine eternity, however, should not obscure its significant import for Barth's actualistic ontology. As Darren Sumner and Paul Jones have argued separately in their respective volumes, God's eternity is the ground, the creation, and the embracing of created time such that all its moments of beginning, middle and end are simultaneously "present" to him. It is precisely for this reason that God is *simultaneously* pre-, supra- and post-temporal vis-à-vis created time that the God-man Jesus Christ can be proleptically identified as the eternal Son, or underscored with an even stronger actualistic emphasis: God in his eternal self-determination constitutes his second mode of being as that of the God-man Jesus Christ.[155] Either way, the point is made that it is this particular facet of Barth's view of divine eternity that funds—philosophically and theologically—his actualistic ontology. Above all, it provides a cogent and viable explanation for how Barth can allow an event in *temporality*—the incarnation of the Son—to be determinative of the divine Son's being in *eternity*. This point, I remind us, forms the basis for the core argument of Barth's actualistic ontology argued in this chapter.

Second, a deeper probe privileges a reading of Barth's actualistic ontology that maintains a logical priority or precedence of triunity over election. The argument runs as follows. Upon deeper enquiry, Barth's view of divine eternity evinces what seems to be a three-tiered understanding of eternity and time.[156] There is the first tier understanding of the pre-temporal, or better, extra-temporal eternity God has *in se*, consisting in the movement and life of the triune persons. As Langdon stated: "Since God's immanent life is the differentiation and perichoretic relation of Father, Son, and Spirit—containing its own movement, order and succession—then eternity is its own

---

154. *CD* II/1, 608.

155. See Sumner, *Karl Barth and the Incarnation*, 120–28, and Jones, *Humanity of Christ*, 99–102. That Sumner and Jones share this common viewpoint, however, should not obscure the finer differences between them. Compare the following two quotes between them: "Just as God embraces creaturely time, in its entirety, in God's eternal life, so too . . . does God embrace the particular time (and space) of Christ, as a human, and make it *constitutive* for the being of the divine Son" (Jones, *Humanity of Christ*, 101 [added emphasis]), and "[I]f God is human in time . . . then God is human also in the eternity which comprehends time . . . . In God's time, the Son's historical becoming is already *contained* within the eternal moment (even as its creaturely temporality has not yet come to pass)" (Sumner, *Karl Barth and the Incarnation*, 123 [added emphasis]). Between the two, Jones is less hesitant to use "constitutive" language to describe the actualistic determination, while Sumner seems to be more comfortable with the language of "identification" and "containment."

156. Smith, "God's Self-Specification," 17.

particular time."[157] Better, as Barth himself says: "Eternity is the dimension of God's own life, the life in which He is self-positing, self-existent and self-sufficient as Father, Son and Holy Ghost."[158] It is in this sense that Griswold is right to assert that "the doctrine of the Trinity is deeply formative for Barth's concept of eternity."[159]

It is within this first tier understanding of the pure divine time of the Father and the Son in the fellowship of the Holy Spirit that there takes place the second tier of Barth's understanding of eternity: the readiness and openness of God to our time. This results in the familiar point by now that in God's eternity lies the simultaneity of pre-, supra-, and post-temporality. Griswold goes further to ground this simultaneity of temporality in God's triunity via the divine processions: "Because God in God's own being has these distinctions of *origin, begotten,* and *sent* without suffering disunity, it is fully consonant with this that God would have within God's own being the supremely temporal distinctions of beginning, succession, and end without suffering loss of duration."[160] Hence, God's eternity, far from being the negation of time, is in fact the grounding and basis of time.[161] The fact of the second tier understanding of eternity flowing from the first tier is captured elegantly in the following quote from Hunsinger:

> Barth presupposes . . . that God's trinitarian life includes a form of beginning, middle, and end peculiar to itself. The beginning, middle, and end that God possesses simultaneously and totally are, first of all, peculiar to the trinitarian *perichoresis*, to the eternal process of becoming, in which God moves from perfection to perfection in and for himself. *This eternal becoming*, in which his own absolute beginning, succession, and end are all present to God simultaneously—that is, his own eternal self-positing of himself as Father, Son and Holy Spirit—in turn *serves as the basis* on which all *creaturely time can be and is taken up by God and made present to himself in its totality simultaneously*.[162]

Equally noteworthy is the point that within this second tier understanding of God's eternity consisting in the simultaneity of pre-, supra-, and post-temporality, there occurs the appointment of the eternal Son for

---

157. Langdon, *God the Eternal Contemporary*, 3.
158. *CD* III/2, 526.
159. Griswold, *Triune Eternality*, 222.
160. Griswold, *Triune Eternality*, 210 (added emphasis).
161. Griswold, *Triune Eternality*, 204, 240–41.
162. Hunsinger, "*Mysterium Trinitatis*," 200 (emphasis mine). See also *CD* II/1, 640.

the temporal world.¹⁶³ In Jesus Christ, both electing God and elected human, stands "the beginning," the genesis of the theatre of created reality distinct from God yet which God interacts with in all his ways and his works. That Barth distinguishes between these two tiers in God's pre-temporal eternity is evident in the following statements of his: "[Jesus Christ] is the beginning of God before which there is no other beginning apart from that of God within Himself,"¹⁶⁴ and "[a]s the subject and object of this choice, Jesus Christ was at the beginning. He was not at the beginning of God, for God has indeed no beginning. But He was at the beginning of all things, at the beginning of God's dealings with the reality which is distinct from Himself."¹⁶⁵ Together, these two tiers of understanding coalesce to depict God's extra-temporal eternity as, stated by Langdon, the "measurement of God's being that includes the *perichoretic* and *electing* life of the Father, Son, and Spirit."¹⁶⁶

The first and second tiers of God's eternity function as the source of Barth's third tier of understanding of eternity and time. This time round, the focus is on our "time." Our time is a created, earthly time, a derived temporality based on God's own temporality. As derived, it does not share in the simultaneity of duration that God's eternity enjoys. But because our gracious God has eternally willed himself to participate in it (as seen from the second-tier understanding), our time—what Barth goes on to call our "lost time" and our "wounded time"—is taken up into his divine being and healed of its wounds.¹⁶⁷

The preceding paragraphs have outlined what I regard as the three tiers of Barth's view of eternity and time, with the first two tiers focusing on eternity and the third on time. Now remains the task of seeing how this three-tiered understanding bears on the actualistic ontology proposed here in this chapter. To repeat: at the core of this actualistic ontology lies the notion that both the divine processions and the divine missions happen in the same divine act in God's eternity, or to put it another way, God's triunity

---

163. *CD* II/1, 622 reads: "[T]his pre-time is the pure time of the Father and the Son in the fellowship of the Holy Spirit. And in this pure divine time there took place the appointment of the eternal Son for the temporal world, there occurred the readiness of the Son to do the will of the eternal Father, and there ruled the peace of the eternal Spirit."

164. *CD* II/2, 94.

165. *CD* II/2, 102.

166. Langdon, *God the Eternal Contemporary*, 66 (added emphasis).

167. The reference to "lost time" can be found in *CD* III/1, 72, while the reference to "wounded time" can be found in *CD* II/1, 617. See also Griswold, *Triune Eternality*, 226–27.

in eternity is *equally basic* and *primordial* as God's divine act of election in eternity. Bringing this one divine act of self-determination into relation with Barth's two-tiered understanding of God's divine eternity leads to the assertion that it is in this one divine act that the possibility of time is *founded*. On this account, eternity stands in relation to time as the founding "moment" to all subsequent temporal moments, rather than a "timelessness" of its own. The final outcome is that the following threefold equation can be maintained: God being the triune God in eternity is *equal* to God's divine act of election in eternity, which, in turn, is also *equal* to the founding "moment" of all subsequent temporal moments.

The above threefold equation bears two further implications for our conception of Barth's actualistic ontology. On the one hand, because it is *extra-temporal* eternity we are talking about, talk of chronology fails. This means that it is just not possible to attribute any kind of *chronological* sequence between God's act of self-differentiation as the triune God and his act of turning towards the world in Christ Jesus, since both happen in extra-temporality within God's eternity. Instead, the crux of Barth's actualistic ontology, as exemplified in Jüngel's thesis, is that both God's *ad intra* turning in triune self-relation and his *ad extra* turning in relation to the world arise not as two separate acts but from one and the same divine act.

On the other hand, the distinction between Barth's first and second tier understanding of divine eternity—moreover, that *the second tier stems from the first*—means that one cannot reverse the *asymmetrical relation* Barth sees between God's eternity consisting in his inner triune life (first tier) and that consisting in the simultaneity of his pre-, supra- and post-temporality in which the gratuitous election of Jesus Christ is located (second tier). Cast in terms of a logical priority, one could say that *God's eternity in Godself is the basis of God's eternity for the world*.[168]

By way of an analogous application of Jüngel's concept of the "double-structure of God's being" from the previous section, I posit a corresponding "double-structure of God's extra-temporal eternity." Stated simply: God's extra-temporal eternity found in the perichoretic and differentiating relations between the three modes of being in God's triune life reiterates itself in the extra-temporal eternity consisting in the simultaneity of pre-, supra- and post-temporality, in which Jesus Christ is posited as the

---

168. Webster, *Confessing God*, 166, describes God's relationship to the world as "not the first but a second movement" of God's being in his extra-temporal eternity. Furthermore, the "first" here must not be conceived as having precedence in time (since it is extra-temporality on view here), but precedence in logical priority. Gunton, similarly, in "Karl Barth's Doctrine of Election," 97, recognizes the "double movement within the Trinity and *ad extra*, which is yet one single movement."

"beginning" of all of God's works and ways with a reality distinct from himself.[169] In the same way that God's one eternal divine act of setting-himself-in-relation takes place in both an inward and outward direction with the inward directing the outward, the resultant extra-temporal eternity that the divine act takes place in likewise has two terms, and similarly, the inward term directs the outward.[170]

The upshot of drawing Barth's notion of time and eternity into the argument and of positing this "double-structure of God's pre-temporal eternity" is that the asymmetrical relationship between the two "determinations" is reinforced and maintained. I stress again: while the two "determinations" take place in a concurrent and coterminous manner in the one same divine act, the *ad intra* "determination" of God's setting-himself-in-relation within the triune persons in the divine Godhead is reiterated in the *ad extra* "determination" of God's setting-himself-in-relation to the world via election. In this case, the *logical* priority is preserved: the life of God *in se* overflows to the life of God for the world; the divine missions, although contained in the divine processions, nonetheless flow from and correspond to the divine processions.

The Validating Question—What about the *Logos asarkos*?

One last issue remains unresolved, that is, do we have a way of validating the particular reading of Barth's actualistic ontology presented thus far? I think we do. It involves answering what I see as the key question: "What then do we do with the *Logos asarkos*?" By that, I do not mean the *Logos asarkos* who is the *Logos incarnandus* at the same time, in other words a *logos-asarkos-and-incarnandus* as described under the actualistic ontological framework argued so far.[171] Instead, I am referring to the *Logos asarkos* "in himself,"

---

169. Jüngel, *God's Being*, 83. Jüngel actually nowhere discusses explicitly in *God's Being* the conditions of eternity in which God's "determination" occurs. The closest we have is on pp. 111–12 where he states that the correspondence of God's being as Father, Son, and Holy Spirit takes place as "God *makes space* within himself for *time*" (original emphasis), and that "this making-space-for-time within God is a *continuing* event" (added emphasis). Such a statement would align Jüngel's view of eternity closer to what has been presented here rather than, say, a "timelessness" view of eternity within the life of God *in se*.

170. The same can be said with regard to divine spatiality. God has his own space arising from the differentiation of the divine persons of the Trinity, and it is divine spaciousness that forms the presupposition and antecedent condition of the space given to the creature. See Rae, "Spatiality of God," 70–86.

171. To clarify, this is McCormack's understanding of the *Logos asarkos*. He has

whose identity is already complete apart from the humanity to be assumed; I am referring to a *logos-asarkos-and-aincarnandus*. As seen from the first chapter, although there are portions in *CD* where Barth disavows such a concept of the *Logos asarkos*,[172] there are also other portions where he seemingly allows for the existence of it, even portions located in what has been acknowledged as the mature phase of his "post-metaphysical" theology. For example, Barth states in one of the sections in the fine print of *CD* IV/1:

> In this context [of reconciliation] we must not refer to the second "person" of the Trinity as such, to the eternal Son or the eternal Word of God *in abstracto*, and therefore to the so-called λόγος ἄσαρκος. What is the point of a regress to Him as the supposed basis of the being and knowledge of all things? In any case, how can we make such a regress? The second "person" of the Godhead in Himself and as such is not God the Reconciler. In Himself and as such He is not revealed to us. In Himself and as such He is not *Deus pro nobis*, either ontologically or epistemologically. *He is the content of a necessary and important concept in trinitarian doctrine* when we have to understand the revelation and dealings of God in *the light of their free basis in the inner being and essence of God*.[173]

How does one make sense of Barth's perplexing move here, given that he not only allows for a *Logos asarkos* "in himself," but attributes to that *Logos asarkos* "a necessary and important concept in trinitarian doctrine"?[174]

There are basically two options available to account for Barth's move that keep within the range of Barth's actualistic ontology as proposed in this chapter.[175] The first is that taken by Bruce McCormack. McCormack

---

frequently been accused (wrongly in my mind) of rejecting wholesale the idea of a *Logos asarkos*. Instead, what McCormack asserts is that the *Logos asarkos* is always and has always been the *Logos incarnandus* at the same time. See McCormack, "The Identity of the Son," 155–72. Someone whom I can only mention in passing who genuinely maintains there is no such subject as the *Logos asarkos* is Robert Jenson. See Jenson, "Once More the *Logos Asarkos*," 130–33.

172. E.g. *CD* IV/1, 66.

173. *CD* IV/1, 52 (my emphasis).

174. Another major passage whereby Barth seemingly affirms the same would be *CD* III/1, 54: "It has to be kept in mind that the whole conception of the λόγος ἄσαρκος, the 'second person' of the Trinity as such, is an abstraction. It is true that *it has shown itself necessary to the christological and trinitarian reflections of the Church*" (added emphasis).

175. There is a third option, although it would take us outside the reach of Barth's actualistic ontology. That is, Barth's objection to the *Logos asarkos* was only on noetic or epistemic grounds and not on an ontic ground. So, for example, Hunsinger states:

is bemused by this statement of Barth to the extent that he infers Barth "either did not fully realize the profound implications of his doctrine of election for the doctrine of the Trinity, or he shied away from drawing them for reasons known only to himself."[176] McCormack sees what he perceives as a return to a "metaphysical" or "essentialist" way of thinking as a momentary lapse on Barth's part.

Now, McCormack's proposal is certainly plausible, especially if the developmental account of Barth's thinking is taken into consideration and the clincher of the argument is given to his latest and final word on the subject matter. Soon after the publication of *CD* IV/1, Barth is known to have spoken to a group of students the following: "Do not ever think of the second Person of the Trinity as only *Logos*. That is the mistake of Emil Brunner. There is no *Logos asarkos*, but only *ensarkos*. Brunner thinks of a *Logos asarkos*, and I think this is the reason for his natural theology. The *Logos* becomes an abstract principle."[177] Since this statement follows chronologically after *CD* IV/1, it could be taken as Barth's ultimate denunciation of the concept of a *Logos asarkos* abstracted from the incarnation he would assume in time. Of greater significance, in my judgment, is that this is the only coherent option available to McCormack, given his assertion of the logical priority and precedence of election over triunity.

Another option is open though, and I stand by this second option. However, this option requires a logical priority or precedence of triunity over election. Barth's retention of the *Logos asarkos* "in himself," that is, a *logos-asarkos-and-a*incarnandus reveals the keen maintenance of his chief descriptor of the being of God: that God is the one who *loves* in *freedom*. The *logos-asarkos-and-a*incarnandus is Barth's way of safeguarding notions of necessity intruding into his thoughts on divine ontology. That is to say, the *logos-asarkos-and-a*incarnandus functions to exclude that line of thinking that goes as follows: because God being triune and his divine decision of election occur in a coincident and coterminous manner, the incarnation of the Word is therefore necessary. Rather, the *logos-asarkos-and-a*incarnandus maintains the incarnation as an entirely free and gratuitous event, even as the divine decision of election (and corresponding to that the decision to be incarnate) is coterminous with God being the triune God.

"What [Barth] rejects is the idea that, as a matter of contingent fact, we might still have access to a *Logos asarkos* above and beyond the *Logos ensarkos*" (Hunsinger, "Election and the Trinity," 188). This third option entails that Barth still maintained the presence of a *Logos asarkos* "in himself and as such."

176. McCormack, "Grace and Being," 102.
177. Barth, *Table Talk*, 49.

Restated slightly differently: we have seen from our earlier consideration that Barth still allows for a divine freedom that is defined *via negativa* as freedom from external constraint and conditioning, that is, from any form of necessity. This is despite Barth's relegating this form of freedom to a position of secondary importance and priority. The presence of this "secondary" divine freedom in turn carries the logical implication that some form of the concept of divine possibilities within the divine self and divine will must be allowed for. The *logos-asarkos-and-*a*incarnandus* is the divine possibility that expresses the concomitant truth going alongside divine freedom which specifies that "the mystery of revelation might have taken place in a different way," as Sumner states.[178]

Having said the above about divine possibilities, however, what matters finally for Barth is the *reality* that God has given to himself and to us, and that straightaway relegates the divine possibility of the *logos-asarkos-and-*a*incarnandus* to a position of secondary and inferior importance vis-à-vis the reality of the *logos-asarkos-and-incarnandus* actualized. That this is the case can be teased out from the following quote by Barth: "[I]t would be senseless to allow the possibility of a reality not actually given . . . to become a rival, so to speak, of the possibility realized in the actually given reality."[179] For Barth, this "actually given reality" is that of the actualistic nature of God's being as a being in a self-determinative act, so much so that God's triune being is never separated from his being the God who reveals, reconciles and redeems in Christ Jesus. In this way, the Word has eternally assumed a human nature, in the sense that the Word is always the *Logos incarnandus*. Because of this, Barth no longer speaks of a *logos-asarkos-and-*a*incarnandus* as a concrete possibility or, even more regrettably, as an independent being. Instead, the *Logos* to Barth is, as Sumner states, "a concept that has meaning only within the larger reality of Jesus Christ."[180]

To reiterate the main point: an allowance for the *Logos asarkos* "in himself"—even if this *logos-asarkos-and-*a*incarnandus* is merely a divine possibility whose significance and importance is totally overshadowed and overpowered by the concrete reality of the *logos asarkos* who is always

---

178. Sumner, *Karl Barth and the Incarnation*, 90.

179. *CD* I/2, 39.

180. Sumner, *Karl Barth and the Incarnation*, 103. The discussion of divine possibilities in light of the freedom of God corresponds to Barth's understanding of divine power. See *CD* II/1, 539–41. The upshot is that while Barth's insistence on the irreducibility of God's divine power to his omnicausality leads to the positing of divine possibilities, his equal insistence on the *potentia absoluta* (God's absolute power) being expressed as the *potentia ordinata* (God's ordained power) leads to the deep relativization of these divine possibilities in terms of their significance and importance.

incarnandus—is possible only on the premise of a logical priority or precedence of triunity over election. That Barth does allow for the idea of a *logos-asarkos-and-a*incarnandus gestures toward such a logical priority for him.

Conclusion

We have traversed much ground—some in the immediate terrain of Barth's theology but also in neighbouring terrain—to uncover what I hope counts as a faithful reading of Barth's actualistic ontology. I am convinced that Barth did espouse an actualistic ontology in that his fundamental perception of God's being is of a *being-in-act*. That is, God is a divine subject whose very being is determined or even constituted in the one act of self-determination that he undergoes. This one act of self-determination, in turn, has an "inward" and "outward" term. The "inward" term is God's eternal relation within himself as the God who is triune—Father, Son and Holy Spirit—while the "outward" term is God's turning toward humanity and the world in his eternal self-election to be the God-who-is-for-us in Christ Jesus. Furthermore, because these *two* terms take place in the *one* act in God's *extra*-temporal eternity, both triunity and election are equally *ontologically* "basic" and "primordial" to who God is. Attempts to prioritize *chronologically* between the two simply fail. Yet, the insight evident in our exploration of the four areas above—especially from Jüngel's reading of Barth and Barth's own view of time and eternity—leads, I believe, to the *logical* priority of triunity over election. That is to say, as a further clarification, when we think of God's being, even though we cannot *ontologically* or *chronologically* separate God's triune being from his being the God-who-is-for-us in Christ Jesus, we should *sequentially* or *logically* think of his triunity first before his election. It is my belief that the preceding description summarizes what I consider to be the core of Barth's actualistic ontology, and it is this reading that will serve as the premise for our further explorations of Jesus' incarnate obedience in the rest of the volume.

Part II

The Present Orientation of the Obedience of Jesus Christ as It Is in the Incarnation

3

The Obedience of Jesus Christ in Karl Barth's Christology in the *Church Dogmatics*

FOLLOWING THE WORK OF the previous two chapters in exploring Barth's tendentious notion of the obedience of the eternal Son within the intra-triune life of God, the present and following three chapters press on to the second part of this volume—a probe into the obedience of Jesus Christ as displayed in his incarnation. In other words, if the first part explored the outcome of Barth drawing the incarnate obedience of Christ "backward" into the triune life, this second part looks at the incarnate obedience of Christ "as it is."

In this regard, the present chapter serves one singular purpose: to elucidate the place belonging to and the role played by Jesus' incarnate obedience within Barth's Christology. The enquiry will be conducted via a "broad" reading of the motif as it is developed at the two key junctures of Barth's "early" and "later" Christology in *CD*. With this overview in mind, chapter 4 presses on to a deeper exploration of that obedience by attending to key metaphysical questions surrounding Jesus' incarnate obedience; chapter 5 explores the question of the Spirit's role in Jesus' obedience; and chapter 6 looks at the function of Jesus' obedience in Barth's doctrine of the atonement.

Stated another way, the previous two chapters reveal that Barth's doctrine of election and the accompanying actualistic ontology lead Barth to identify and present the eternal Son *as* the God-man Jesus Christ, who, with his human will in a proleptic and actualistic manner, renders obedience to the Father by accepting his divine mission from all eternity. Barth's actualistic logic follows through: if the eternal Son is identified as the God-man Jesus Christ, then the obedience of Jesus Christ in his incarnation *is* the obedience of the eternal Son. That such is the case for Barth points to the significance of Jesus' obedience in his incarnate life. Therefore, this present chapter devotes itself to the task of explicating the significant and crucial role played by Jesus' incarnate obedience in Barth's Christology.[1]

---

1. See my comment in chapter 1 explaining the rationale for my decision to begin with divine obedience within the immanent Trinity rather than the Son's incarnate obedience in the economy.

That said, the task itself is not easy and lays upon us exigent demands. For one, Christology filled every corner and permeated every crevice in Barth's theology, and that in itself already points to the overwhelming nature and difficulty of the task of explicating the role of Jesus' incarnate obedience within Barth's Christology in a single chapter. The following account hence promises neither to be comprehensive nor does it pay equal attention to the topics it does cover.[2] Instead, the treatment inevitably bears a stochastic nature, delving in at two particular points that I consider critical in pinpointing the place and significance of Jesus' incarnate obedience, namely, the early and later stages of Barth's Christology. The exploration will also be limited to *CD*.[3]

Christology in CD I/2 §15—Jesus Christ as *"vere Deus, vere homo"*

I begin with Barth's "early" Christology in *CD* I/2 §15. Having affirmed the objective possibility of revelation in §13, Barth is concerned at this point to identify the subject at the center of that objective revelation. In other words, Barth is answering the question "Who is Jesus Christ?"[4] to which he provides the immediate emphatic answer: Jesus Christ is *vere Deus vere homo*.[5] The heart of Barth's Christological discussion is thus found in

---

2. Examples of topics not covered include Barth's understanding of the relation between Christology and the "historical Jesus," diachronic developmental issues pertaining to Barth's Christology, and methodological or *prolegomenon* questions. Specific topics covered under methodology include Barth's relationship to Traditional Christology, in particular "Chalcedonian" Christology, or his relationship to the modern liberal German Christology of his day. Important as these topics are, limitations prevent even a cursory treatment. Instead, I can but commend the following resources: i) for Barth's relationship to Tradition, see Brown, "Scripture and Tradition," 3–19; Webster, "Theology of Reformed Confessions," 41–65. Webster's essay is a commentary on Barth, *Theology of Reformed Confessions*, a vitally important book providing key insights into Barth's relationship with the Reformed tradition; ii) for Barth's relationship to "Chalcedonian Christology," see the formative essay by Hunsinger, "Karl Barth's Christology," 127–42; McCormack, "Historicized Christology"; Sumner, *Karl Barth and the Incarnation*, 155–93, and iii) for Barth's relationship to the modern liberal theology of his day, see Dorrien, *Kantian Reason and Hegelian Spirit*.

3. See Sumner, *Karl Barth and the Incarnation*, 74–84, for a good overview of Barth's Christology in his *Unterricht in der christlichen Religion*; *Die christliche Dogmatik im Entwurf*, and in his Lectures on John's Gospel—all of Barth's earlier works prior to *CD*.

4. *CD* I/2, 123.

5. Jones, *Humanity of Christ*, 33–34, suggests that *vere Deus vere homo* has come to be Barth's preferred expression to replace the Chalcedonian formulation of "one person, two natures."

§15.2 "Very God and Very Man." That Barth would anchor his exploration around the central New Testament statement of John 1:14 "The Word was made flesh" is unsurprising, considering that Barth had earlier lectured on the Gospel of John during his time at Münster (1925/26) and Bonn (1933).[6] In three further subsections, Barth revolves his discussion around the triadic axis of i) the subject of the incarnation (Ὁ λόγος, the "Word"), ii) the object of the incarnation (σάρξ, "flesh"), and iii) the process of the incarnation itself (ἐγένετο, "became").[7] The following four features should be borne in mind, especially as they relate directly to the topic of enquiry: Jesus' incarnate obedience.

The Divine Subject Who Assumes the Incarnation in Freedom

First, Barth makes it clear that it is a *divine* subject who assumes the incarnation, and that this divine subject remains *free* in doing so. It was not "deity in itself and as such that was made flesh," Barth reminds us, but rather it was the triune God in his second mode of being, "the Son or Word of God that was made flesh."[8] This "becoming" of the Word rests neither upon any inner necessity of human history nor any evolutionary possibility within creation, nor even upon any necessity in the divine nature or the intra-Trinitarian relations, but is rather to be regarded as a *novum* creation.[9] No doubt the

---

6. The first chapter of John from those lectures subsequently came to be translated and published as Barth, *Witness to the Word*. Sumner, *Karl Barth and the Incarnation*, 79–80, notes the significance of the John lectures in that "they bridge Barth's thought in the 1920s and the Christology of the *Church Dogmatics*." Webster, "Witness to the Word," 65–85, equally highlights the significance of the John lectures not only for Barth's Christology, but also for how he sees the task of theological *Erklärung*. Webster states: "What Barth finds in John . . . is materially and formally fundamental to his Christology; and the exegesis of John 1.1–18 afforded him an opportunity to attain a clarity in his thinking on the matter which he was not subsequently to abandon" (79).

7. Interestingly, the order between the second and third sub-divisions is switched from Barth's earlier exposition of this verse in his John commentary. See Barth, *Witness to the Word*, 84–93.

8. *CD* I/2, 133. Sumner, *Karl Barth and the Incarnation*, 86n58, notes the shift in Barth's language from "the Word" to "Jesus Christ" as the primary subject of his Christology between *CD* I/2 and *CD* IV/1. I suggest that the context determines the usage. Barth at this point is describing his Christology using John 1:14 as an anchor passage, hence his frequent mention of "The Word." Furthermore, the Christological treatment here is also carried out in the wider context of Barth's doctrine of revelation. Nonetheless, Sumner highlights a valid and interesting point, that is, Barth does move increasingly towards using "the Son of God" as his main referent for the divine subject in the incarnation in the later volumes of *CD*. Balthasar, *Theology of Karl Barth*, 114, might have been among the first to highlight this key development.

9. *CD* I/2, 134–35.

incarnation takes place in the domain of the love of God for man, a love which Barth reminds us is "originally grounded upon the eternal relation of God, Father and Son," but just as that love is "free and unconstrained in God Himself, so, too . . . is it free in its realisation towards man."[10] Barth's keenness to maintain the divine freedom of the Word in his incarnation leads to the following statements: "His Word will still be His Word apart from this becoming, just as Father, Son and Holy Spirit would be none the less eternal God, if no world had been created,"[11] and "The Word is what He is even before and apart from His being flesh."[12]

Clearly, these two immediately preceding statements do not sit comfortably with Barth's actualistic ontology. If, as seen from the previous chapter, God so self-determines his being in election—including that of the being of the Eternal Son—to be the God who is for us in Christ Jesus, in what way then could the Word still be what He is even before and apart from His being flesh? The larger question is whether there is a "shift" between the Christology of *CD* I/2 and that of the later volumes such that they really become two disparate Christologies? This is a question I will return to in due course.

The Anhypostasis-Enhypostasis Distinction

Second, Barth's treatment of Christology here in *CD* I/2 displays his endorsement of the established *anhypostasis-enhypostasis* distinction first offered by the ancient church and then maintained throughout its tradition.[13] For Barth, *anhypostasis* asserts the negative, that is, Christ's human nature has its existence or its subsistence only in the *hypostasis* or mode of being of the divine Word. Apart from its concrete existence in God in the event of the *unio personalis* (personal union), the humanity of Christ has no existence of its own. Conversely, *enhypostasis* asserts the positive. Because of the *unio personalis*, the human nature of Christ does have a concrete existence that is given by the divine mode of being.[14]

10. *CD* I/2, 135.
11. *CD* I/2, 135.
12. *CD* I/2, 136.
13. Barth makes an initial explicit mention of the clause in the third sub-section while discussing the nature of the "becoming" (ἐγένετο in John 1:14). See *CD* I/2, 163–65.
14. Jones, *Humanity of Christ*, 24, mentions that Barth's definition of the *anhypostasis-enhypostasis* clause was heavily dependent on Heinrich Heppe's construal, which read a definition that did not exist, and was never intended to do so, among the early Christian writers' construal of the clause. The debate remains as to whether the modern

Paul Dafydd Jones, however, has cautioned against overstating the significance the formula has for Barth's later theology. In following McCormack, Jones does not disagree that the Barth of the early 1920s came to discover in the *anhypostasis-enhypostasis* model of Christology the mooring he needed for the veiling and unveiling dialectic that Barth employed in his doctrine of revelation then. The paired clause endorses a *unio personalis* that does not compromise the distinction between God and humanity.[15] Yet, Jones is concerned that the description of Jesus' humanity as *anhypostatic* could threaten the integrity of Barth's own Christology that seeks to affirm Christ as fully human.[16] As such, Jones reduces the significance of the *anhypostasis-enhypostasis* formula for Barth's mature Christology, especially as it pertains to the elucidation of Christ's humanity.[17]

Jones' postulation bears an element of truth. Following its first explicit mention in *CD* I/2, the *anhypostasis-enhypostasis* formula receives scarce and very brief explicit references before reappearing in a somewhat longer discourse in *CD* IV/2.[18] There, interestingly however, Barth defends the doctrine against the allegation that the doctrine somehow compromises the humanity of Christ. He states: "[I]t is hard to see how the full truth of the humanity of Jesus Christ is qualified or even destroyed by the fact that as distinct from us *He is also a real man only as the Son of God.*"[19] Clearly, Barth does not see the description of Jesus' humanity as *anhypostasic* as a hindrance to the state of Jesus being fully human. Therefore, Barth has not totally discarded the *anhypostasis-enhypostasis* formula in his mature Christology. Moreover, as we have seen from the previous chapter and as put forward by Jüngel, it is the *anhypostasis-enhypostasis* doctrine that funds Barth's actualistic assertion of the "pre-existing God-man" without conceiving or implying in any way the eternal presence of a "heavenly" *man*.[20]

---

thinkers have appropriated the usage correctly as intended by the Church Fathers (see Shults, "Dubious Christological Formula," 431–46; Lang, "Anhypostatos-Enhypostatos," 630–57). But as Sumner, *Karl Barth and the Incarnation*, 93n85, reminds us, the material content of the doctrine as Barth appropriates it should not be dismissed.

15. Jones, *Humanity of Christ*, 22–23. Jones takes his guidance from McCormack's exposition of Barth's development of his theology during his Göttingen days. See McCormack, *Critically Realistic Dialectical Theology*, 358–371.

16. Jones, *Humanity of Christ*, 25. For example, Jones questions if Barth might have "foregrounded the primacy of God qua Son in a way that hobbles subsequent elucidations of Christ's human decisions and actions."

17. Jones, *Humanity of Christ*, 51.

18. The few instances are *CD* I/2, 193; *CD* I/2, 216, and *CD* III/2, 69–70.

19. *CD* IV/2, 49 (added emphasis).

20. Jüngel, *God's Being*, 96.

In agreement with Jones then, the importance of the doctrine is curtailed in Barth's mature Christology. By that stage, Barth has found other resources that enable him to speak of the genuine humanity of Christ, namely, the *communicatio gratiarum*, the *communicatio operationum*, and the powerful concept of *Entsprechung* ("correspondence"). It is the form and content of these other resources that Barth draws upon in his later Christology.

The Assumption of a Fallen yet Sinless Humanity

The third feature of Barth's Christology in *CD* I/2 that warrants our attention is that the Word in assuming σάρξ ("flesh") assumes fallen humanity, or in what becomes prominent in the following chapter, a fallen nature. Barth is unambiguously clear in construing the humanity God assumes in the incarnation as a humanity under judgment. He emphasizes: "[T]here must be no weakening or obscuring of the saving truth that the nature which God assumed in Christ is identical with our nature as we see it in the light of the Fall."[21] The following reasons suggest why Barth sees this as the case.

First, Barth exegetes and reads σάρξ in the New Testament to embody "the *concrete* form of human nature marked by Adam's fall."[22] Second, Barth's understanding of Jesus Christ as the revelation of God in the "flesh" calls for such a reading as well. Barth deems that for Jesus Christ to be the true revelation of God to us, he must be "flesh" in the sense of being fallen flesh just as we are.[23] Third, if Jesus recapitulates and relives the history of Adam—and not only Adam but also Israel as we shall see in chapter 7—then, according to Barth, Jesus must take on the concrete form of our "flesh" in "solidarity and necessary association with our lost existence."[24]

But yet—and here is a point Barth insisted on—Christ taking on *fallen* humanity is of a piece with him taking on a *sinless* humanity. How is this possible? The answer Barth provides surprises us. His reasoning rests on the logical consequence arising from the truth that it is a *divine* subject that undergoes the incarnation. Because it is *the Son of God* who became as we are, Barth reminds us, he "is *the same* in quite a *different* way from us,"[25] the main difference being that Christ enjoys the sanctification and blessing of a sinless being. Barth asserts the following:

---

21. *CD* I/2, 153.

22. *CD* I/2, 151 (added emphasis). Two crucial New Testament passages for Barth are 2 Cor 5:21 and Gal 3:13.

23. *CD* I/2, 152.

24. *CD* I/2, 152.

25. *CD* I/2, 155 (added emphasis).

> In [the Incarnation] God Himself is the Subject. How can God sin [*sic*] deny Himself to Himself, be against Himself as God, want to be a god and so fall away from Himself in the way in which our sin is against Him, in which it happens from the very first and continually in the event of our existence?... Therefore in our state and condition He does not do what underlies and produces that state and condition, or what we in that state and condition continually do. *Our unholy human existence*, assumed and adopted by the Word of God, is *a hallowed and therefore a sinless human existence* . . .[26]

For Barth, the fact that *God himself* becomes incarnate and enters into the form of our human essence—even if it is the same concrete fallen form—means that the way he lives in that mode of existence will nevertheless be one that is, by virtue of God acting, a sinless mode of existence.

Barth's logic, however, leads to another difficulty, and one that pertains centrally to our topic of enquiry. Does the fact that it is the divine subject of the Son of God who assumes human nature in the incarnation compromise Christ's human agency and actions? Is there still a place for the genuine humanity, and *arising from it the genuine obedience*, of Jesus Christ? Some scholars have made the charge that Barth espoused an enfeebled account of Christ's humanity.[27] Meriting our attention in this regard is the view held by Charles Waldrop.

Waldrop's study evaluates Barth's Christology according to the categories of Alexandrian or Antiochian. Waldrop opts for the former. According to Waldrop, Barth's basic Alexandrian position emphasizing the divinity of Christ results in an insufficient account of Christ's humanity. Specifically, that God—and God alone—is the bearer of the human nature of Jesus Christ means that Jesus' humanity inevitably will have an "Apollinarian appearance." Waldrop views that the absence in Jesus Christ of *a human subject bearing a human nature* means that the independence of Jesus' human nature is not sufficiently preserved.[28] A consequence would be that the genuinely human obedience of Christ fails to be secured. Waldrop states:

26. *CD* I/2, 155–56 (added emphasis).

27. Among others, see Baillie, *God Was in Christ*, 53, where Barth is deemed not to have a truly incarnational theology because of his general non-interest in studies of the historical Jesus (for a response, see Jones, *Humanity of Christ*, 52–59); Hartwell, *Theology of Karl Barth*, 185–86, where he states erroneously (in my opinion): "The proposition that the Son of God is the Subject of the person of Jesus Christ casts a doubt upon the true humanity of Jesus Christ"; McGrath, *Making of Modern German Christology*, 114; Macquarrie, *Jesus Christ in Modern Thought*, 13–14, though he qualifies his statement later on p. 287.

28. Waldrop, *Karl Barth's Christology*, 173.

> It is difficult to see how this human nature can fail to obey and serve God. Since the human nature comes into being only because God begins to act humanly and since the human nature exists only as the form of revelation, without having an independent existence, it seems to be merely an aspect or a part of God's being and act. It is so integrally taken up and assumed into God's being that its purely human existence is denied . . . . It serves and attests God because God determines it to be that which serves and attests him.[29]

The above quote results in Waldrop struggling to conceive how it could be said that Jesus was really tempted, much less actually moved to commit sin. Waldrop concludes: "Thus, for Barth, the claim that Jesus Christ was tempted cannot be systematically correlated with the fact that he is the Son of God."[30] Clearly, Waldrop has presented a vocal demurral to the claim of the authentic and genuine nature of Christ's incarnate obedience, and his objection needs to be addressed.

I will leave the question of the relation between Jesus' sinlessness and his impeccability (or otherwise) to the following chapter, and of the nature of Jesus' temptation and struggle to chapter 7. In the meantime, I offer the following points by way of response to Waldrop.

First, Waldrop's underlying premise that Barth espoused an Alexandrian position in his Christology has been challenged. Hunsinger, for example, prefers to see Barth's Christology as employing a "strategy of juxtaposition," alternating between an Alexandrian and Antiochian position without falling definitively in line with either position.[31] Jones goes further to posit that labels like "Alexandrian" or "Antiochian" fail to capture sufficiently the totality of Barth's Christology.[32] These insights render questionable Waldrop's simplistic categorization of Barth's Christology as Alexandrian.

Second, as we have seen from the central argument of the first two chapters, Barth's conception of *who* the divine subject assuming the incarnation is undergoes a substantial development following his actualistic ontology deriving from his doctrine of election by the time he wrote *CD* II/2. The identity of the divine subject is no longer just the *logos-asarkos-and-aincarnandus*, but is the *logos-asarkos-and-incarnandus*. Granted that it is still a *divine* subject that assumes the incarnation, Barth's actualistic ontology which reads and identifies this divine subject *as* the God-man Jesus

---

29. Waldrop, *Karl Barth's Christology*, 174.
30. Waldrop, *Karl Barth's Christology*, 174.
31. Hunsinger, "Christology," 130.
32. Jones, *Humanity of Christ*, 47–50.

Christ means that greater latitude and prominence is given to the humanity of Christ. In other words, Barth's actualistic ontology led him to see that the eternal Son—in the triune self-determination of God to be Father, Son, and Holy Spirit—*is*—in the same electing self-determination of God to be the God who-is-for-us—Jesus Christ. Such a thought immediately opens up leeway for the humanity and obedience of Jesus Christ to be brought to the forefront in a way that exceeds what Waldrop's position could afford. After all, a traditional "Alexandrian" reading of the incarnation would not be so quick to identify the second mode of being of the triune God as the *God-man* Jesus Christ in the same way that an actualistic ontology would.

Third, even at this specific point in *CD* I/2 without Barth's actualistic ontology fully in play, Barth still considers Jesus' humanity and his obedience in particular to be of a genuine nature and to play a substantial role in his Christology. This notion reverberates in *CD* I/2 at two distinct points. The first is Barth's endorsement of dyothelitism. In what counts as the first explicit mention of this doctrine, Barth upholds in Jesus the exercise of a human will.[33] This is crucial for two reasons: i) *the exercise of a human will* is what stands at the center of *human agency* and ii) the presence of an independent will brought into submission (to another will) is what *constitutes the very action of obedience*. I will elaborate on these two crucial ideas in the following chapter, but even at this point, Jones is fully justified in saying that "running through §15 . . . is a powerful affirmation of Christ's distinctive human agency, understood expansively to encompass cognitive and affective processes, decisions, and the realization of intention."[34] The second point where Barth affirms Christ's genuine humanity (and obedience) in *CD* I/2 is seen in the way Barth conceives the coordination between divine and human action. In a brief but revealing statement, Barth evinces his thinking: "[T]he reality of Jesus Christ is that God Himself in person is actively present in the flesh. God Himself in person is the Subject of a real human being and acting. And *just because God is the Subject of it, this being and acting are real.* They are *a genuinely and truly human being and acting.*"[35] For Barth, as Jones states: "Divine action does not displace human action. Divine action grounds and enables human action, making that action coterminous with it, though still ontologically distinctive."[36] Clearly, there is a fundamental difference in the way Barth views the divine-human interrelation as compared

---

33. *CD* I/2, 158.
34. Jones, *Humanity of Christ*, 41–42.
35. *CD* I/2, 151 (my emphasis).
36. Jones, *Humanity of Christ*, 42 (original emphasis).

to Waldrop. For Barth, the divine initiative engenders the human response, rather than hinder the genuine flourishing of human action.

The fourth point of response is that for Waldrop, genuine humanity requires a *human* subject to bear the human nature. Otherwise, Waldrop struggles to count that humanity as genuine. So, in the case of the incarnation, because it is a divine subject who bears the human nature, Waldrop struggles in conceiving a genuine humanity in the person of Jesus Christ. Waldrop's underlying premise runs counter to Barth's own view on this matter. There are good grounds to believe that Barth did not see the lack of a human personhood as detrimental to the authenticity of that humanity. For Barth, the question of personhood broaches on the issue of *existence*, while the issue of genuineness or authenticity lies in the *nature* of that humanity.[37] Barth's position is supported by recent developments in Philosophical Theology. Several recent essays have argued a similar case: the lack of human personhood in Christ need not put into question the authenticity of Christ's humanity.[38]

In all, the importance of this point for the central argument of this chapter cannot be over-emphasized, and we will find ourselves repeatedly returning to this principal notion of Barth's: the Son's assumption and indwelling of Christ's human essence in the *unio personalis* goes hand in hand with the genuineness of this human essence. The *anhypostatic* or *impersonalitas* nature of Jesus' humanity need not subvert the reality or authenticity of Christ's human being and acting.

---

37. So, besides Barth's statement in *CD* IV/2, 49 where Barth states that the *anhypostatic* nature of Jesus' humanity in no way jeopardizes the authenticity of that humanity, I refer also to Barth, *Table Talk*, 49. When asked by one of his students if the lack of "personality" in a human nature discounted the genuineness of that human nature, Barth replied: "Individuality is necessary to human nature, but not Person. A person exists in human nature. Of course Christ had a 'centre of consciousness'. Personality means just this or that man. It can only be applied to the *existence* of a particular man. His thisness or thatness is his personality. If the old Christological doctrine denied personality to Christ, it meant to deny that there was a man as such and then the Word became that man. No, this man never existed except as Son of God—from the beginning. . . . Personality means the *existence of a man*" (original emphasis).

38. Morris, *Logic of God Incarnate*, 62–70; Leftow, "A Timeless God Incarnate," 273–99, and Crisp, *Divinity and Humanity*, 34–71.

Jesus' Sinlessness and Obedience and His "Divine Enburdenment" of Sin

I arrive at the fourth and final feature gleaned from Barth's Christological treatment in *CD* I/2 and it is in this fourth feature that Barth pinpoints the location of Jesus' sinlessness and obedience:

> [I]f we ask where the sinlessness, or (positively) the obedience of Christ, is to be seen, it is not enough to look for it in this man's excellences of character, virtues or good works.... Jesus Christ's obedience consists in the fact that He willed to be and was only this one thing with all its consequences, God in the flesh, the divine bearer of the burden which man as a sinner must bear.[39]

Jesus' willingness to take upon himself the "divine enburdenment" carries on to be expounded by Barth under the recapitulation motif, whereby Jesus is portrayed unmistakably as the "second Adam" (1 Cor 15:45), who "made good what Adam perverted."[40] By putting himself in the sinner's position, Jesus "bowed to the divine verdict and commended Himself solely to the grace of God." It is, however, in doing so that Jesus paradoxically "judged sin in the flesh."[41] All this, Barth reminds us again, constitutes "His hallowing, His obedience, His sinlessness."[42] Yet, Barth is equally quick to affirm that Jesus' sinlessness does not deny him the experience of a genuine struggle.[43] How Barth reconciles this apparent paradox requires further elaboration, which I will attend to in the chapters ahead.

In summary, our survey of Barth's "early" Christology in *CD* I/2 has yielded four insights of relevance to our central enquiry about the obedience of Jesus Christ. First, that it is God himself in the mode of being of the Son who is the *divine subject* at the center of the incarnation reminds us of the divine initiative realized through the incarnation. Moreover, that it is the divine Son who becomes incarnate serves as the authentic ground of the real human being and acting of Jesus Christ. Second, Barth's endorsement of the *anhypostasis/enhypostasis* formula shows his willingness to allow the tradition to serve as a basic guide in safeguarding his Christological exposition from falling into the dangers of either adoptionism or a raw Nestorianism. Third and fourth, the paradoxical position of the fallen

---

39. *CD* I/2, 156.
40. *CD* I/2, 157.
41. *CD* I/2, 157. The language of Barth here anticipates what he will cover in *CD* IV/1 §59 2. "The Judge judged in our place."
42. *CD* I/2, 157.
43. *CD* I/2, 158–59.

humanity, on the one hand, and the sinless humanity, on the other hand, that Christ assumes forms the context in which to understand the obedience of Christ Jesus. That Christ would enburden himself in an Adamic being and state of fallenness so as to disburden sinners of the same, Barth reminds us, counts as the definitive act of Jesus' obedience. These four points remain with us throughout the *Dogmatics*, undergoing repetition in some instances and refinement and revision in others. What Barth gestures towards here in *CD* I/2 becomes in his mature Christology in *CD* IV/1 and 2 a full-bodied construal of the divine and human "essences" couched in the language of decision and action.

The Bridge between Barth's "Early" and "Later" Christology: The Doctrine of Election in *CD* II/2 §33

There is much truth in Jones' observation that the Christological domain of *CD* II/2 has gained a considerable measure of freedom from the "ontological reservation" that characterized much of *CD* I/2.[44] That is, if *CD* I/2 still displays vestiges of preserving a distinction between God in his eternal being and God in his revelatory activity, that distinction is attenuated in *CD* II/2. As seen, Barth via his doctrine of election in *CD* II/2 reaches the zenith of his actualistic ontology, ascribing to God self-determination to such a degree that in his freedom and love, God eternally wills not just to be the God who is *for us* in Christ Jesus, but to be the *God* who is for us in Christ Jesus.

It is not my intention to rehearse again the treatment of Barth's actualistic ontology undertaken in the earlier two chapters. The novel point that I wish to highlight is that Barth's doctrine of election serves as the bridge between his "early" and "later" Christology. Drawing on the two descriptions Barth gives to Jesus Christ in his doctrine of election—"electing God" and "elected human"—and bringing in what I see as a third implicit description—Jesus as "the electing human who elects God"—I wish to briefly state the significant effects Barth's doctrine of election has on his understanding of Jesus' incarnate obedience at this point of development in *CD* II/2.

Jesus Christ as "Electing God"

First, flowing from the nomenclature of Jesus Christ as "electing God," Barth underscores the point mentioned earlier from *CD* I/2 that it is a divine subject who is at the center of the incarnational event. Barth's descriptor

---

44. Jones, *Humanity of Christ*, 64.

of "electing *God*" serves to ground what Jones calls the "personally simple but ontologically complex person of Jesus Christ"[45] in a divine origin, and along with that a divine initiative and prerogative. That Barth paid attention and gave precedence to the divine prerogative is found encapsulated in the following quote:

> We cannot over-emphasise God's freedom and sovereignty in this act. We cannot assert too strongly that in the election of grace it is a matter of the decision and initiative of the divine good-pleasure, that as the One who elects God has absolute precedence over the One who is elected . . . . [T]he theme of the divine election is primarily the relationship between God and man in the person of Jesus Christ. Who has the initiative in this relationship? Who has the precedence? Who decides? Who rules? God, always God. God founds and maintains the union between Himself and man.[46]

Not only does Jesus Christ as "electing God" evoke the notion that election is ultimately a divine initiative, it also reminds us that the entire act of election (and hence incarnation) is carried out in grace. Barth reminds us that God does not owe it to anyone (us or even himself) to have carried out any of his particular ways or works *ad extra*. God would have been satisfied with his inner triune glory—one that abounds in his freedom and love—but, as Barth states, "the fact that He is not satisfied, but that His inner glory overflows and becomes outward, the fact that He wills the creation, and the man Jesus as the first-born of all creation, is grace."[47] Barth employs two expressions—"sovereign grace" (*souveräne Güte*) and "eminent grace" (*eminenter Gnade*)—to intensify his description of the grace of God. Together, the two terms refer to God's generous decision to allow his "inner glory," otherwise described as his triune fellowship (*Gemeinschaft*),[48] to "overflow" and extend outwards to creation. The term "overflow" (*überströmt*) in itself carries the connotation that this outward extension of God's glory and fellowship happens not out of lack or insufficiency, but follows from an over-spilling of the perfection within.[49]

45. Jones uses this expression frequently throughout Jones, *Humanity of Christ*.
46. *CD* II/2, 177.
47. *CD* II/2, 121.
48. *CD* II/1, 275. There, Barth states carefully: "As and *before* God seeks and creates fellowship with us, He wills and completes this fellowship in Himself" (added emphasis).
49. In *CD* II/1, 280, Barth states that "this overflowing is conditioned by the fact that although it could satisfy itself, it has no satisfaction in this self-satisfaction, but as love for another it can and will be more than that which could satisfy itself." This

The grace of God extends not only to fellowship with the creaturely other, but also includes God's act of divine self-determination whereby he actually incorporates the being of this other into his own eternal being qua Son.[50] That is, as Barth reminds us, likewise grace. The sum of it all is that in relation to God allowing his inner glory to overflow, he *did not have to do it*, but he *did it*. And he did it *this way*. Read in tandem with Barth's statement that "the man Jesus as such has nothing to bring before the electing God which would make Him worthy of the divine election or make His election necessary,"[51] Barth reminds us that the election of God is one conducted only and totally in the realm of grace.

Jesus Christ as "Elected Human"

Second, the nomenclature of Jesus Christ as the "elected human" carries with it the following major theological import: the man Jesus was elected to suffer and to die.[52] Reinforcing the central point gleaned from *CD* I/2, Barth asserts: "The very obedience which was exacted of Him and attained by Him was His willingness to take upon Himself the divine rejection of all others and to suffer that which they ought to have suffered."[53] That said, the specific locale where this point is made—in the context of Jesus as the "elected human"—renders explicit a major truth. The fact that God takes the consequences of fallen man's actions upon himself in *the person of the elected man Jesus* means that *great import is given to the human obedience of the elected man Jesus Christ*.

Taking in view the above consideration, a pellucid picture begins to emerge. Although Barth gives due place to divine action in recognizing the eternal Son as the directive being-in-act constitutive of the person of Jesus Christ, he never does it at the expense of an equal affirmation of human action, namely, the human obedience of Jesus Christ. For Barth, *divine command* and *human obedience*—the latter of which under Barth's actualistic

---

"overflowing" of God's fellowship and glory, not out of need but out of excess, is another reason for me to posit the logical priority of triunity over election within Barth's actualistic ontology.

50. Barth states in *CD* II/2, 121: "[I]n His Son He makes the being of this other His own being."

51. *CD* II/2, 121.

52. *CD* II/2, 122. Barth states it bluntly: "The election of the man Jesus means, then, that a wrath is kindled, a sentence pronounced and finally executed, a rejection actualised."

53. *CD* II/2, 123.

thought is counted as *divine obedience*—are coterminous with one another, even though Barth is emphatic that *the divine engenders the human response*.

This coterminous coordination of the divine and human response is, in turn, seen in the idea of the divine and human steadfastness (*Beharren*) predicated of the electing God and elected man respectively. "On God's side," Barth states, "it is the steadfastness of grace even in the judgment to which He condemns the Elect.... It is the steadfastness of election even in the midst of the rejection which overtakes Him." Conversely, "on the side of the Elect, it is the steadfastness of obedience to God, and of calling only upon Him, and of confidence in the righteousness of His will."[54] Barth at this point asserts a key statement pertaining to Jesus' incarnate obedience, but one that makes full sense only in the light of *CD* IV/2, where he treats the Reformed idiom of the *communicatio operationum*. Barth states: "It is in the *unity of this steadfastness both divine and human* that we shall find the peculiar secret of the election of the man Jesus."[55] If election has to do with divine ontology, this rather perplexing statement gestures toward a state of affairs where we uncover the gratuitous generosity of God in allowing human obedience to play a part in God's own self-determination, even as the divine precedence and initiative is maintained throughout.[56]

Jesus Christ as "the Electing Man Who Elects God"

The third way in which Barth's doctrine of election bears on his notion of Christ's obedience derives from the third nomenclature applied to Jesus Christ—"The electing man who elects God."[57] Strictly speaking, Barth nowhere in this portion of writing in §33 applies this title to Christ, but a gloss of the contents of this section nonetheless reveals an accurate usage of the nomenclature.[58] This section finds itself in a broader context

---

54. *CD* II/2, 125.

55. *CD* II/2, 125 (added emphasis).

56. Barth's maintenance of the divine precedence and initiative is seen clearly in *CD* II/2, 176, where Barth states: "The Son of Man... testifies that what takes place between God and man according to God's predestination has its source wholly and utterly in the divine initiative. It is not that God and man begin to have dealings with each other, but that God begins to have dealings with man. Without any qualification the precedence is with God. There can be no question of any activity on man's part except upon the basis of the prior activity of God, and in the obvious form of a human response to this prior activity."

57. *CD* II/2, 175–81.

58. Both McCormack, "Karl Barth's Version," 122, and Jones, *Humanity of Christ*, 104, refer to the work of the German scholar Goebel, *Vom freien Wählen Gottes und des Menschen*, who organizes his monograph on election and analogy around the four

whereby the discussion revolves around the nature of God's eternal will.[59] Barth presents the eternal will as "identical with the election of Jesus Christ" and as "a divine activity in the form of the history, encounter and decision between God and man."[60] Barth is adamant that the experience of history (*Geschichte*), encounter (*Begegnung*), and decision (*Entscheidung*)—three terms paramount to the discussion here—is first applied to Jesus the elected one, before it is secondarily applied to us mankind, and even then only as we are "in him."[61]

Together, the three terms "encounter," "decision" and "history" draw attention to the nature of Jesus' human activity before God and provide useful information about his human agency.[62] "Encounter," as Jones suggests, speaks concurrently of the command of God that the man Jesus is confronted with as the "elected human" and God's call for Jesus Christ to enact a uniquely particular identity. "Decision" denotes the effective response Jesus gives, which is one of active realization of the identity God has intended for him as he lives and constitutes himself as an authentic human being.[63] After all, as Barth states: "The man Jesus is not a mere puppet moved this way and that by God. He is not a mere reed used by God as the instrument of His Word. The man Jesus prays. He speaks and acts.... In His wholehearted obedience, in His electing of God alone, He is wholly free."[64] In the quote, one traces a subtle rebuke of the "instrumentalization" view of the incarnation where Jesus is merely portrayed as the "instrument" of the Word.[65] The quote also hints at Barth's basic construal of the relation between obedience and freedom, namely, that true freedom is found in obedience. Finally, "history" signifies at its most basic level the being and existence of Jesus Christ as one that carries the character of an

---

inter-related claims of i) Jesus Christ is the electing God ii) Jesus Christ is the elected man iii) Jesus Christ is the electing man, and iv) Jesus Christ is the elected God.

59. *CD* II/2, 145–94.
60. *CD* II/2, 175.
61. *CD* II/2, 175–76.
62. Jones, *Humanity of Christ*, 105. Jones recognizes that his gloss of the terms, which I am indebted to, does to some degree artificially prize the terms apart.
63. Jones, *Humanity of Christ*, 108–9.
64. *CD* II/2, 179.
65. It could be said that the "instrumentalization" view of Jesus' incarnation was held by some of the early church fathers, e.g., Athanasius. See Athanasius, *On the Incarnation of the Word*, §43–44; *Four Discourses Against the Arians*, II.7, where the earthly flesh of Jesus that the Word puts on is likened to the priestly robes that Aaron put on, and in 4:III.53 where the body is described as the temple in which the presence of the Lord dwelt. See Sumner, *Karl Barth and the Incarnation*, 19–37, for an overview on how the incarnation was perceived in the Early Church to post-Chalcedon.

event, more specifically, an event that bears a timely and historical form.[66] The three terms added together constitute the confounding truth that even as God wills to bring men into reconciliation with him, he does not keep at arm's length human volition, but God qua Christ Jesus humanly participates in the most terrifying moment of this reconciliatory program, taking upon himself the deadly enburdenment of sins, including its most excruciating historical moment of death on a cross.[67]

In all, the doctrine of election in the hands of Barth undergoes an enriching and, in fact, revolutionary revision. Moved from its traditional locale of being something God does via a hidden *decretum absolutum*, it now becomes something God *does* that affects the core of who He *is*. Simply stated, election expresses the sublime truth that God does not will to be God other than in relationship with mankind, so much so that he ordains the concrete life of Jesus Christ to condition his own eternal being.[68] Taken in turn, that Jesus of Nazareth is the "elected man" means his human action and response play a secondary but indispensable function.

One final step remains before we move to Barth's "later" or "mature" Christology, and that is to clarify the relationship between Barth's "early" and "later" Christology. Given the doctrine of election acts as the bridge between the two phases of Barth's Christological thought, does the actualistic ontology stemming from his doctrine of election effectively lead to two disparate Christologies? Or are there more points of continuity between the two? I am inclined towards the latter opinion. Rather than seeing Barth's "later" Christology in *CD* IV/1–3 as disparate from that of *CD* I/2, it is preferable to see material consistency across the whole of *CD*, while allowing for an organic growth and development of Barth's actualism.[69] To be sure, Barth's actualistic ontology—burgeoning in *CD* II/2 and certainly in place by

---

66. For a chronological account of the development of "history" in Barth's theological thought, see Wu, "Concept of History." Wu submits that the concept of history grows in significance in tandem with Barth's Christocentrism, reaching its acme in *CD* IV/2, where the being of God is "historicized"—in God becoming incarnate in human time and history—and human history is "ontologized"—in that the movement of humanity and its history is brought forth from "below" to "above."

67. That is the essence of what Barth states in *CD* II/2, 141: "In [God's] case [the defeat of this evil power] must take on the character of an event. It must become the content of a history: the history of an obstacle and its removing; the history of a death and a resurrection; the history of a judgment and a pardon; the history of a defeat and a victory."

68. *CD* IV/1, 7.

69. In this way, I agree with Sumner, *Karl Barth and the Incarnation*, 88, who states: "*CD* I/2 belongs as much to the later *Dogmatics* as it does to the early Barth; the changes evident later in the project were already in development here."

CD IV/1—would entail a revision to some of his earlier Christological statements in *CD* I/2. However, I believe those statements need not be retracted. Statements like "His Word will still be His Word apart from this becoming"[70] and "The Word is what He is even before and apart from His being flesh"[71] can still be contained within the confines of Barth's actualistic ontology as set forth in the previous chapter. To reiterate: this is an actualistic ontology that contends for the ontological and chronological simultaneity of God being the triune God and he being the electing God who-is-for-us-in-Christ Jesus, while positing a logical precedence and priority of triunity over election. Similar to our discussion on the *logos-asarkos-and-aincarnandus*, I propose that Barth's "early" Christological statements quoted above should be read at best as a divine possibility intended to protect the freedom of God and reveal his non-dependency in relation to creation. It is clear, however, that the significance of such statements has been deeply relativized in light of the reality of the self-determining act of God in election.

Christology in *CD* IV/1—Jesus Christ, the "Lord as Servant"

In this section and the next, I explore the role and function of the incarnate obedience of Christ as described within the domain of Barth's "mature Christology" as seen in *CD* IV/1–3. I declare at the outset that our exploration will be restricted to certain portions of *CD* IV/1–2. While *CD* IV/3 carries on the Christological discussion—presenting an explication of Jesus' prophetic office and the content of his prophetic word as "Jesus is victor"—I will not be tapping on it in contributing to the discussion of Christ's human obedience.[72] As such, *CD* IV/3 will not have an exclusive coverage of its own, and any references will serve a supplementary role in relation to the existing cluster of ideas from *CD* IV/1–2. I will also reserve the weighty discussion on Barth's conception of the relation between Jesus' incarnate obedience and his doctrine of the atonement to chapter 6, where the subject matter will receive the full attention it deserves. Instead, what I will highlight here are three aspects of *CD* IV/1 that in my view have a significant bearing upon Jesus' incarnate obedience—the concept of covenant, history, and the *duplex*

---

70. *CD* I/2, 135.
71. *CD* I/2, 136.
72. Interestingly, both Jones, *Humanity of Christ*, and Sumner, *Karl Barth and the Incarnation*, also refer minimally to *CD* IV/3 in comparison to *CD* IV/1–2. For a work dealing in divine and human freedom that covers *CD* IV/3 in quite some depth, see Leigh, *Freedom and Flourishing*, especially chapters 3–5.

status of humiliation and exaltation. In the following section, I will carry on the exploration to *CD* IV/2, where I believe the notion of Jesus' incarnate obedience within Barth's Christology receives its clearest illumination, namely via Barth's creative and novel recovery of Protestant Orthodoxy's theological idioms, namely, the *communio naturarum*, the *communicatio gratiarum* and the *communicatio operationum*.

Jesus Christ as Covenant-Lord and Covenant-Partner

I begin with Barth's concept of the covenant as it is treated in *CD* IV/1. Barth's mention and exposition of the covenant right at the beginning of his doctrine of reconciliation (§57) sends an unambiguous signal about the pivotal role covenant has in his theology.[73] For Barth, the simple (but not simplistic) message lying at the heart of the Church's dogmatics and Christian faith, love, and hope is "the covenant fulfilled in the work of reconciliation."[74] The covenant forms the presupposition of the atonement, in the sense that Jesus Christ in carrying out the atonement was fulfilling none other than God's original covenant with man.[75] The pre-eminence of the motif of Jesus Christ as the fulfiller of the covenant means that Christ's existence and work follows neither from the act of creation nor the act of divine providence; on the contrary, it is for the sake of Jesus Christ that creation takes place and God rules as the preserver and controller of world-events.[76] Barth's revised "supralapsarian" position is clearly on display.[77]

Following from the above, if Jesus' fulfilment of the covenant takes logical precedence over creation itself, and if the reality that lies behind the covenant is captured by an Old Testament phrase particularly favoured by Barth: "I will be your God, and ye shall be my people,"[78] then somehow or another—ineffably—*humanity is drawn into eternity via Jesus Christ*. In

---

73. *CD* IV/1, 22–78.

74. *CD* IV/1, 3.

75. *CD* IV/1, 37.

76. *CD* IV/1, 50. Grebe, *Election, Atonement, and the Holy Spirit*, 103, highlights creation and providence as two secondary elements in Barth's theology kept separate from one another, with the election of grace as the "root" common to both doctrines. Together, the doctrines of creation and providence build the external basis of the covenant.

77. See *CD* II/2, 127–45, for Barth's evaluation between the "supralapsarian" and "infralapsarian" positions, with Barth himself eventually coming down on the side of a revised "supralapsarianism," reconstructed along the Christological lines that Barth himself advocates in his doctrine of election.

78. *CD* IV/1, 22. Barth refers to Jer 7:23; 11:4; 30:22; 31:33; 32:38; and Ezek 36:28.

Jesus Christ, we uncover the one who as electing God is the covenant-Lord and who as elected man is the faithful covenant-partner. This much is clear from the following quote by Barth:

> In [the] free act of the election of grace there is already present, and presumed, and assumed into unity with His own existence as God, the existence of the man whom He intends and loves from the very first and in whom He intends and loves all other men . . . . In this free act of the election of grace the Son of the Father is no longer just the eternal Logos, but as such, as very God from all eternity He is also the very God and very man He will become in time . . . . He in whom the covenant of grace is fulfilled and revealed in history is also its eternal basis.[79]

The above quote asserts a crucial truth and sounds a cautionary word at the same time. On the one hand, the covenantal will of God concurrently establishes the ontological determination of both Jesus Christ and humanity at large. On the other hand, the fact that God's eternal determination for covenant with creatures is *grounded antecedently in his divine election* safeguards the precedence and priority of the ontological determination of Jesus Christ (as human) before that of humankind. That Jesus Christ is the elected human, the first and true covenant-partner of God means that *insofar as humankind finds its ontological determination in being God's covenant-partner, it does so only according to the humanity of the Son*. Yet, equally true is the converse fact that because in divine election God self-determines a human existence for himself, humankind never had a moment where it was not the covenant-partner of God. The almost too sublime truth is that God has, in a profoundly inexplicable manner, determined to express his love to the creaturely other *even in the moment when the creation of this other has not been realized*.[80]

In relation to the above, here is a facet of Barth's discussion crucial to our thesis. While expounding on the significance of Jesus in relation to his covenant keeping, Barth states: "The *divine* and the *human fulfilment of the covenant are one and the same in the act of obedience on the part of Jesus*, in this final crisis of His saving work."[81] The significance of the above statement is that it situates *Jesus' obedience as the locale wherein both the divine and*

---

79. *CD* IV/1, 66.

80. The immediate significance is that if Jesus Christ is the first and true covenant-partner and we as humankind receive our ontological determination as covenant-partners with God only *in him*, then the fulfilment of the covenant within human history will inevitably take on the character of atonement (*CD* IV/1, 67–68). See chapter 6 for a further elaboration of this point.

81. *CD* III/2, 214 (added emphasis).

the human aspects of the covenant are fulfilled. The divine aspect is fulfilled, in that the triune God decides in eternity to allow his love to overflow to the creaturely other even before the realization of this other; moreover, to overflow to the degree that God would qualify his own being qua Son to include the being of Jesus Christ. From eternity, the being of the Son is the very God and very man he will become in time. Furthermore, the humanity of the Son is expressed in the form of a humble servant obedient unto death (Phil 2:6-8). This is the extent that God goes to in order to express his desire to be the covenant-Lord over his people.

Similarly, the human aspect is fulfilled, in that the man Jesus Christ shows himself unreservedly as the man who is for God and fellow man.[82] As the man Jesus lives in gratitude unto God, calls upon him, and obeys him right to the very end of surrendering his life (as attested by the New Testament), Jesus proves himself as the pre-eminent covenant-partner of God, both elected and called. Thus, both covenant-Lord ("I will be your God") and covenant-partner ("ye shall be my people") meet and find their fulfilment in the one person of Jesus Christ.

As Sumner states, the covenant could be said to be in Barth's theology "the exegetical connective tissue between [his] doctrines of election and reconciliation."[83] Election is God's eternal determination for covenant with creatures, covenant is the presupposition of reconciliation, and reconciliation is the fulfilment of that covenant.[84] Our consideration highlights the further dimension that *it is the obedience (unto death) of Jesus Christ that holds the key to the fulfilment of the covenant.*

The History of Jesus Christ—Where the History of God and the History of Man Meet

The concept of covenant segues into the second feature that I would like to highlight—that of the history (*Geschichte*) of Jesus Christ. My central contention is that Barth's appropriation of *Geschichte* and the role he gives to it within his overall theology parallels that of the covenant, namely, as the nexus between the doctrines of election and reconciliation.

---

82. *CD* III/2, 208.

83. Sumner, *Karl Barth and the Incarnation*, 114. Grebe, *Election, Atonement and Holy Spirit*, 101, goes so far as to posit that the covenant of grace in Jesus Christ could be the unifying thread bringing together all the different strands of *CD*.

84. Sumner, *Karl Barth and the Incarnation*, 114.

It is well established that Barth begins his treatment of atonement in §59 with a foundational declaration of the importance of history in understanding the atonement. Barth avows:

> The atonement is history. To know it, we must know it as such. To think of it, we must think of it as such. To speak of it, we must tell it as history. To try to grasp it as supra-historical or non-historical truth is not to grasp it at all. It is indeed truth, but truth actualised in a history and revealed in this history as such. . . . [T]he atonement is the very special history of God with man, the very special history of man with God. . . . To say atonement is to say Jesus Christ. To speak of it is to speak of His history . . . . For He is *the history of God with man* and *the history of man with God*.[85]

In the above passage, we find the acme of Barth's usage of *Geschichte*—a term he started appropriating in *CD* II/2 and increasingly preferred in subsequent volumes. For Barth, *Geschichte* as a locution appropriately captures core facets of his actualistic ontology. This is evident as early as *CD* II/2, where Barth spoke of God in his movement as covenant-Lord towards his covenant people in terms of the "primal history" (*Urgeschichte*) that is between God and the one man Jesus, and through this one man, the people that are represented in him.[86] Given that this "primal history" describes the dynamics of the inner-triune being of God and his relation to an external reality, it is accurate to say that God pre-temporally anticipates his relationship with the human creature. As Jones affirms: "In that the divine Son is never not becoming the person of Jesus Christ, God is always intending a history between God and humankind, anchored in the life of Christ."[87]

Reiterating the same point but from the opposite perspective: the concrete history of Jesus Christ is constitutive of the identity of Jesus Christ, and that, in turn, is constitutive of the eternal identity of God qua Son. That the history of Jesus Christ constitutes his identity recalls and reaffirms Barth's refusal to separate the person of Christ from his work.[88] Yet, that the identity of Jesus Christ constitutes the identity of the eternal Son adds further import in tandem with Barth's actualistic intuitions. God's "incorporation" of the concrete and realized history of Jesus Christ into the divine life means that

---

85. *CD* IV/1, 157–58 (added emphasis).

86. *CD* II/2, 7–9.

87. Jones, *Humanity of Christ*, 190.

88. *CD* IV/1, 128 where Barth states: "His being as this One is His history, and His history is this His being. This is the truth which must light up the doctrine of reconciliation as Christology." See also *CD* IV/3.1, 179.

God has allowed—as part of his divine self-determination—for a qualitatively distinct ontological and agential reality to be included within the divine triune life in pre-temporal eternity via the Son's assumption of that reality. This is why Barth is emphatic that our understanding of "Godhead" cannot be divorced from Jesus Christ: "It is a matter of the Godhead . . . [that] Jesus Christ is Himself God as the Son of God the Father and with God the Father the source of the Holy Spirit, united in one essence with the Father by the Holy Spirit. That is how He is God. *He is God as He takes part in the event which constitutes the divine being.*"[89] In the last statement, one finds again the core assertion of Barth's actualistic ontology: God's self-determination as the triune Godhead of Father, Son and Holy Spirit is ontologically "coincident" and "coterminous" with his decision to become incarnate.

The next aspect of *Geschichte* makes a further contribution. If Barth's usage of *Geschichte* parallels that of covenant, then *Geschichte* furthers Barth's interest by "concretizing" the covenant. The one history of Jesus Christ becomes, on the one hand, the intersecting point of God's history and mankind's history, and, on the other hand, the locale where the covenant is fulfilled. Both concepts of covenant and *Geschichte* are intertwined in the person and work of Jesus Christ.[90] This explains why if the fulfilment of the covenant takes on the nature of atonement,[91] then Jesus Christ in living out the history of man necessarily takes on a history of suffering.[92] This has two further implications. First, recalling that the history of Jesus Christ is the history of *God*, God himself is embroiled in suffering, as ineffable as such a notion seems.[93] Second, this also means—recalling that the history of Jesus Christ is at the same time the history of *man*—Jesus' history of suffering will involve the action of obedience, whereby he willingly submits in obedience to the Father's call for him. In so doing, that is how Jesus Christ determines the being of mankind represented in him as the faithful covenant-partner of God. The upshot of our enquiry is that inasmuch as the history of Jesus Christ involves wholeheartedly the history of

89. *CD* IV/1, 129 (added emphasis).

90. The bringing together of the concepts of *Geschichte* and covenant is seen explicitly in the following quote found in Barth, "The Humanity of God," 46: "In Jesus Christ there is no isolation of man from God or of God from man. Rather, in Him we encounter the history, the dialogue, in which God and man meet together and are together, the reality of the covenant *mutually* contracted, preserved, and fulfilled by them" (original emphasis).

91. *CD* IV/1, 68.

92. *CD* IV/1, 175.

93. I am aware that my statement immediately raises the question of Barth's take on the doctrine of God's impassibility. This is a topic beyond the scope of discussion. For more on this topic, see Sumner, *Karl Barth and the Incarnation*, 218–23.

God and the history of man, both *the divine and human actions play their part in animating the one history of Jesus Christ*.⁹⁴

The Twofold State of Exinanitionis and Exaltationis

One of the refreshing distinct features of Barth's doctrine of reconciliation is its dynamic sense of *movement* and *event*, resourcefully and faithfully captured under the rubric of the *status duplex* consisting in the humiliation and exaltation of Christ. This move is already evident in Barth entitling the first sub-section of §59 as "The Way of the Son of God into the Far Country," capturing the movement of humiliation, and his entitling the second sub-section of §64 as "The Homecoming of the Son of Man," capturing the corresponding movement of exaltation.⁹⁵

Consistent with Barth's employment of other theological idioms, he appropriates the *status duplex* with the following two innovative tweaks. First, the *status duplex* serves Barth's larger commitment to join the two treatments of the person and work of Christ. On Barth's view, the *status duplex* serves to convey the sense of movement intrinsic to the very essence of who Christ Jesus is as true God, true man, and true God-man.⁹⁶ As Barth affirms, if Jesus Christ is the God who "can give Himself up and does give Himself up . . . to the suffering of the human creature . . . dying the death which they have deserved,"⁹⁷ this "downward" movement of *exinanitionis* (humiliation) captures the humility intrinsic to God himself.⁹⁸ Likewise,

---

94. See especially *CD* IV/1, 300.

95. This is not to ignore the place that the *munus triplex* (the threefold mediatorial office of Christ as prophet, priest and king) occupies in Barth's presentation of the doctrine of reconciliation, but in agreement with Johnson, "Servant Lord," 159–73, it is to ascribe to the *munus triplex* a limited and, at best, secondary role. Johnson establishes his case by arguing that Barth's hamartiology, in particular his description of sin as pride, sloth and falsehood, does not tally with the "office" of priest, king and prophet respectively (164–66). Instead, Barth's hamartiology coheres better with Barth's own entitling of his presentation: "Jesus Christ, the Lord as Servant," "Jesus Christ, the Servant as Lord," and "Jesus Christ, the True Witness" (cf. *CD* IV/1, 135). Johnson's article checks against claims that the *munus triplex* forms a controlling or central motif in Barth's presentation of reconciliation, and in this way also highlights a point of contrast between Barth and John Calvin's doctrine of atonement. For the centrality of *munus triplex* in Calvin's Christology, see *Inst.*, II.15.

96. Barth adumbrates all three aspects by way of providing an overview to his doctrine of reconciliation in *CD* IV/1, 128–38.

97. *CD* IV/1, 130.

98. Allen, *Karl Barth's Church Dogmatics*, 141n2, expresses the idea well when he states that for Barth, God is not the type of God who "though he is God, he became incarnate." Rather, God is the God who "because He is God, he became incarnate."

if Jesus Christ is true man, then what has happened in him, Barth states, "is the conversion of all of us to God and the realisation of true humanity . . . . In Him humanity is exalted humanity, just as Godhead is humiliated Godhead."[99] Once again, the "upward" movement of *exaltationis* (exaltation) captures the sense of glory intrinsic to Jesus Christ as the true man elected in eternity, and by virtue of us being in him, shared with the rest of humanity. In this way, the *status duplex* serves as a powerful vehicle to carry the movement of humiliation and exaltation and present it as an organic whole in the one being of God and man qua Jesus Christ.

Second, that Jesus Christ is always the one God-man means that the two states of humiliation and exaltation should not be conceived as two "states" which succeed one another, but as two sides or directions, or better, a twofold action of the one work of Jesus Christ.[100] Humiliation and exaltation are rightly to be thought of as *simultaneous* in the one event and existence of Jesus' incarnation: Jesus Christ as the Son of God is never the humiliated one without being also, at the same time, the exalted one as the Son of Man, and vice versa. The state of exaltation always has its origin and grounding only in the state of humiliation, and occurs as *a response of gratitude* to the grace of God, while the state of humiliation occurs as *a divine initiative* of grace.[101] Barth affirms elsewhere: "Without the condescension of God there would be no exaltation of man. As the Son of God and not otherwise, Jesus Christ is the Son of Man. His sequence is irreversible."[102]

Taking a step further, the actualistic trope of Barth's theology actually permits the simultaneity of humiliation and exaltation to be true not only of Jesus Christ in time, but also in eternity. God qua Son via the divine determination in election has always been both the *eternally* humble and exalted one. Added further to this is the fact that Barth consciously reversed the objects of predication of the two states such that it is the Son of *God* who is *humiliated* and the Son of *Man* who is *exalted*.[103]

---

99. *CD* IV/1, 131.

100. *CD* IV/1, 133.

101. *CD* IV/2, 47.

102. Barth, "Humanity of God," 48.

103. *CD* IV/1, 134. A typical account of the *status duplex* can be found in Heppe, *Reformed Dogmatics*, 488–509. Heppe's account tends to present the two states as chronological and sequential (494) and certainly limits the two states to that of Christ's state in the assumed flesh (488). It should be mentioned that Barth, who wrote the foreword, displayed his gratitude to Heppe's overall work. Yet, at the same time, Barth recognized that a strict return to Protestant Orthodoxy would not be possible (vi–vii). For a varied account advocating the same argument but drawing in wider biblical exegesis and the views of John Calvin, see Treat, "Exaltation in and through Humiliation," 96–114.

Of key consequence to our central enquiry is the observation that *the core action underpinning the movement of humiliation and exaltation is none other than the obedience rendered by Jesus Christ in his incarnation*, specifically, his obedience in taking upon himself the divine enburdenment of humankind's sin. Obedience forms the apex of Jesus' humility in the downward movement of humiliation. More than that, given Barth's actualistic ontology, it forms the eternal humility of God qua Son. Likewise, the upward movement of exaltation as the Son of Man is only premised upon Jesus' obedience. By rendering that obedience, Jesus establishes himself as true man who lives as the faithful covenant-partner of God.

More could be said: if the humiliation of Jesus as the Son of God specifies the divine self-determination of God, and likewise, the exaltation of Jesus as the Son of Man specifies the divinely given determination of mankind, then it could be suggested that it is in the obedience of Jesus Christ that both the divine and human determination are "actualized." What remains implicit at this stage becomes explicit when we cross over to the Christological domain of *CD* IV/2, a consideration that will now occupy our attention.

Christology in CD IV/2—Jesus Christ, the "Servant as Lord"

Barth's treatment of Christology in *CD* IV/2 focuses substantially though not exclusively on the humanity of Christ, who is the "royal man" in his upward movement of exaltation. This, Barth does via his discussion of the theological idioms arising from Protestant Orthodoxy: the *communio naturarum* (the communion of natures) and from there, the trio of idioms that discuss the effects of the hypostatic union—the *communicatio idiomatum* (communication of idioms), the *communicatio gratiarum* (the communication of graces) and the *communicatio operationum* (communication of operations).[104] It is especially in the discussion of the *communicatio operationum* and in the idea of the "common actualization of the divine and human essences" that we find the climactic description of the role Barth gives to the incarnate obedience of Jesus Christ within his Christology.

---

104. McCormack, "'We Have Actualized,'" 182, states that Barth's order differs from the source-book of Heinrich Heppe who dealt with the *communicatio gratiarum* before the *communicatio idiomatum* so as to "front-load Reformed polemic against the Lutheran Christology." McCormack reads Barth's different order as indicating his non-interest in confessional differences.

That Barth begins his discussion in *CD* IV/2 by reprising the doctrine of election is an observation not to be hurried over.[105] In doing so, Barth issues the reminder that the discussion to follow concerning the humanity of Christ is founded on God's eternal election of grace manifested concretely in the election of Jesus Christ.[106] Jesus Christ being not only the electing God but the elected man entails that the humanity of Christ, particularly his human history and earthly life, is "therefore primarily and finally basic—an absolutely necessary concept—in exactly the same and not a lesser sense than that of His true deity," as Barth boldly asserts.[107] Throughout his treatment of the theological idioms, Barth evinces a delicate balance in maintaining the divine initiative and priority, even as he gives a generous and substantial role to the human response and action.

Barth's discussion of the three idioms finds its place in an exposition of what it means for God to be have become incarnate in Christ. It is worthwhile to recap briefly Barth's main points. First, he states: "[T]his One, God, the Son, became and is also man."[108] Barth here rehearses much of his earlier Christological considerations in *CD* I/2, affirming the freedom of God and asserting God the Son as the acting subject in this event.[109] His second point emphasizes that the incarnation involves taking on the existence of a man. God the Son exists not only in His divine essence, but also in human being and essence, in our nature and kind.[110] Barth reaffirms his assent to the *unio hypostatica* (hypostatic union) as that which undergirds all subsequent discussions of the *communio naturarum* and the *communicatio idiomatum*.[111]

The Communio Naturarum

Barth's third point affirms the unity of both divine and human essences in Jesus Christ.[112] At this point of the discussion, Barth brings in the

105. *CD* IV/2, 31–36.
106. *CD* IV/2, 31.
107. *CD* IV/2, 35.
108. *CD* IV/2, 45.
109. *CD* IV/2, 46–47.
110. *CD* IV/2, 50.
111. *CD* IV/2, 52. Barth affirms that for all the differences between the Lutherans and the Reformed in terms of their understanding of the *communio naturarum* and the *communicatio idiomatum*, they agree that all thinking must start from the basis of the hypostatic union.
112. *CD* IV/2, 60. In the following page, Barth defines divine and human "essence" (*Wesen*) as that which "Jesus Christ has in common with the Father and the Holy Spirit as the Son of God" and that which Jesus Christ "has in common with all other human

communio naturarum (communion of natures) which he defines as the union from the two-sided participation of the divine and human essence in Jesus Christ.[113] Barth appeals to the four established terms of the Chalcedonian Definition—"inconfusedly," "unchangeably," "indivisibly," and "inseparably"—in defining the parameters of understanding the union.[114] "Inconfusedly" and "unchangeably" restrain us from conceiving the union in the sense of a fusion, while "indivisibly" and "inseparably" impels us to view the union as a genuine two-sided participation in which there is "a real and strict and complete and indestructible union."[115] Yet, inasmuch as the *communio naturarum* speaks of the genuine participation of the divine and human essence in a union, it is *only in the act of the divine subject that there takes place this union*.[116] In this manner, Barth grounds the *communio naturarum* in the hypostatic union enacted by *God qua Son*, maintaining the divine initiative in the process.

Barth carries on to his fourth point as follows: Jesus Christ, with the incarnation, exalted human essence in himself.[117] Barth considers the task of explicating the exaltation of the human essence in Christ Jesus to be one undertaken with great precision and careful delimitations.[118] To that end, Barth utilizes the language of "determination." What Barth means by this key term is elaborated in the following quote:

> [I]n the Son of God, and therefore by the divine Subject, united in His act, *each of the two natures*, without being either destroyed or altered, *acquires and has its own determination*. By and in Him the divine acquires a determination *to* the human, and the human a determination *from* the divine. The Son of God takes and has a part in the human essence assumed by Him by giving this a part in His divine essence. And the human essence

---

creatures as the Son of Man" respectively. Though intending a similar meaning as the word "nature" (*Natur*), Barth prefers "essence" because "nature" on Barth's view has a danger of connoting a known or knowable idea of deity or humanity apart from the specific revelation of both realities in Christ Jesus (see *CD* IV/2, 26). One has also to be aware of not drawing in notions of "substance" into Barth's usage of "essence." Instead, Barth's usage of the term approximates that of his usage of *Existenz* (existence), a term that captures the dynamic quality Barth intends. See Sumner, *Karl Barth and the Incarnation*, 170–74, for a fuller discussion.

113. *CD* IV/2, 63.
114. *CD* IV/2, 63–65.
115. *CD* IV/2, 64.
116. *CD* IV/2, 65.
117. *CD* IV/2, 69.
118. *CD* IV/2, 70.

assumed by Him takes and has a part in His divine by receiving this from Him.[119]

Barth's language at this point is inevitably provocative: what does he mean by the divine (nature) acquiring a determination *to* the human (nature), and the human *from* the divine? To say the least, Barth here is gesturing towards a notion that he will formulate fully when he expounds on the *communicatio operationum*, that of the "common actualization" of the divine and human essence in the one existence of Jesus Christ. But even at this point, Barth's words are carefully chosen. He speaks of the "mutual" participation of the divine and human essence and an inter-acquisition of the "determination" the natures share between each other in the one divine subject. Yet, the prepositions "to" and "from" clearly vouchsafe an asymmetrical relation.[120] Jones captures the idea well when he states: "[T]he essences in question are 'determined' to comprise, and actively do comprise, a numerically simple person: the determination coming (preveniently) *from* God and being given *to* Christ's human essence, with this human essence realizing God's determinative intention in seamless unity with the Word."[121] Barth is adamant that there is no point in which the human essence is "divinized" to become divine essence, or that it usurps the divine initiative.[122]

In adhering to his goal of speaking about the human essence in Jesus with great precision, Barth proceeds to examine three theological idioms arising from the "old orthodoxy," which as a cluster, attests to the effects of the hypostatic union. They are the *communicatio idiomatum* (communication of idioms), the *communicatio gratiarum* and the *communicatio operationum*. While the commentary on the *communicatio idiomatum* yields an interesting discussion on its own, our central enquiry into the incarnate obedience of Jesus Christ leads us to focus on the latter two idioms.[123]

---

119. *CD* IV/2, 70 (added emphasis). McCormack, "'We Have Actualized,'" 189, views that the term "determination" serves as the primary category to express Barth's actualized Christology.

120. *CD* IV/2, 70–71.

121. Jones, *Humanity of Christ*, 135 (original emphasis).

122. *CD* IV/2, 71. It is with this meaning that Barth speaks of the "humanity of God," an expression he was growing increasingly fond of. The human essence of the Son of God will always remain human essence, although it is united and brought into full harmony with the divine essence common to Father, Son and Holy Spirit (*CD* IV/2, 72). For Barth's increasing emphasis on the humanity of God, see his essay by the same name, "The Humanity of God," delivered as a lecture in 1956, a year following the publication of *CD* IV/2. Barth states: "It is precisely God's *deity* which, rightly understood, includes his *humanity*" (46, original emphasis).

123. Barth's commentary on the *communicatio idiomatum* runs from pp. 75–83 of *CD* IV/2, covering related topics such as the *genus majestaticum* and its opposite, the

The Communicatio Gratiarum

Barth's commentary on the *communicatio gratiarum* runs for almost twenty pages in *CD* IV/2—not the longest by far—yet it contains discussion apropos to our central enquiry. The *communicatio gratiarum*, at its core, points to the movement that is initiated to the human essence by virtue of the concrete union of the two natures in Jesus Christ.[124]

Barth begins by highlighting the primary determination of divine essence, and in the process illuminates what he meant earlier when he stated that the divine essence acquires a determination *to* the human essence. The key lies in returning to Barth's doctrine of election and grasping that in the eternal counsel, "God does not first elect and determine man but *Himself.*"[125] Election, even before it is to be understood as the election of Jesus as the elected man, is to be comprehended first and foremost as God's eternal determination of himself to be the God *of man*, in that the Son of God should exercise grace by becoming the Son of Man.[126] In this way, God so determines the divine nature that it should acquire its *telos* in man.[127] Barth states: "This is why we cannot possibly maintain that the participation of the two natures in Jesus Christ is only one-sided, that of the human in the divine. In the first instance, indeed, it is that of the divine in the human. And in the fact that it is this first it has its ultimate depth and unshakeable solidity as a participation of the human in the divine."[128]

It is with the above preamble that Barth turns to the aspect of the determination of the human essence in Jesus Christ. The *communicatio gratiarum*, Barth defines, is "human essence . . . determined wholly and utterly, from the very outset and in every part, by the electing grace of God."[129] For

---

genus tapeinoticum, and "kenotic" theories of the nineteenth century. For a fuller treatment, see Jones, *Humanity of Christ*, 146–50 and 267–69, and Sumner, *Karl Barth and the Incarnation*, 129–31. The question of Barth's accurate interpretation of the Lutheran understanding of the *communicatio idiomatum* remains. See Muller, *DLGTT*, 72–74, for a reading of the Reformed and Lutheran conception of the *communicatio idiomatum* as defined in Protestant Orthodoxy. McCormack, "'We Have Actualized,'" 185, further contends that Barth refuses to choose between the older Reformed or the older Lutheran understanding of the *communicatio idiomatum* because Barth finally demurs in relation to the metaphysical basis on which the differences between the Reformed and Lutherans were generated.

124. *CD* IV/2, 84.
125. *CD* IV/2, 84 (added emphasis).
126. *CD* IV/2, 84, 87.
127. *CD* IV/2, 87.
128. *CD* IV/2, 87.
129. *CD* IV/2, 88.

Barth, the *communicatio gratiarum* speaks of the human essence when it is effectively *confronted* with the divine, "so that without itself becoming divine it is an essence which exists in and with God, and is adopted and controlled and sanctified and ruled by Him."[130]

Specifically, Barth goes on to delineate five ways in which the human nature of Jesus is determined by the grace of God in its confrontation with the divine: i) the grace of the man Jesus Christ's origin ii) the grace of the sinlessness of his human essence iii) the grace of presence and effective working of the Holy Spirit iv) the grace to be the organ of the work of the Son as mediator between God and man and the grace to receive power for this work, and v) the grace of glory whereby in Jesus Christ, human essence is exalted to share in the glory of the divine nature.[131] Clearly, the scope of this present chapter constrains us from elaborating on all of the graces described. I will return, however, to a fuller examination of the second and third aspects of the communicated grace in subsequent chapters. Suffice in the meantime to make the following two general observations.

First, a cursory glance of the five communications of grace reveals Barth's basic adherence but also his innovative expansion of traditional accounts of the *communicatio gratiarum* framed by Protestant Orthodoxy. In those accounts, the grace communicated typically falls under two major categories—the *gratia unionis* (grace of union) otherwise termed *gratia eminentiae* (grace of eminence) and the *gratiae habituales* (habitual graces).[132] The former refers to the grace that elevates Jesus' humanity above all other creatures while the latter refers to the gracious dispositions conferred by the Holy Spirit on the human nature of Christ resulting in the man Jesus possessing true knowledge, and soundness and perseverance of the will beyond the natural capacity of human beings.[133] Barth covers the same ground as the traditional treatment does, but his actualistic ontology leads him to innovate in the following two ways. First, Barth resists the older Reformed idea of understanding the Spirit's work in Jesus as a "state" of grace, a *gratiae habituales*. To do so in Barth's opinion would be too approach the particular determination of Jesus' human essence in too "static" a manner; it would be to consider the particular determination "apart from the act in which it was given and received"—here, Barth is referring to the particular

---

130. *CD* IV/2, 88.

131. *CD* IV/2, 89–103.

132. For example, see Heppe, *Reformed Dogmatics*, 434–35, and Muller, *DLGTT*, 72.

133. Muller, *DLGTT*, 72.

history which took place in Jesus Christ—[134] and to focus instead on the effects of the state of Jesus' (elevated) human essence.[135] Second, Barth extends the *communicatio gratiarum* from its time-bound application limited to the incarnation to moor the doctrine in God's prevenient eternal election. This election, as we recall, is what constitutes the determination of the divine and human essence in Christ Jesus simultaneously—but as Barth maintains—not symmetrically.

The second observation to be made of Barth's treatment of the *communicatio gratiarum* is that Barth appropriates the five graces toward the end of securing Jesus' human obedience, while maintaining that obedience as a genuine human response. Consider the first grace of origin. While not involving or effecting any alteration in the human essence as such, the grace of origin exalts Jesus' human essence to "that harmony with the divine will, that service of the divine act, that correspondence to the divine grace, that state of thankfulness ... [and] true human freedom."[136] The point to be underscored is that these descriptions of the human essence are exalted to count for Barth as the characteristic markers of obedience. Similarly, the grace of sinlessness and the grace of the Holy Spirit have a paramount role to play in securing the "success" of Jesus' obedience while positing that obedience as a genuine human response. Even the fourth aspect of the communicated grace—what is traditionally termed the *potestas officii* (power for his work)—Barth regards as a *divine empowerment* and *not a divine negation* of the necessary creaturely medium (of human essence). Barth states clearly his reason for maintaining fully the genuine humanity of Christ:

> This work concerns man and the world. It therefore demands a human soul and a human body, human reason and human will, human obedience and human humility, human seriousness and anger, human anxiety and trust, human love for God and the neighbour. And it demands all this in an existence in our own human and created time. The speaking and acting, the suffering and striving, the praying and helping, the succumbing and conquering have all to be in human terms. That is why human essence is necessary to Him.[137]

---

134. *CD* IV/2, 89.

135. As McCormack, "'We Have Actualized,'" 191, states: "'Determination,' 'address,' 'confrontation'—all of this language belongs to the sphere of divine *action*—which means that even when Barth takes up the problem of the effects of the divine communication of grace to the humanity of Christ, he is still thinking within the sphere of act."

136. *CD* IV/2, 92.

137. *CD* IV/2, 99.

The upshot is that Barth's appropriation of the *communicatio gratiarum* gravitates towards a picture, as painted by Jones, whereby the human essence of Jesus in its *confrontation with* the divine and determination *from* the divine leads to Christ qua human *being spurred to act humanly*. "And he does so act," states Jones, "He presents himself as a human cognizant of, and responsive to, God's gratuitous advance; he *gives* thanks. In so doing, he qualifies each human as an agent capable of grateful decision making and action."[138]

The Communicatio Operationum and the Common Actualization of the Divine and Human Essences

I turn finally to the last of the triadic idioms that Barth utilizes from Protestant Orthodoxy: the *communicatio operationum*. Once again, Barth adopts but concurrently innovates what the Tradition has laid down in this regard.[139] The innovation of interest to us lies in the way Barth broadens the *operatio* to cover not just the divine-human work of atonement (as thought within the tradition) but to include *the determination of the human and divine essences themselves*. Similar to the *communicatio gratiarum*, Barth expands the doctrine from its specific application in the duration of the incarnation and extends it "retrospectively" to the eternal determination of God qua Son. This, Barth conveys through the notion of the "common *actualisation* of divine and human essence" in the existence of Jesus Christ.[140]

Barth is cognizant that he stands on risky ground in expressing things this way, and immediately qualifies the point to indicate that by itself, the divine essence as the eternal essence of the triune God—"of course" (Barth's emphasis)—[141] did not and does not need any actualization. The divine

138. Jones, *Humanity of Christ*, 140–41 (original emphasis).

139. See Heppe, *Reformed Dogmatics*, 445–46, and Muller, *DLGTT*, 72–74, for definitions of the *communicatio operationum* as understood in Protestant Orthodoxy, also termed the *communicatio apotelesmatum* (the communication of mediatorial operations in and for the sake of the work of salvation) by the Reformed. The debate revolves around the Lutheran preference to view the *apotelesma* (divine-human work) as resulting directly from the *communicatio idiomatum*, hence arguing for a third "class" of the *genus apotelesmaticum*, rather than a separate *communicatio apotelesmatum*, as per what the Reformed were inclined to. Barth, in an excursus in *CD* IV/2, 104–5, displays awareness of the debate and offers his own take, concluding with a respectful tone: "A mere battle of words? A splitting of hairs? That may be our reaction. But surely it is better to respect the care with which the older theologians, instead of making wild assertions, marked off their positions even to the final details."

140. *CD* IV/2, 113 (original emphasis).

141. *CD* IV/2, 113.

essence of the Son did not need his incarnation to become actual. Yet, *in the eternal self-determining election of God qua Son to be the God-man he will become in time, the divine essence needed a special actualization in its union with human essence.*[142] Barth affirms the same for human essence. By itself, human essence in general is actualized—albeit not self-actualized but God-actualized—but *in its union with the divine essence in the person of Jesus Christ whereby human essence is exalted into fellowship with God, therein lies the need for a special actualization.*[143] The "special" actualization of both the divine and human essences takes place in the *communicatio operationum*, in their *common* actualization in the singular work of all that Jesus Christ does and says as the one Son of God and Son of Man. This point is forcefully captured in the following quote:

> [The divine and human essences] are co-ordinated—commonly actualised—in His work. It is where the divine rules and reveals and gives that the human serves and attests and mediates. The one Word of Jesus Christ is His self-expression as God's eternal Word, and it is also the . . . word of the proclamation of this man as humanly articulated and conditioned. *The one will of Jesus Christ is the eternal will of God and it is also . . . the motivated human will which determines the way of this human life as such.* The one power of Jesus Christ is the omnipotent power of God and it is also the . . . power . . . in which this man as such does signs and wonders. The one death and passion of Jesus Christ is the final depth of the self-humiliation of God and it is also, following and completing it as a human death and passion, the way which the man Jesus entered . . . even to the extremity of misery and need as prepared for Him, not by men, but by God Himself. And the glory of Jesus Christ . . . is the triumph of God Himself,

---

142. *CD* IV/2, 113. Interestingly, McCormack, "'We Have Actualized,'" 196–97, views Barth's point concerning the divine essence of the triune God needing no actualization as a lapse on Barth's part back into "metaphysical" thinking. McCormack traces the root of Barth's inconsistency to the fact that Barth "repeatedly makes election to be a 'free' act in which God gives to His 'essence' a 'determination' which was not original to it" (197). McCormack's comment is unsurprising given his reading of Barth's actualistic ontology. Here, the differences between McCormack and my reading surface again. McCormack's maintenance of a logical priority or precedence of election over trinity leads him to redefine notions of "freedom" and "necessity" from how they are commonly understood. My own reading which allows for a logical priority or precedence of triunity over election allows for the idea of divine possibilities associated with the idea of a divine freedom which is free from any form of compulsion or necessity within the triune life. These divine possibilities are maintained no matter how relativized and secondary they are compared to the divine actuality that is realized.

143. *CD* IV/2, 114.

the end of all His ways in His work of atonement, and also His human life in obedience, with the answer revealed to His human life in the public coronation of His resurrection from the dead. *In the work of the one Jesus Christ everything is at one and the same time, but distinctly, both divine and human . . . . The divine and the human work together.* But even in their common working they are not interchangeable. The divine is still above and the human below. Their relationship is one of genuine action.[144]

The above quote lifts Barth's appropriation of the *communicatio operationum* to its crowning point, and concurrently reveals the pinnacle that Barth ascribed to Jesus' incarnate obedience within his Christology. Barth's highlighting of the divine and human aspects of the work of the one Christ points not only to their distinction—the human and divine aspects of the work are not interchangeable—but also to their coordination. In their common working, we find not only the *apotelesma* of the reconciliation of the world with God fulfilled, but also the very actualization of the divine and human essences as they exist in the one person of Jesus Christ. And in accordance with Barth's actualistic ontology, the *communicatio operationum* is not just about the common actualization of the divine and human essences at the point of incarnation, but is nothing less than *the actualization of the very being God has eternally determined for himself qua Son via the election— to be one and the same time the electing God and the elected man*. The main import for our enquiry is that the *communicatio operationum* holds Jesus' obedience in high esteem.

Seen in the light of the actualization of being, the following can be said: though God qua Son, with the Spirit, is the one who anteriorly actualizes and brings Christ's humanity into existence, Christ's human essence must still, as Jones stated, "take up and enact, and *does* take up and enact, the identity that God proposes."[145] This is an enactment that is started and completed only in the full obedience the man Jesus of Nazareth renders. And seen in the light of reconciliation, God's Christocentric self-determination reveals his decision that salvation should be effected by two coordinated but asymmetrically related agential realities. In the reconciliatory endeavor, God generously and graciously includes Christ's human agency, particularly his human response of obedience.[146]

---

144. *CD* IV/2, 116 (added emphasis).
145. Jones, *Humanity of Christ*, 143.
146. Jones, *Humanity of Christ*, 144, 146.

Jesus Christ, the Royal Man

The above discussions on the theological idioms take us to the edge of Barth's Christological treatment in *CD* IV/2 §64.2. In §64.3, Barth carries on to speak of Jesus Christ as the "Royal Man," following the Synoptic Gospels' attestation.[147] He defines the royal man as one created "after God" (κατὰ θεόν), one who as a man "exists analogously to the mode of existence of God. In what He thinks and wills and does, in His attitude, there is a *correspondence*, a parallel in the creaturely world, to the plan and purpose and work and attitude of God."[148]

The crucial word to take note of is "correspondence" (*Entsprechung*), a word which as Jones states "suggests that Christ's human activity goes hand in hand with Christ's divine activity; that the act and being of the Son, rather than displacing human agency, enables its exercise."[149] The import of the notion of *Entsprechung* is captured in the following statement of Barth's: "[T]he man [Jesus] . . . in His own person was and is and will be the kingdom and lordship of the God who reconciles the world with Himself. . . . *[God's] kingdom and lordship and dominion are concretely the kingdom and lordship and dominion of this man.*"[150] Jesus Christ is hence presented unambiguously as the royal man, the one who is "[God's] creaturely and earthly and historical correspondence."[151] He is the one who in his very human existence realizes God's intention and completes God's work of divine love by rendering it covenantal, most of all through his offering of a full and complete obedience to God.

Conclusion

Major swathes of Barth's "early" and "later" Christology have been considered in this chapter in order to identify accurately the place and significance Barth ascribed to the incarnate obedience of Jesus Christ. Our survey has yielded the following composite picture: Barth allocates to the human obedience of Jesus Christ a far more significant place and position than what has commonly been recognized. As early as his first major Christological exposition

---

147. *CD* IV/2, 156.

148. *CD* IV/2, 166 (added emphasis).

149. Jones, *Humanity of Christ*, 151.

150. *CD* IV/2, 155 (added emphasis). See also Jüngel, *Karl Barth*, 128–29, for a different presentation of essentially the same point: the speaking of God leads to the speaking of the royal man, Jesus, which in turn leads to the speaking of humankind. The royal man, Jesus, "moves" God's own eternal being (129).

151. *CD* IV/2, 181.

in *CD* I/2 §15, Barth's basic position already evinces itself. Even though it is the *divine* subject of God qua Son who becomes incarnate, Christ's genuine humanity and consequently his actions of obedience are by no means diminished. This, Barth tells us, is an obedience that receives its fullest definition in Jesus Christ taking upon himself the burden of our sins.

The above-mentioned picture forms the basic core of the conception that Barth has of the role and place of Jesus' obedience, even as his theology underwent further development, especially in the maturing of his actualistic ontology. Via the doctrine of election, Barth came to envisage God qua Son as the one who self-determines himself to be both "electing God" and "elected man." Self-determination in *this* way has ontological implications. In tracing these implications, it is interesting to note the weight Barth gives to the obedience of Christ. So, while the clause "Jesus as the electing God (in eternity)" highlights the divine initiative and points to election as an act grounded from start to finish in the grace of God, the counterpart clause "Jesus as the elected man" and consequently "the man who elects God (equally in eternity)" also serves to highlight the role played by the human obedience of Jesus. From eternity, this history, encounter and decision between God and man, albeit in *this* man Jesus Christ, is *already* present in the primal history of God. Even as God carries out his will to bring man into a reconciliatory relationship with him, God qua Jesus of Nazareth *humanly* participates in the program via his obedience, most of all in its most terrifying and excruciating moment of the cross. Here lies the confounding truth that this participation happens in a proleptic manner in eternity in the self-determination of God to be the God *for us*.

Already then, in *CD* II/2, we have a sense of the increasingly dominant trope of Barth's actualistic theology pressing upon his conception of Jesus' obedience. Just as Barth's actualistic ontology reaches its full maturity in *CD* IV, so similarly the significance and importance of Jesus' incarnate obedience finds its crescendo in *CD* IV/1, especially in the critical role given to it in the three inter-related concepts of covenant, history and the *status duplex*. That Jesus Christ can be both the faithful covenant-Lord and covenant-partner; that there can be found in Jesus Christ's history the history of God and the history of man, and that in Jesus Christ we find the concurrent humiliation of the Son of God and the exaltation of the Son of Man, all this is—as Barth repeatedly emphasized—made possible by the *prior divine initiative* and *action*. It is *God* who wills to be covenant-Lord, who "allows" his *Geschichte* to be conditioned by the *Geschichte* of the man Jesus of Nazareth, and who as the Son of God first stoops low in humility and in humiliation.

Yet, the divine initiative never displaces the human response, in fact creating a genuine space for human action to co-exist in. Germane to our argument, *the main human action rendered in that space is specifically that of obedience*. So likewise, it is *Jesus Christ the elected man* who responds in obedience, proving himself to be the faithful covenant-partner who is for God and for fellow man, who in taking on the history of suffering shows his obedience to the Father's will, and who by that course of obedience, is the Son of Man exalted. Barth indeed makes generous allowance for the articulation of Jesus' human obedience. Furthermore, when Barth's actualistic ontology is factored in, the latitude of that articulation is all the more increased: God qua Son is the *eternal* covenant-Lord and covenant-partner, the one in whom is found the *primal history* (*Urgeschichte*) of God and man, and the one who exists *eternally* in his twofold simultaneous state of humiliation and exaltation.

The accentuation given to the obedience of Jesus Christ reaches its maximum expression in *CD* IV/2 in Barth's consideration of the *communio naturarum*, the *communicatio gratiarum* and the *communicatio operationum* derived from Protestant Scholasticism. In Barth's hands, the three idioms serve as a vehicle of expression to capture not only the coexistence of the divine and human action, but also the "common actualization" of the divine and human essences.

On this account, Barth is a daring theologian, but not careless. He recognizes that the "common actualization" spoken of is purely on the basis of the common union of the divine and human essences in the one person and existence of Jesus Christ. Notwithstanding this point, the significance Barth gives to the obedience of Jesus Christ as he treats the *communicatio operationum* must not be lost on us. Barth here really ascribes to the human obedience of Jesus Christ a *co-participatory* role whereby the human response of obedience actually has a part to play in the common actualization of the human and the divine essences, although it is a secondary and derivative role in relation to the divine initiative. Furthermore, from the perspective of Barth's actualistic ontology, this co-participatory role is one that extends to the eternal divine self-determination of God to be the electing God and the elected man. Barth's description of the obedience of Jesus Christ reaches its climax at this point. Even though God brings about the humanity of Christ Jesus, the man Jesus of Nazareth must still, via his human essence, accept the identity proposed to him and obey the path of suffering ordained for him.

In all, Barth gives maximal space within his Christology for the articulation and expression of the genuine incarnate human obedience of Christ. The deeper truth that this chapter sheds is that it is Barth's actualistic ontology that generously funds this rich account of Jesus' obedience. Regardless of the approval or disapproval one shows towards Barth's actualistic ontology, it cannot be denied that via this strand of thinking, the human obedience of Jesus Christ is given a significance in eternity that far outweighs its immediate import within the circumscription of time and space surrounding Jesus' incarnate life. In Barth's scheme, Jesus' obedience is "stretched" back in eternity even to the point of God's self-determination. In this way, the notion of Jesus' incarnate obedience is heightened to a stage of development that has not been done previously.

This chapter has sought to establish the above findings with its "wide" reading of Christ's obedience within the bookends of Barth's "early" and "later" Christology in *CD*. What remains the task of the next chapter is to engage in a "deep" reading of Christ's obedience through an examination of certain metaphysical dimensions of that obedience. This will be done in the hope of shedding further light on the notion of the obedience of the one who is *vere Deus, vere homo*—Jesus Christ.

4

Karl Barth's Reading of the Metaphysics of the Obedience of Jesus Christ

THE PREVIOUS CHAPTER SURVEYED the importance of the incarnate obedience of Jesus Christ in connection with a reading of Barth's "early" and "later" Christology. The findings reveal that Barth accords to Christ's obedience a far more important place than what has usually been recognized. In tandem with Barth's full-fledged actualistic ontology, the incarnate obedience of Christ is elevated to a status where its significance is seen not just in the economy of salvation, but also within the eternal being of God himself. Notwithstanding the primal and gratuitous basis of the divine initiative, Jesus' human response of obedience is co-opted in such a manner to have a participatory role in the eternal self-determination of God. This is a self-determination wherein God being the triune God is coterminous with him being the electing God and elected man at the same time.

Having detailed the above moves in the previous chapter, I turn now to address three perennial questions of a metaphysical nature that arise whenever the incarnate obedience of Jesus is considered. The first question concerns the state of the human nature that Jesus assumed: whether it was "fallen" (postlapsarian) or "unfallen" (prelapsarian) human nature. Our earlier cursory reference to Barth's position of a "fallen" human nature leaves itself open for further exploration. Second, Barth affirms that Christ was without sin. The scriptural affirmation that Jesus Christ was "tempted in every way, just as we are—yet was without sin" (Heb 4:15) is a doctrinal axiom that Barth, alongside many others, would accept without dispute.[1] Yet, how Jesus was without sin is a question that remains. Was Jesus, to employ the common scholastic notion, *posse peccare et non peccare* (able to sin but did not sin), that is, he was "sinless"? Or was he *non posse peccare* (not able to sin in the first place), that is, he was "impeccable"? And how would the viewpoint adopted affect the way one conceives Jesus' incarnate obedience? Third, given that an act of obedience involves two distinct

---

1. See Davidson, "Pondering the Sinlessness," 383–91, for an exposition of the key scriptural texts that attest to the sinlessness of Jesus Christ.

expressions of volition, is the obedience of Jesus Christ to be found in the submission of his singular will to the Father's will or in the submission of Jesus' human will to his divine will, which is similar in turn to the Father's will? To phrase the question in the above fashion is to foreground the discussion of Monothelitism vs. Dyothelitism, especially its implications for the obedience rendered by Jesus Christ.

These three queries are the deeper metaphysical questions that inevitably need to be addressed for a thoroughgoing enquiry into the incarnate obedience of Jesus Christ, and so they frame the discussion that follows. I begin by addressing the first two areas together, that of the fallen nature Jesus assumed and the question of whether Jesus was impeccable or merely sinless. By highlighting insights from Barth's mature Christology and correspondingly the actualistic ontology his Christology is framed in, I show that, while drawing from the Tradition, the answer Barth provides finally takes us in a new direction, especially as it pertains to the latter issue of how Jesus remained without sin. Following this I consider the implications that maintaining a monothelite or dyothelite position holds for the obedience of Jesus Christ. I explain why, despite Barth's relative reticence over a discussion of this topic, a dyothelite position would more profitably serve Barth's understanding of the incarnation and the place of obedience within it.

To restate this chapter's purpose: while the previous chapter argued for the importance of the obedience of Jesus Christ within the broad canvas of Barth's Christology, this chapter adds "depth" and "thickness" to that specification by concerning itself with the larger metaphysical questions at hand.

"Like Us and Unlike Us": Barth's Discussion of the Fallen vs. Unfallen Human Nature that Jesus Assumed and the Impeccability vs. Sinlessness Debate

I commence with the first two questions: the first concerning the type of human nature assumed in the incarnation, and the second, the manner in which Jesus remained without sin. Before turning to Barth's treatment of these two questions, it would be profitable to paint the background and provide an overview of the specific issues associated with each viewpoint.

Background and an Overview of the Issues

The question of whether the Son of God assumed a fallen or unfallen human nature in the incarnation is certainly not an article of faith by which the church stands or falls,[2] but it has generated much discussion. On the one hand, those of the "fallen" persuasion have the task before them of explaining how it is that fallenness and corruption does not in any way entail sin and sinfulness, given the common association of fallenness with the notions of original sin and guilt.[3] For advocates of the "unfallen" position, on the other hand, their task is to explain how Jesus Christ in his incarnation truly became *one of us* and not merely *like* us. The latter notion consists in the idea that although Jesus took on a nature that is genuinely human in kind, it is nevertheless one extracted from the concrete situation of fallenness and corruption that humanity has found herself in. Although it is clearly preferable to employ the language of "fittingness" instead of "necessity," that is, it was not necessary for Jesus to have assumed a fallen human nature, proponents of the "unfallen" camp still have to answer to the claim that given the actual and concrete situation humanity is now in, it is certainly fitting that Christ should assume a condition that is humanity's very own.[4]

The issue remains an area of debate when it comes to what the tradition has to say, but it is somewhat safer to assume that the tradition's inclination is toward the "unfallen" position. According to McFarland, the patristic era was just beginning to formulate the question and hence did not have at hand the categorical tools needed to achieve the level of definition and specificity evident in later discussions. It was Augustine who introduced into the discussion the key categorical tool of the notion of original sin and guilt, directly linking fallenness with sinfulness in a way that had not been done so far and which subsequently could not be ignored. This move led, during the medieval period, to the explicit affirmation that Christ assumed an unfallen nature, a view that held sway over Reformation and post-Reformation Protestant orthodoxy. It was only in the eighteenth and nineteenth century that a certain number of theological voices began to advocate for the "fallen" position.[5] McFarland affirms of this alternate theological voice: "While their

---

2. See McFarland, "Fallen or Unfallen?," 399.

3. I take the point from Kapic, "Son's Assumption," 163.

4. McFarland, "Fallen or Unfallen?," 405–8. In this regard, McFarland states rightly that Gregory of Nazianzus' soteriological axiom—"The unassumed is the unhealed"—cannot be appealed to without great difficulty. Granted that the effects of the Fall damaged and corrupted human nature, they are by definition not essential to and constitutive of that nature. Hence, strictly speaking, fallenness does not need to be assumed in order to redeem it (406). McFarland contends that the language of fittingness is more appropriate in this case.

5. McFarland, "Fallen or Unfallen?," 401–5. Kapic, "The Son's Assumption," 156, records others who have attempted to revisit the past and argue, to the contrary, that the patristic Fathers could be read as maintaining a "fallen" position. Notably, Kapic cites Dorries, "Nineteenth Century British Christological Controversy," and Torrance,

position can hardly be said to have carried the day, it has proved enormously influential in contemporary academic theology."[6]

Barth takes his stand with the minority report: Jesus took on a fallen human nature. Before looking at his argument in greater depth, it would be worthwhile to pay more detailed attention to the arguments of the opposite camp, in order that Barth's position might be more clearly appreciated. To do that, I turn briefly to Oliver Crisp's essay "Did Christ have a fallen human nature?"[7]

At its nub, Crisp's argument is clear: there is no way to make sense of the notion that Christ had a fallen human nature but was not sinful. The reason for this, as Crisp argues, is that the notion of "fallenness" even in its "weakest" form as understood within the tradition already entails the idea of sinfulness.[8] Expanded, Crisp's argument comprises an engagement with the two constituent elements of original corruption and original guilt derived from the wider umbrella of Reformed Orthodoxy's assertion of the doctrine of original sin. In his case, Crisp emphasizes an *imputed* rather than an *inherited* (via natural generation) corruption and guilt. Crisp defines original corruption as a propensity or proneness to actual sin, whereby human beings inevitably sin without the intervention of divine grace.[9] The discussion revolving around original guilt is more complicated—the details of which need not detain us at this point—but the final outcome is that according to the claim of Reformed Orthodoxy, original guilt must be logically imputed prior to corruption.[10] In accordance with this strict logic, advocates of the "fallen" position have to account for how Jesus can remain sinless when

---

Trinitarian Faith, 153. Mention should also be made of Weinandy, *In the Likeness of Sinful Flesh*, who argues in favor of the "fallen" position, although his ambiguous treatment of the crucial question of the relationship between the assumed nature to original sin and guilt renders his proposal broad enough to be accepted by many, including those who might rest in the "unfallen" camp. On this point, McFarland, "Fallen or Unfallen?," 402n9, remains unpersuaded of Weinandy's presentation of Christ assuming a fallen human nature as a matter of consensus among the patristic fathers.

6. McFarland, "Fallen or Unfallen?," 405.

7. First published as Crisp, "Did Christ Have a Fallen Human Nature?," 270–88; reprinted in *Divinity and Humanity*, 90–117. Future citations will be to the work located in *Divinity and Humanity*.

8. Crisp, *Divinity and Humanity*, 93.

9. Crisp, *Divinity and Humanity* 96–97.

10. Crisp, *Divinity and Humanity,* 98–103. Crisp states: "All human beings post-Fall have imputed to them Adam's guilt, and, as a consequence of this, Adam's corruption. It is not the case that all post-Fall humanity has a corrupt nature passed down to it via natural generation, and, as a consequence of this, incurs an inherited guilt" (103).

Jesus assuming a fallen human nature entails that he is imputed beforehand with original guilt.

To be sure, the above argument is premised on a tight correlation between the concept of original sin and original guilt. Not all who espouse a doctrine of original sin, however, embrace equally this particular correlation.[11] Interestingly, Crisp himself agrees that there are inherent difficulties with a concept of original guilt, namely, the "transference" problem. That is to say, how can guilt be transferred, even imputed, from one party to another?[12] This explains why Crisp takes his argument to another level. Allowing for the possibility of Christ assuming a "fallen" human nature wherein the state of fallenness does not include the notion of original guilt, Crisp contends that such a fallen nature would still admit of original corruption, and on Crisp's terms, the very possession of an originally corrupt human nature would entail the possession of a morally corrupt human nature. That, in effect, would have been enough to render Christ sinful, since Christ with a morally corrupt human nature would be considered "loathsome in the sight of his heavenly Father."[13] Compounding the issue further is the metaphysical notion that it would have been impossible anyway for the impeccable divine nature of the Word to be hypostatically joined with a fallen human nature. Because the nature assumed by the Word becomes a "part" of the Word, if the Word were to assume a fallen (and corrupt) human nature, the Word would cease to be impeccable at that moment.[14] According to Crisp, the fallenness position at best can only cohere with a version of Nestorianism, where "the Word is not hypostatically united with his human nature, but lives a sort of parallel existence to it."[15] The above difficulties lead Crisp to firmly assert the fallenness position as untenable.[16]

So far, I have highlighted the issues at stake in considering whether Christ assumed a fallen or unfallen human nature. For the second and related question concerning the specific manner in which Jesus was without sin, I turn similarly to another essay by Crisp. In "Was Christ Sinless

---

11. An example would be John Calvin, whose doctrine of original sin is aimed at depravity and corruption, rather than any notion of an inherited or imputed guilt. See Allen, "Calvin's Christ," 382–97.

12. Crisp, *Divinity and Humanity*, 99. Crisp reaffirms the difficulty in "On Original Sin," 257–58, 264 thesis 4.

13. Crisp, *Divinity and Humanity*, 112.

14. Crisp, *Divinity and Humanity*, 113.

15. Crisp, *Divinity and Humanity*, 113.

16. Crisp, *Divinity and Humanity*, 115–16 goes on to contend that the best position is the traditional position, like that taken by Augustine, wherein Christ's sinless and unfallen human nature was affected by the Fall without being actually fallen.

or Impeccable?" Crisp argues for the "impeccable" position as opposed to merely the "sinless" position, meaning: Jesus Christ was not only able to not sin (*posse non peccare*), but he really was not able to sin (*non posse peccare*) in the first place.[17] In establishing his position, Crisp distinguishes between the two positions of *succumbing to a particular temptation* and *the capacity to succumb to temptation*, emphasizing that the version of impeccability he advocates allows for the latter position while denying the former.[18] In this way, Crisp controverts the common idea that impeccability automatically entails the notion of immunity to temptation. Likewise, Crisp insists that his version of impeccability allows for Christ to have a "psychological configuration" that is consistent with him feeling the "pull" and the "lure" of the temptations that Jesus is reported in the New Testament accounts to have endured.[19]

Having cleared his view of impeccability of the two prime misconceptions, Crisp moves on to argue the key difference between his view and the "sinless" view. On Crisp's account, the final difference lies in the issue of whether Christ *could actually have sinned* when presented with temptation. The impeccable position states a resolute "No," because *the divine nature would have prevented such an outcome or would prevent it* if it became necessary, although one could say that such an eventuality never arose because the Holy Spirit was always at work within the human nature of Jesus to ensure he withstood every instance of temptation.[20] The same, however, cannot be said of the "sinless" view. Crisp argues that the "sinless" view cannot answer with the resolute "No" the way the impeccable position could. The "sinless" view instead must allow for possible situations where Christ could have sinned (although he did not actually do so).[21] On Crisp's account, this is tantamount to saying Christ had the capacity to sin *qua* human and *qua* divine. Adherents of the "sinless" position would—in the process

---

17. First published as Crisp, "Was Christ Sinless or Impeccable?," 168–86; reprinted in *God Incarnate*, 122–36. Future citations will be referring to the version found in *God Incarnate*.

18. Crisp, *God Incarnate*, 127.

19. Crisp, *God Incarnate*, 128. Crisp, however, rightly qualifies that these temptations would have to be externally generated by some other agent rather than internally generated by Christ himself. Furthermore, the temptations would have to belong to the category of what Crisp calls "innocent" temptations rather than "sinful" ones. The difference between the two is that the former does not require an existing psychological configuration that is already in a state of sin itself to find the "pull" of the temptation appealing. Finally, Crisp allows that the "innocent" temptations Christ endured do not in any way render him morally culpable before God for being subjected to those temptations themselves (129–32).

20. Crisp, *God Incarnate*, 128–29.

21. Crisp, *God Incarnate*, 133.

of differentiating themselves from the impeccability position—find themselves inevitably locked in this precarious state of insinuating the capacity to sin on the part of the divine person.[22]

Survey of Barth's Exposition in the Dogmatics

Having sketched the background and identified the issues at hand, I turn to a deeper exploration of Barth's own take on this specific matter. In the following section, I will draw out what I see as Barth's unique contribution to the ongoing debate.

As seen in the earlier chapter, as early as *CD* I/2, Barth states unequivocally his claim that the human nature assumed by the Word is that of postlapsarian fallen human nature.[23] To recap, three reasons were cited for Barth's unusual move vis-à-vis the Tradition: i) Barth's reading of σάρξ in the New Testament ii) the "revelation" reason, wherein the event of the Word made flesh calls for a state of affairs whereby the flesh assumed by the Word is to be the same nature as that found in those to whom the Word is revealed and iii) the "recapitulation" reason, that is, since Jesus Christ comes to recapitulate the history of Adam and Israel, it is perfectly fitting that he should assume the flesh and human nature of those whose history he recapitulates.[24] Especially in the last two reasons, one finds strong resonances with the "fittingness" theme. While there is no soteriological necessity for Christ to have assumed a fallen human nature, nonetheless it is certainly fitting that he should have done so, given *this is the concrete form of human nature* that humanity has embedded herself in since the Fall.[25]

At the same time, *CD* I/2 reveals a Barth who maintains that while Christ took on fallen human nature, he nonetheless was without sin. Moreover, Christ was without sin in a manner and for a reason resembling very closely impeccability. Because it is the divine subject, the Son of God, who assumes human nature—even fallen human nature—the singular person of the Lord Jesus Christ *would not* and *could not* have sinned anyway.[26] Barth's consideration of the fact that Jesus was without sin at this stage admits of a dialectical tension which Barth does not seem concerned to resolve. At one

---

22. Crisp, *God Incarnate*, 134.
23. *CD* I/2, 153.
24. *CD* I/2, 152–53.
25. McFarland, "Fallen or Unfallen?," 406–8.
26. I reiterate Barth's crucial statements in this regard: "In [this being] God Himself is the Subject. How can God sin [sic] deny Himself to Himself, be against Himself as God . . ." (*CD* I/2, 155).

end of the dialectical pole is Christ's facing of real inward temptation and trial, a genuine struggle to obey involving tears to God and wrestling with God in real inward need.[27] At the other end of the dialectical pole lies the fact that, for Barth, Jesus was without sin because "Jesus cannot sin" and that he was "bound to win in this struggle."[28] At this second end of the pole one finds Barth's argument closely aligned with the "impeccable" position, although Barth might have overplayed his rhetoric to the degree that it seemingly clouds his affirmation of the genuine nature of Jesus' temptation and struggle.[29] But overall, this was a dialectical tension Barth was keen to maintain throughout his writings: Jesus was sinless in that he *would not* and *could not* sin, but his impeccability in no way negates the genuine struggle arising from the temptations he faced. The paradoxical tension Barth presents could be pithily summarized by the basic axiom that Jesus Christ is both "*like* us and *unlike* us" in his incarnation. Barth states: "In becoming the same as we are, the Son of God is the same in quite a different way from us."[30]

This central axiom—Jesus is "like us and unlike us"—receives a further bolstering in *CD* III/2. In discussing the subject matter of theological anthropology, Barth highlights the point that a true understanding of human nature in humanity must begin first with Jesus Christ and the human nature found in him.[31] Not discounting the difference that human nature in fallen humanity has been distorted by sin and concealed in its reality, Barth asserts that it is in the sinlessness of Jesus that the difference between Jesus' human nature and ours is founded. In expanding on that trait of sinlessness, Barth states that Jesus' human nature "is not different from our own, and does not simply exclude the possibility of the corruption to which it has fallen victim in us."[32] Jesus' human nature "might have become a prey to the corruption

27. *CD* I/2, 158.
28. *CD* I/2, 158.
29. For example, what did Barth mean when he said that "the eternal Word of God is immune from temptation even in the flesh" (*CD* I/2, 158), or that Jesus "really had no awareness of sin" (*CD* I/2, 159)? Most likely, given Barth's intention to maintain the genuine struggle of Jesus, Barth meant, in relation to the first statement, Jesus' immunity from falling and succumbing to temptation as opposed to an immunity to experiencing the "pull" or "lure" of temptation itself. In relation to the second statement, I surmise that Barth meant the awareness of the notion of actually sinning against God. Because God is the divine subject of the incarnation, God cannot, as Barth stated earlier, deny himself against himself. This once again does not mean, however, that Jesus fails to experience the "pull" of temptations, especially as it applies to Jesus being faced with the temptation to will a different course.
30. *CD* I/2, 155.
31. *CD* III/2, 50.
32. *CD* III/2, 51.

which was its fate in us. For even in Him it is still creaturely, not creative and divine, and therefore not precluded from sin."[33] In this way, Barth affirms the genuine danger and liability posed to Jesus by the temptations he faced. The emphasis here is that Jesus' sinlessness does not consist in *any special quality of his humanity that would have rendered Jesus physically incapable of sin*.[34] Instead, "the secret of the sinlessness of Jesus" lies in *the particular way in which he is man* as the Son of God, the Creator and Lord. Barth states: "In becoming man God remained true to Himself."[35] The two ends of the dialectic are shown again: Jesus assumed a fallen human nature that according to Barth includes even the possibility of corruption. But yet, he remained sinless, with the basis of his sinlessness reposing in the fact that it is a divine subject who bears that humanity. Therefore, at this stage, one could say that Barth still conceived the quality of Jesus being without sin to arise from the impeccable nature of the divine subject. Barth states slightly further on: "Sinlessness and the power to be sinless are divine qualities."[36]

In *CD* IV/1–2, Barth continues to give substantial attention to Jesus' sinlessness. At this point, however, Barth's treatment evinces a turn not to be missed. In *CD* IV/1, Barth links Jesus' sinlessness to his obedience. Defining the supreme expression of obedience in the specific act of Jesus taking our place as sinners, Barth asserts that the sinlessness of Jesus must be construed in the light of this obedience, and not as a sinlessness consisting in "an abstract and absolute purity, goodness and virtue."[37] He elaborates in a crucial passage a little further on:

> [Man's] unwillingness to repent is the constant renewal of his sin. The sinlessness of Jesus Christ consists in the fact that He does not take part in this game. He was a man as we are. *His condition was no different from ours. He took our flesh, the nature of man as he comes from the fall.* In this nature He is exposed every moment to the temptation to a renewal of sin—the temptation of impenitent being and thinking and speaking and action. *His sinlessness was not therefore His condition. It was the act of His being* in which He defeated temptation in His condition which is ours, in the flesh.[38]

33. *CD* III/2, 51.
34. *CD* III/2, 51.
35. *CD* III/2, 52.
36. *CD* III/2, 52.
37. *CD* IV/1, 258.
38. *CD* IV/1, 258–59 (added emphasis).

The above quotation is important on two counts. First, given that the purpose of this chapter is to address certain metaphysical aspects of Jesus' incarnate obedience, consequently ascertaining the genuineness and authenticity of his obedience, the remarkable observation is made that Barth reverses the direction of thought! On Barth's terms, it is not so much a matter of Jesus' sinlessness bearing on his obedience as it is Jesus' obedience reinforcing and grounding his sinlessness. I mention this point not to nullify the current enquiry—in my mind, there is a valuable place for discerning the metaphysical conditions of Jesus' incarnate obedience—but simply to highlight the different epistemological starting point between Barth and this chapter's specific enquiry. Barth is less concerned with establishing the metaphysics of Jesus' incarnate obedience than he is with taking at face value the truth of Jesus' obedience and drawing out its implications, chief of which is Jesus' sinlessness.

Second, Barth's consideration of Jesus' sinlessness at this point emits a more palpable actualistic tone. The sinlessness of Jesus is certainly not a special quality of the humanity he assumed—a fact Barth consistently maintained—but rather is "the act of his being."[39] In distinction from previous expositions, Barth locates explicitly the sinlessness of Jesus in the *act* and *actions* of his being, as opposed to the *state* of his being. This latter notion of the state of Jesus' being bears the idea that since it is an impeccable divine subject who assumes humanity, the person of Jesus Christ is therefore sinless. This, of course, is not to suggest that Barth no longer upheld the idea of an impeccable divine subject who becomes incarnate, but under the actualistic framework that Barth is increasingly operating from, that notion no longer takes center stage for him.

The actualistic turn receives its climactic treatment in *CD* IV/2, the last of Barth's major sections treating the sinlessness of Christ. As seen in the previous chapter, under Barth's treatment of the *communicatio gratiarum*, the second of the graces communicated to the human nature of Jesus within the hypostatic union is that of the grace of the sinlessness of Jesus' human essence.[40] Barth reiterates that the sinlessness of Jesus is not a quality that stems or flows automatically from Jesus' human essence. Rather, Jesus' sinlessness, his being "without sin" means that "in our human and sinful existence as a man *He did not sin*."[41] Repeating his fundamental "like us yet unlike us" axiom, Barth states: "He made our human essence His own even

---

39. *CD* IV/1, 259.
40. *CD* IV/2, 92 onwards.
41. *CD* IV/2, 92 (added emphasis).

in its corruption, but He did not repeat or affirm its inward contradiction."[42] Having arrived at the fullness of his actualistic ontology by this juncture, Barth extends the actualistic strand of his thinking into his conception of Jesus' sinlessness as shown in the following quote:

> [T]he sinlessness of Jesus was not a condition of His being as man, but *the human act of His life working itself out in this way from its origin*. And on this aspect, too, the determination of His human essence by the grace of God does not consist in the fact that there is added to Him the remarkable quality that He could not sin as a man, but *in His effective determination from His origin* for this act in which, participant in our sinful essence, *He did not will to sin* and *did not sin*.[43]

Barth here continues the actualistic emphasis by underscoring the sinlessness of Jesus as a matter of the act and action of his being, as opposed to the state of Jesus' being. Barth carries on further to correlate the act of Jesus' sinlessness with the notion of freedom, stating that Jesus did not sin, because from the origin of his humanity—which in this context would refer to the determination of his human essence by the divine grace of God—Jesus lived as a man in the true human freedom for obedience, for "harmony with the divine will."[44] On Barth's reading, this human freedom for obedience entails that Jesus "had no place for sinful action."[45] He affirms: "[T]here could be no question of it ever becoming His act. Because and as He was man only as the Son of God, it was excluded from the choice of His acts. *In virtue of this origin of His being, He was unable to choose it.* Therefore *He did not choose it.* And *He did not do it.*"[46]

From the survey of key passages taken from the *Dogmatics*, we see an unequivocal pronouncement on Barth's part that Jesus Christ took on a fallen human nature, despite being cognizant that such a view stood along the lines of a minority report in the tradition. Christ has made this fallen human nature his own, with all its weaknesses and infirmities and if possible, even its corruption—that is the degree to which Barth would go—but as he also insists, Christ did not make its *inward contradiction* his own and commit sin. Instead, in fully participating in human nature, Jesus sanctifies and restores that human nature, exalting it to sinlessness and freedom from sin. This explains why, for Barth, the notion of Jesus taking on a fallen human

42. *CD* IV/2, 92.
43. *CD* IV/2, 92–93 (added emphasis).
44. *CD* IV/2, 93.
45. *CD* IV/2, 93.
46. *CD* IV/2, 93 (added emphasis).

nature is always of a piece with Jesus being without sin, which in the final analysis, is predicated on Jesus' impeccability. Because the subject bearing the humanity is the divine Son of God, the human nature of Jesus receives a determination of grace from the divine, such that the singular person of the Lord Jesus Christ working out his humanity from this divinely-determined origin is one that *would not* and *could not* sin. As Sumner summarizes, Barth's doctrine of the human nature assumed by Jesus can simultaneously be described as both fallen and divinely determined. Though conditioned by the fall, in virtue of the *communicatio gratiarum*, it was not left in a state of being peccable, but in fact rendered impeccable.[47]

Evaluation of Barth's Position

Jesus' Assumption of a Fallen Human Nature

Having detailed Barth's stand, it remains in the rest of this section to evaluate Barth's position vis-à-vis the tradition. I begin with Barth's stand on Jesus' fallen human nature. To recall, Crisp has highlighted certain major difficulties with the "fallenness" position.

The first difficulty concerns the association of original guilt with the idea of original sin embedded within the notion of a fallen human nature.[48] The obvious predicament, in this case, is that in assuming a fallen human nature, Jesus would not only bear what Barth terms the "alien guilt" of others,[49] but he would bear his own guilt, hence disqualifying himself from being our sinless Savior.[50]

In response, although Barth subscribes to both the doctrine of original sin—albeit in a revised form as we shall soon see—and the concept of guilt within his hamartiology, he keeps the two separate and nowhere integrates in a manner after Reformed Orthodoxy the second element as part of the first. That is to say, Barth's doctrine of original sin does not involve at all the

---

47. Sumner, "Fallenness," 195, 205.
48. Crisp, *Divinity and Humanity*, 103.
49. *CD* IV/2, 92.
50. The notion of imputed guilt in association with original sin as propagated under Reformed orthodoxy is often complemented with or predicated upon a version of federal or natural headship. Both views essentially see Adam as the representative of the whole human race. Either Adam acted on our behalf so that the entirety of the human race is treated as if we have actually and personally done what he as our representative did, or the entirety of the human race was present in seminal or germinal form in Adam such that the rebellion of Adam is counted as that of the entire human race. The definition of federal and natural headship comes from Erickson, *Christian Theology*, 578.

idea of original guilt.⁵¹ Instead, the notion of guilt from sin and wrongdoing in Barth's thought is one in which guilt is accrued by individual human beings on the basis of their entire lives. Due to man's wretched pride, the whole of his life becomes one of guilt.⁵² Once the connection between original guilt and a fallen human nature is severed, Crisp's first difficulty with the fallenness position would present itself as a non-issue in Barth's eyes. In fact, as mentioned earlier, Crisp himself does not espouse a notion of original guilt in his understanding of original sin.⁵³

Crisp's second difficulty with the "fallenness" position pertains to the idea that even if the notion of original guilt is somehow removed, the idea of an inherited corrupt nature passed down via propagation or imputation to the entirety of Adam's subsequent offspring still poses an insurmountable difficulty on its own. Even if, hypothetically speaking, no actual sins were committed, the possession of a fallen human nature would by itself mean that a morally vitiated and corrupt nature is sinful and loathsome before God's presence. The upshot is that Jesus in assuming such a fallen human nature would already have been sinful, even if no actual sins were committed.⁵⁴

---

51. Barth's non-subscription to the notion of original guilt has to do, in large part, with the way he sees Adam as the representative of the human race vis-à-vis that of Reformed Orthodoxy. Barth sees Adam as the representative more in a typological as opposed to an ancestral-forebearer sense. See Barth, *Christ and Adam*, for a more detailed exposition of the Adam-man and the Christ-man relationship. It could be said further that Barth's specific view of the Adam-man relation is predicated upon the more fundamental relation between Adam and Christ. Adam is not the ancestral-forebearer representative of humanity, because for Barth, the Adam-man relationship forms not the primary but only the secondary anthropological truth and ordering principle. The primary principle is found in the relationship between Christ and us, such that man's essential and original nature is to be found in Christ, not Adam (17). In this sense, Barth states that "Christ who seems to come second, really comes first, and Adam who seems to come first really comes second" (46).

52. See *CD* IV/1, 489.

53. Even some theologians in the Reformed Tradition, e.g., John Calvin, likewise denied the idea of inherited guilt within his concept of original sin (*Inst.*, II.1.6) But Calvin affirmed inherited corruption (*Inst.* II.1.8). My surmise is that this explains why Calvin is equivocal in whether Christ assumed a fallen nature. Calvin's upholding of hereditary corruption would have made it difficult for him to affirm Christ's assumption of a fallen human nature in an outright manner. There is a way, however, and it is by extending the sanctifying work of the Holy Spirit (mentioned in *Inst.* II.13.4) to the very moment of "conception" of the human nature of Jesus, such that despite being a fallen and morally corrupt nature, it was sanctified so that it would not be, on Crisp's account, loathsome before the presence of God. See Ahn, "Humanity of Christ," 145–58, who interprets and presents Calvin as supporting a fallen human nature position.

54. Crisp, *Divinity and Humanity*, 112.

Once again, by way of response, we note that Barth subscribes to the notion of original sin,[55] but a key modification he implements is to excise any elements of hereditariness or inheritance from his understanding of original sin. He states: "However we may conceive and express this, there can be no doubt that the idea of a hereditary sin (*Erbsünde*) which has come to man by propagation is an extremely unfortunate and mistaken one."[56] As Barth sees it, the main problem is that hereditary sin detracts from the notion of sin the component of one's own active act and determination, and presses instead towards an alternate picture of sinful human beings as victims.[57] In view of this grave misconception, Barth prefers to abandon the notion of hereditary sin altogether and speak only of original sin (*Ursünde*). By this term, Barth means "the sin of every man, *the corruption which he brings on himself* so that as the one who does so . . . he is necessarily and inevitably corrupt."[58] In other words, Barth maintains a doctrine of original sin, but one that has been excised of any vestige of an inherited or imputed corruption passed down from mankind's originator to his line of descendants like a hereditary disease. In this sense, Barth's doctrine of original sin identifies itself more closely with the notion of total depravity.[59]

---

55. In *CD* IV/1, 499, under §60 The Pride and Fall of Man, Barth states: "The substance of this second proposition is co-extensive with what the earlier confessions of the Church all called the original sin of every living man consequent upon the fall of the first man."

56. *CD* IV/1, 500.

57. Barth writes: "In this imprisonment God speaks to him and makes Himself his liberator in Jesus Christ. But it is still his *peccatum*, the act in which he makes himself a prisoner and therefore has to be a prisoner. This is the point which is obscured by the term hereditary sin (*Erbsünde*). *What I do as the one who receives an inheritance is something that I cannot refuse to do, since I am not asked concerning my willingness to accept it*" (*CD* IV/1, 500, added emphasis). A little further on, Barth states that the nub of sin is its deliberateness. When linked to the notion of inheritance, it comes to have a "hopelessly naturalistic, deterministic and even fatalistic ring" (*CD* IV/1, 501).

58. *CD* IV/1, 501 (added emphasis).

59. Webster, *Barth's Moral Theology*, 73–74, states that Barth is aware that his voluntarist account of (original) sin draws him near to the Pelagian position, and hence offers two qualifications. First, Barth affirms alongside the radicalness and totality of human sin its universality, and hence, the experience of solidarity with others. Barth states: "[M]y conclusion in disobedience may be my own affair, but as such it is also a common affair in which I was bound in solidarity with all others" (*CD* IV/1, 504). Second, Barth presents the sin of human beings as involving an enslavement to malign and lordless forces. Thinking he can control his own life apart from God as a manifestation of his self-mastery, the sinner finds himself entrapped and enslaved in his sin instead (see *ChrL*, 214 onwards). Whether these two qualifications are sufficient to ward off charges of Pelagianism is a judgment left to the reader.

Returning to Crisp's second difficulty, it is observed that the notion of original corruption is foundational to the crux of the difficulty: as long as one is born of the seed of Adam, one is born with this fallen and inherited/imputed corrupt human nature. This fallen human nature, when inhering in a human being, has a deep propensity for actual acts of sin and is by itself morally repulsive to God. However, once the connection between a fallen human nature and inherited/imputed hereditary corruption is excised, the second difficulty loses much of its argumentative weight.

The above is what happens on Barth's account. By repudiating the notion of hereditary sin, Barth is able to freely attribute to Jesus *a fallen human nature without incurring the notion of sinfulness that is usually attendant with the concept of inherited/imputed corruption or hereditary sin*. Applied to the *sui generis* case of the incarnation, Barth asserts that Jesus assumed a fallen human nature, yet one that is without corruption and its accompanying sinfulness. Barth bases his assertion on two reasons. First, there is no *hereditary* corruption from Adam that comes along with this fallen human nature, and second, as the obedient Son of God, Jesus is the unique sinless one, who by his obedience defies the *natural* corruption that fallen humanity inevitably brings upon herself.

The two reasons provided by Barth explain for two further phenomena that we noticed in the earlier survey of Barth's thoughts on this subject matter. First, Barth displays due diligence in his writings not to associate Jesus' fallen human nature with corruption. In stressing the sameness of Jesus' human nature to ours, Barth states that the human nature assumed by Jesus could have fallen prey to corruption, and in this way comes very close to associating Jesus' fallen human nature with corruption, but he stops short at that point.[60] Second, Barth's affirmation of the fallen human nature that Jesus assumes goes hand in hand with his affirmation of Jesus being without sin. Affirming the latter is how Barth maintains that despite assuming a *fallen* human nature, Jesus is cleared of the *natural* corruption that the rest of humanity brings upon and owns for herself.

The upshot of the discussion is that Barth can continue to associate fallenness with corruption—which he does—while affirming that this corruption is a *natural* corruption that humanity brings upon herself rather than a *hereditary* corruption inherited or imputed from Adam. Insofar as the above equation pertains to the whole of humanity, Crisp is right: fallenness equates to sinfulness. But when it comes to Jesus Christ, the *sui generis* instance of the divine hypostasis of the second mode of being of the triune God assuming even a fallen human nature, the equation does not obtain.

---

60. *CD* III/2, 51.

It is further observed that much of Barth's argument at this point resonates with that of McFarland's, who distinguishes between the hamartiological concepts of fallenness and sinfulness. McFarland assigns fallenness to become a descriptive property of "nature" ("*whatness*") and sinfulness that of "hypostasis" ("*whoness*"). In this way, fallenness does not necessarily entail sinfulness.[61] Upon closer examination, McFarland's argument hinges on the concept of the will. Insofar as the will is a feature of human nature, a fallen human nature implies a fallen will. Yet, this fallen will is only expressed and subsequently experienced as sin by an individual human being *hypostatically*, as part of the individual's own agency. When that happens, the fallenness of the human nature correlates with the sinfulness of the hypostasis. In the *sui generis* case of the incarnation, however, because Christ's *hypostasis* is the second person of the Trinity, his human will is deified. This means that Christ's will is at every point turned towards God, so that his willing is shaped by God's will for him. Importantly, this means that Jesus' assumption of a fallen human nature need not imply that he was sinful, since sinfulness is more appropriately described as a predicate of *hypostasis* than of nature.[62]

The above findings, however, lead to a deeper question: given that a fallen human nature neither equates to sinfulness nor corruption for Barth, what then could the theological signification of fallenness be for Barth? I believe two interwoven motifs undergird Barth's stress on the theological signification of fallenness. First, in turning back to *CD* I/2, Barth provides a definitive elucidation of what a fallen human nature signifies: "[W]hat the New Testament calls σάρξ includes not only the concept of man in general but also . . . man who is liable to the judgment and verdict of God," who, because of his sin, "must incur wrath."[63] This is the situation of the "man of sin" that every member of humanity has found herself in because of her voluntary and responsible acts of sin.[64] *The idea of being under the judgment and wrath of God*—this, I propose, is the central and basic signification intended by Barth when he speaks of Jesus possessing a fallen human nature. In this regard, I agree with Dustin Resch who highlights that the theological import of fallenness for Barth is that it signifies the eternal Son of God assuming a

---

61. McFarland, "Fallen or Unfallen?," 412.

62. McFarland, "Fallen or Unfallen?," 409–12.

63. *CD* I/2, 151.

64. The term "man of sin" comes from Barth's first round of exposition on his hamartiology in *CD* IV/1 §60. Consistent with his Christocentrism, Barth states that it is only in the face of the knowledge of Jesus Christ that we can know that "man is the man of sin, and what sin is, and what it means for man" (389).

human nature as it exists in a peculiar relationship or situation with God, that is, the situation of being under his judgment and wrath.[65]

A further question follows through. That is: given that, according to Barth, Jesus assumes a fallen human nature but one that is devoid of *personal* guilt, corruption and sinfulness, in what way does Jesus still carry the theological signification of being under the judgment and wrath of God? This question is especially pertinent since there must be the constitution of either guilt or corruption for one to be under the judgment and wrath of God.

The answer provided by Barth is that Jesus does not find himself to be the "man of sin" via the process of *natural* corruption like the rest of humanity does. Being without sin and having committed no sin—to be more precise, possessing neither *hereditary* nor *natural* corruption—the only way is for Jesus to *voluntarily* assume human essence as it exists under the form of this "man of sin," and *to be counted as* this "man of sin" with a guilt, corruption and sinfulness that is not his own. As Barth states:

> Unlike Adam, as the "second Adam" He does not wish to be as God, but in Adam's nature acknowledges before God an Adamic being, the state and position of fallen man, and bears the wrath of God which must fall upon this man, not as a fate but as a righteous necessary wrath. He does not avoid the burden of this state and position but takes the conditions and consequences upon Himself.[66]

To be sure, the successful outcome of Jesus' work of substitution is not presupposed or dependent upon Jesus' assumption of a fallen human nature; the assumption of an unfallen or prelapsarian human nature would equally count as a valid basis for Jesus' work of substitution.

That brings me to the second interwoven motif that undergirds Barth's stress on the theological signification of fallenness. Barth's speaking of Jesus assuming a fallen human nature is not only to signify being under the wrath and judgment of God, but also to signify the "concrete" way in which Jesus arrives at that particular state and to denote the "depth" of his identification with us, while at all times keeping to the language of "fittingness" rather than "necessity." In Jesus' coming to us, he does not come as one superseding our condition, but he comes to us *exactly where we are*, challenging and opposing sin not simply *by* his person, but *in* his person, and finally removing sin not from *without* but from *within*, specifically, by bearing it away.[67] McFarland might have made the utterance, but the following statement

---

65. Resch, *Virgin Birth*, 119–20.
66. CD I/2, 157.
67. Sumner, "Fallenness," 205.

could easily fit with Barth and serve as an appropriate summary of Barth's position: "[I]f the nature that God assumes is itself damaged and yet is taken on by God as God's own humanity, then the damage our natures suffer is clearly not an occasion for divine revulsion."[68]

Jesus Being without Sin

I turn now to the question of Jesus being without sin, whether this unique occurrence should best be attributed—to use the earlier terminology of Crisp—to Jesus' impeccability or his mere "sinlessness."

Here, on the one hand, there is a significant overlap observed between Barth and Crisp. Both affirm a basic version of impeccability: Jesus Christ was *non posse peccare*; he *could not* sin.[69] Both also maintain that the impeccability of Christ does not exclude him from experiencing the "pull" and lure of the temptations he faced, hence affirming the genuine struggle of Jesus in obeying—a struggle common to all other men.[70] Furthermore, both are explicit in not attributing impeccability to a special quality residing in the human nature of Jesus.[71]

On the other hand, the difference between Barth and Crisp shows for itself in the differing emphasis that they place on where they finally locate the impeccability of Christ. Crisp consistently grounds the impeccability of Jesus in the *divine nature* of the divine subject (read: *hypostasis*) who becomes incarnate. For him, Jesus' impeccability arises from the fact that "Christ's divine nature would ensure that his human nature never sins, were his human nature about to sin."[72] From this comment, it would be right to gather that Crisp views impeccability as a state in which an entity is incapable of sin *under any circumstances*; it is part of the *nature* of an entity.

To be certain, Barth's early Christology likewise admits of a similar predilection, locating the impeccability of Jesus in the fact that because it is the Son of God—a *divine* subject—who assumes human nature, Jesus Christ *could not* have sinned.[73] Yet, as noticed in our survey, Barth, in tandem with his full-fledged actualistic ontology, takes the actualistic turn in *CD* IV and locates the source of Jesus being without sin in the *act* and

---

68. McFarland, "Fallen or Unfallen?," 413.

69. Crisp, *God Incarnate*, 124; *CD* IV/2, 93 where Barth explicitly attributes to Jesus the state of being "*non peccare* and *non posse peccare*."

70. Crisp, *God Incarnate*, 127–28; *CD* I/2, 158.

71. Crisp, *God Incarnate*, 128–29; cf. *CD* III/2, 51; *CD* IV/1, 258, and *CD* IV/2, 92.

72. Crisp, *God Incarnate*, 129.

73. See again *CD* I/2, 155; *CD* III/2, 52.

actions of Jesus. This actualistic turn receives its climactic expression in *CD* IV/2. Having been confronted and effectively determined in his human essence by the divine, Barth states that Jesus "did not will to sin and did not sin" while carrying out the actions of his human life. In fact, by virtue of the origin of his being—that "[Jesus] was man only as the Son of God"—Jesus *could not choose* sin.[74] The language in the immediate preceding sentence is still within the domain of impeccability, even on Crisp's terms where Jesus *cannot sin under any circumstances*. Yet, the interesting move Barth makes is to shift the source of that impeccability from *nature* to *volition/ act*, such that, as Sumner states it, Jesus' impeccability is specified in "functional" rather than "essential" terms.[75] There are good grounds to suggest that, in the final analysis, *Barth conceived the impeccability of Jesus not on the basis of his metaphysical make-up but by virtue of his act*. This view is further vouchsafed by a key comment from Barth, spoken about the same time as the writing of *CD* IV/2:

> [T]he sinlessness of Christ is a *deed*, not a quality . . . . "*Non posse peccare*" is a deed of God, not a quality. When this is understood, then you can speak of volition. There is a real will in this deed. Temptation was very real for Jesus, but a temptation that could not be followed by a new "Fall," because now God has chosen to be man. . . . Nevertheless, the reality of a sanctified life was a *fight*, not just a being. Jesus had to *obey*. But it was a fight that could not have another result.[76]

The reverberations of Barth's move in finally attributing Jesus' impeccability to his act and actions should not be lost on us. As seen from the above quote, to bring an actualistic dimension to the consideration of Jesus' impeccability is to say, with Sumner, that Jesus being without sin is contingent upon his obedience, even if that obedience is a foregone conclusion by virtue of his divine identity.[77] Importantly, it is to affirm that *the exercise*

---

74. *CD* IV/2, 93.

75. Sumner, "Fallenness," 205.

76. Barth, *Table Talk*, 68–69 (emphasis original).

77. Sumner, "Fallenness," 210–11. Sumner, however, maintains that Barth would not hold Jesus to be impeccable in the sense according to Crisp, stating that "[Jesus'] sinning was not impossible in theory, but impossible in actuality" (211). I differ from Sumner and view that Barth, because he held onto the notion that "[Jesus] was man only as the Son of God" even in his mature Christology (*CD* IV/2, 93), would still maintain that it is impossible for Jesus to sin in theory, despite his clear emphasis by then on the impossibility of Jesus to choose sin in actuality. It is for this same reason that I am somewhat disquieted by the view of Sonderegger, "Sinlessness of Christ," 267–75. Toward the end of her essay (273–74), Sonderegger presents Barth as finally espousing

of Jesus' human agency especially seen in his obedience comprises a necessary constituent of his being without sin. As Jones writes: "Christ humanly applies the decision for sinlessness throughout his life."[78]

With the above fundamental difference in emphasis between Barth and Crisp in mind, the implication of considering the manner in which Jesus remains without sin as they bear on our exploration of Jesus' obedience comes into full light. Although both maintain a basic position of impeccability, Crisp's "essentialist" account runs a greater risk of either downplaying or altogether bypassing the role of Jesus' obedience from the discussion. That Jesus is *non posse peccare* because his peccable (human) nature is subjected to the impeccable (divine) nature of the Son of God reduces the focus and leaves less room for the prime descriptor of Jesus' obedience. By contrast, Barth's "actualistic" account of Jesus' impeccability, which emphasizes that Jesus is *non posse peccare* because he did not will to sin, did not sin and in fact more than that *could not* choose sin, lays the trump card of Jesus' obedience clearly on the table. It is to guarantee Jesus' sinlessness in a way that does not bypass his human agency and obedience.

The remark that Jesus could not choose sin, however, at first glance appears to debilitate the picture of Jesus' obedience by limiting or even withdrawing the freedom of choice he had. This, however, is not the case. It should be borne in mind that on Barth's terms, obedience is not predicated on the possession of the freedom of choice between alternatives, but living and acting in a way following and corresponding to the decisions of God. That, for Barth, is what constitutes true freedom.[79] Hence, the fact that Jesus could not choose sin is not due to a lack of freedom, but precisely the opposite: it is because Jesus is truly free before God that his freedom consists in his obedience. In that one's freedom is circumscribed by the bounds of an identity he has taken upon himself,[80] Jesus' inability to choose sin negates neither the exercise of his volition—he still had to *will* not to sin—nor the freedom he had, speaking pointedly instead to the kind of freedom Jesus abounded in. "He did not sin," Barth reiterates, "because from this origin He lived as a man in this true human freedom—the freedom for obedience—not knowing or having any other freedom."[81]

---

a position of *posse peccare* for Jesus Christ—he could have sinned but in fact did not disobey. I believe that Sonderegger could do with a stronger emphasis on the perspective that sinning for Jesus was impossible in actuality.

78. Jones, *Humanity of Christ*, 175.

79. *CD* IV/1, 257.

80. Jones, *Humanity of Christ*, 173.

81. *CD* IV/2, 93.

Our evaluation of Barth's account of Jesus' impeccability has shown up the following novel turn: Barth is not so much occupied over the question of how the impeccability of Jesus bears on Jesus' obedience than to claim that obedience as the climactic display and expression of Jesus' impeccability. By emphasizing impeccability as a deed as opposed to it being a quality of the divine nature, Barth's account provides a segue for a deeper engagement with the place of the will and volition in Jesus' obedience.[82] It is to this particular discussion of Jesus' will that I now direct our attention in the second major section of this chapter.

"Not My Will but Yours Be Done": Barth's View on the Monothelitism vs. Dyothelitism Discussion

Clarifying the way Barth conceives of the relation between Jesus' volition and his obedience is neither an unimportant nor superfluous exercise, especially as it pertains to the central enquiry of this thesis. Given that the action of obedience requires an act of willing in response to another, and granted that Barth throughout maintains the one will and volition of the triune Godhead, the only way that Barth can consistently attribute to the divine Son an eternal obedience to the Father is by counting the Son's willed act of obedience in *temporality* as that rendered in *eternity*.

A cognizance of the above point, however, does not automatically undo the difficulties associated with the relation between Jesus' volition and his obedience. Two prime difficulties spring to mind. The first concerns the question of whose will and volition is in play in the moments wherein obedience is demanded. So, in the case of the prime example, when Jesus utters in the Garden of Gethsemane what is widely regarded as the overriding manifestation of his obedience: "Not my will but yours be done" (Luke 22:42),[83] *whose* volition or volitions—as predicated by the pronouns "my" and "yours"—are in view? Furthermore, what does that imply about the number of wills and centers of volition present in the one incarnate Christ: was it one will (Monothelitism) or two wills (Dyothelitism)?[84] The second

---

82. Barth, *Table Talk*, 69, again: "'*Non posse peccare*' is a deed of God, not a quality. When this is understood, then you can speak of volition."

83. Cf. the Matthew version "Yet not as I will, but as you will" (Matt 26:39) and the Markan version "Yet not what I will, but what you will" (Mark 14:36).

84. As Davidson, "'Not My Will,'" 188, states: "Chalcedon's confession of 'one and the same Christ . . . acknowledged in two natures' in itself says nothing about whether there are two distinct centres of willing that continue to subsist in the one *hypostasis* or *prosopon* of the incarnate one, and if so what this may imply for the relationship between his two *physeis*, or whether there is only one centre of willing in him, and if so how that single centre might be characterized."

difficulty pertains to the struggle Jesus underwent in the midst of his active volition to be obedient. Scripture attests to this struggle being filled with "sorrow to the point of death" (Mark 14:34; Matt 26:38); one in which—according to certain later manuscripts—Jesus' sweat was "like drops of blood falling to the ground" (Luke 22:44). Yet, if as ascertained, Jesus' obedience is secured by virtue of the divine determination of his human origin, wherein lies the struggle? I will respond to the first difficulty (the question of monothelitism or dyothelitism) in the remainder of this chapter. The second difficulty (the particular location of Jesus' struggle) will be left to chapter 7 for reasons that will be evident later.

Dyothelitism vs. Monothelitism

Turning to a discussion of monothelitism or dyothelitism, the historical development leading to these two positions extends beyond the direct scope of our enquiry and need not detain us at this point.[85] Instead, I draw our attention to Barth's explicit, albeit passing, references to the debate and his basic support of the dyothelite position.

The first mention appears in *CD* I/2, where Barth affirms "how right was the attitude of those who in the so-called monothelite controversy of the seventh century upheld and eventually led to victory the doctrine that along with the true human nature of the God-Man there must likewise not be denied His true, human will, different from the will of God although never independent of it."[86] The second reference appears in *CD* II/2, where in a discussion on the genuine freedom of Christ Jesus consisting in his obedience, Barth states: "The Early Church knew what [obedience] was about when in the monothelite controversy it insisted on the distinction and confrontation of the divine and human will in the person of Jesus. It did this in the light of the temptation story and Gethsemane, where it emerges clearly enough that the freedom in which Jesus obeys is real obedience."[87]

Two scant references and a cursory endorsement—strangely, that is all Barth affords to dyothelitism within his voluminous writings in the *Dogmatics*. Surely Barth could have said more, but I believe that the absence of any further elucidation reflects Barth's priority of locating the definitive expression of obedience not in a metaphysical description of the will, but in the act of prayer. This is a point I will develop in chapter 8. Nevertheless, Barth's minimalistic comments belie the significant role dyothelitism plays

85. For a full discussion, see chapters 1 and 2 of Bathrellos, *Byzantine Christ*, 9–98.
86. *CD* I/2, 158.
87. *CD* II/2, 605–6.

for him. In both references, the neighboring discussion revolves around Christ's obedience. The significant point is that, for Barth, obedience presupposes a dyothelite position: there is not only a human will arising from the human nature of Christ, but this human will stands juxtaposed to the divine will in the one person of Jesus Christ. It is under such a condition that Barth affirms the genuine obedience of Christ Jesus. In other words, although Barth stopped short of a detailed exposition, it could safely be said that a dyothelite position undergirds his assertion of Christ's genuine obedience. To see why this is so, one has to look further beyond—more precisely before—Barth, namely, to the foremost advocate of the dyothelite position, Maximus the Confessor.[88]

The Dyothelitism of Maximus the Confessor

Maximus the Confessor (c. 580–662) championed the cause of dyothelitism throughout his theological writings, and right through a period where monothelitism was the prevalent argument of the day. It could be said that Maximus' dyothelitism is founded on two central pillars, one advancing a positive, and the other, a negative element.

First, since human beings are created rational and possess an intrinsic sense of self-determination, Maximus attributes the will to a quality of nature, and he considers the will to be characteristic of all who share in the same nature.[89] Maximus' locating the will in the nature of a being is motivated by his view of the will as a faculty, integral to all rational beings, in virtue of which they are capable of willing and in the process fulfilling the aspect of self-determination. Both a divine and human nature encompass these facets of rationality and self-determination.[90] On this ground Maximus maintains that Christ possesses both a human and divine will. To him, the main repercussion of denying to Christ a human will would be the implication that the Word

---

88. Congdon, "Afterword," 255–78, comments that an interesting conversation yet to take place is between that of Maximus the Confessor and Karl Barth (257). Congdon highlights specifically an area that could yield a fruitful conversation would be that of Maximus' and Barth's respective treatments of Gethsemane. Congdon cites Jones, *Humanity of Christ*, 41, 234, 242, as initiating that conversation. As we shall see, chapter 7 serves what I hope to be a further step toward that direction.

89. As stated in Bathrellos, *Byzantine Christ*, 130. Bathrellos draws his conclusion in turn from *Opusc.* 15, 157C and *Opusc.* 1, 28C. The counter question could be raised that if the will is tethered to the nature, why is it that we as individual humanity will differently, given that we all share in one common human nature? Maximus' reply would be that what differs and changes is not the will, but the mode of willing (Bathrellos, *Byzantine Christ*, 133).

90. Bathrellos, *Byzantine Christ*, 124, 126.

did not become a true man; stated more severely, that he did not become a man at all.[91] Such a thought naturally carries a soteriological ramification of disastrous proportion. It would be in effect to affirm, as Maximus puts it, that "[God] either condemned his own creation as something that is not good . . . or he begrudged us the healing of our will, depriving us of complete salvation," since "whatever is not assumed is not saved."[92]

Second—here Maximus proceeds along the negative argument—the monothelite position has immense difficulties specifying a proper name to the alleged one will. If we were to call it divine, it would amount to the claim that Christ was only God; if theandric or composite, that this will differed from the will of the Father and Spirit; if natural, that it confuses Christ's natures; if hypostatic, that we introduce three wills in the Trinity corresponding to the three hypostases, and finally, if we refuse to give this will any nomenclature at all, that would lead to a position of absurdity.[93] Maximus employs the positive and negative arguments to argue for dyothelitism.

Maximus' Dyothelitism Applied to Jesus' Prayer in the Garden of Gethsemane

When applied to Jesus' prayer in the Garden of Gethsemane, Maximus' dyothelitism leads him to frame *both* portions of the prayer—"Yet *not what I will*, but *what you will*" (Mark 14:36)—as having to do with the humanity of Christ and the exercising of his human will. In other words, it is Christ as Savior, the *Logos as man*, addressing the Father in Gethsemane and with the utterance of the prayer "[confessing] the ultimate concurrence of his human will with the divine will."[94] Maximus summarizes the essence of his position in the following quote:

> [C]learly the negation here—*Not what I will*—absolutely precludes opposition and instead demonstrates harmony between the human will of the Saviour and the divine will shared by him and his Father, given that the Logos assumed our nature in its entirety and deified his human will in the assumption. It follows, then, that having become like us for our sake, he was calling on his God and Father in a human manner when he said, *Let not what I will, but what you prevail*, inasmuch as, being God by

---

91. *Opusc.* 3, 49A–B, as found in Louth, *Maximus*, 194.

92. Bathrellos, *Byzantine Christ*, 131. The quote is from *Disputatio*, 325A–B. Maximus here is appropriating the well-known axiom of Gregory of Nazianzus.

93. Bathrellos, *Byzantine Christ*, 135. Bathrellos draws from *Opusc.* 24, 268D–269C.

94. *Opusc.* 6, 68A, as found in Maximus, *On the Cosmic Mystery*, 174.

nature, he also in his humanity has, as his human volition, the fulfilment of the will of the Father.[95]

As Bathrellos correctly identifies, the gem of Maximus' dyothelitism applied to his reading of Gethsemane is that it profitably accentuates *the human obedience of the Son to the Father* in a way that exceeds previous interpretations of Gethsemane.[96] In assuming a human will, which he submits to his divine will that is shared with the Father, Jesus offers us a perfect example of obedience for the sake of our salvation. The one hypostasis of the *Logos* (as God) willed by his divine will, and the same *Logos* (as man) obeyed the divine will by his human will.[97]

Importance of Dyothelitism for Barth's Account of Christ's Incarnate Obedience

The preceding discussion reveals why dyothelitism counts as an important presupposition in considering Barth's account of Christ's incarnate obedience. It is dyothelitism that provides a conducive and fecund environment to conceptualize the incarnate obedience of the Son and the eternal ramifications of that obedience within the triune Godhead; monothelitism fails to achieve this desideratum. It either renders the portrayal of Barth's concept of the obedience of the eternal Son proffered so far problematic, or it fails to fully secure Barth's way of understanding the incarnation.

The above statement stands in need of further clarification. I explore first the monothelite position that affirms the singular will of Jesus as a *divine* will. In this case, the Gethsemane prayer in its negation "Not what I will" is uttered wholly and solely out of an act of the single *divine* volition on the part of the Son. This notion, I suggest, is problematic because it finally posits a situation where distinct and possibly even opposing wills exist within the divine hypostases in the triune Godhead. In this case, the *divine* will of the Son—"Not what *I* will"—is seemingly different from that of the divine will of the Father—"but what *you* will." As seen in the earlier chapters, the very idea

---

95. *Opusc.* 6, 68C, as found in Maximus, *On the Cosmic Mystery*, 176 (emphasis original).

96. Bathrellos, *Byzantine Christ*, 147. Previous interpretations tended to dispense with the reality of Christ's desire to avoid the cup (Gregory of Nazianzus), or suggest a kind of monothelitism in order to strengthen the unity of Christ (Apollinarius and Themistius), or allow for an opposition between the denial of the cup by the flesh and the fiat that allegedly belonged to the Logos as God, or attributed the fiat to "the form of the servant" (Theodoret).

97. Bathrellos, *Byzantine Christ*, 171.

of the divine will of the Son being *distinct* from the divine will of the Father already contravenes the central Trinitarian axiom that Barth maintained of Father, Son, and Spirit sharing in one common will and volition, let alone the difficulties involved in the Son having a distinct divine will that is *different* and *opposed* to the Father.[98] For this reason, a monothelite interpretation of the Gethsemane prayer along the lines of a strictly *divine* volition presents itself to be at odds with Barth's own account.

I explore next the monothelite position that affirms the singular will of Jesus as a *human* will, in which case the Gethsemane prayer is entirely and solely attributable to Jesus' single *human* volition. At first sight, this reading appears similar to that undertaken by Maximus, who likewise read the prayer in both its negatory and affirmative portions as an act of the human will in submission to the divine will. The difference, however, lies in *the identification and location of the divine will*. The monothelite, in distinguishing himself from the dyothelite, would have to identify the divine will strictly as the Father's will, and locate that divine will "external" to the one (and only) human will possessed by the incarnate Son. The dyothelite position, on the other hand, is able to identify the divine will as Jesus' very own that he nonetheless shares with the Father. Moreover, the dyothelite is able to identify this divine will as "internal" within the one person of the incarnate Son—borrowing Chalcedonian terminology—without confusion or changeability and yet without division or separation from the human will. Although I concede that the monothelite position is equally able

---

98. One who would not see the Son's distinct and different divine will from the Father as a difficulty would be Jürgen Moltmann; see his *Trinity and the Kingdom*, 76 onwards. Moltmann interprets Gethsemane and Golgotha as events that introduce a rift or division into the divine life. Specifically, he reads Jesus' prayer as a plea for the removal of the cup of suffering. In God not answering Jesus' prayer, God leaves Jesus to a state of forsakenness and abandonment (76). As Lauber, *Barth on the Descent*, 118, states: "For Moltmann, Gethsemane depicts an opposition and conflict of wills—the will of the Son, Jesus Christ, and the will of his Father." To be sure, Moltmann's reading of Gethsemane is consistent with his wider theology, which so stresses the love of the triune God for the creaturely other that the love between the Father and Son is transformed into infinite pain and suffering, even "the death of God" (*Trinity and the Kingdom*, 80). This divine experience is so intense that if not for the Holy Spirit, the triune unity would not have been safeguarded (82). Moltmann, however, qualifies his statement of the opposing wills. Ultimately, the Gethsemane story signals too the "inner conformity between the will of the surrendered Son and the surrendering will of the Father," but does so "precisely at the point when the Son is furthest divided from the Father, and the Father from the Son." (82). As will be evident in chapter 7, Barth's interpretation shares certain points of similarity with Moltmann, but finally heads in a totally different direction in ascertaining the genuine obedience of Jesus Christ. Barth does not introduce any form of rift or division between the Father and the Son whereas this is the precise notion that Moltmann capitalizes on.

to achieve an account of the genuine obedience of the incarnate Son, the monothelite position somehow attenuates the truth that in the incarnation, *God* was in Christ Jesus, reconciling the world to himself (2 Cor 5:19). Even if the Chalcedonian idiom that Christ Jesus possessed a full divine nature is maintained, because the one will Jesus had was a human will alone, the *divine determination arising from the divine will of God*, instead of arising directly *from* and *in* Jesus Christ as his own divine will, would only be enacted *indirectly upon* him as the divine will of the Father. *Divine agency, in this case, would not be direct, but mediated.* The major drawback of such a schema is that it calls into question the status of Jesus' divinity. A divine nature that has the crucial property of self-determination abstracted from it leaves up in the air the status of the fullness of its divinity.[99]

By contrast, the dyothelite position espoused by Maximus allows for the *self-determining component of both the human and divine wills to act directly in the one person of the incarnate Christ*. At this point, however, Maximus should not be misread as advocating a position wherein the natures either exercise the act of willing in abstraction of a person (*hypostasis*), or that the divine will in Christ moves the human will without any reference to the person of the Logos. The former resounds of Nestorianism while the latter risks detracting particular acts of willing from the human will of Christ, hence effectively rendering that human will as a non-actualized faculty.[100] Rather, it is more the case that the self-determining component of *both* the divine and human wills are actualized in particular acts of willing in the one person of the Logos. The incarnate Christ as God willed by his divine will to save mankind, and the same one *hypostasis* of the incarnate Christ as man willed by his human will to obey. In this manner, Jesus allowed his own human will to be "moved" by his divine will, in turn identical to the divine will of the Father.[101] To sum up, Maximus is not saying that willing is done by the nature in abstraction of the person, but rather the person who wills does so according to his nature—its rationale and self-determining aspect. In Jesus Christ, both the divine and human willing occur in accordance with the divine and human natures fully inhering within him.[102]

---

99. The late British theologian Colin Gunton held a view similar to the monothelite position presented above. See Gunton, *Act and Being*, 29, and *The Christian Faith*, 95. See also the response to Gunton's view by Spence, "Person as Willing Agent," 49–64.

100. Bathrellos, *Byzantine Christ*, 162.

101. Bathrellos, *Byzantine Christ*, 173.

102. The question remains as to how the existence of two self-determining faculties (the human and divine wills) within a single person can be envisaged. Loke, "On Dyothelitism," 1–7, advocates a Divine Preconscious Model (DPM). The DPM posits that within the incarnate Christ resides a divine preconsciousness in which certain

Overall, while I admit that Barth nowhere approaches the finesse that Maximus displays in expounding the dyothelite position, it could be argued nonetheless that much of Maximus' argument is congenial to Barth's own theology. For sure, Maximus' dyothelite position captures more accurately an understanding of the incarnation according to Barth as compared to the monothelite position. For the latter position, even if the one human will was acted upon and directed by the Father's divine will (external to the incarnate Christ's being), such a principle of mediation as a reading of divine agency sits further afield from Barth's own viewpoint. As far as I can see, Barth operates from a principle of direct divine action and agency while neither attenuating nor nullifying the human response.[103] Although unstated, I infer it is for this reason that Barth affirmed dyothelitism.

Conclusion

The investigation undertaken in this chapter complements that of the previous chapter. While the previous chapter established the significant function the incarnate obedience of Jesus Christ has within Barth's Christology, this chapter explores the deeper metaphysical underpinnings of Barth's conceptualization of Jesus' obedience. The investigation involved

---

divine properties (e.g., omniscience, omnipotence) continue to repose. These divine properties are not currently in the (one) consciousness of the incarnate Christ, but can be accessible to consciousness by directing attention to them (2). According to the DPM, Christ, in having one self-consciousness, is one "willer." He has a human will, having desires natural to human nature immediately aware to his consciousness. But he also has a divine will, in that he has divine desires and determination as and when he accesses his divine preconscious. In this manner, the human self-determining faculty and the divine self-determining faculty can be maintained in the one "willer" of Jesus Christ, the former by virtue of his consciousness and the latter by virtue of his consciousness having access to his divine pre-consciousness (5). For a fuller account of the DPM, see Loke, *Kryptic Model*.

103. In Webster, "Gunton and Barth," 17–31, he highlights Gunton's criticism of Barth for "[compacting] divine action and the humanity of Christ together, so that 'incarnation' becomes 'immanence', with the result that Jesus' freedom and identity as agent in space and time are compromised" (26). Webster views this criticism as a misunderstanding of Barth, arguing that Gunton had "seriously underestimated the significance which human time and history held for Barth" (27). In fact, Webster further contends that to speak of the humanity of Christ as if it were separate and independent of divine action and agency, or to think of the "humanity" of God in the incarnation as a separate category from the humanity of Jesus the man, is to fall into the danger of believing that Jesus' humanity needs to be somehow protected from the determination of the Word if it is to have integrity (28). As seen from the previous chapter, the opposite seems to be more the case for Barth. It is because of divine determination from the Word that the authenticity of Jesus' humanity is guaranteed.

answering three questions that framed the discussion in the chapter. In relation to the first question regarding the type of human nature assumed in the incarnation, Barth gives a resounding affirmation of the minority report—Jesus assumed a "fallen" postlapsarian human nature following after Adam, yet *one that was without sin*. That Barth is (logically) able to assert the second half of his position is due to his decoupling of both concepts of original guilt and corruption from the doctrine of original (or universal) sin that he espoused. As a result, a fallen human nature comes to signify for Barth the truth of mankind as the "man of sin" under the definitive judgment of God and the "concreteness" of the incarnation. The former situation is a situation Jesus *voluntarily* enters into via *substitution*, rather than a *hereditary* situation he finds himself in. This explains why Barth's assertion of Jesus' assumption of a fallen nature is always accompanied by an equal affirmation of Jesus' sinlessness. More important to our enquiry, Barth asserts *it is only under these conditions of finitude and fallenness—similar to ours—that Jesus works out his obedience*.[104]

In relation to the second question pertaining to the manner of Jesus being without sin, Barth adopts a generic form of the impeccability argument: Jesus *could not* sin. However, a closer examination reveals that Barth places his emphasis of the impeccability of Jesus certainly not in a special quality of his human nature, nor even in the divine nature of the distinct *hypostasis* of the Son of God that has assumed the human nature—true as that is—but in a kind of "functional" impeccability. Having his human origin effectively determined by the divine, Jesus humanly lives out every moment of his life applying the decision for sinlessness. He would not and, in fact, *could not* choose sin. To speak this way is already to reverse the direction of enquiry. Instead of asking how the impeccability of Jesus impacts the genuineness of his obedience, for Barth, it is more a question of how Jesus' obedience serves as the key expression of his impeccability.

The third and final question revolves around figuring out the implications that monothelitism or dyothelitism holds for a construal of Christ's obedience. While the question appears to border on theological nit-picking, and acknowledging Barth's relative silence, I argued that a dyothelite position would better serve Barth's theological intentions in relation to his portrayal of the obedience of Jesus Christ. On the one hand, a monothelite reading of Jesus' single will as a purely *divine* act of volition leads to a positing of distinct, even different and opposing, wills within the Trinity, clearly contravening Barth's basic Trinitarian understanding. On the other hand,

---

104. *CD* IV/1, 216, where Barth states: "[Jesus] had to achieve His freedom and obedience as a link in the chain of an enslaved and disobedient humanity."

although a monothelite reading of Jesus' single will as a purely *human* act of volition neither negates nor lessens his incarnate obedience in any way, it leads to a scenario wherein divine agency is exercised at best in a *mediated* or *indirect* way. This, I contend, is further from Barth's understanding of the incarnation where he sees the person of Jesus Christ exercising his divine agency in a *direct* manner.

The metaphysical dimension and depth that has been added to Barth's portrayal of Jesus' incarnate obedience from our findings in this chapter hopefully puts us in good stead for the next segment of our investigation, that of seeing how the obedience of Christ functions in Barth's atonement theology. But first, I turn to address what might be alleged as a shortcoming in our inquiry thus far; that is, the portrayal has been suspiciously "binitarian." Does Barth have anything to say about the role of the Spirit in his account of the obedience of the Son of God, be it as the eternal Son or the incarnate Lord? It is to this crucial question that I turn to in the next chapter.

5

The Spirit in Relation to the Son's Incarnate and Intra-Trinitarian Obedience to the Father

It is now commonplace within the guild of Barth scholarship to find the entrenched criticism that Barth's treatment of the person and work of the Holy Spirit remains lacking.[1] Even Philip J. Rosato, in his seminal work on Barth's pneumatology *The Spirit as Lord* admitted to several deficits in Barth's Spirit theology.[2] This is surprising considering that Rosato advanced the tendentious notion—back then and still now—that Barth was just as much, if not more, of a pneumatic theologian than a Christocentric theologian![3] At the heart of the criticism lies the relationship between the "person" of the Spirit and the "person" of the incarnate Christ our Lord qua his humanity, even as it is recognized that Barth espoused a predominant "Logos" Christology.[4] Gunton highlights the concern well: the alleged underweighting of Barth's pneumatology in the soteriological and ecclesial dimensions might find its roots in Barth's conception of the more primal relationship between the Spirit and the incarnate Christ.[5]

---

1. The criticism itself has ranged from mild critique—the Spirit is present, but is "underweighted" or "eclipsed" by the Son—to strict censure—the Spirit is "absent" for substantial stretches of Barth's thinking. Gunton, "Salvation," 152, and Rogers, "Eclipse," 173–90, serve as examples of the former category, while Jenson, "You Wonder," 296–304, serves as an example of the latter category.

2. From Rosato's perspective, Barth's Spirit theology lacks eschatological insights, fails to give credence to the (direct) interaction between the divine Spirit and the human spirit, and has no allowance for a natural theology of any kind (*Spirit as Lord*, 132–55). All three criticisms arise from what Rosato perceives as Barth's fundamental error: the Spirit is denied his own independent role as *Spiritus Creator*, but instead is the former insofar only as he is the *Spiritus Redemptor*.

3. Rosato, *Spirit as Lord*, 3.

4. The immediate comment should not detract from the original revision that Barth brings via his actualistic ontology: the Logos and second person of the Godhead from eternity would have been Jesus the God-Man foreseen *actualistically* and counted *proleptically*.

5. Gunton, "Salvation," 152; Gunton, "God the Holy Spirit," 114.

Taking the criticism one step deeper, the relation between the Spirit and Jesus could be further predicated upon the *identification* of the Spirit and the *location* of his activity vis-à-vis the triune Godhead—[6] what I term as an "immanent pneumatology." Phrased in this manner, the difficulty surfaces: Barth's basic conception of the Trinity follows after the Western Augustinian model whereby the Spirit is shown to be the bond of love and unity between the Father and the Son. The perennial struggle for Western Latin Trinitarianism is this: how does the Spirit being the bond of love and unity properly account for the distinguishable *hypostasis* the Spirit is? Barth, in being beholden to the Western Trinitarian model, struggles with the same issues.[7] The basic criticism held against Barth's pneumatology emerges clearly enough: difficulties in articulating the relation between the Spirit and the incarnate Christ (and consequently, between the Spirit and the church) can be traced back to difficulties in identifying—or better, "*hypostasizing*"— the Spirit and locating his activity vis-à-vis the triune Godhead.

The issues highlighted above are by no means meant to complicate matters, but are instead meant to provide the background to our central enquiry in this chapter. For our own inquiry into Jesus' obedience within Barth's doctrine of reconciliation could be subjected to the same charge that Barth has perpetually faced: the language and terms of discussion have been suspiciously "binitarian" thus far. Hence, in the wider scheme, this chapter is vital in addressing the role of the Spirit first in relation to the Son's incarnate obedience and second the Son's intra-Trinitarian obedience to the Father.

To the above stated end the chapter proceeds via the following sections. The first section, largely of a descriptive nature, focuses on selected portions of outstanding significance within *CD* where Barth outlines the role of the Spirit with respect to the incarnate Christ. The second section evaluates Barth's presentation in interaction with the account of the Spirit-Christ relation offered by the English Puritan John Owen (1616–83). The third section shifts the attention from the obedience displayed in the incarnation to that rendered by the eternal Son to the Father within the triune Godhead. Partly descriptive, partly constructive, this section delineates

---

6. Gunton, "God the Holy Spirit," 105.

7. In fact, according to Robert Jenson, even more so. Jenson contends that Barth does not suppose he *ought* to conceive an independent salvation-historical initiative of the Spirit in the first place ("You Wonder," 300). Insofar as the inner-Trinitarian relations are portrayed as a concrete salvation-historical relationship between the Father and the Son under the command-obedience rubric, the Spirit as the bond (*vinculum*) between the two parties of Father and Son already connotes the idea that he is excluded from being a *party* in the triune actuality itself ("You Wonder," 301). Smith, *Theology of Third Article*, 5, articulates the difficulty well: "We might say that the Spirit actualizes the Father-Son history; he is not an actuality with the Father and Son in history."

Barth's own specification of the distinct *hypostasis* the Spirit is, or Barth's "immanent pneumatology" (so to speak). It also outlines ways later interpreters of Barth constructively build on his reading. Finally, I conclude in the fourth section with a preliminary attempt at constructive theology by advocating a minor adjustment to the way the inner-triune relations are conceived within the Western (Latin) Trinitarian model that Barth inherited. In my opinion, this is a tweak that neither detracts from the essence of the Western Trinitarian model nor jeopardizes Barth's existing conception of the Spirit within the triune Godhead.

The Relation between the Spirit and the Incarnate Son in the *Church Dogmatics*

I begin by detailing significant points where Barth speaks of the relation between the Holy Spirit and the incarnate Christ. The first substantial point comes in *CD* I/2 §15.3, where Barth considers the Virgin Birth of Christ. Here, the Spirit is given a vital role in terms of the Son's assumption of a *human nature* and *existence*. Under the consideration of the creedal statement "*conceptus de Spiritu sancto*" ("conceived by the Holy Spirit"), Barth asserts that the statement reveals *the human existence of Jesus Christ as one that belongs peculiarly to the work of God the Holy Spirit*.[8] But why particularly the Holy Spirit? Barth's answer points to his presentation of the Holy Spirit as God himself, who in the freedom exercised in his revelation, avails Himself to be present to his creature. Through the Holy Spirit, man can be there for God and be a recipient of his revelation.[9]

Seen in the above light, the appropriateness of the conception of Jesus Christ as *an act of the Holy Spirit* comes through. If the Holy Spirit is the freedom of God who prepares and avails man for the revelation of God, it is all the more fitting that *this* Spirit be involved in the incarnation of the Word of God so that man—above all *this* man Jesus Christ—is there and is freed for God.[10] Following a further safeguard where Barth lays the stricture against erroneously viewing the work of the Holy Spirit as an act of copulation in lieu of the male,[11] Barth turns to the specific action of the Holy Spirit in the miraculous conception of Jesus Christ. Strangely, he offers but a cursory and almost perfunctory comment—even so one that he

8. *CD* I/2, 196.
9. *CD* I/2, 198.
10. As Barth states: "Through the Spirit this Man can be God's Son and at the same time the Second Adam" (*CD* I/2, 199).
11. *CD* I/2, 200–201.

simply quotes from the scholastic J. Gerhard—in place of what could have been a fuller exposition. Barth states:

> The first is the unmediated energy which gave to the virgin the ability to conceive a foetus without a male seed, beyond the order of nature. The second is the miraculous sanctification which sanctified that matter from which the body of the Son of God was formed, that is, purified it from sin. The third is the indescribable unification, which made the divine and the human nature into one person.[12]

Dustin Resch, having undertaken a full-scale study of Barth's interpretation of the Virgin Birth, suggests a possible reason for the baldness of the account. Barth had, in the course of developing his understanding of the Virgin Birth, increasingly read the miraculous birth as a "sign," with the corollary that the import of the spiritual conception now lies in that to which the sign *refers*, rather than in the details of *how* the conception occurred.[13] In fact, to speak too definitively on the latter incurs for Barth the fear of detracting from the sheer miraculous nature of the event of the incarnation.[14] Nonetheless, Barth's brevity should not be misconstrued as a rejection of the scholastic schema, to which he gave, at the very least, a sympathetic reading.[15] More importantly, the brevity of Barth's account belies the significant understanding he had of the spiritual conception of Jesus as one intricately tied to who the Spirit is in eternity. In particular, the third action of the Spirit in uniting the divine and human natures in one person parallels the activity of the Spirit in the triune Godhead. In the same way that the Spirit is the "bond and boundary" between the Father and the Son, so the Spirit is likewise the bond and boundary between the human and divine essence of Jesus.[16]

The next major segment that considers in some detail the Spirit-Christ relation is found in Barth's anthropological treatment in *CD* III/2 §46. Here, Barth seeks to present Jesus as *the* man who is so uniquely related to the Holy Spirit as the Messiah and the Son of God that he forms the paradigmatic

12. *CD* I/2, 201–2 (translated).

13. Resch, *Virgin Birth*, 130.

14. Resch, *Virgin Birth*, 131.

15. This is seen in the fact that Barth's comments here in *CD*, albeit abbreviated, and in his earlier cycle of lectures in *Göttingen Dogmatics* §6, 166–67, follow what has been elaborated at greater length by the Reformed Scholastics. See e.g. Heppe, *Reformed Dogmatics*, 424–27.

16. Resch, *Virgin Birth*, 136. Resch draws his understanding of the Spirit as the "bond and boundary" from Guretzki, *Karl Barth on Filioque*, 179–83.

model by which to understand mankind, who as body and soul are created, preserved and regenerated by the Holy Spirit so as to relate to God as covenant partner.[17] Garnering from a swathe of mainly New Testament passages,[18] Barth posits Jesus to stand in an "absolutely unique relationship to the Holy Spirit."[19] Jesus possesses the Holy Spirit not in an occasional, transitory, or partial manner like any other man would (if bestowed the Spirit), but "lastingly and totally." Moreover, Jesus' unique relation to the Spirit is predicated on the enigmatic statement—one that Barth simply states without further explanation—that Jesus "not only has the Spirit, but primarily and basically He is Spirit as He is soul and body. For this reason and in this way He lives."[20] For Barth, it is this *dual* event of *the Logos becoming flesh* and *the Spirit resting upon this man* that "[human] flesh is slain in its old form and is quickened and comes alive in its new."[21]

Already then, the contours of Barth's Spirit-Christ relation emerge. On Barth's count, it is both components of *the Logos becoming flesh* and *the Spirit resting upon this man* that wholly define Jesus' human existence in a definitive and paradigmatic way that consequently opens up to the rest of human existence the similar possibility of the Spirit dwelling within us. In particular, the Spirit is seen to play a paramount role in the "passion and action in the flesh" that Jesus comports himself in throughout the course of his life.

It is this immediate concept that Barth amplifies in *CD* IV/1. Here, he offers a strong statement that in my opinion undoubtedly secures a place for the Spirit in the outworking of Jesus' *objective* achievement of reconciliation.[22] Barth states: "The particular existence of the Son of God as man,

---

17. This particular expression of Barth's overall anthropological thrust is taken from Cortez, "Body, Soul, and (Holy) Spirit," 328–45. At the same time, Barth is clear of the relational order: it is not because of Jesus' unique relation with the Spirit that he becomes the Messiah and Son of God, but the reverse is true. It is already because Jesus is the Messiah and the Son of God that He stands in this special relationship with the Holy Spirit. See *CD* III/2, 333.

18. The passages include Isa 11:1; 1 Kgs 3:6; John 1:32; Luke 4:1; Matt 12:18; Luke 4:18; John 3:34; 6:63; Rom 1:3; 1 Pet 3:18; 2 Cor 3:17, 1 Cor 15:45, and the key annunciation passages like Luke 1:35 and Matt 1:18, 20. Mangina, *Karl Barth*, 43, states that throughout this excursus, Barth's strategy is to focus on the total impression generated by the biblical narratives rather than on the close exegesis of individual passages. In this way, Barth's argument builds on the way the "overall shape and pattern of the text" portrays Jesus.

19. *CD* III/2, 334.

20. *CD* III/2, 334.

21. *CD* III/2, 337.

22. Barth's view of the Spirit in terms of the *subjective* apprehension of revelation and reconciliation is debated on two counts. First, critics have questioned if the work

and again the particular existence of this man as the Son of God, the existence of Jesus Christ as the Lord who becomes a servant and the servant who becomes Lord . . . is itself ultimately grounded in the being and work of the Holy Spirit. He is *conceptus de Spiritu sancto*."[23] Barth continues to recount the role of the Holy Spirit in Jesus' accomplishment of salvation in CD IV/2. As seen, in expounding on the theological idiom of the *communicatio gratiarum*, Barth lists the presence and effective working of the Holy Spirit as one of the graces determined to the human essence of Jesus Christ as he is confronted by the electing grace of God. Rejecting the idea of a transferred condition or an infused habit that is given to the determination of the human essence—so that the human essence possesses this quality anteriorly— Barth attributes Jesus' *habitus* to "the grace of the Father's Yes and the Spirit's power."[24] Yet, this grace in no way alters Jesus' humanity, transforming his human essence into one that is dissimilar and alien to ours. An interesting observation is that in much of what Barth described as the other graces communicated to the human essence, there is a major similarity and overlap with the person and work of the Holy Spirit, so much so that the Spirit could just as easily find his place there in those descriptions.

Barth continues to interject at subsequent points in CD clear statements concerning the role the Spirit plays in Jesus' life and mission.[25] It is, however, in §64.4 "The Direction of the Son" that we find the climax of his presentation. In speaking of Jesus as the one who sets a new direction for us in his exaltation as the royal man, Barth highlights the Holy Spirit as the power who awakens men to see themselves in Jesus Christ, to be set in this new direction of living and speaking, and to be gathered as the church to be witnesses of Christ.[26] The crucial link is this: the Spirit is the power simply because the Spirit is none other than the presence and action of Jesus Christ himself. Better: the Spirit is the power of Jesus Christ because He is in the first place *the very power by which Jesus is empowered* to carry out the incarnational mission of reconciliation. Barth states unambiguously:

---

of the Holy Spirit in "applying" the salvation achieved by Jesus Christ is given its due weight, considering that all the Spirit does is to "awake" people and cause them to acknowledge the new state of salvation they have *de jure* found themselves in. The second issue concerns whether Barth's account of the Spirit unwittingly robs man of his genuine human freedom in either accepting or rejecting God's gracious activity. See Rosato, *Spirit as Lord*, 141–48, for an example of the second criticism.

23. *CD* IV/1 148.
24. *CD* IV/2, 94.
25. *CD* IV/2, 167.
26. *CD* IV/2, 319–20.

> He [i.e., the Spirit] is the power of the Son of God and Son of Man: the power in which He humbled Himself in order that in His humiliation as God He might be exalted and true man . . . . It was in the power of the Spirit that He went to His death; and it was also in the power of the Spirit that He was raised again from the dead in order that what happened in His death should not be hidden but revealed. Thus the Spirit who makes Christians Christians is the power of this revelation of Jesus Christ Himself—His Spirit.[27]

Barth then proceeds in a relatively long excursus to argue for the way the New Testament directs us to see the Holy Spirit as the Spirit of Jesus Christ.[28] Drawing on a host of New Testament passages,[29] Barth's exposition culminates in a portrayal of Jesus as the beloved Son of God, who from the outset and throughout his existence is the spiritual man, "the true and exalted and royal man who lives by the descent of the Spirit of God and is therefore wholly filled and directed by Him."[30]

Evaluation of Barth's Account of the Spirit-Christ Relation

An evaluation of Barth's presentation of the Spirit-Christ relation is in order. I begin by highlighting four points that act by way of summary to distil the major contours of Barth's account.

First, Barth had a "Spirit Christology," if by the term's most basic description we mean a Christology shaped by Christ's relation to the Spirit. As seen from the above, Barth did have something substantial to say about that relation. Second, Barth also had a "Spirit Christology," if by that term we refer to its usage in recent theological discussions.[31] "Spirit Christology,"

---

27. *CD* IV/2, 323.

28. *CD* IV/2, 323–30.

29. John 3:6; 2 Cor 3:7; 1 Cor 15:45; Matt 3:16; John 3:34; Mark 1:12; Heb 9:14; 1 Pet 3:18; Rom 1:3 and 1 Tim 3:16.

30. *CD* IV/2, 324.

31. The term "Spirit Christology" has, regrettably, obtained a nebulous status and so requires a clear definition. In following Habets, *Anointed Son*, 4–5, Spirit Christology is a Christological model that seeks to define the relationship between the "person" of the Holy Spirit and that of the Son, chiefly in the incarnation and in the work of redemption, and from there, extending to the intra-Trinitarian relations. In certain circles, Spirit Christology is pitted as an alternative to Logos Christology. Following Habets (*Anointed Son*, 5), I see Spirit Christology as complementary to Logos Christology, rather than replacing the latter.

or an "Inspirational Christology" as it is alternatively termed, emphasizes viewing Jesus Christ as a person in whom God has acted lavishly through His Spirit, strengthening him in his spiritual life and empowering him in his mission.[32] This, Barth exudes in his treatment. The Holy Spirit is presented as the one who enacts the *novum* creative work in preparing and furthering the assumption of the human nature by the Son of God (*conceptus de Spiritu sancto*); he is the one who communicates no less than himself under the *communicatio gratiarum* such that Jesus is the one who not only has the Spirit in an unparalleled way to any other human being, but is Spirit as He is soul and body. The Spirit is the one who so wholly fills Jesus' life that one could say every moment and aspect of Jesus' existence is directed by the Spirit, inasmuch as the Spirit is the power of Jesus to live his incarnational mission from the cradle to the cross, to the empty grave, and to the heavenly ascension at the right hand of God the Father. In all of this—the point is central to our thesis—the Spirit is the one who enables *the man Jesus to take every step of the way in sinless obedience to be the faithful covenant partner of God*. Surely, a depiction of the Spirit-Christ relation as vivid as this would qualify for Barth to be counted as espousing a "Spirit Christology," going by its technical theological nomenclature.

Third, Barth saw his Spirit Christology as of a piece with his predominant *Logos* Christology. Primarily and essentially for Barth, the incarnation is a Trinitarian divine act that terminates upon the Son who as the divine subject assumes human nature into the distinct *hypostasis* he is. Seen in this light, the train of thought of Barth's Spirit Christology complements the leitmotif of his *Logos* Christology. Inasmuch as Jesus Christ is understood as the Word made flesh and the Son of God, he is also the Son of Man who is the Spirit-filled one. And insofar as God the Son is the divine subject of the human nature he assumed, the man Jesus is also the one who by the power of the Spirit obeys and lives the incarnational mission at every point. In this way, Barth runs counter to the increasing tendency in modern Christological discussions to portray Spirit Christology as antithetical to and as a replacement for *Logos* Christology.

Fourth, Barth upholds both a *Logos* and Spirit Christology and presents both in concert within the span of *CD*—sometimes separately, at other times concurrently within the same segment of writing—without any conscious attempt to reconcile the two streams of thought. Instead, Barth allows the dialectical tension arising from the concurrent endorsement of the two Christological models to remain.[33] Daniel Migliore calls it "Barth's dialectic of

---

32. Spence, *Incarnation and Inspiration*, 3.
33. In this way, one is reminded of George Hunsinger's remarks in Hunsinger, *How*

Christology and pneumatology."[34] In a manner not dissimilar to what Hunsinger suggested Barth did with his "Chalcedonian" Christology,[35] Barth could be said to have employed a "strategy of juxtaposition," alternating between a *Logos* and Spirit Christology, and in this way drawing out in all its fullness the richness of an incarnational-inspirational way of thinking about Christology. Frank Macchia is hence not wrong to suggest: "Barth's strong christological determination of pneumatology and his concomitant accent on Spirit Christology . . . can help to mediate between [those] who are christocentric and those who want to give equally strong emphasis on the Spirit."[36]

Barth in Interaction with John Owen

I turn very briefly now to draw out a specific insight arising from another account of Spirit Christology, that of the English Puritan John Owen (1616–83). In his work *Pneumatologia* II.III–IV,[37] Owen contends that "the only singular immediate *act* of the person of the Son on the human nature was the *assumption* of it into subsistence with himself" and that the "only *necessary consequent* of this assumption of the human nature . . . is the *personal union of Christ*."[38] Owen avers that all other acts of God in the person of the Son towards the human nature were *voluntary* and not the result of the hypostatic union because "there was no transfusion of the properties of one nature into the other, nor real physical communication of divine essential excellencies unto the humanity."[39] In this way, Owen is able to explain Jesus' moment of dereliction (Matt 27:46) or his moments of ignorance (Mark 13:32) as purely the experiences of Jesus in his human nature, neither affected nor "encroached upon" by the actions of God the Son in his divine

---

to Read, ix, in recognizing paradox and dialectic as built into the heart of Barth's argument. In addition, one recalls the argument of McCormack, *Critically Realistic Dialectical Theology*, where in countering the thesis of Hans Urs von Balthasar, McCormack contended that Barth maintained his dialectical method throughout his career.

34. Migliore, "*Veni Creator Spiritus*," 172.

35. Hunsinger, "Christology."

36. Macchia, "Spirit of God," 159.

37. *Pneumatologia* can be found in volume 3 of Owen, *Works of John Owen*. Hereafter future references are cited as *Works* 3 followed by page reference.

38. *Works* 3, 160 (added emphasis).

39. *Works* 3, 161. Crisp, "John Owen," 11, highlights that Owen employs the Reformed Tradition's understanding of the *communicatio idiomatum*—where any communication of attributes between the human and divine natures happens through the person of Christ, rather than directly between the two natures—to ground his assertion.

nature.⁴⁰ Owen contends instead that it is the Holy Spirit who is the "the *immediate, peculiar, efficient cause* of all external divine operations."⁴¹ Being "the Spirit of the Son,"⁴² he is the one who executes the divine actions of the Triune God on the incarnate Son. Once again, Owen delimits carefully, stating: "Hence is [the Spirit] the immediate operator of all divine acts of the Son himself, *even on his own human nature. Whatever the Son of God wrought in,* by, or upon the human nature, *he did it by the Holy Ghost*, who is his Spirit, as he is the Spirit of the Father."⁴³

To guard against a misguided view of the Spirit's work as isolated and separatist in nature, Owen appeals to the venerated doctrinal principle *Opera Trinitatis ad extra sunt indivisa* (the external works of the Trinity are undivided). On this principle, the acts of the Holy Spirit on the human nature of Christ may be the Spirit's, but it is not "without the concurrence" of the Father and the Son.⁴⁴ Owen continues to expound on what he calls the "especial actings" of the Holy Spirit towards Jesus Christ via ten detailed thesis statements. As insightful as the statements are, they need not detain us at the point. Rather, the upshot is that in the writings of John Owen, we find an alternate account of the Spirit-Christ relation. This is an account that, as Alan Spence noted, occurs within the context and not at the expense of a *Logos* Christology. To that end, Spence credits Owen as being one of the first theologians (since Irenaeus) to hold together, on the one hand, a proper depiction of the incarnation, and on the other hand, a picture of Christ as a man who was thoroughly inspired by the Holy Spirit.⁴⁵

Moving forward, I return to Karl Barth while still keeping an eye on Owen. Specifically, I return to a question generated by a comment Rosato made in relation to Barth's account of the Spirit-Christ relation. Rosato stated that the most Barth could do was to enhance his basic *Logos* Christology with intermittent references to the Spirit working in Jesus' humanity.⁴⁶ Notwithstanding the validity of Rosato's observation, his comment begets the question: could Barth have said more?

Certainly, Barth would not have said what Rosato would have liked him to say. With Rosato and a number of other contemporary Spirit Christology proposals, the starting point begins with a consideration of

40. *Works* 3, 161.
41. *Works* 3, 161.
42. *Works* 3, 162.
43. *Works* 3, 162 (added emphasis).
44. *Works* 3, 162.
45. Spence, *Incarnation and Inspiration*, 59.
46. Rosato, *Spirit as Lord*, 175.

Christology from an *inspirational* basis, before moving in a direction that gradually accounts for the *incarnational* component in a secondary way.[47] Barth's Christocentric sensibilities would have caused him to balk at such an approach. On Barth's terms, Christology moves in the opposite direction, beginning firmly with the *incarnational* component before encompassing or accounting for the *inspirational* aspect.[48] Given this is so, the following question remains: what if in beginning with Barth's "incarnational" starting point we took Barth's Spirit-Christ relation further down the "inspirational" direction, that is to say, in a direction akin to Owen's Spirit-Christ relation? Would Barth have been open to that?

I do not think so. Oliver Crisp has highlighted a fundamental difficulty with Owen's specification of the Spirit-Christ relation that I believe Barth would concur with. That is, Owen's pneumatology ultimately introduces, as Crisp states, "a theologically damaging cleavage between God the Son and his human nature."[49] Specifically, the cleavage happens between, on the one hand, *the subject of the incarnation—God the Son*, and on the other hand, *his agency* "in" and "through" his human nature at all moments following the first moment of assumption of the human nature. Upon closer examination, this cleavage arises because of Owen's precise and detailed specification that

---

47. Take for example Rosato's own Spirit Christology proposal. In *Spirit as Lord*, 178–79, Rosato sketches a "tentative improtu outline" of the Spirit Christology he advocates. It begins with the "living Christian community" and moves (backwards) to "the paschal mystery" and then to "the ministry, baptism and incarnation of Jesus." Rosato states of his intended Spirit Christology: "Jesus' meaning is set in the current pneumatic framework of the Church, in the pneumatic context of the Scriptures and in the pneumatic setting of Israel's messianic expectations. *Consideration of Jesus' ontic being follows an examination of His singular historical function*" (179, added emphasis). I draw our attention to the last line. A *Logos* Christology that begins with the incarnation is, at best, secondary, in Rosato's scheme.

48. In this regard, one must read with caution Barth's well-known comment written in a postscript to a text on Schleiermacher. The comment reads: "What I have already intimated here and there . . . would be the possibility of a theology of the third article, in other words, a theology predominantly and decisively of the Holy Spirit" ("Concluding Unscientific Postscript," 278). This statement has often been misconstrued as an indication on Barth's part that he was inclined to pursue a pneumatic *as opposed* to a Christocentric theology, if given the time and opportunity to begin all over again. I disagree with such an interpretation. Instead, Barth was expressing his desire for theology to be reworked and rethought in terms of the person and work of the Holy Spirit in the same way and not as a replacement of the manner he had done so with the work and person of Jesus Christ. Perhaps, Hunsinger's statement best provides an insight to what Barth meant by a "Third Article theology." Whereas from the standpoint of reconciliation, the work of the Spirit was presented as serving the work of Christ, from the standpoint of redemption (if Barth had managed to write it), the work of Christ would have been presented as serving the work of the Spirit. Hunsinger, "Mediator of Communion," 150.

49. Crisp, "John Owen," 7.

God the Son does not act directly upon his human nature, but only in a mediate manner, through the agency of the Holy Spirit.[50] The consequence is that, as Crisp reminds us, "God the Son is one step removed from his own human nature."[51] This notion detracts somewhat from our understanding of the incarnation wherein the second person of the Trinity is clearly the subject at the center of the (incarnational) action, and is the one in whom the incarnation terminates. If the human nature is *God the Son's* by virtue of the hypostatic union—if God the Son "owns" the human nature assumed— then, as Crisp suggests, "there appears to be no metaphysical room for the interposition of another divine person between the intentions of God the Son (i.e., his agency) and the intentional actions brought about in his human nature."[52]

Neither would it do to appeal to Owen's usage of the *Opera Trinitatis ad extra* principle.[53] It could be argued through the principle that since the Spirit is part of the triune Godhead and not a numerically distinct deity, and furthermore is the Spirit of Christ, God the Son would still be involved in the actions of his human nature despite the mediation of the Spirit.[54] Thinking in this fashion would be to misapply the Trinitarian principle, whose original formulation was to safeguard the doctrine of the Trinity while allowing for particular actions to terminate on particular divine persons of the Godhead. So the principle cannot be used to justify the Holy Spirit as the one upon whom actions carried out in the human nature of Christ terminate, when, as Crisp argues, "the Incarnation is the work that terminates upon the *Son*."[55]

More important to our discussion is Barth's own reading of the subject matter. The general drift of *CD* I/2 §15, *CD* IV/1 §59.1 and *CD* IV/2 §64.2— segments within *CD* that detail Barth's treatment of the incarnation—all point toward Barth seeing the incarnation as an act or event wholly "owned" by the Son and in whom the action terminates. The alternate view of the incarnation as an occurrence of a partial terminus resting upon the Son (in terms of his assumption of human nature) and the remaining terminus resting upon the Spirit (in terms of the execution of the acts of that human nature) seems adrift from Barth's way of thinking. To take Barth's Spirit-Christ relation further in an Owenite direction would mean that Barth would have

---

50. Crisp, "John Owen," 15.
51. Crisp, "John Owen," 17.
52. Crisp, "John Owen," 20–21.
53. *Works* 3, 162.
54. Crisp, "John Owen," 21.
55. Crisp, "John Owen," 21.

to qualify one way or another his core conviction that the incarnation, from start to finish, is an act "owned" by the Son of God. He is the *terminus a quo* and the *terminus ad quem*.

The more accurate picture is one where Barth is content to present in concert both aspects of his Christological model—Jesus Christ is the Son of God who assumes human nature in the incarnation, and he is also the Son of Man who is the Spirit-filled one—without delving into the intricacies of demarcating the limits of agency and terminus for the Son and the Spirit respectively. In line with his overall theological methodology, Barth would rather let the dialectical tension remain than to smooth over the tension in the manner that Owen's sharp and precise delineation between the (direct) act of the Son of God and the subsequent (mediated) acts of the Spirit on the human nature of Christ allows for.

The Distinct *Hypostasis* of the Spirit within the Immanent Trinity according to Barth and His Recent Interpreters

It will profit us in this section to trace out Barth's own specification of his "immanent pneumatology" (as I have termed it earlier), that is, to outline the identity of the distinct *hypostasis* that the Spirit is and consequently to denote his activity within the immanent Trinity. Since Barth drew the incarnate obedience of the Son "backwards" into the triune Godhead such that it counts as the obedience of the eternal Son, naturally, the role or relation the Spirit has to this intra-Trinitarian obedience warrants our close attention.

I begin with *CD* I/1 §12.2, where the bulk of Barth's "immanent pneumatology"—"the Eternal Spirit"[56] as he terms it—is found.[57] Barth's specification in that section largely follows after the Western (Latin) Trinitarian tradition largely bequeathed by Augustine.[58] Barth conceives the

---

56. This is the title Barth gave to the sub-section within §12: "*Der Ewige Geist*."

57. In beginning at *CD* I/1, however, one has to address the following methodological question: can Barth's "immanent pneumatology" in *CD* I/1 still hold in the latter volumes post-*CD* II/2, given the momentous ramifications Barth's doctrine of election holds for his doctrine of the Trinity? While agreeing with the insights highlighted by Williams ("Triune God," 129) and McCormack ("Lord and Giver," 247) that Barth's Trinitarian discourse in the latter volumes trades on a greater plurality in the differentiation of the three modes of being, my opinion is that the revisions are not seismic enough to call for a retraction of Barth's earlier statements in *CD* I/1. Barth's central contention in his doctrine of the Trinity holds steadily across his writings: the triune God is a singular divine subject in three modes of being.

58. See McIntyre, *Shape of Pneumatology*, 145–55, where he especially highlights Barth's indebtedness to Augustine.

Holy Spirit as "the common element . . . the fellowship, the act of communion, of the Father and the Son," immediately carrying on to mention that "[the Holy Spirit] is the *act* in which the Father is the Father of the Son or the Speaker of the Word and the Son is the Son of the Father or the Word of the Speaker."[59] How is one to understand this "act" that the Spirit is? Barth, in the immediate excursus to follow, draws from Augustine directly, and identifies the Spirit as the "bond of peace," the "love," the "charity," and the "gift" between the Father and the Son. He sees the Spirit as a "special divine mode of being."[60] Most likely, what Barth means by this phrase is that he sees the common being and work of the Father and the Son as a mode of divine being distinct from the Father and the Son, thereby conceiving the Spirit as a *special* divine mode of being. Furthermore, since there is no higher "principle" from which the Father and Son find themselves together in the "bond of peace" other than their own divinity, the Spirit must be acknowledged as a *divine* mode of being in his own right.[61]

The message is clear: if Barth "roots" (*Wurzel*) the doctrine of the Trinity in the concept of revelation where "God reveals himself as the Lord,"[62] and if the doctrine of the Trinity really serves to answer the question what God must be in order for God's revelation to be as it is, then the answer Barth provides is that God must be "'antecedently in Himself' the act of communion, the act of impartation, love, gift. For this reason and in this way and on this basis He is so in His revelation. Not *vice versa*!"[63] Special attention must also be referenced to Barth's identification of the Spirit as the "Spirit of the Son" not only in time but also in eternity, a reference made in the context of Barth upholding the importance of the immanent *Filioque*.[64]

---

59. *CD* I/1, 470 (added emphasis).
60. *CD* I/1, 470.
61. *CD* I/1, 470.
62. *CD* I/1, 306. We must take note of Hunsinger's comment on the proper way to understand "root" as used by Barth, not signifying an epistemological direction, but more of a logical or conceptual basis. In other words, revelation presupposed the doctrine of the Trinity, even as the Trinity interpreted the concept of revelation. See Hunsinger, "Karl Barth's Doctrine of Trinity," 296.
63. *CD* I/1, 470-71.
64. *CD* I/1, 481. Barth's point is that if the Spirit is not the Spirit of the Son in eternity, then the communion between God and man does not have "a guarantee in the communion between God the Father and God the Son as the eternal content of its temporal reality." McIntyre, *Shape of Pneumatology*, 155, states it as follows: "[I]f the Spirit is not the Spirit of the Son within the Godhead, then . . . the communion between God and human beings . . . will have no ultimate ground in the being of God himself, and will yield no actual revelation of the content of God's being."

So far, Barth's "immanent pneumatology" has shown itself to be embedded within an Augustinian Trinitarian framework. This bears two implications. First, Barth will be subjected to the same critique that Augustine's Trinitarian model has perennially received, that is, the nebulous definition of the Spirit as a distinct *hypostasis*. The argument is often put forward that it is not altogether clear how the depiction of the Spirit as the "love" or as the "act" of their communion between Father and Son specifies the Spirit as fully a *subject* in this third mode of being.[65] Not all is lost for Augustinian Trinitarianism though. In recent literature, there have been persuasive attempts to reread Augustine as arguing against the common perception that he asserted the unity of God at the expense of the diversity of the persons.[66] Others have suggested revisions to Augustine's basic framework that tend towards a sharper specification of the Spirit's identification and role.[67] The refinement I propose in the final section of this chapter itself trades on what is essentially an Augustinian framework. The second implication of Barth's "immanent pneumatology" operating essentially from an Augustinian framework in *CD* I/1 would mean that talk of the Spirit's role in the intra-Trinitarian obedience is absent, since Augustine did not conceive the relation between the Father and the Son in terms of obedience.

Things, however, take a different turn with *CD* II/2. Alongside Barth's positing of an intra-Trinitarian obedience from the Son to the Father is evinced the Spirit's role in that obedience. A key specification is found in

65. McCormack, "Lord and Giver," 238. The case might, at first glance, be further exacerbated by Barth's comment in *CD* I/1, 469: "Thus, even if the Father and the Son might be called 'person' (in the modern sense of the term), the Holy Spirit could not possibly be regarded as the third 'person'. In a particularly clear way the Holy Spirit is what the Father and the Son also are." Barth's comment appears to deny to the Spirit the status of a "divine person," but it is more likely that Barth was simply hesitating in applying what he deemed to be an amorphous term—"person"—to the Spirit, in the same way he hesitated applying that term to the Father and Son, preferring to use the term *seinsweisen*.

66. I am thinking mainly of Ayres, *Augustine and Trinity*, in particular chapter 10. Ayres masterfully traces through the portrayal of the Spirit as the bond of love between the Father and the Son in *De trinitate*, depicting Augustine as maintaining the balance between speaking of the Spirit (as love) as both irreducible "person" and as the essence of Father and Son. The following quote summarizes what Ayres is aiming at: "That the Spirit is named as love . . . [means] we must say both that Father and Son are in their essence love *and that* the Spirit is the love of Father and Son and fully another beside and in them" (259, original emphasis).

67. By drawing on Richard of St. Victor's crucial insight that love limited to any two persons is intrinsically incomplete, Gunton, "God the Holy Spirit," 126, attributes to the Holy Spirit the dynamic of divine love. The Spirit is the one (hypostasis) within the divine eternity who perfects the love of Father and Son by moving it beyond itself to embrace the creaturely other.

what could possibly count as Barth's manifesto of his doctrine of election. Just as it was the Father's choice (in the beginning) to establish a covenant with mankind in the fulfilment of his grace, and just as it was the Son's choice (in the beginning) to be obedient to this grace, likewise (in the beginning), it was the "*resolve* of the Holy Spirit that the unity of God, of Father and Son should not be disturbed or rent by this covenant with man, but that it should be made the more glorious."[68] Barth undertakes a similar specification of the Spirit's role in the intra-Trinitarian obedience in *CD* IV/1, describing the Spirit as "a Third" in the "same perfect unity and equality" within the one triune Godhead, who "affirms the one and equal Godhead through and by and in the two modes of being . . . who makes possible and maintains His fellowship with Himself as the one and the other."[69] The same affirmation is repeated in the prime passage where Barth tethers the command-obedience relation between the Father and the Son to their eternal relation of begetting-and-being-begotten: "The Father is not the Father and the Son is not the Son without a mutual affirmation and love in the Holy Spirit."[70]

From our consideration of the above key passages, it could be said that, on the one hand, Barth's construal of the Spirit's role in the intra-Trinitarian obedience continues to retain an essentially Augustinian flavor: the Spirit remains the bond of unity within the triune Godhead even as the Son renders obedience to the Father. This, I suggest, is the best Barth can do as he adopts the right move in limiting the command-obedience relation to one that is exclusively between that of the Father and the Son. Therefore, Barth correctly nowhere states that the Spirit is obedient to either the Father or the Son. On the other hand, even as Barth's doctrine of the Trinity begins to trade on a greater plurality in the differentiation of the three modes of being, Barth also attempts a clearer "*hypostasizing*" of the Spirit. To speak of the "resolve" (*Beschluß*) of the Spirit in maintaining the triune unity is to render to the Spirit (as a mode of being) the most pronounced sense of "being-a-subject" one could afford, while not contravening Barth's basic rubric of the Trinity as a singular divine subject in three modes of being. After all, only an acting subject can "resolve" to be or do something. It is to posit the bond of unity ensuing from the dynamics of the command-obedience (or the self-positing-and-being-posited) relation experienced between the first two modes of being as one that is fully another beside and in them; in other words, it is to posit the bond of unity as a third mode of being. To articulate things in this manner is, as Jones states, to go for a maximal intensification and sharpening

---

68. *CD* II/2, 101 (added emphasis).
69. *CD* IV/1, 202–3.
70. *CD* IV/1, 209.

of God's triune self-differentiation, while not embracing anything like the idea of three centers of consciousness or volition.[71]

The question remains though: how would Barth's actualistic ontology—as described in this thesis—affect the way one construes Barth's "immanent pneumatology"? Unfortunately, Barth remained silent on this question, leaving it to subsequent interpreters to suggest some constructive possibilities. I will briefly highlight and evaluate two such proposals, before moving to develop my own proposal in the last section of this chapter.

The first proposal comes from Paul Nimmo, and the gist of his argument runs as follows: because Jesus Christ is the "electing God," we cannot view the *logos asarkos* in abstraction, but we always see him as the *logos incarnandus* destined to be in the flesh. In the same way, because the Spirit is also the "electing God" (as "electing Spirit"), we cannot view the Spirit as the *pneuma anecclesion* in abstraction, but we likewise see the Spirit as the *pneuma inecclesiandus*, the Spirit destined to be "enchurched."[72] Nimmo asserts: "[A]s the eternal determination to incarnation is part of the determination of the eternal being of the Son, so the mediating activity of the Spirit in time between Jesus Christ and the community of God is part of the eternal determination of the Spirit."[73] In other words, God's very mode of being as Spirit is determined with his temporal activity in view.[74]

It is clear that Nimmo operates from a "strong" reading of the Trinity-election relation. That is to say—following Nimmo's train of thought—not only is God being the triune God coincidental and coterminous with his election to be the God who saves in Jesus Christ, that decision of election actually (logically) precedes triunity. While remaining controversial, it is this very premise that enables Nimmo to attribute to the Spirit a defined and distinct identification and role in the Trinity. After all, on Nimmo's terms, he is the Spirit who is determined as the third mode of being in the triune Godhead *because* He is the Spirit who summons the church and is "enfleshed" in the church. Paralleling an actualistic ontology, the concept of an "actualistic ecclesiology" receives its maximal invigoration in the hands of Nimmo.

While I share in a general reading of Barth's actualistic ontology, in that act and being are both *ontologically* and *chronologically* equal and basic to who God is, I have my reservations about Nimmo's "strong" reading. My own account, as seen earlier, is predicated on a *logical* precedence of

---

71. Jones, *Humanity of Christ*, 212. It is acknowledged that Jones made this statement in a slightly different context.

72. Nimmo, "Barth and Election-Trinity," 178.

73. Nimmo, "Barth and Election-Trinity," 174–75.

74. Nimmo, "Barth and Election-Trinity," 172.

triunity over election. In spite of this difference, I believe the central insight of Nimmo can be retrieved without subscribing to the "strong" actualistic ontology he espouses. If God being the triune God and being the God-who-is-for-us-in-Christ-Jesus is coincidental and coterminous in the one eternal event of his self-determination, it is possible to illumine Barth's earlier "immanent pneumatology" in this actualistic light. The "Spirit of the Son"[75] is at one and the same moment the "Spirit of Jesus Christ," who is not only the Spirit that is with the Son of God in his incarnation, but is also the power of Jesus Christ who continues to summon and be "enfleshed" within the community of the church.[76] And just as the Spirit is the bond of unity between the Father and the Son, the Spirit is also one and the same moment the one who binds the community to Christ, uniting the ascended Christ to his people.[77] Under this reading, Barth's "actualistic ecclesiological" commitments receive the same pronounced attention while maintaining a logical precedence of triunity over election.[78]

It is this notion of the Spirit as "the Spirit of the Son" that the second proposal capitalizes on. Bruce McCormack has advocated that one should not speak of "the Spirit as the act of communion between the Father and the Son which is not also, and at the same time, the act of turning towards the world in creative and redeeming power."[79] Building on the notion of what he terms a "Reformed Kenoticism" (briefly outlined in chapter 2), McCormack moves to specify in what way the Spirit is "the Spirit of the Son" not just in temporality but also in eternity. The nub of McCormack's proposal trades on Barth's actualistic ontology and involves (as McCormack admits) taking the further step Barth himself did not undertake: what the Spirit does in and through the incarnate Son in time is determined to be what the Spirit does in eternity, via a proleptic foreseeing and an actualistic reckoning. If the Son or Logos is related to the man Jesus in the mode of receptivity, and this receptivity is an *eternal* receptivity arising in turn from the eternal humility and obedience of the Son, it must carry the following two

---

75. *CD* I/1, 481.

76. Holmes, *Holy Spirit*, 152, captures the idea in the following manner: "The Spirit's work in relation to Jesus and his body reflects . . . who the Spirit is in eternity, that is, the Spirit of Jesus Christ."

77. Holmes, *Holy Spirit*, 159.

78. In fact, Holmes, "Church and Presence of Christ," 269, argues that a basic consideration of Barth's Christology in itself leads to an actualistic ecclesiology. Barth's Christology, specifically the twofold movement of the humiliation of the Son of God and the exaltation of the Son of Man, unfolded in the language of "event," by itself already generates a concrete ecclesiology, in that the account of the church is already worked into the identity of the resurrected and ascended Christ.

79. McCormack, "Lord and Giver," 231.

implications. First, the identity of the Son in eternity is (already) constituted by the act of looking forward to what he will be in time, namely Jesus Christ. And second—here is where McCormack brings in the pneumatological twist—"[the Son's] willed non-use of the omnipotent power He shares with the Father and Spirit *in time* must correspond to a willed non-use of that power *eternally*."[80] This opens the door for the Spirit to be posited as the one "breathed forth [from the Father and the Son] to be the effective agent of all that is done by the triune God in relation to the world, creation and redemption,"[81] the mediator of *all* of the Son's otherwise *indirect* work.[82] In other words, the personal property of the Holy Spirit as the third mode of God's being is defined as being the effective agent of all that is done by the Father and the Son in relation to the world.[83] McCormack garners support from the pneumatological considerations of John Owen that we came across earlier, in fact going beyond Owen to suggest that even the assumption of human nature should not be viewed as a direct work of the Son.[84]

Although Barth's "immanent pneumatology" receives a sharp specification through McCormack's constructive proposal, certain reservations remain on my part. Following largely from a similar concern over Owen's pneumatology highlighted earlier in the chapter, I wonder if Barth would agree to such a construal of the incarnation. The Son of God is finally seen as an indirect and passive subject in the incarnation, whose actions (if any) can only be carried out *indirectly* and in a *mediated* manner through the Spirit. In my mind, to insist that the Son's humility and receptivity constitutes the whole of his activity in the person of Jesus Christ is to tend toward monothelitism, or, at best, to a severely muted dyothelitism wherein *the divine will (arising from the divine nature of the Son of God) ceases to feature directly in the Son's incarnate life*. Even if the divine will does play a role, it only features because of the mediated activity of the Spirit.[85] As expressed in the previous chapter, I surmise that a mediated view of divine agency fails to capture Barth's own view of direct divine agency in relation to the incarnation.[86]

80. McCormack, "Lord and Giver," 250 (added emphasis).
81. McCormack, "Lord and Giver," 250.
82. McCormack, "Lord and Giver," 251.
83. McCormack, "Lord and Giver," 251.
84. McCormack, "Lord and Giver," 251. McCormack's commendation of Owen's pneumatology appeared on two other previous occasions: McCormack, "'With Loud Cries and Tears,'" 38–40, and "God Who Graciously Elects."
85. See Jones, *Humanity of Christ*, 214n62, for a somewhat similar concern.
86. McCormack, "Lord and Giver," 251, appeals to the *opera trinitatis ad extra sunt indivisa* axiom to maintain that the acts of the Spirit may rightly be said to have been

A Proposed Refinement to Barth's Conception of the Spirit's Identity and Role within the Trinity

After outlining two constructive proposals seeking greater integration between Barth's actualistic ontology and his pneumatology, I turn in this final section to attempt my own proposal. The constructive element involves making a minor refinement to the Augustinian Trinitarian framework that Barth inherited and largely operated from. To be more precise, the refinement involves tweaking Augustine's famed positing of the Spirit as the bond of love between the Father and the Son. Integrated with Barth's actualistic ontology, the refinement allows us to articulate the Spirit's work with respect to the incarnate Son while upholding Barth's dialectical conception of the Spirit-Christ relation as presented thus far.

The refinement is actually not novel and has been developed by Roman Catholic theologian Thomas Weinandy in his book *The Father's Spirit of Sonship*. Without delving into the finer details but covering enough to suffice for our purpose, the central claim of Weinandy's proposal concerns the way we conceive the divine processions. His basic contention is that within the Trinity, the Father begets the Son *in or by* the Holy Spirit, with the Spirit thus proceeding simultaneously from the Father as the one *in whom* the Son is begotten. The Son, being begotten *of* the Father *in* the Spirit, simultaneously loves the Father in the same Spirit by which he himself is begotten (is loved).[87] I will highlight four key premises and features of Weinandy's proposal in a bid to flesh out his thesis.

First, Weinandy works within the keystone principle—one that Barth tenaciously maintained too—that the Trinity *ad intra* is revealed in the Trinity *ad extra*, and that the way we come to discern the inherent Trinitarian ontology of the former is by paying careful attention to the functional, economic expression of the Trinity *ad extra* found in the Scriptural passages.[88] The twofold economic pattern revealed in the New Testament involves firstly, the Spirit conforming Jesus to be the faithful Son on earth (and herein lies Weinandy's promotion of the Spirit-Christ relation),[89] and, secondly, the Spirit enabling our adoption as sons and daughters of God.[90] Together, these two themes of the Spirit's work in the economy of salvation is what precipitates

---

done by the Son. As argued earlier, however, the employment of the axiom does not address the problem of the indirect nature of the divine agency of the Son.

87. Weinandy, *Father's Spirit of Sonship*, 17.
88. Weinandy, *Father's Spirit of Sonship*, 22.
89. Weinandy, *Father's Spirit of Sonship*, 25–33.
90. Weinandy, *Father's Spirit of Sonship*, 33–38.

Weinandy to postulate the same within the triune Godhead, that is to say, the Spirit conforms the Son as *the Son* within the Trinity.

Second, Weinandy's proposal arises from his relocation of the signification of the Godhead from one resting either on the Father alone (the tendency of Eastern Orthodox Trinitarianism), or in a solitary substance distinct from the Trinity (the tendency of Western Trinitarianism), to one founded in the Trinity.[91] As Weinandy states: "The being of God . . . *is* the Trinity which is the one act of the Father begetting the Son and spirating the Spirit. The eternal constituting of the persons takes place within (and not outside of) the one being of God, and therefore is the one being of God."[92] Although Weinandy's move is not unprecedented,[93] the genius (to some) and equally the tendentiousness (to others) of his initiative lies in the fact that he infuses a sense of dynamic mutuality and reciprocity through the "*perichoresis* of *action*" that takes place among the divine persons of the Godhead. This *perichoresis* extends to *who* they are as *hypostases*—Father, Son and Spirit.[94]

When expanded, the notion of a "*perichoresis* of *action*" runs as follows. From the viewpoint of *the Father*, the Father is the Father in the one eternal action consisting of the distinct but mutually inherent acts of begetting and spirating whereby the Son is begotten of the Father and the Spirit proceeds simultaneously as the love undergirding that begetting. Weinandy inserts the following crucial statement in this regard: "The Father does not, even logically, first beget the Son and then love the Son in the Spirit. The begetting of the Son and the proceeding of the Spirit are simultaneous and, while distinct, mutually inhere in one another."[95] Similarly, from the viewpoint of *the Son*, the Father eternally begets the Son and by that act of filial love enacted in the Spirit of sonship makes him the Son. But conversely, the Son, in being begotten of the Father, loves the Father and so as Son helps conform the Father *as Father*. In both relations, what holds together the fatherly act of lovingly begetting the Son and the filial act of the Son loving the Father is the

---

91. Weinandy, *Father's Spirit of Sonship*, 60.

92. Weinandy, *Father's Spirit of Sonship*, 64 (original emphasis).

93. It could be said that Aquinas initiated the move by stating that since relations existing in God cannot have the status of an accidental existence but only that of a substantial existence, relations in God are really the same as his essence (ST I., q. 28, a. 2; cf. q. 39, a. 1). Aquinas's thoughts prepare the way for one like T. F. Torrance to develop the notion that the one divine *ousia* is (actually) the communion-constituting activity of the three *hypostases*. See Torrance, *Christian Doctrine of God*, 124.

94. Weinandy, *Father's Spirit of Sonship*, 78.

95. Weinandy, *Father's Spirit of Sonship*, 71.

action of the Holy Spirit.[96] And finally, from the viewpoint of *the Spirit*, the Spirit principally proceeds from the Father as the love in which the Father begets the Son, and in that way conforms the Father as *the Father (who loves)*. Equally true, although derivatively, is the fact that the Spirit also proceeds from the Son as the Spirit by which the Son loves the Father, and so conforms the Son as *the Son (who is loved and who loves in return)*.[97] The main upshot is that this "*perichoresis* of *action*" bearing on the relations of origin within the Godhead facilitates a conception of the divine processions that shifts away from a "linear" sequence—the Father begets the Son, *followed by* the spiration of the Spirit. Instead, our conception of the divine processions is directed toward "one simultaneous, non-sequential, eternal act in which each person of the Trinity subsistently defines, and equally is subsistently defined by, the other persons."[98]

Third, Weinandy believes that his proposal has constructive ecumenical implications by offering resources for resolving, or at least abating, the *filioque* controversy.[99] On the one hand, by maintaining that the Father is the principal source from whom the Spirit proceeds, Weinandy secures the "monarchy" of the person of the Father, albeit a monarchy considered not in isolation but within the one being of the triune God. Furthermore, because it is only in the simultaneous procession of the Spirit that the Father begets the Son (in love), the distinct procession of the Spirit from the Father is secured at the same time.[100] On the other hand, Weinandy's proposal also allows for a derivative procession of the Spirit from the Son. The Son, being begotten by the Father, is conformed as the Son by the Spirit (of love and sonship) who himself proceeded from the Father. In so doing, the Spirit also proceeds from the Son as the identical Love for the Father in whom he is begotten.[101] Weinandy's proposal holds potential as a possible point of convergence for the needs and concerns of the Eastern and Western church to be met.

Fourth, apropos to our topic, Weinandy depicts a picture of the divine processions whereby the Son and the Spirit play active and symmetrical roles within the Trinity. If such is the order of being within the Trinity *ad*

---

96. Weinandy, *Father's Spirit of Sonship*, 73.
97. Weinandy, *Father's Spirit of Sonship*, 74.
98. Weinandy, *Father's Spirit of Sonship*, 14–15. Weinandy admits (*Father's Spirit of Sonship*, 72n33) that this way of thinking does away with the precedence and "logical priority" deriving from an Aristotelian framework that the "linear" sequential view is built upon—the Son must "first" be known "before" he is loved.
99. Weinandy, *Father's Spirit of Sonship*, 87–100.
100. Weinandy, *Father's Spirit of Sonship*, 95.
101. Weinandy, *Father's Spirit of Sonship*, 96.

intra, it is unsurprising that the pattern and order will be repeated in the Trinity *ad extra*. By highlighting the vital role the Spirit plays within the triune life, Weinandy underscores and provides credence to the significant and vital nature of the Spirit's work first on the incarnate Christ and then within his body, the Church.[102] Pertinently, just as the Spirit in eternity conforms the Son *as the Son* in his being begotten of the Father, and just as the Spirit subsequently conforms us as obedient sons and daughters of God in Christ, so the Spirit likewise in the "middle" conforms Jesus as the obedient Son even to the point of shedding his blood as man.[103] There is nowhere to be found any idea of the subordination of the Spirit to the Son. But the reverse is equally true: there is also nowhere to be found the subordination of the Son to the Spirit. Since the Son loves the Father in the same Spirit in whom he is begotten, the Spirit is also the Spirit of the Son. Thus even the Spirit's work on the incarnate Christ is to bring glory to Jesus, and through that, to the Father (John 16:12–15).

In all, Weinandy's proposal seeks to hold out a robust Christology and pneumatology without sacrificing or privileging one over the other. Better: Weinandy's proposal offers great fecundity in outlining a pneumatological *Christology* or a Christological *pneumatology*, sourcing its basis for doing so all the way back into the life and relations within the triune Godhead.[104]

The key question awaits: would Barth be sympathetic to such a proposal? Judging from Barth's writings, the immediate answer would be in the negative. Towards the end of *CD* I/1 §12 where he discusses the *Seinsweise* of the Holy Spirit, Barth broaches the crux of Weinandy's proposal: since the Spirit proceeds from the Father and the Son, could not the reverse be said of the Son, that he likewise proceeds from the Father and the Spirit?[105] Barth's answer "No" stems largely from his underlying stance that, first, *perichoresis* was never employed as a term to describe the mutuality of origins, but only the modes of being of the one God. As a description of the *homoousia* of Father, Son, and Spirit, *perichoresis* has nothing to do with begetting or spiration as such.[106] Second, Barth sees the relation of procession, in this case from the Spirit, as applying—if possibly to anything—only to the humanity of Jesus Christ and not to the eternal Son of God himself.[107] His reasoning

---

102. Weinandy, *Father's Spirit of Sonship*, 99.

103. Weinandy, *Father's Spirit of Sonship*, 52.

104. For a somewhat similar thesis, see also Tanner, "Beyond the East/West Divide," 198–210.

105. *CD* I/1, 485.

106. *CD* I/1, 485.

107. *CD* I/1, 486.

rests upon the distinction between, on the one hand, the begetting (of the Son) from the Father and the proceeding (of the Spirit) from the Father and the Son, and on the other hand, the bringing forth or procession from the Holy Spirit. In the first instance (the divine processions), what is brought forth is not of another essence, but is of the same essence as the Father (in the case of begetting) and the Father and the Son (in the case of spirating). In the second instance, however, what is brought forth is of some other essence whose existence does not concern an "eternal relation of origin." Based on this premise, Barth argues that the procession from the Holy Spirit *in relation to the Son in revelation* is incommensurable with and of a wholly different category from either the "begetting" of the eternal Son or the "proceeding" of the Spirit from the Father and Son.[108]

I would like to issue a challenge to Barth's reasoning on this subject, being convinced that Weinandy's proposal is sufficiently nuanced to avoid the pitfalls that concern Barth. I see no difficulty in extending *perichoresis* to a mutuality of origins, as Weinandy has done. If Father, Son and Holy Spirit exist as the modes of being of the one triune God, and if the concept of *perichoresis* at heart involves—as defined by Barth himself—the "definite ... [and] complete participation of each mode of being in the other modes of being,"[109] then it is not conceptually impossible for *perichoresis* to be extended back to the point of origins, since it is solely by virtue of their *different relations of origins* that each mode of being is defined and distinguished from the other two in the first place. Barth is cognizant of this point too, recognizing that "the modes of being are in fact *identical with the relations of origin.*"[110] If this is the case, I find it surprising that Barth delimits *perichoresis* to apply to the mutuality of the modes of being only and not to the mutuality of their origins, given the close identification between the two.[111]

Perhaps Barth's concern—and this constitutes an objection one might raise to Weinandy's proposal—is that applying *perichoresis* to the mutuality of origins obfuscates the distinct and unique "properties" peculiar to each mode of being, namely, that the Father begets, the Son is begotten, and the Spirit is spirated (*filioque*). If that is so, Weinandy's careful and deliberate choice of words in advancing his proposal must be noted. Nowhere is the *perichoretic* action of the Spirit on the Son (in relation to the Son's being begotten) described as a "procession" of the Son from the Spirit. Instead, the *perichoretic* action is strictly delineated in *instrumental*, and not in

108. *CD* I/1, 485.
109. *CD* I/1, 370.
110. *CD* I/1, 370 (added emphasis).
111. *CD* I/1, 485.

causative, terms: the Father eternally begets the Son *in*, or *by*, the Holy Spirit. This means that, in Weinandy's scheme, the eternal properties pertaining to each mode of being arising from their different relations of origin are still effectively preserved: to the Father, paternity, to the Son, filiation, and to the Spirit, procession. Relevant to our concern here, the Father as a mode of being is still distinguished uniquely as the one who begets the Son (as the second mode of being), as he does so through the instrumentality of the third mode of being of the Spirit. In fact, one could further argue the case that this "*perichoresis* of action" extending to the mutuality of origins parallels that of the Tradition, which posits that the Father eternally begets the Son in *love*. This is the reason why I see Weinandy's proposal essentially as a modification of Augustine's basic framework of the Spirit as the bond of love between the Father and the Son.[112]

More positively, and in closing, I remain persuaded of the gains that could be achieved in relation to Barth's Trinitarianism and his construal of the Spirit-Christ relation if Weinandy's proposal was adopted. Primarily, a more perspicuous account of the person of the Spirit and a specification of his divine activities vis-à-vis the triune Godhead would be achieved. No longer would the Spirit function merely as the passive bond of love or the gift shared between the Father and the Son. Instead, the Spirit, under Weinandy's proposal, takes on the role of an acting subject in being the love that the Son is (instrumentally) begotten *in*. The Spirit is now defined as the Spirit who proceeds from the Father in that concurrent "moment" of the begetting of the Son in love and hence is the divine person whose activity conforms the Son as *the Son*. He is also the same Spirit who proceeds from the Son as the love returned to the Father and thus is the divine person whose activity too conforms the Father as *the Father*. The Spirit now has subjective "*hypostasizing*" depth because of his defining activity as a divine person who conforms the other two divine persons to be who they are, even as the Spirit himself is conformed in the *perichoretic* process of doing so.[113]

---

112. The key difference is as follows though: as Weinandy rightly pointed out, a Western Augustinian Trinitarianism is predicated on an Aristotelian epistemology which asserts that a thing cannot be loved until it is known. On this account, Western Trinitarianism sees the Father as logically and sequentially begetting the Son before he spirates the Spirit. The Father begets the Son, and *only when the Son is first begotten does the Spirit proceed*, from the Father as his love for the Son and from the Son as his love for the Father. It is this logical and sequential presupposition that Weinandy's proposal critiques and revises (*Father's Spirit of Sonship*, 8–10). Interestingly, Ayres, *Augustine and Trinity*, 265–66, allows for the possibility of Augustine's Trinitarianism leading to a supposition of the Spirit's work in the begetting of the Son from the Father, although he admits Augustine nowhere discusses this notion.

113. Weinandy, *Father's Spirit of Sonship*, 8.

Integrated with Barth's fully-developed actualistic ontology, Weinandy's refinement of the language of the divine processions gains further descriptive depth. It does so in a manner that preserves the *logical* priority of triunity over election, since it begins with the divine processions. Following the rubric of Barth's actualistic thought, the Spirit is not just the one who maintains the fellowship between the Father who commands in majesty and the Son who obeys in humility.[114] Neither is the Spirit merely the mutual affirmation and love between the two. But being the Spirit in whose divine mode of being and *instrumentality* the Son is begotten—who himself proceeds from the Father in that begetting—the Spirit should be seen more correctly as the one who has an active role to play in *conforming both the Father as the self-positing Father who commands*, and *conforming the Son as the posited Son who is the eternally obedient one*. The divine missions involving Father, Son and Spirit are contained in the divine processions.[115] In the words of Barth himself, the Holy Spirit is the "actual rendering of a perfect obedience."[116] The Spirit, by dint of the active role he has within the mutual "determination" of the relations of origins, is "a *party* in the triune actuality."[117]

The key consequence arising from this clearer specification of the person and activity of the Spirit is that the Spirit and the Son are now seen as on a par with one another within the divine triune life. The Spirit is neither subordinate to the Son (since it is in the instrumentality of the Spirit that the Son is begotten of the Father), nor is the Son subordinate to the Spirit (since the Spirit proceeds from the Son as the love returned to the Father). That the Spirit has this role and activity in relation to the Son within the Trinity *ad intra* in turn founds the relation between Christ and the Spirit in the economy. This calls in turn for an account of the incarnation that offers an in concert and equal presentation of the person and work of both Christ and the Holy Spirit. *This*, I suggest, is what Barth's presentation of the Spirit-Christ relation proffers. Barth's dialectic of Christology and pneumatology, where his depiction of Jesus Christ as the Son of God become flesh is juxtaposed with the Son of Man who is the Spirit-filled one, seeks to maintain an equal emphasis on both Christ and the Spirit. Weinandy's proposal acts as a timely complement to provide Barth the antecedent and primal basis and justification for his specific presentation of the Spirit-Christ relation.

---

114. *CD* IV/1, 202–3.
115. *CD* IV/1, 209–10.
116. *CD* IV/1, 209.
117. In response to Jenson, "You Wonder," 301.

6

The Obedience of Jesus Christ in Barth's Doctrine of the Atonement

INSOFAR AS THIS TREATISE provides a specification of the obedience of Jesus Christ in Karl Barth's doctrine of reconciliation, we converge in this chapter on what could count as the crowning point of our inquiry, namely the role and function occupied by Jesus' obedience in relation to Barth's doctrine of the atonement.[1] In what follows, I contend that the obedience of Jesus is assigned an indispensable and foundational role in Barth's doctrine of the atonement—in a way that extends beyond what the tradition could offer—especially when the doctrine is read in the light of Barth's actualistic ontology.

A successful demonstration of the above contention requires an acquaintance with Barth's doctrine of the atonement. A significant portion of this chapter will hence be devoted to that task. Barth's doctrine of the atonement, as will be seen, is capable of embodying the diversity and plurality of approaches and understandings Scripture and the tradition of the church have to offer when it comes to explaining the atonement, yet without losing the sense of unity that holds these various explanations together. In this way, Barth's doctrine holds potential for a proper account of what Adam Johnson terms the problem of the "one and the many" within atonement doctrine. Johnson is referring to the need to discern the unity underlying the numerous portrayals of Christ's saving work.[2] This, Barth does despite his unmistakable centering of the doctrine of the atonement under the judicial framework.[3] There are good reasons for Barth's choice of the judicial framework, but I am convinced that Barth's doctrine of the atonement remains open to other frameworks besides the judicial one.

The above conviction is based, in turn, on the further contention that the operative force of Barth's doctrine of the atonement lies not in the

---

1. I will address in a moment the difference between the terms "reconciliation" and "atonement" within Barth's theology.

2. Johnson, *God's Being in Reconciliation*, 3.

3. *CD* IV/1, 211–83 "The Judge Judged in Our Place."

judicial imagery itself or for that matter in any other framework, but in the "pattern of exchange" lying behind and in fact presupposing the judicial framework he employs. This "pattern of exchange" revolves around the central concept of "substitution" (*Stellvertretung*), the idea that Christ's death was in some manner "for us and in our place" (2 Cor 5:21).

Furthermore, as I seek to demonstrate, this "pattern of exchange" is intrinsic to Barth's doctrine of election. If election on Barth's account specifies that God had from eternity self-determined to be at the same moment the electing God and elected man in Christ Jesus, then Christ's election could be denoted as including the purpose of undergoing our rejection in order that we might be elected in him. Therein already lies a "pattern of exchange" which involves at its core the actuality of the atonement. In this way, atonement comes to be bound up with an event in God's being and his own divine history. It is at this point that the obedience of Jesus Christ radiates through: via the rendering of obedience by the eternal Son on our behalf in this primordial "pattern of exchange" found within divine election, the salvation of humanity is established. An elucidation of the above-mentioned points forms the substantial consideration of this chapter.

An outline of Barth's doctrine of the atonement is therefore in order. In providing such an outline, however, one is immediately confronted by a pressing definitional question. Given that the German word for "reconciliation" and "atonement" is the same throughout *KD*—*Versöhnung*—but in *CD* is translated as the two English terms, did Barth espouse a doctrine of the atonement in contradistinction to his doctrine of reconciliation?[4]

The answer depends in large part on the theological definition supplied to the English terms. While many have defined the two terms as virtually synonymous with one another with the meaning hovering around the concept of bringing to peace two estranged parties (in this case God and humankind),[5] Paul Fiddes has correctly highlighted a "time-and-place" focus particularly applicable to the atonement. After all, the etymology of the word "at-one-ment" connotes the idea of "making one" at one moment and one place in time.[6] The doctrine of atonement could hence be seen as a narrower subset of the doctrine of reconciliation concerning

---

4. The fact that Bromiley translated *Versöhnung* as "reconciliation" and "atonement" indicates that he perceived Barth as differentiating, although not separating, the doctrine of the atonement from his doctrine of reconciliation. He writes: "[T]he word *Versöhnung* . . . is given by Barth a rich content that includes both 'atonement' and 'reconciliation'. . . . [B]oth [words] are used in in the body of the text according to the requirements of the context" (*CD* IV/1, vii).

5. See for example the entries for the two terms in *EDB*, *BTDB* and *PDTT*.

6. Fiddes, "Salvation," 178.

the specific subject matter of how the death of Jesus Christ on the cross of Calvary achieves reconciliation between God and humankind, bringing about salvation for the latter.

I contend that such a distinction is also present in Barth's doctrine of reconciliation in *CD* IV. According to Barth, §59.1 "The Way of the Son of God into the Far Country" primarily concerns the question *Quo iure Deus homo* ("How is it that God became man"), while §59.2 "The Judge Judged in Our Place" largely concerns the question *Cur Deus homo* ("Why did God become man").[7] So, without pressing the distinction too finely, it could be said that Christology—*who* it was that went to the cross—forms the main subject matter of consideration in §59.1, while atonement—*what* the cross of Christ achieved and *how* that achievement was brought about—is the topic of discussion in §59.2. In this way, it could be said that Barth did espouse a doctrine of the atonement distinct but not separated from his wider doctrine of reconciliation.

With the definitional preamble clarified, a delineation of Barth's doctrine of the atonement now awaits us. My aim is to outline four main features in Barth's atonement doctrine in the four sections to follow in this chapter. Together, these four features provide the background needed for a consideration of the role the obedience of Christ plays within Barth's doctrine of the atonement, and that will occur in the fifth section. For a sense of completion, the chapter concludes with a sixth section evaluating Barth's doctrine of the atonement.

Locating the Atonement as an Event in God's Triune Being via Barth's Doctrine of Election

In my mind, the following point serves as the most striking feature of Barth's doctrine of the atonement: through the doctrine of election, Barth locates the atonement as an event in God's triune being and in his own divine history (*Geschichte*). Barth states: "Jesus Christ . . . is a being, but a being in

---

7. See *CD* IV/1, 184 (in §59.1) where Barth writes: "*Cur Deus homo* is the question we shall have to deal with in the second part of this section—the question concerning the necessity of the incarnation of the Word. But it presupposes that we have already answered the question concerning its possibility from the standpoint of God: *Quo iure Deus homo* [sic]." The "second part of this section" Barth was referring to is §59.2. There, Barth clearly states: "But now we enter a whole sphere of new considerations . . . . [W]e had to begin with this side—the doctrine of the "person of Christ"—because it is the presupposition of everything that follows . . . . That is one thing. Quite another is the answer to the question: Why did He become a servant? . . . In other words: *Cur Deus homo*" (*CD* IV/1, 211–12).

a history. The gracious God is in this history, so is reconciled man, so are both in their unity. And what takes place in this history, and therefore in the being of Jesus Christ as such, is atonement."[8]

In order to accentuate the distinctiveness of Barth's atonement doctrine, I draw our attention to the work of Paul Jones who in two separate essays compares the doctrine of the atonement as set out in Anselm and Calvin to Barth.[9]

Between Anselm and Barth, the former sees the atonement as a gift that the incarnate Son offers to the Father on behalf of sinful humanity,[10] while the latter sees the atonement as the event where Christ on the cross draws into his being the totality of human sin and wickedness and wherein sin and the sinner are rejected, crushed and conclusively "killed off."[11] But more fundamental than the way atonement is portrayed lies the difference of what the atonement means for God's eternal being. While he acknowledges that the cross decisively reveals God as *pro nobis*, Anselm—according to Jones—does not suppose that God's economic action in and through the Son bears on God's immanent being.[12] Barth, however, by virtue of his treatment of election that resulted in a reconceptualization of the identity of the eternal Son, affirms the passion Christ endured on the cross as "an event in the divine life that also happens in the context of creaturely time and space."[13]

Jones similarly identifies in Calvin what he sees as an "ontological deficit" in Calvin's theology. That is to say, Calvin's reluctance to articulate an ontology of the divine being corresponding to his assertion of God's primordial love for his people leaves open the door as to whether God's economic activity is truly consonant with his eternal identity.[14] The way forward—Jones suggests in an underlying appeal to Barth—is to take more seriously the fact that God's love is elective, with election having not so much to do with an apportionment of grace in pre-temporal eternity as it has to do

---

8. *CD* IV/1, 126.

9. Jones, "Barth and Anselm," 257–82; Jones, "The Atonement," 44–62. It is recognized that the comparison with Barth is explicit in the first case (with Anselm) and implicit in the second case (with Calvin).

10. Jones, "Barth and Anselm," 257. Even here, Jones offers a variation to the common "transactional" reading given to Anselm that presumes the "insult" of sin requiring a proportional compensation. Jones argues to the contrary that in offering his life as a gift to the Father, Christ provides a fitting parallel to God's own unnecessitated and gracious attitude towards his creatures (258).

11. Jones, "Barth and Anselm," 258, 276.

12. Jones, "Barth and Anselm," 259.

13. Jones, "Barth and Anselm," 280.

14. Jones, "The Atonement," 49.

with the doctrine of God itself, concerning the very *pro nobis* identity that God assigns himself.[15]

In all, Jones has identified what sets Barth's doctrine of the atonement apart from the Tradition. For Barth, atonement is an event that is "drawn into the time and space of God's eternal being."[16] The following statement from Barth confirms this view: "[I]n this event [of atonement] God allows the world and humanity to take part in *the history of the inner life of His Godhead*, in the movement in which from and to all eternity He is Father, Son and Holy Spirit, and therefore the one true God."[17] This is why Kevin Vanhoozer is essentially right—in an essay mapping out the current landscape of atonement within modern theology—to label Barth's doctrine as having to do with divine self-determination under the wider category of "The Cross as an Event in God's Being."[18]

Clearly, Barth's doctrine of election is key in facilitating him seeing the atonement as an event in God's being. Notwithstanding our prior treatment of this central doctrine in chapters 1 and 3, our task now is to spell out which aspects of election in Barth's account lead him to see the atonement as such. Specifically, I posit that the link lies in Barth's basic axiom that "Jesus Christ is the electing God, and that He is also elected man,"[19] and following on as a corollary, that he is the elected and the reprobate one. I will highlight key implications of these two statements in the paragraphs to follow.

Jesus Christ as Electing God

The novelty and ingenuity of Barth's postulation that Jesus Christ is the electing God and therefore the subject of election can neither be overstated, nor its central import overemphasized. Jesus Christ as the electing God is a game changer for any theological thinking on election. Election is no longer confined to a secret *electio Patris* (election of the Father) according to an unknown *decretum absolutum* (absolute decree) in which the Son is reduced merely to the role of being an executor of this election. Rather, whenever "predestination" or "election" is now mentioned, the immediate referent must be the God who is self-determined in the person of Jesus Christ.[20] This means that Jesus Christ is the active Elector in the divine election, and as Barth emphasizes:

15. Jones, "The Atonement," 51.
16. Jones, "Barth and Anselm," 257.
17. *CD* IV/1, 215 (added emphasis).
18. Vanhoozer, "Atonement," 191–96.
19. *CD* II/2, 103.
20. Gibson, *Reading the Decree*, 48.

"[T]hat election is also His election; that it is [Jesus Christ] Himself who posits this beginning of all things . . . who executes the decision which issues in the establishment of the covenant between God and man."[21]

The revolutionary impact of Jesus Christ being the electing God can only be fully appreciated when juxtaposed with the tradition. As David Gibson has shown, John Calvin could similarly be read as positing Christ who according to his divine nature acts as the "author" of election, over and above Calvin's better-known designation of Christ as the "mediator" of election.[22] Utilizing Calvin's concept of the *Logos incarnandus* as being the perfect expression of the *Logos asarkos* in relation to the harmony between the divine essence and the divine act, there is a sense in which Calvin could be read as positing the divine Son as the *Logos incarnandus* who actively partakes in the divine electing.[23] This comes close to Barth's own position of Jesus Christ being the electing God. However, a deeper examination reveals that Barth's understanding and appropriation of the correlation between the *Logos incarnandus* and Jesus Christ goes further and deeper than Calvin does. For Calvin, the *Logos incarnandus* is seen more as an act of the divine will expressed eternally with no essential bearing on the *Logos asarkos*. But for Barth, the *Logos incarnandus* is conceived actualistically as *a divine mode of being* wherein the God-man Jesus Christ that the Son of God becomes in time is allowed to exert significant pressure on the ontological identity of the Son in eternity.[24] Another way of stating the difference is that Barth would claim the "stronger" statement of Jesus Christ being the *Logos incarnandus* while Calvin at best the "weaker" statement that the *Logos incarnandus* can be seen as Jesus Christ. It is this actualistic strand within Barth's thought that enables him to assert unequivocally:

> [W]e can be absolutely certain that *in Jesus Christ we have to do immediately and directly with the electing God*. If this is not the case, we are exposed always to the doubt that in the election we have to do perhaps with the will of a God who has not bound

---

21. *CD* II/2, 105 (added emphasis).

22. Gibson, *Reading the Decree*, 31. Gibson's argument is grounded on Calvin's exegesis of John 6:70–71 and 13:18 from his commentaries, and from *Inst.* III.22.7.

23. Gibson, *Reading the Decree*, 56.

24. Gibson, *Reading the Decree*, 56. There is a second difference concerning the object of election. On Calvin's account, the *Logos incarnandus* still elects a certain number from mankind for salvation, but on Barth's account, the chief object of election is Jesus Christ himself as man. For other alternate accounts of election within the Reformed and post-Reformed tradition which allow for Jesus Christ to be the ground and cause of election rather than just merely being the mediator of election, see Crisp, "Election of Jesus Christ," 34–55.

> Himself in covenant with us and who is not gracious towards us
> .... [O]ur own election is truly revealed to us in the election of
> the man Jesus ... in Him we have to do not merely with elected
> man, but with the electing God ...²⁵

As seen from the above quote, the upshot of Jesus Christ being the electing God for Barth comes down to a matter of the assurance of our own election. Unfortunately, this was an assurance that, in Barth's view, neither the *decretum absolutum* nor the tradition could provide. In all, if it is said—as McCormack affirms—that "the greatest contribution of Karl Barth to the development of church doctrine ... [is] in his doctrine of election,"²⁶ then I contend that it is precisely in this notion of *Jesus Christ being the electing God* that the central weight of Barth's contribution is to be found.

Jesus Christ as Elected Man

Jesus Christ as the subject of election—the electing God—is however only half the equation for Barth. The other half of Jesus Christ as the object of election—the elected man—is just as important, although Barth rightly gives logical precedence to the first half of the equation.²⁷ That said, the cruciality of Jesus Christ as elected man is nowhere attenuated:

> [W]e must now formulate the second statement with rather more precision. It tells us that before all created reality ... in the pre-temporal eternity of God, the eternal divine decision as such has as its object and content the existence of this one created being, the man Jesus of Nazareth, and the work of this man in His life and death, His humiliation and exaltation, His obedience and merit.... [T]his man is the object of the eternal divine decision and foreordination. Jesus Christ, then, is not merely one of the elect but *the* elect of God.²⁸

The above quote is significant on two counts. First, once again, Barth distinguishes himself from the tradition. The tradition undoubtedly promulgated Jesus Christ as the object of election, but it did so by way of affirming that Christ in his humanity was *one* of the elect or—at best—the *first* of the

---

25. *CD* II/2, 108 (added emphasis).

26. McCormack, "Grace and Being," 92.

27. Barth states in *CD* II/2, 116: "[T]he second assertion [i.e., Jesus as elected man] rests on the first [i.e., Jesus as electing God], and for the sake of the second the first ought never to be denied or passed over."

28. *CD* II/2, 116.

elect.²⁹ As long as the *decretum absolutum* holds sway, the primary object of election will always be the certain finite number of humanity that the triune God has decreed to save out of his good pleasure and unquestionable will.³⁰ This is not the case with Barth. As the above quote reveals, Barth perceives the *sole* object of election to be the man Jesus Christ. Humanity if they are seen as the elect are only so because they are derivatively elected "in" and "through" him. In this way, the idea of a *decretum absolutum* is crowded out and replaced by the name of Jesus Christ.³¹ Coupled with the earlier statement of Jesus Christ as the electing God, election in Barth's hands comes to be, as Webster pronounces, a term that refers "not to a decision of God in which the human race is divided into the elect and the reprobate, but to God's self-election and God's election of humanity, both actual in Jesus Christ."³²

The second point of significance is that the truth of Jesus Christ as the elected man already contains within it the actuality of the atonement. That Jesus Christ is the elected man in the self-electing determination of God means that, as mentioned in the quote above, Jesus' life and death, his humiliation and exaltation, his obedience and merit are all factored within the divine self-determination God undertakes in election.³³ As the elected man, Barth states: "Jesus was foreordained to suffer and to die."³⁴ The sum of the matter is that "[t]he election of the man Jesus means, then, that a wrath is kindled, a sentence pronounced and finally executed, a rejection actualised."³⁵

---

29. *CD* II/2, 107, 110, and 116.

30. The above holds true regardless whether one espouses what is loosely termed a "limited atonement" or "unlimited atonement" position. In any case, because salvation in the final call is only effectual for those elected "in" and "through" Christ, the primary object of election would still be the finite group of human individuals destined for salvation. For a succinct iteration of the "unlimited atonement" position and how it pertains to the doctrine of election, see Crisp, "Election of Jesus Christ," 44–45.

31. *CD* II/2, 103. Grebe, *Election, Atonement and Holy Spirit*, 28, states it as such: "The sentence 'Jesus Christ is the electing God' displaces and replaces the idea of a *decretum absolutum* and is substituted by Jesus, the *decretum concretum*."

32. Webster, *Barth*, 91.

33. Barth is very careful at this point. Despite mentioning and affirming the obedience and merit of Christ Jesus, Barth does not allow that obedience and merit to precede the man Jesus' election to divine sonship (*CD* II/2, 118). Instead, as stressed earlier in chapter 3, the entire act of election is one carried out in unnecessitated grace, captured in the truth of Jesus Christ as the electing God (*CD* II/2, 121–22).

34. *CD* II/2, 122.

35. *CD* II/2, 122.

Jesus Christ as the Elected One and the Reprobate One

The notion of atonement as founded within Barth's doctrine of election is further sharpened when we consider the corollary statement: Jesus Christ is the elected and reprobate one. Doing what he customarily does best, Barth takes the established concept of double predestination found within Reformed Theology—especially that belonging to a Calvinistic trajectory—modifies it, and relates it to God's own being.[36] Notwithstanding the surprise already present in his revisionist move of positing Jesus Christ as electing God and elected man, Barth further astounds with his treatment of double predestination. "[W]e may say already that in the election of Jesus Christ which is the eternal will of God," Barth states, "God has ascribed to man the former, election, salvation and life; and to Himself He has ascribed the latter, reprobation, perdition and death."[37] In other words, stated simply: "God wills to lose in order that man may gain."[38]

The rationale for this peculiar reversal is more readily grasped when two other factors are considered. First, Barth sees that it is fallen man that God has elected to be with in Christ Jesus. He states:

> [T]he man with whom the eternal will of God has to do is . . . this man, not good as God created him, but fallen away from God. In fact, then, the risk taken by God was far greater. His partner in this covenant is not man on the brink of danger but man already overtaken by it; man for whom the impossible has become possible, and the unreal real, and the fulfilment of evil an actual occurrence. . . . It is the lost son of man who is partner of the electing God in this covenant.[39]

Second, flowing from the first point, God being who He is—just in his mercy—means that God wills to "treat evil seriously, to judge it and to sentence it, to reject and to condemn its author, delivering him over to death."[40] Yet, because God is also merciful in his justice, God "took the author of evil to His bosom, and willed that the rejection and condemnation

---

36. Gockel, *Barth and Schleiermacher*, 161.

37. *CD* II/2, 163.

38. *CD* II/2, 162.

39. *CD* II/2, 164. This is not an insignificant point to be hurried over. It is essentially on this basis of Jesus Christ electing himself to be *fallen* man that the bold thesis of Tseng, *Karl Barth's Infralapsarian Theology*, is advanced. Going against the consensus, Tseng argues that Karl Barth should be thought of as being "basically infralapsarian," since the object of double predestination is *homo lapsus*, in contrast to the basic supralapsarian position which states the object of double predestination is unfallen (30).

40. *CD* II/2, 167.

and death should be His own."[41] In God's eternal purpose, it is God himself who elects his own rejection and suffering in his Son. As a result, Barth affirms that "[r]ejection cannot again become the portion or affair of man."[42] Inhering within the concept of double predestination is the act of atonement, as captured in the following quote from Barth: "Predestination means that from all eternity God has determined upon man's acquittal at His own cost. It means that God has ordained that in the place of the one acquitted He Himself should be perishing and abandoned and rejected—the Lamb slain from the foundation of the world."[43]

To recapitulate: the doctrine of election is that which grounds the unique vantage point espoused by Barth when it comes to thinking about the atonement. That is, via his doctrine of election, Barth sees the atonement as an event in the time and space of God's eternal being. Given that election is for Barth an act of self-determination of God's eternal being to be the God who is for us fallen humankind, the self-determining election of Jesus Christ already contains the actuality of the atonement.[44]

The "Pattern of Exchange" Present in Barth's Doctrine of Election Expressed in the Atonement

The second point follows from the first and in fact deepens it by specifying the underlying pattern that lies at the heart of Barth's doctrine of election. Travis McMaken has termed it the "pattern of exchange," stating that "Christ is elected for the purpose of undergoing our rejection so that we

41. *CD* II/2, 167.
42. *CD* II/2, 167.
43. *CD* II/2, 167.
44. Grebe (*Election, Atonement and Holy Spirit*, 250) agrees with Barth's positing of Christ as both electing God and elected man, but differs in relation to Jesus Christ being the reprobate one. Grebe arrives at his position via his theological exegesis of Lev 16 over against Barth's exegesis of the same passage (94–99). This leads Grebe to prefer a cultic framework advocating participation to a forensic one promoting imputation. On his view, Jesus does not bear sin and is not substitutionally judged for it. Instead, by going to the cross, Jesus takes humanity's sinful existence with him into his death, but through the resurrection brings humanity into contact with God (253). Grebe may be right in spotting inconsistencies with Barth's theological exegesis of Lev 16. But I maintain that Barth's positing of Jesus Christ as the reprobate one arises as a natural corollary following from Jesus Christ as the electing God and, in particular, the elected man. Barth's positing of Jesus Christ as the reprobate one circumvents the risk of presenting sin as divorced from the sinner and dealt with on the cross separate and "external" of the person involved in the sin. Conversely, it reinforces the idea that Jesus as the elected man identifies not just with the sin, but more importantly with the sinner (while not committing any sin himself).

might be elected in him; that is, Christ bears our rejection, and we receive the benefits of his election."[45] This pattern of exchange is that which, on the one hand, occasions the actuality of the atonement to be instated in Barth's doctrine of election in the first place and, on the other hand, undergirds subsequent formulations of Barth's atonement doctrine that ensues as he ventures into later volumes of the *Dogmatics*. In other words, this pattern of exchange that obtains in the eternal divine life through the divine election is manifested in the context of creaturely time and space expressed as Barth's doctrine of the atonement.

In appropriating the pattern of exchange, McMaken—taking his lead from Hans Frei's initial usage of the term—has formulated his understanding primarily within a cultic setting, especially the cultic rituals of ancient Israel where there is "the mysterious exchange of guilt with self-sacrificing purity."[46] Based on this, McMaken observes that despite being a fundamentally cultic concept, the pattern of exchange is presented predominantly under judicial categories in Barth's doctrine of the atonement.[47]

Even though McMaken makes a valid move in seeking recourse in a cultic setting for the origin of the pattern of exchange, I question whether this needs to be the case. In my mind, the origin of the pattern of exchange transcends any contextual settings that could be thought of—judicial, cultic, marketplace, battlefield—and instead is to be found inherently and intrinsically in the notion that God is *pro nobis*. The notion of the God who is "for us" by itself already calls for some form of substitution and exchange, given that the "us" is sinful humanity who has broken the covenant. On this reading, the pattern of exchange governs the various contextual settings that frame the doctrine of the atonement; it is just that Barth particularly chooses the judicial (for good reasons which I will come to in a moment).

More germane to our discussion is the way this substitutionary pattern of exchange is expressed in subsequent articulations of Barth's doctrine of the atonement. Ensuing from the fundamental axiom of Jesus Christ being the electing God and the elected man, the pattern of exchange extends to Barth's other Christological descriptions. For example, the pattern of exchange underlies the Christological headings Barth gives to *CD* IV/1 "the Lord as Servant" and *CD* IV/2 "the Servant as Lord." More specifically, it underlies the central notion holding both volumes together: Jesus is the Son of God who goes out into the "Far Country" in order that Jesus as the Son of Man

---

45. McMaken, "Election and the Pattern of Exchange," 209.

46. McMaken, "Election and the Pattern of Exchange," 203. The quote is from Frei, *Identity of Jesus Christ*, 74.

47. McMaken, "Election and the Pattern of Exchange," 214.

can return in "homecoming."[48] This pattern of exchange, of course, finds its climactic expression in the famed heading Barth gave to his specific elaboration of the doctrine of the atonement: "The Judge Judged in Our Place."

In advocating this "pattern of exchange," however, McMaken issues a precaution. While election and the pattern of exchange are intricately tied to one another in what McMaken terms "a relationship of unity-in-distinction,"[49] there is an ordering principle in this relationship that results in an asymmetry in favor of election. This means that it is election that lends the pattern of exchange its efficacy; it is only because God has elected to be *Deus pro nobis* that the pattern of exchange actualizes.[50] So, even as it is proper to uphold the pattern of exchange as a critical element in Barth's doctrine of the atonement, McMaken reminds us that the pattern must not be isolated as an independent principle abstracted from the God who elects, for it is in election that the exchange is rendered efficacious in the first place.

"The Judge Judged in Our Place": The Judicial/Forensic Pattern of Exchange in Barth's Doctrine of the Atonement in CD IV/1

Barth's Choice of the Judicial Framework

The pattern of exchange obtaining in eternity in the divine being of God via his self-determining act of election is unmistakably expressed in terms of a judicial framework when it comes to Barth's culminating treatment of atonement in *CD* IV/1. Before delving into a deeper exploration, it is appropriate to first address the question: "Why did Barth choose a judicial framework?"

Barth's choice of a judicial framework is, from the outset, neither arbitrary nor accidental. Rather, as McCormack has argued, the judicial or forensic imagery presents itself as a natural choice flowing from Barth's

---

48. Allen, *Karl Barth's Church Dogmatics*, 75n5, mentions that the "Christological metaphysics" involved in Barth's doctrine of election (Jesus Christ is electing God and elected man) translates to the statement that Jesus is Lord and Servant simultaneously in *CD* IV/1–3. Bloesch, *Jesus Is Victor!*, 50, also refers to this "exchange" present whereby "God condescends to man while man is taken up in the unity of the life of Jesus Christ." What is interesting—as I highlighted in chapter 3—is Barth's conscious reversal of the objects of predication of the two states: it is the Son of God who is humiliated and the Son of Man who is exalted. The pattern of exchange is situated in that reversal.

49. McMaken, "Election and the Pattern of Exchange," 216.

50. McMaken, "Election and the Pattern of Exchange," 217.

doctrine of election.[51] McCormack contends that the work carried out by the forensic concept of "imputation" in the older Protestant theology is carried out in Barth's theology by the doctrine of election, such that when "the divine verdict is pronounced in time, it is the manifestation of a decision already made in eternity."[52] In this manner, "forensicism" becomes "the frame of reference that is basic to the whole of [Barth's] soteriology."[53] Election means Jesus Christ as the electing God taking upon himself as elected man reprobation, perdition, death, such that a certain conceptual affinity arises between the two constructions of "electing God and elected man" and "the judge judged in our place," with the latter construction flowing quite naturally from the former.[54]

Inasmuch as the above is true, I surmise that Barth's final reason for choosing the judicial framework rests on his reading of the (Synoptic) Gospels. In the early pages of his exposition of the judicial framework, Barth offers what he calls "the outline of the evangelical history . . . especially in the form in which it is presented in the synoptic Gospels."[55] Barth divides the history into three parts.

In the first part, we have a record of the sayings and acts of Jesus Christ amidst his disciples, the multitudes, and the religious and political leaders of his day. More significantly, Jesus through his proclamation and work shows himself to be their Judge.[56] In contrast to the first part, there is a surprise in the second part starting from Gethsemane where "Jesus no longer seems to be the subject but the object of what happens. His speech is almost exclusively that of silence and His work that of suffering."[57] In a brisk sequence of activities consisting of "an arrest, a hearing and prosecution in various courts, a torturing, and then an execution and burial,"[58] the theme pervades throughout the narrative that the Judge (as read from the first part) is the one who is now judged (as read in the second part), while those who are to be judged (as read again from the first part) are the ones given the leeway to judge (as read again in the second part).[59]

---

51. McCormack, "*Justitia Aliena*," 167–96.
52. McCormack, "*Justitia Aliena*," 192.
53. McCormack, "*Justitia Aliena*," 192.
54. Highlighted by McMaken, "Election and the Pattern of Exchange," 214.
55. *CD* IV/1, 224.
56. *CD* IV/1, 224–25.
57. *CD* IV/1, 226.
58. *CD* IV/1, 226.
59. *CD* IV/1, 226. Barth sees the most forceful expression of this reversal of roles in the Barabbas episode.

It is only with the third part, the Easter story, that a commentary is given and the first two parts are comprehended in their unity and completeness. By raising Jesus from the dead, God declares Jesus of Nazareth to be "the Son of God, [who] as man, took our place in order to judge us in this place by allowing Himself to be judged for us."[60] Barth clearly sees a "transference" of judgment happening: "[T]he divine subject of the judgment on man as which Jesus appears in the first part of the evangelical record becomes the object of this judgment from the time of the episode in Gethsemane onwards. If this judgment is fulfilled at all . . . then it is with this reversal."[61] Barth's reading of the Synoptic Gospels indubitably leads him to conceive the judicial framework as a felicitous choice for expressing the pattern of exchange central to the doctrine of the atonement.[62]

Barth's Exposition of the Four Points of His Judicial Framework

I turn now to Barth's doctrine of the atonement as presented within the judicial framework. In answering the question that Barth perceives as the driving force behind the doctrine of the atonement—*Cur Deus homo*—he states:

> Why did the Son of God become man, one of us, our brother, our fellow in the human situation? The answer is: In order to judge the world . . . to show His grace in the execution of His judgment . . . . *That is how God has actually judged in Jesus Christ.* And that is why He humbled Himself. That is why He went into the far country as the obedient Son of the Father.[63]

Implicit within the quote is the pattern of exchange underlying the judicial framework, which will be more explicitly revealed as Barth expounds his judicial framework under four noteworthy and non-negotiable points. These four points explain how Christ is "for us." We now turn our attention to the salient features of these four points.

---

60. *CD* IV/1, 228.

61. *CD* IV/1, 238. Barth sees the judgment Jesus proclaims and which he subsequently undergoes as an eschatological judgment. This is demonstrated by Barth's reading of Jesus' submission to the baptism of John the Baptist; a baptism that serves as "the sign of penitent expectation of the Judge and His *dies irae* (day of wrath)" (*CD* IV/1, 218).

62. For a fuller argument of how Barth's reading of the Gospel accounts leads to his doctrine of substitutionary atonement, see MacDonald, "Karl Barth's Narrative Doctrine," 91–117. MacDonald in fact maintains the view that Barth provides what he believes as "the most powerful and persuasive version of the biblical doctrine of the atonement" (92).

63. *CD* IV/1, 222 (added emphasis).

Jesus as Judge

First, Barth states: "Jesus Christ was and is 'for us' in that He took our place as our Judge."[64] Identifying the root and origin of sin as the arrogance by which we as humankind unanimously engage in the activity of being our own and each other's judge, Barth highlights that God in Christ Jesus "reseizes" and reasserts his rightful function as judge.[65] On the one hand, this means the abasement and jeopardizing of every man: I am totally displaced from the domain where I (self-) judge and am placed instead in a domain where I learn what that judgment should be.[66] On the other hand, Jesus Christ as judge carries the liberation and hope of every man, in that judgment is now out of my hands and placed into the hands of one infinitely more just than I could ever be.[67] Taken this way, the overall rubric of Barth's doctrine of the atonement "The Judge judged in our place" is decidedly appropriate. God as the judge in carrying out his act of judgment regains his rightful place to judge, taking over our wrongful place in the first instance (the word "judged" in this case would be understood in its active sense as "judging"). The fact that God is the rightful judge who judges also parallels the statement that God is the electing God.

Jesus as the Judged

Second, Barth continues: "Jesus Christ was and is for us in that He took the place of us, sinners."[68] Barth reiterates the point that in taking our place as judge, Jesus—unlike us—did not do anything illegitimate, but carried out the activity of judging as part of the divine prerogative that rightfully only belongs to him. Yet, in a strange twist, Jesus "acts as Judge in our place by taking upon himself . . . that which we do in this place," in the process not only "[giving] Himself . . . to the fellowship of those who are guilty . . . but [making] their evil case His own."[69] Barth even goes so far as to say that Jesus Christ has made our sin his very own; our sin now becomes "His sin, the sin of Jesus Christ."[70] This is certainly an inconceivable and mysterious outworking of the divine affairs, but it is precisely in this outworking that

---

64. *CD* IV/1, 231.
65. *CD* IV/1, 232.
66. *CD* IV/1, 233.
67. *CD* IV/1, 234.
68. *CD* IV/1, 235.
69. *CD* IV/1, 236.
70. *CD* IV/1, 238.

our sin ceases to be our sin. It is here at this point that the pattern of exchange is rendered most explicitly in judicial language:

> [The cessation of our sin] means that it became His way: His the sin which we commit on it; His the accusation [*Anklage*], the judgment [*Urteil*] and the curse [*Fluch*] which necessarily fall on us there. He is the unrighteous amongst those who can no longer be so because He was and is for them. He is the burdened amongst those who have been freed from their burden by Him. He is the condemned [*Verurteilte*] amongst those who are pardoned because the sentence which destroys them is directed against Him. He who is in the one person the electing God and the one elect man is as the rejecting God, the God who judges sin in the flesh, in His own person the one rejected man, the Lamb which bears the sin of the world that the world should no longer have to bear it . . . that it should be radically and totally taken away from it.[71]

Once again, the apposite and versatile titling of "The Judge judged in our place" as an encapsulation of Barth's atonement doctrine is displayed: God as the Judge in carrying out his act of judgment unexpectedly turns out to be the one who is judged in our place. In this case, the word "judged" would refer to its passive sense of "being judged." The signification of a twofold active and passive judgment happening at the same time but whose occurrence is governed by the fact that both judgments are "in our place" is ingeniously well conveyed by the title. This, in turn, is rendered possible by Barth's parallel reading of the forensic notion of judgment carried over from his doctrine of election. In the same way that Jesus is the electing God who *in his election elects for himself rejection*, Jesus is the Judge who *in his judging allows himself to be judged*. "He judged, and it was the Judge who was judged, who let Himself be judged," as Barth affirms.[72]

Jesus Judged in Our Place

Third, "Jesus Christ was and is for us in that He suffered and was crucified and died."[73] Barth here focuses on the passion of Jesus Christ. This merits our close attention because it is in the passion that we discover "the true fulfilment of what God had to do for us in Jesus Christ."[74] Barth highlights

71. *CD* IV/1, 236–37 / *KD* IV/1, 260.
72. *CD* IV/1, 222.
73. *CD* IV/1, 244.
74. *CD* IV/1, 244.

three aspects of the passion: i) even though Jesus, the subject of the Gospel story, renders himself an object, Barth reminds us that "in the passion we [still] have to do with an action [of Jesus']," for that self-surrender happens out of his freedom and his volition;[75] ii) in the passion, "we are dealing with an act which took place on earth, in time and space, and which is indissolubly linked with the name of a certain man."[76] It is an act whose definitive nature in world history cannot be exchanged for any other. And iii) the passion is still to be understood as the action and, therefore, the passion of God Himself.[77] The last point is not to be skimmed over. For Barth, the mystery of the passion is located in the fact that it is the eternal God who gives himself in his Son to be man, and as man to take upon himself this human passion and suffering. As such, God does not merely preside over the occurrence of the passion "at a distance," but draws close by giving himself to be the human person acting and suffering in the passion.

Two other aspects pertinent to the argument I am making mark Barth's discussion of this third point and warrant a discussion.

The Aufgehoben of Sin and the Sinner as the Center of the Atonement

The first is that Barth spells out clearly what he sees lying at the center of the atonement:

> The very heart of the atonement is the overcoming [*Beseitigung*] of sin: sin in its character as the rebellion of man against God . . . . It was to fulfil this judgment on sin that the Son of God as man took our place as sinners. He fulfils it—as man in our place—by completing our work in the omnipotence of the divine Son, by treading the way of sinners to its bitter end in death, in destruction, in the limitless anguish of separation from God, by delivering up sinful man and sin in His own person to the nonbeing which is properly theirs, the nonbeing, the nothingness to which man has fallen victim as a sinner and towards which he relentlessly hastens.[78]

"Sin" (*Sünde*) and the way of sin to "its bitter end" resulting in "death" (*Tod*); "destruction" (*Verderben*); "separation from God" (*Gottesferne*);

---

75. *CD* IV/1, 244–45 (quote is from p. 244).

76. *CD* IV/1, 245.

77. *CD* IV/1, 245.

78. *CD* IV/1, 253 / *KD* IV/1, 278. Lauber, *Barth on the Descent*, 33, interprets the mention of Christ "treading the way of sinners to its bitter end" as an implicit reference to Christ's descent into hell.

"non-being" (*Nichtsein*); "nothingness" (*Nichtigkeit*), and especially associated with the last two terms, *das Nichtige*—God confronts and deals with all of these in the person of Jesus Christ on the cross.[79] Again, in a neighboring passage, Barth asserts plainly what God is confronted with on the cross:

> We are not dealing merely with any suffering, but with the suffering of God and this man in face of the destruction which threatens all creation and every individual . . . . We are dealing with the painful confrontation of God and this man not merely with any evil, not merely with death [*Sterben*], but with eternal death [*ewigen Tode*], with the power of that which is not [*der Gewalt des Nichtigen*]. Therefore we are not dealing merely with any sin, or with many sins . . . . We are dealing with sin itself and as such [*die Sünde selbst und als solche*]: the preoccupation, the orientation, the determination of man as he has left his place as a creature and broken his covenant with God; the corruption which God has made His own, for which He willed to take responsibility in this one man. Here in the passion in which as Judge He lets Himself be judged God has fulfilled this responsibility. In the place of all men He has Himself wrestled with that which separates them from Him. He has Himself borne the consequence of this separation to bear it away.[80]

From the above quotes, one is warranted to deduce that the actuality of the cross for Barth consists in this removal and abolishment (*aufgehoben*) of both the sin and the sinner in Christ's own person.[81] In this pattern of exchange where the Judge allows himself to be judged in our place, we find the concentration of the entirety of human wrong-doing in a single person, but there in that one moment and one person, we find also the annihilation of sin, the sinner and *das Nichtige*, and consequently, the natal instantiation of the new man reconciled and at peace with God.[82]

---

79. *CD* III/3, 305: "The true nothingness is that which brought Jesus Christ to the cross, and that which He defeated there."

80. *CD* IV/1, 247 / *KD* IV/1, 272.

81. *CD* IV/1, 253 / *KD* IV/1, 279.

82. Jones, *Humanity of Christ*, 222–23, states it compellingly when he contends that on the cross, "God [wills] that *das Nichtige* and sin be drawn into God's own life . . . . God hereby turns its [i.e., *das Nichtige*] chaotic menace upon Godself, concentrating it in the time and space of God's being, where it simply *cannot* be" (emphasis original).

Did Barth Hold onto Penal Substitutionary Atonement?

The second pertinent aspect concerning Barth's doctrine of the atonement that I wish to explore deeper takes its bearing from the first. That is, it is only in subservience to the presiding concept of the *aufgehoben* of sin and the sinner on the cross that the language and terminology of "punishment" or the related notion of "satisfaction" find their place in Barth's atonement theology. Since we are at this particular juncture, it is appropriate to address the question as to whether Barth's doctrine of the atonement could be counted as penal substitutionary atonement, and through the discussion, identify the role of "punishment" and "satisfaction" in Barth's account.

Opinions divide as to whether Barth's doctrine of the atonement can be properly classified as belonging to the family of penal substitutionary atonement.[83] In his essay on Barth's doctrine of the atonement, Garry Williams surveys the landscape, and notes that opinion ranges from non-espousal, to endorsement, to venturing beyond penal substitutionary atonement, and even to "retrieval" or "rescue" of the doctrine. Williams himself settles for the view that Barth has altered penal substitution beyond recognition.[84]

In many respects, one can understand the diversity of opinion over this matter. On the one hand, Barth employs terminology characteristic of *penal* substitutionary atonement. As seen, terms such as "judgment" (*Urteil*; *Gericht*), "accusation" (*Anklage*), "condemnation" (*Verurteilung*), and "punishment" (*Strafe*) are prevalent in his exposition.[85] Barth's free usage of such penal language warrants the observation that he sees punishment as necessary. Earlier in *CD* II/1 where Barth considers the divine perfection of God's righteousness (and its associated pairing, God's mercy), he speaks approvingly of Anselm's basic insight that if *iniustitia* (injustice) remained unpunished and God simply forgave sins *sola misericordia* (by sheer mercy alone), then *iniustitia* would in a way harbor "the character of a second Godhead in the face of God."[86] A little further on, Barth affirms the notion of *iustitia distributiva* (distributive justice), stating that because it is a real righteousness of God revealed in Christ Jesus, it will be a righteousness that condemns and punishes while not ceasing to be merciful.[87] Throughout his

---

83. See Vanhoozer, "Atonement," 196–99, for a succinct summary of the background of the debates in relation to penal substitutionary atonement. For a fairly recent defense of penal substitutionary atonement, see Jeffery, Ovey, and Sach, *Pierced for Our Transgressions*.

84. Williams, "Karl Barth and Atonement," 256–57.

85. An example passage where such terminology abounds would be *CD* IV/1, 223.

86. *CD* II/1, 380.

87. *CD* II/1, 391–92.

treatment, Barth distinguishes but refuses to separate the two divine perfections of mercy and righteousness, emphasizing that "the condemning and punishing righteousness of God is in itself and as such the depth and power and might of His mercy."[88]

Moreover, alongside his affirmation of penal language, Barth equally emphasizes the other major component of a penal substitutionary atonement, that is, its *substitutionary* context. This, Barth reminds us, is a punishment, an *iustitia distributiva* given out and borne and suffered by "no other than *God's own Son*, and therefore *the eternal God Himself* in the unity with human nature which He freely accepted in His transcendent mercy."[89] Barth states: "The wrath [*Zorn*] of God which we had merited . . . was now in our place borne and suffered as though it had smitten us and yet in such a way that it did not smite us and can no more smite us."[90] Barth is adamant that the concept of substitution is at play here: "Our position is such that we can be rescued from eternal death and translated into life only by total and unceasing substitution [*Stellvertretung*], the substitution which God Himself undertakes on our behalf."[91]

In fact, Barth further underscores the point that it is only because it is fully God and fully man acting in Jesus Christ that this substitution is possible and efficacious in the first place. It is because Jesus Christ is fully man that he could, as Barth states, "take our place with . . . effectiveness," possessing "the freedom and power to be in His humanity . . . the Head [*Haupt*] and Representative [*Vertreter*] of us all."[92] Taking our place in this case means that God in the man Christ Jesus—even though he knew no sin—becomes the "object of His own anger (*Zorn*), the victim of His own condemnation (*Verurteilung*) and punishment (*Strafe*)."[93]

Stated plainly: on the cross, God enters his own wrath. Yet, equally important is the fact that because Jesus Christ is fully God he could effectively take our place as our substitute without being annihilated in the process.[94]

---

88. *CD* II/1, 393.

89. *CD* II/1, 397 (added emphasis).

90. *CD* II/1, 397 / *KD* II/1, 446. See also *CD* II/1, 398 for a further underscoring of the "in our place" language.

91. *CD* II/1, 399 / *KD* II/1, 449. There is discussion as to whether the German word "*Stellvertretung*" should be translated into English as "substitution" or "representation." I agree with Bromiley's decision to translate "*Stellvertretung*" as "substitution" (*CD* IV/1, vii–viii).

92. *CD* II/1, 403 / *KD* II/1, 454.

93. *CD* II/1, 398 / *KD* II/1, 447.

94. Barth states: "There could happen there [what took place on the cross] . . . that which could not have happened to us without causing our annihilation" (*CD* II/1, 399).

As Barth asserts, being God, Jesus Christ could subject himself to the severity of God without succumbing to it.

More importantly, it is this fact that God is fully present and acts in the substitution of Christ Jesus that safeguards Barth's understanding of penal substitution from falling into the same errors that more crude and superficial renderings of penal substitutionary atonement have been susceptible to. Barth writes:

> [W]e do not have here . . . a raging indignation of God, which is ridiculous or irritating in its senselessness, against an innocent man whose patient suffering changes the temper of God, inducing in Him an indulgent sparing of all other men, so that all other men can rather shamefacedly take refuge behind his suffering, happily saved but quite unchanged in themselves. We do not have here an abstract justice of God which is later changed into an equally abstract compassion and indulgence. On the contrary, it is the actual and terrible wrath of God which rules according to God's free good-pleasure in the fulfilment of what is from the first His merciful righteousness, and it does not need any change of mood or weakening, but in its strictest fulfilment it is the self-expression of the eternal unchangeably good will of God.[95]

Clearly, the acuity of Barth's treatment of penal substitutionary atonement located under his consideration of the divine perfections of mercy and righteousness is seen in the above quote. God's divine righteousness is his divine mercy and vice versa, and both are equally functions of his divine loving.[96]

Based on the above considerations, one could be excused for concluding that Barth espouses wholesale a version of penal substitutionary atonement in its quintessential expression. Yet, to hold Barth down to such a conclusion would be premature. Despite resonating with both penal language and the substitutionary motif, Barth does exhibit some striking differences that set him in contradistinction to the classical doctrine. Three key differences come to mind.

First, as stated above, Barth does use penal language in his discussion of the atonement, but is intransigent about not giving center stage or pride

---

95. *CD* II/1, 402. For a defense of a "classical" version of penal substitutionary atonement against similar misrepresentations of penal substitution, see Jeffery, Ovey, and Sach, *Pierced For Our Transgressions*, 228–33; 279–85.

96. See *CD* II/1, 376 for an affirmation of this point.

of place to the concept of punishment in the manner often done under classical expressions of penal substitutionary atonement.[97] He asserts:

> [W]e must not make this [i.e., punishment] a main concept as in some of the older presentations of the doctrine of the atonement (especially those which follow Anselm of Canterbury), either in the sense that by His suffering our punishment we are spared from suffering it ourselves, or that in so doing He "satisfied" or offered satisfaction to the wrath of God. The latter thought is quite foreign to the New Testament.[98]

In Barth's thought, the punishment of sin is clearly subordinated to the more dominant concept of the *aufgehoben* and annihilation of sin and the sinner in Christ's own person.

The second and third differences have been alluded to in the above quote. Undoubtedly, running through Barth's specification of atonement under the judicial framework is the irrefutable notion of substitution, but this substitution should not be conceived in a manner so as to say that since Jesus Christ has suffered the punishment humanity deserves, humanity is consequently spared from suffering it. As a result, humanity remains totally divorced and external from all that happens in Christ, simply "[taking] refuge behind his suffering, happily saved but quite unchanged in themselves," as Barth states of this erroneous understanding of substitution.[99] Lauber calls such a view "a strong version of substitution."[100]

Rather, incorporated in the version of substitution Barth has in mind is the idea of participation, wherein humanity as a whole somehow or other "participates" in the death of Christ, even as it is Christ alone who stands in our place as the judged one. Nowhere in *CD* II/1 or *CD* IV/1 does Barth state that the judgment, condemnation, punishment and suffering that fell upon the Lord Jesus falls also on us. In this sense, Barth preserves the truth that Jesus Christ's suffering is unique and that he alone endures the judgment of God. Here, one sees the *substitutionary* aspect at work. But in the one unique passion and death of our Lord, humanity finds their sin and their status as sinners *aufgehoben*, and finds their ontological status transformed from sinners to saints. Here, one finds the *participatory* element at work.

---

97 For example, Jeffery, Ovey, and Sach, *Pierced for Our Transgressions*, 21, opens with an unambiguous definition: "The doctrine of penal substitution states that God gave himself in the person of his Son to suffer instead of us the death, punishment and curse due to fallen humanity as the penalty for sin."

98. *CD* IV/1, 253.

99. *CD* II/1, 402.

100. Lauber, *Barth on the Descent*, 34.

As a reminder, this is an *aufgehoben* and transformation pre-determined in eternity in the electing of Jesus Christ to be *elected man*, but actualized in the one event of Good Friday and Easter Sunday. That Barth's atonement theology comprises both the substitutionary and participatory strands is borne out in the following quote:

> The decisive thing is not that He has suffered what we ought to have suffered so that we do not have to suffer it, the destruction . . . and therefore the punishment which we deserve. . . . This is true, of course. But it is true only as it derives from the decisive thing that in the suffering and death of Jesus Christ it has come to pass that in His own person He has made an end of us as sinners and therefore of sin itself by going to death as the One who took our place as sinners.[101]

Once again, this is a "participation" not based on our initiative, but premised upon *Jesus Christ's first election of himself* to participate fully not just in our sin but also in our status as sinners while remaining throughout the Son of God who had no sin (2 Cor 5:21). This harks back to the earlier idea that it is fallen man that God has elected to be with in Christ Jesus, and explains, as seen in chapter 4, Barth's insistence that it is fallen human nature that the Son of God assumed in the incarnation.

Third and perhaps the most outstanding difference of all, Barth is very careful to say that any satisfaction made through the atonement is certainly not satisfaction made to the wrath of God, nor even to the righteousness of God, but if anything, it is satisfaction to the love of God. The crucial passage again:

> [T]he worst had to happen to sinful man: not out of any desire for vengeance and retribution on the part of God, but because of the radical nature of the divine love, which could "satisfy" itself only in the outworking of its wrath against the man of sin, only by killing him, extinguishing him, removing him. Here is the place for the doubtful concept that in the passion of Jesus Christ, in the giving up of His Son to death, God has done that

---

101. *CD* IV/1, 253. Recall the central contention of Grebe, *Election, Atonement and Holy Spirit*. A significant reason for Grebe's preference of a cultic framework over a judicial framework (250) is because, in his opinion, the former allows for the notion of participation while the latter does not. This, as hopefully demonstrated above, is premised on a false dichotomy between substitution and participation when there is none in Barth's presentation of the judicial framework. As Bromiley insightfully observes, Barth's use of *Stellvertretung* "enshrines the notions both of representation and substitution, and never the one without the other" (*CD* IV/1, vii).

which is "satisfactory" or sufficient in the victorious fighting of sin to make this victory radical and total.[102]

It is this decisive move of Barth in ordering satisfaction to the love of God rather than to the wrath or righteousness of God that led McCormack to attribute to Barth the prestigious status of being the first one to "overcome the deficiencies in the satisfaction theory as traditionally set forth in Reformed theology and to give it a more solid foundation."[103] To be sure, McCormack contends that Barth's finest contribution only came to its full light in his mature conception of the atonement evinced in *CD* IV/1, for Barth in *CD* II/1 still mistakenly considered the death of Christ to be a satisfaction of the divine righteousness. This is despite his overall commendable move of dialectically pairing divine righteousness with divine mercy and classifying both under the heading of the perfection of the divine loving.[104]

The problem with conceiving satisfaction as offered to the divine righteousness is, as McCormack elaborates, the love of God inevitably "drops from view at the decisive point" and fails to show itself as "operative at every step along the way in the accomplishment of our redemption."[105] Worse: it risks introducing a fissure in the being of God between his mercy and his righteousness. The impression is inevitably drawn that God's mercy is non-operative until his righteousness has first been fully satisfied. Conversely, God's righteousness is seemingly portrayed as possessing an independent status requiring its own act of satisfaction apart from and prior to the outworking of divine mercy.

But where satisfaction is offered to the divine love, the picture changes. It is no longer divine hostility to sin that is satisfied, for God does not require retribution for sin for the sake of himself and his own justice. As Barth himself affirms: "[T]he worst had to happen to sinful man [but] *not out of any desire for vengeance and retribution* on the part of God."[106] Rather, it is divine love that is satisfied from beginning to end as God does all that is needed to bring human sin to an absolute end. Under this viewpoint, the

---

102. *CD* IV/1, 254.

103. McCormack, "For Us and Our Salvation," 303.

104. McCormack, "For Us and Our Salvation," 305–6. See *CD* II/1, 396 and 400 where Barth still views satisfaction as offered to the righteousness of God.

105. McCormack, "For Us and Our Salvation," 302.

106. *CD* IV/1, 254 (added emphasis). Barth argues, in *CD* IV/1, 486–87, that God does not need retribution to take place as a separate act that satisfies his righteousness before he can forgive. Here, he departs from Anselm who maintained that there must be a prior satisfaction for the hurt done to the divine glory before divine forgiveness could take place. On this basis, Anselm deduced the necessity of the incarnation of God. It is this very basis that Barth questions.

wrath of God is seen in its proper place. It does not possess its own independent existence, but is present only as the means to the end of accomplishing God's love, even if it is a *necessary* means in virtue of the *holy* love of God. The wrath of God is, as Barth puts it memorably, "the fire of His love."[107] More importantly, the entire act and language of satisfaction is grounded in the context of God's holy *love*. God has done all that is needed in satisfying the full demands of his love (in the annihilation of sin) and fulfilling the full measure of that love (in the loving restoration of *Gemeinschaft* with what were once his sinful human creatures).[108]

On account of the three key differences, is it still valid to say that Barth held onto penal substitutionary atonement? It is my view that he does. After all, the judicial framework "The Judge judged in our place" chosen by Barth provides a natural home for penal substitutionary atonement, and Barth does include the core elements of "penal" and "substitution" in his account. Nevertheless, Barth's "yes" to penal substitutionary atonement has to be qualified by his heavily nuanced appropriation of the terms "punishment" and "satisfaction" that distinctly set him apart from more classical formulations of the doctrine.[109] I concur with Johnson's conclusion: "Barth's doctrine of reconciliation includes within it all that penal substitution affirms, while offering [a] larger and more encompassing account of Christ's substitutionary work."[110]

Going further, I suggest that Barth's particular narration of penal substitutionary atonement retrieves much of the good intended by the theory, and in this way serves as a profitable contemporary restatement of the doctrine, given that penal substitutionary atonement today as a whole has fallen on hard times. It is, however, beyond the scope of this present work to prove and demonstrate this intuition.

Jesus Acted Justly in Our Place

I turn now to the fourth and final point in Barth's exposition of his judicial framework: "Jesus Christ was and is for us in that He has done this before God and has therefore done [it] right."[111] That is to say, in carrying out this

---

107. *CD* IV/1, 94.

108. McCormack, "For Us and Our Salvation," 307.

109. Lauber, *Barth on the Descent*, 35, arrives at a similar conclusion: "We may conclude that if one wants to view Barth's interpretation of the passion of Jesus Christ as a form of 'penal substitution', then one must account for his specific use of the term 'punishment.'"

110. Johnson, *God's Being in Reconciliation*, 95n7.

111. *CD* IV/1, 256.

action, "Jesus Christ was amongst us and lived and acted for us as the just or righteous man: 'the just for the unjust' (1 Pet. 3:18)."[112] In this section, Barth expounds the obedience of Christ Jesus and shows how the obedience serves as the establishment of Jesus' righteousness, seen in Jesus taking the judgment upon himself in the judging of the Judge.[113] As mentioned in chapter 4, this obedience serves at the same time as the definitive attestation of the sinlessness of Jesus, an obedience enacted amidst the presence of great and genuine temptations facing Jesus.[114] Barth brings this final point to a climax with an in-depth exploration of what he deemed to be the ultimate temptation facing Jesus: the event of the Garden of Gethsemane.[115] For reasons that will be clarified later, I reserve Barth's treatment of this crucial milestone in Jesus' journey of obedience to the next chapter.

"Theories" of the Atonement vs. the "Sache" of the Atonement: Barth's Openness to Other Approaches to the Doctrine of the Atonement[116]

With the four main points of his judicial framework covered, Barth concludes his exposition with a closing comment:

> We are now at the end of the important section dealing with the general question . . . asked by Anselm: *Cur Deus homo?* and with the particular question what Jesus Christ was and did *pro nobis*, for us and for the world. To this question we have given four related answers. He took our place as Judge. He took our place as the judged. He was judged in our place. And He acted justly in our place. It is important to see that we cannot add anything to this . . . . All theology, both that which follows and indeed that which precedes the doctrine of reconciliation, depends upon this *theologia crucis*. And it depends upon it under the particular aspect under which we have had to develop it in this first part of the doctrine of reconciliation as *the doctrine of substitution*. Everything depends upon . . . *this fourfold "for us"* . . . . For that reason this is the place for a full-stop. Many further

---

112. *CD* IV/1, 257.
113. *CD* IV/1, 258.
114. *CD* IV/1, 258.
115. *CD* IV/1, 259–73.
116. The following section first appeared in Fong, "'The One and the Many,'" 142–45. The portion of the article is used by permission of The Pennsylvania State University Press.

statements may follow, but the stop indicates that this first statement is complete in itself, that it comprehends all that follows, and that it can stand alone.[117]

With such a rousing comment affirming the adequacy of the judicial framework in covering the doctrine of the atonement, one is somewhat bemused to find in the immediately following pages a reiteration of the doctrine, but this time couched within a cultic framework. Barth speaks of Jesus Christ as i) the priest who represented us ii) the one who gave himself up to be offered as a sacrifice to take away our sins, and iii) the one who in doing so offered a perfect sacrifice.[118] Worthy as the task is, a more detailed exposition of Barth's cultic framework would take us beyond the scope of this current work.[119]

I draw attention instead to the point that, taken together, Barth's closing comment and his reiteration of the doctrine of atonement under a cultic framework reveals a penetrating insight not to be missed. That is, rather than locating the crux of the atonement in the judicial framework or metaphor, Barth situates the non-negotiable core of the doctrine in the substitutionary reality operating behind the judicial framework. This operating reality is, as stated in Barth's own words, the "doctrine of substitution (*Stellvertretung*)" or the "fourfold 'for us' [*vierfachen 'Für uns'*]."[120]

It would thus not be incorrect to say that, for Barth, the emphasis is found not so much in the particular framework adopted to present the doctrine of the atonement as it is in the greater reality and actuality happening behind the chosen framework, and to which the framework points. The immediate observation gains confirmation in Barth's earlier *Dogmatics in Outline*. In his discussion of the passion of the Christ, Barth states: "Let me add that no doctrine of this central mystery can exhaustively and precisely grasp and express the extent to which God has intervened for us here. Do not confuse my theory [*Theorie*] of the reconciliation with the thing itself [*der Sache selber*]. All theories of reconciliation can be but pointers."[121]

That said, the above statements should not be taken to imply that Barth's choice of the judicial framework is arbitrary. As seen, Barth had good reasons for preferring the judicial framework.[122] Notwithstanding these good reasons, the central thesis remains that Barth would not have

---

117. *CD* IV/1, 273 (added emphasis).
118. *CD* IV/1, 274–83.
119. I refer interested readers to Drury, "The Priest Sacrificed in Our Place."
120. *CD* IV/1, 273 / *KD* IV/1, 300.
121. *DO*, 116 / *DG*, 137.
122. *CD* IV/1, 275.

occluded the possibility of other frameworks or *Theorien* of reconciliation—be they drawn from the financial, military or cultic—expressing the *Sache* or the subject matter lying at the core of the doctrine of the atonement, namely, the fourfold substitutionary "pattern of exchange."[123]

A deeper probe behind the "pattern of exchange" lends credence to the claim that for Barth it comes down ultimately to the fact that God is *pro nobis*. Barth himself indicated that the standpoints and terminologies adopted serve "our systematic reflection on the *pro nobis*."[124] In this way, Barth indicates that the *Deus pro nobis* is the very *Sache* he has in mind when it comes to the doctrine of the atonement. As Johnson affirms:

> Barth's argument . . . is not that the work of Christ is unified because it is substitutionary, but rather that it is unified because God is the one present in Christ making this substitutionary work effective . . . . This explains why Barth begins his doctrine of reconciliation with an account of "God with us" (*CD* IV/1, 3), and only explicitly formulates a doctrine of substitution as such in what nearly amounts to an appendix to his argument.[125]

In fact, the doctrine of substitution and the notion of God who is for us need not be viewed in opposition, but the two are congruous with each other. To recall a key idea from the preceding discussion: God *pro nobis* means that in eternity, this merciful God in an act of pure gratuity already self-determined via election to be the God who "does not will to be God without us,"[126] preferring instead in Jesus Christ to be present with us in the fullness of his divine perfections. By itself, this description already embodies a substitutionary "pattern of exchange," given that Barth is clear that it is

---

123. Barth's non-occlusion of other frameworks forms my main reservation with Terry, *Justifying Judgment of God*. Terry argues, on the basis of Barth, for judgment to be seen as the paradigmatic metaphor of atonement "that so fully and profoundly expresses the atonement that the other metaphors should be treated as subordinate to it" (169). I fear that Terry's development of judgment as the paradigmatic metaphor might be moving in a direction that Barth showed no inclination of moving towards. Barth displays neither the interest nor intention to arrange the various metaphors according to relations of headship and subordination.

124. *CD* IV/1, 274.

125. Johnson, *God's Being in Reconciliation*, 124. This is why Johnson spends two chapters of his volume looking at the doctrine of the Trinity and the doctrine of the divine perfections in Barth before turning to his doctrine of the atonement. The importance of considering the divine perfections in relation to a doctrine of the atonement is further underscored by Holmes, "A Simple Salvation?," 35–46. In the essay, Holmes shows how misconstruals of the atonement can be prevented by a conscious effort to maintain divine simplicity.

126. *CD* IV/1, 7. See also *CD* II/2, 7, 42–3 for a similar emphasis.

fallen humanity that God determines to be in covenantal relationship with. The doctrine of atonement for Barth hence is really an account of how this "pattern of exchange" eternalized in the divine election is actualized within the ambit of our time and space.

All of the above adds up to the central insight that the judicial framework, while being a focal point for Barth's doctrine of the atonement, is neither a dead nor unmovable center. Instead, following Johnson's lead, I am persuaded that Barth's doctrine of the atonement remains munificently open to other approaches or frameworks conveying this key doctrine, as long as the fourfold substitutionary framework Barth developed on the basis of Christ's work serves as the guiding principle for these explorations.[127] Along with Johnson, I agree that Barth would have been amicable to the idea of further developing the doctrine of the atonement not only on "lines of approximation" founded scripturally (in this regard Barth provides an example from the cultic sphere),[128] but also on other "lines of approximation" appropriated either from the different divine perfections considered as single perfections,[129] or even from Barth's account of hamartiology.[130] Johnson carries on to supply concrete examples of these new "lines of approximation," rearticulating Barth's doctrine of the atonement from the perspective of the divine patience and divine omnipresence,[131] and from an aspect of Barth's hamartiology, specifically, the understanding of sin as envy in which the work of René Girard is engaged.[132] The point I wish to register is that the suggestive input Johnson offers forms the basis of the next chapter, where I present my own account of Barth's doctrine of the atonement that particularly emphasizes the obedience of Christ. Here is an account of the atonement where Jesus Christ is himself "The Obedient One, Obedient in Our Place."

---

127. Johnson, *God's Being in Reconciliation*, 124.
128. The phrase "lines of approximation" is taken from *CD* IV/1, 274.
129. Johnson, *God's Being in Reconciliation*, 127.
130. Johnson, *God's Being in Reconciliation*, 148.
131. Johnson's account of the doctrine of the atonement from the perspective of divine patience is found in *God's Being in Reconciliation*, 127–32, while that based on the divine omnipresence is found in his concluding chapter, "A Temple Theory of The Atonement" (164–96). Another theologian who has recently commented on the divine perfection of patience, though not directly with respect to atonement, is Jones, "On Patience," 273–98.
132. Johnson, *God's Being in Reconciliation*, 158–63. Johnson is not the first to initiate an interaction between Barth and Girard. See Hunsinger, "Politics of the Nonviolent God," 21–41, and Mikkelsen, *Reconciled Humanity*, 187–96.

Obedience as That Which Renders Effective the "Pattern of Exchange" in Time and in Eternity

The above elaboration of the main contours of Barth's rather intricate thinking on the atonement has prepared the way to conceive the role and function of the obedience of Jesus Christ with a renewed perspicuity and import. Stated plainly, the central argument is this: it is the obedience of Jesus Christ that facilitates the "pattern of exchange" and renders that substitutionary pattern effective. McMaken captures the point well: "It is this displacement or exchange that, *joined with the obedience that Christ renders on our behalf* in this exchange, establishes the salvation of humankind."[133] As affirmed by Barth himself:

> The atonement is therefore positively the removal of this unrighteousness by the existence of the one obedient and therefore free man.... [T]he righteousness of Jesus of Nazareth for us as the obedient Son of God consists simply in His complete affirmation of this reversal, this execution of judgment in the judging of the Judge. It consists in the fact that He delivered Himself up to this.... [This] point is decisive for a true understanding: *Jesus Christ was obedient in that He willed to take our place as sinners and did, in fact, take our place.*[134]

From the above, Barth contends that the obedience of Jesus Christ plays a causative role in securing the salvation of humanity and their reconciliation with God: it is *because* the Lord Jesus Christ "humbled himself and became obedient to death—even death on a cross!" (Phil 2:7) that salvation was won for us. Moreover, this causality is at the same time instrumental, that is, it is also *by* the Lord humbling himself and being obedient to death that salvation is won. One could therefore affirm minimally the obedience of Jesus Christ as having both a *causative* and *instrumental* role in Barth's doctrine of the atonement.

That Jesus' obedience plays this causative and instrumental role in the act of atonement is a claim theologians of all orthodox stripes affirm. John Calvin, for example, similarly captures both the causative and the instrumental senses in his account of Jesus' obedience, as shown in the following quote:

---

133. McMaken, "Election and the Pattern of Exchange," 215 (added emphasis).

134. *CD* IV/1, 258 (added emphasis). See also earlier references in *CD* IV/1, 237 and 244.

> The second requirement of our reconciliation with God was this: that man, who by his disobedience had become lost, should by way of remedy counter it with obedience, satisfy God's judgment, and pay the penalties for sin. Accordingly, our Lord came forth as true man and took the person and the name of Adam in order to take Adam's place in obeying the Father, to present our flesh as the price of satisfaction to God's righteous judgment, and, in the same flesh, to pay the penalty that we had deserved.[135]

Calvin also insists rightly that Jesus' obedience is to be extended to the whole course of his life, and that obedient life to be counted as part of his atoning work.[136]

Thomas Torrance serves as another example of one in whom the obedience of Christ plays a pivotal role in his atonement theology. Torrance writes that, as attested in the Gospels, Jesus presents himself as one who is obedient to the will of God and the Old Testament scriptures,[137] whose sinlessness consists in his obedience,[138] and who fulfills the Scriptural motifs of the servant-son, the "son of the house" and the new Adam.[139] In addition, Torrance affirms the active and passive obedience of Jesus in which is imputed to us a correspondent active and passive righteousness.[140] What proves particularly interesting in Torrance's treatment is his correlation of the threefold office of Christ to the obedience of Christ: the *prophetic* office corresponds to the *incarnational assumption of our humanity*, the *priestly* office corresponds to the *passive obedience* of Christ, and the *kingly* office corresponds to the *active obedience* of Christ.[141] Finally, Torrance also relates Jesus' resurrection to his obedience, correlating Jesus' passive

---

135. *Inst.* II.12.3. Based on this, Peterson, *Calvin and the Atonement*, 61–68, posits that part of Calvin's multi-faceted doctrine of the atonement involves conceptualizing Jesus Christ as the obedient second Adam, even as Calvin concurrently presents Christ as the victor, legal substitute, sacrifice, our merit and our example.

136. Calvin states in *Inst.* II.16.5: "[Jesus] has achieved [salvation] for us by the whole course of his obedience.... In short, from the time when he took on the form of a servant, he began to pay the price of liberation in order to redeem us."

137. Torrance, *Incarnation*, 18.

138. Torrance, *Incarnation*, 64.

139. Torrance, *Incarnation*, 69–73.

140. Torrance, *Incarnation*, 80–81, and reinforced in *Atonement*, 22, 31–32. Torrance means by "active" obedience the positive fulfilment of God's saving will in the life of Jesus and by "passive" obedience the submission of Jesus to the judgment of the Father in relation to his sin-bearing work.

141. Torrance, *Atonement*, 59–60.

obedience to the fact that he *was raised* and correlating Jesus' active obedience to the fact that he *rose*.[142]

In this regard, Barth joins the ranks of Calvin and Torrance, affirming likewise the causative and instrumental functions of Jesus' obedience in relation to the atonement. Yet, I contend that to leave the matter at that would fail to do justice to the obedience of Jesus Christ in Barth's thought. Barth could and is able to say *more* in view of his wider theology. Under the full bearing of the actualistic ontology stemming from Barth's doctrine of election, the causative and instrumental role of the obedience of Christ is untethered from its traditional limits of being circumscribed within *the economy of salvation* to ramify all the way down to the level of the *immanent divine ontology*.

The point asserted immediately above carries a weighty claim that requires substantiation. This can be achieved through further consideration of John Webster's essay, "'It was the will of the Lord to bruise him.'" Webster advocates rightly that soteriology inevitably broaches upon the theological metaphysics of the triune God *in se*, such that it "stretches both backwards and forwards from this central event [of the cross,] . . . [tracing] the work of salvation back into the will of God, and forward into the life of the many, who by it are made righteous."[143] Webster proceeds to highlight the covenant of redemption and the divine processions and missions as two profitable areas of exploration wherein soteriology takes as its starting point a specification of the doctrine of the immanent Trinity. In relation to the first area, the covenant of redemption grounds our salvation in the perfection of God's own life and vouchsafes the history of the atonement as a history which realizes God's "eternal purpose" (Eph 3:11). In relation to the second area, a fruitful claim can be made that the divine missions are contained in the divine processions, repeating *ad extra* the relations *ad intra*.

So far so good. The difficulty comes when an attempt is made to incorporate the obedience of Jesus Christ into these two concepts functioning at the "higher" level of the immanent divine ontology. The language of obedience as part of the description of the covenant of redemption irresistibly slips into portraying the *pactum* between the Father and the Son as an encounter of wills, leading to a portrayal of the Father and the Son within the triune Godhead as having their own distinct centers of willing.[144] In terms

---

142. Torrance, *Atonement*, 213–16. Another contemporary theologian who likewise devotes substantial attention to the obedience of Christ is Horton, *Lord and Servant*, 208–41.

143. Webster, "'Will of the Lord,'" 15.

144. This is why proponents of the best articulations of the *pactum salutis* are very careful not to confuse the matter as one involving two wills in operation. John Owen,

of the divine processions and missions—as we have seen—the best one can do is to posit the filial-paternity relation arising from the eternal begetting as an ontological ground and basis for the obedience of Jesus Christ that he will come to show in the incarnation, but one is not permitted to speak of this relation as obedience itself.

The beauty of Barth's actualistic ontology, as demonstrated in the earlier chapters, is that it enables him to equate the obedience rendered in the economy of salvation to that rendered by the eternal Son within the triune Godhead. On Barth's account, the eternal Son is actualistically conceived as the God-man Jesus Christ as a second mode of the divine being. In this manner, the difficulties associated with speaking of both areas of the covenant of redemption and the divine processions and missions in the language of divine obedience are transcended, and the incarnate obedience of Jesus Christ finds itself *all the way back* to feature prominently in the eternal antecedent will of God. In so doing, that obedience bears on the ontological divine being and identity of God himself. That Barth gives the incarnate obedience of Jesus Christ the above unmistakable and distinct shape within the domain of the divine ontology and identity is confirmed by his free and unequivocal usage of the language of obedience in relation to the Son's self-election in eternity. The Son is "obedient to grace,"[145] obedient to the Father in electing himself as man to do the will of God.[146]

In fact, as seen in chapter 1, the climax comes in Barth's linking of the obedience of Jesus Christ—an obedience unto death(!)—to the eternal generation of the Son by the Father.[147] This move in particular takes the obedience of Christ as far back as it can go to its utmost limit, the eternal divine processions itself. God in being who He is in virtue of the divine processions—the Father who begets the Son and who together with the Son breathe forth the Spirit—is at one and the same moment the God who is for us in Jesus Christ, whose obedience takes him all the way to death on a cross. Here, the triune being and identity of God is truly coterminous and coincident with the being

---

for example, distinguished between the one will belonging to the Father, Son and Spirit, and the application of that one will unto the distinct and peculiar *acts* of the person of the Father and Son. What is striking is the visible absence of the language of "obedience" in his account. I owe this point to Tay, *Priesthood of Christ*, 41–44. Even in cases where the language of obedience is used, as in Jonathan Edwards, "Economy of the Trinity," 430–43, the obedience is defined carefully as "only that which implies humiliation, or a state and relation to the Father wherein [the Son] descends below the infinite glory of a divine person" (437). Nowhere is there the "dependence of one on the will of another" or "the proper subjection of one to the will of another" (431).

145. *CD* II/2, 101.
146. *CD* II/2, 105.
147. *CD* IV/1, 208–9.

and identity of the God who is for us in Christ Jesus. God's self-constitution as triune (the divine processions) is at one and the same moment his self-turning towards humanity in Jesus Christ (the divine missions), constituting one divine act or event. As a result, any ontological lacuna between who God is *ad intra* and *ad extra* is removed.

In all, the following summary is justified: if the obedience of Jesus plays a vital role in what he carries out in the time and history of his incarnate life, then that obedience via the construal of actualistic ontology resounds throughout the eternal being of God's own perfect divine life.

A Critique and Defense of Barth's Doctrine of the Atonement and His Actualistic Ontological Framework

Barth's doctrine of the atonement, and the actualistic ontology his atonement doctrine is premised upon, has been subjected to a number of criticisms. I will review three such criticisms, listing them in increasing order of weightiness.

The "Privileging" of the Divine Mercy over the Divine Righteousness

First, Garry Williams takes issue with Barth's statement that "the mercy of God must precede His righteousness," highlighting in particular Barth's larger rejection of the picture of the divine perfections as points on the surface of a sphere, all equidistant from the center.[148] In Williams' eyes, this "privileging" of the divine mercy over the divine righteousness signals Barth's forsaking of the classical and Reformed doctrine of God, which maintains the "equal ultimacy of the divine attributes."[149] Furthermore, Barth's position is problematic because it presents the divine mercy as necessary, consequently undermining the intrinsic character of divine mercy as *mercy* and raising problems for the notion of divine freedom. If the divine perfection of righteousness is always preceded by the perfection of mercy, then as Williams asserts: "God cannot be free, either in being or act, to choose whether or not to intend mercy."[150] Such a difficulty, however, does not arise with the perfection of righteousness or justice. To say that justice is necessary would not invoke the same kind of logical contradiction and self-destroying argument to the very nature of the attribute under examination

---

148. Williams, "Karl Barth and Atonement," 259, quoting *CD* II/1, 376.
149. Williams, "Karl Barth and Atonement," 259.
150. Williams, "Karl Barth and Atonement," 260.

than an assertion of the necessity of mercy would. The upshot is that the Reformed position (according to Williams) is able to maintain that "the God who is free to act mercifully or not is truly merciful, while Barth has undermined the nature of divine mercy."[151]

By way of response, I concede that at first glance Barth's statement of the divine mercy preceding his righteousness could potentially mislead one into thinking that he ranks the divine perfections according to the importance of their content. But I believe that would be to severely misconstrue Barth's reading of the divine perfections. Barth's systematic presentation of the divine righteousness following after the divine mercy is not, in his own words, concerned "with a second thing side by side with a first; but that in both cases we have to do with one and the same thing . . . . In this one thing, in God Himself, in the plenitude of His being, there is no division and therefore no mutual qualification and augmentation of His attributes."[152] As Barth's emphasis in the header statement of his paragraph on the perfections of God reinforces: each of God's "many individual and distinct perfections . . . is nothing else but God Himself, His one, simple, distinctive being."[153] In other words, the divine perfections, on Barth's account, do not stand as discrete and separate perfections, otherwise clamoring to be fitted into some pattern of unity, but rather, as Holmes states, they "live through and in one another."[154] Together, they speak of the one divine triune subject who—whenever he acts—acts in the unity and fullness of all the perfections proper to his being as God.[155] Any "qualification" and "augmentation" of one attribute to another that Barth allows for only arises because of the process by which "we are allowed to recognise God on the basis of His revelation and in the truth of His unity and plenitude."[156]

I gather what Barth means by this rather puzzling comment is that despite the content of revelation being about the one God in the unity and fullness of his divine perfections, the way this revelation is received by us calls for a certain order. According to that order, "the mercy of God must

---

151. Williams, "Karl Barth and Atonement," 261.

152. *CD* II/1, 375.

153. *CD* II/1, 322.

154. Holmes, *Revisiting Divine Attributes*, 59.

155. Johnson, *God's Being in Reconciliation*, 102, captures well how one should read the divine perfections on Barth's count: "Because each perfection is the perfection of the one essence of God and fully expresses the nature of that one essence, it necessarily includes within it the multiplicity of the other divine perfections in which the one divine essence consists."

156. *CD* II/1, 375.

precede His righteousness, just as His grace had to precede His holiness."[157] Yet, immediately in the next statement, Barth argues that this precedence of mercy does not mean that God is therefore less holy and righteous than he is merciful and gracious, affirming once more: "God is altogether everything that He is. In everything that He is, He is Himself."[158] This, I surmise, also forms the reason why Barth rejects the picture of the perfections being equidistant points on the surface of a sphere. For Barth, the picture fails to capture the relationship of "mutual penetration and consummation" central to a specification of the divine perfections.[159]

The significant point gleaned from the above analysis is that because of their different starting presuppositions, what Williams perceives as a problem will not surface as such at all for Barth. Under Williams' consideration, the divine mercy and divine righteousness are seen as two discrete and distinct entities needing to be correlated in unity, and for that, Williams finds Barth's particular correlation problematic. But under Barth's specific construal of the divine perfections, the divine righteousness is itself a determination of the divine mercy; likewise, the divine mercy will necessarily have the determination of divine righteousness.[160] The precedence of mercy over righteousness (and grace over holiness) on Barth's count pertains to a question of the right emphasis in epistemological order rather than a subservience of ontological content.

Concurrently, Williams' argument of the necessity of mercy impinging on the divine freedom of God consequently leading to the (self-)demolition of the divine mercy as mercy hinges on a common perception of freedom as applied to God. Divine freedom in this case is seen as being able to choose between alternative states of existence and being. But, as argued in chapter 2, the focus on divine freedom in Barth's account is on God *being* in a particular way as defined by the perfect knowing and willing of himself *tout court*, rather than him *choosing* between alternatives and choices. If so, I doubt that Williams' argument poses a serious difficulty for Barth because of the different definitions of divine freedom presupposed by the two interlocutors.

---

157. *CD* II/1, 376.
158. *CD* II/1, 376.
159. *CD* II/1, 376.
160. *CD* II/1, 376.

The "Eternalization" of History and the "Historicization" of Eternity

The second criticism pertains to what I call the "eternalization" of history and the "historicization" of eternity in Barth's account. Barth's fundamental move of identifying the atonement as a historical event in the eternality of God's divine life and being involves substantial modifications to traditional conceptions of the relationship between history and eternity. As Hunsinger notes of Berkouwer's and Jenson's comments on this matter, Barth's theology has the potential, on Berkouwer's reading, to separate eternity from time (and thus history) such that "time never really has a chance," being so overpowered by eternity that it is effectively "eternalized" and absorbed into God in a movement of monism. On Jenson's reading, however, the opposite occurs. The "absolute priority of Jesus' existence" leads Jenson to advance what he deems should be a natural consequence arising from Barth: a "historicization" of eternity to the degree that eternity is effectively identified with history in a dialectic fashion.[161] It is fascinating to note that Barth's theology can be tilted towards approaches that lead in opposite directions.

The same results obtain when the matter is viewed from the perspective of the divine election. It has been demonstrated that the divine election on Barth's count is nothing less than an *Urentscheidung*[162] (primal decision) on God's part involving his *Urgeschichte*[163] (primal history) with the one man Jesus and, through this one man, humankind represented in him. The interplay between these two key terms reveals that when *Urgeschichte* is seen in light of *Urentscheidung*, historicity is introduced into the eternal election. Conversely, when *Urentscheidung* is seen in light of *Urgeschichte* such that the primal history is seen as directly willed by God, and since the primal decision on Barth's terms involves a self-determination of God's divine being, divine ontology comes to be bound up with history.[164] In the first case, history is "eternalized," while in the second case, eternity (at least thought of in terms of the divine ontology) is "historicized."

Whether from the perspective of the relationship between eternity and time (and history), or from the perspective of the divine election, the net results are the same, generating two similar complications that I believe are unavoidable on any reading of Barth's actualistic theology.

First lies the complication of the degree and extent to which historicity conditions eternity or the divine ontology. In other words, if Jesus Christ

161. Hunsinger, *How to Read*, 15–16.
162. *CD* II/2, 76.
163. *CD* II/2, 8.
164. I owe the observation on the relationship between *Urentscheidung* and *Urgeschichte* to an email correspondence from Dr. Roland Chia.

is his history and if Jesus Christ is very God, then the conclusion follows that God is his history. As Barth states: "[God's] being as God [Father, Son, and Holy Spirit] is His being in His own history."[165] This, as Adam Neder reminds us, is a history that has by an act of pure gratuity through the divine election come to include us.[166] To anticipate the question: how far does this "history" go in conditioning or even determining the triune being? This question could arguably be the central question the Trinity-election debate revolves around, and since my own position in relation to the Trinity-election debate has been spelled out in chapter 2, a simple reiteration of the main conclusion will suffice. I believe that Barth posits an *ontological* and *chronological* simultaneity—one that does not call for a precedence or prioritization—between on the one hand the "history" of God's triune being as Father, Son, and Spirit, and on the other hand his (primal) history with us in Christ Jesus. The two are truly coterminous with one another. Yet, within that arrangement, the overall tenor of Barth's theology points towards a *logical* priority of triunity over election.[167]

The second complication runs as follows: does Barth's tilt towards the "eternalization" of history "rob" time and history of its defining quality, that is, sequentiality? Stated differently: what role does the "before" and "after" still have in God's external works and specifically, in the event of the atonement given that time is "eternalized" on Barth's account? In an essay evaluating Barth's actualistic Christology, Horton airs his basic suspicion: "Am I correct in concluding that for Barth the history defined by God's act (*Urgeschichte*) is the sublation of ordinary time (*Historie*) in an eternal moment that knows only the simultaneity of a single event of humiliation and exaltation rather than a succession of events (or 'states')?"[168]

Of significance for Horton are the implications of what he sees as Barth's substitution of sequentiality for simultaneity, and the implications show particularly in the *historia salutis* (history of salvation) and the *ordo salutis* (order of salvation). In relation to the former, Horton maintains that "the genuine narrative structure of the Bible is threatened," since in Barth's account grace is already posited as necessary before the fall.[169] He states: "In this view, history—in fact, creation itself—cannot be the theater in which

165. *CD* IV/1, 205.

166. Neder, "History in Harmony," 154.

167. By way of reminder, a *logical* priority means that when we think of the divine ontology, even though we cannot ontologically or chronologically separate God's triune being from his being as determined by the primal decision to be for us in Christ Jesus, we should logically or sequentially think of his triunity first before his election.

168. Horton, "Covenant, Election, and Incarnation," 131.

169. Horton, "Covenant, Election, and Incarnation," 133.

a genuine drama unfolds, because creation, fall, and redemption are not successive events but different aspects of the same event."[170] Consequently, the monumental and genuine significance of the fall and the event of human sin are deeply relativized or done away with altogether.[171] In specific reference to the atonement, the incarnation and the cross form the real deal while the resurrection, ascension, and *parousia* seem to be relegated to events having merely the status of confirmation or attestation, but not in themselves constituting anything new in redemptive history.[172]

In relation to the latter (the *ordo salutis*), Horton similarly maintains the criticism that the application of redemption in our temporal history is sublated into the accomplishment of the atonement in the eternal "time" of the cross. This results in: i) a weakened or even absent concept of mediation—conversion, justification, sanctification and calling have already occurred for every person, even if they are not aware of it,[173] ii) a relegated pneumatology—the Spirit merely awakes the person out of his or her "salvific slumber," rather than render effectual that salvation (as commonly held under Reformed Theology), and iii) the lack of a clearly demarcated transition from the previous state of condemnation and death to the new state of justification and life.[174]

The censure above is severe, but perhaps—in my view—too severe. That Barth affirms simultaneity is undoubted, but this affirmation does not arise from Barth's stress on a principle of unity, which Horton feels "obtains a controlling status in Barth's dogmatics,"[175] let alone from any *a priori* "universal metaphysical scheme."[176] The immediate suggestion is one that Barth himself would have especially rejected.

Instead, my inkling is that Barth's emphasis on simultaneity over sequentiality flows from his view of eternity, which in turn is thoroughly

---

170. Horton, "Covenant, Election, and Incarnation," 133.

171. Blocher, "Christocentric," 21–54, offers the intriguing observation that having rejected the creation-sin-reconciliation sequence, Barth has to derive an alternate explanation for evil and sin, and how it is that grace and mercy are needed in those primeval and antecedent conditions. For this, Barth seeks recourse in "an ontological interpretation of evil as 'Nothingness' that proceeds necessarily, though indirectly and paradoxically, from God's grace" (53). Berkouwer, *Triumph of Grace*, 381, calls this a replacement of the biblical and Reformed antithesis of "sin vs. grace" to one of "chaos vs. grace."

172. Horton, "Covenant, Election, and Incarnation," 138–40; see also Blocher, "Christocentric," 51–52, and Williams, "Karl Barth and Atonement," 254–55.

173. Horton, "Covenant, Election, and Incarnation," 142.

174. Horton, "Covenant, Election, and Incarnation," 143.

175. Horton, "Covenant, Election, and Incarnation," 135.

176. Horton, "Covenant, Election, and Incarnation," 131.

Trinitarian. Recalling what we have seen in chapter 2, eternity in Barth's view is not a container in which the triune life of God is confined but is a predicate of the triune being itself.[177] Flowing specifically from the divine processions and the Trinitarian *perichoresis* comes, as Hunsinger states, a "beginning, succession and end that God possesses perfectly, simultaneously, and totally in his interminable trinitarian life."[178] It is this simultaneous presence and containment of beginning, succession and end in the triune life of God that ensues in a form of "eternity as readiness for time" expressed concretely in turn as pre-temporality, supra-temporality and post-temporality.[179] Like the Trinitarian *hypostases*, each aspect of temporality embodies eternity as a whole and yet exists in simultaneous coexistence with the others, and, akin to the Trinitarian *perichoresis*, each co-inheres in the other.[180] Finally, the three coexist in union with time in a real simultaneity that is also *a real sequence*.[181] Barth's emphasis on simultaneity does not come at the expense of sequentiality. On Barth's account, even as history and time is "eternalized," the sequentiality so crucial a quality to an authentic definition of human time is taken up into a state of simultaneity but is not dissipated.

The immediate point highlighted above is further reinforced when deeper consideration is given to the key moments in the Biblical narrative that are said to be, under this particular criticism, relegated to secondary importance in Barth's theology. An extensive exposition of the significance of creation, the fall, resurrection, ascension, the mediation or "application" of salvation, and the return and final judgment of Christ in Barth's theology is beyond the scope of this thesis. But a cursory glance at dictionary entries of these topics reveals that Barth values these events as historical events in a genuine sequence bearing a significance of their own that goes beyond merely that of confirmation or attestation, even as these events are "eternalized" in the primal history of God.[182]

Creation, for example, is famously posited as "the external basis of the covenant,"[183] even as its counterpart statement is equally true: the covenant is "the internal basis of creation."[184] The fact that creation is, as Günter Thomas

---

177. Hunsinger, "*Mysterium Trinitatis*," 189.
178. Hunsinger, "*Mysterium Trinitatis*," 200.
179. *CD* II/1, 619.
180. Hunsinger, "*Mysterium Trinitatis*," 205.
181. Hunsinger, "*Mysterium Trinitatis*," 208.
182. An excellent resource for this purpose would be Burnett, *Westminster Handbook to Karl Barth*.
183. *CD* III/1, 94ff.
184. *CD* III/1, 228ff.

asserts, "a first act in the covenant of grace that aims at the story of Jesus Christ," points to creation being a genuine theatre in the realm of time and history that stages the primal and sempiternal meta-drama of God's electing grace and mercy.[185] The Fall, on Barth's account, can be marked as an event in time but with an eternal significance that works both "backwards" and "forwards," prospectively and retrospectively.[186] Posterior to the event of the cross, the resurrection should be seen, as Dawson highlights, as a *novum* in that it constitutes the transition for the turning of Jesus Christ in all that he has accomplished for us, *to* us.[187] Along somewhat similar lines, the ascension signifies the extension of Jesus Christ's lordly agency to reach, as Burgess describes, "into the lives of his people . . . in such a way that they are now made to share *His* time."[188] Short of a deeper exploration, the above cursory survey already yields the crucial finding that these key moments in the narrative of salvation do bear significance for Barth, and they do so in a manner that relies on and preserves sequentiality in time and history.

In the final analysis, the matter turns on whether one accepts or rejects the actualistic ontology that stems from Barth's theology. To accept an actualistic ontology is to allow, at its most basic consideration, for time and history to be inevitably drawn into a complex relationship with eternity, invariably leading to some degree wherein sequentiality is "absorbed" into simultaneity. I am just not convinced that the sublation is so total that all sequentiality is negated, or that the decisive moments of the narrative of salvation are deprived of their unique individual distinction to be reduced merely to different aspects of the singular event of the cross.

Barth's Alleged Universalism

The third and last criticism of Barth's doctrine of the atonement and his actualistic ontology highlighted could arguably be the most weighty and substantial criticism—that of Barth's alleged universalism. As McCormack states: "The problems that have proven to be most intractable [with Barth's theology] all have to do in one way or another with the allegation of universalism."[189] Clearly, once again, any sustained consideration of this

---

185. Thomas, "Creation."

186. This particular conception of the Fall, whose description coheres largely with Barth's, forms one of the key ways to retrieve an Augustinian Theodicy, as advanced by Vorster, "Augustinian Type of Theodicy," 26–48.

187. Dawson, *Resurrection*, 3.

188. Burgess, *Ascension*, 38.

189. McCormack, "So That He May Be Merciful," 227. McCormack states his comment in the context of the reception of Barth's theology within American Evangelicalism.

subject matter is beyond the scope of our central enquiry.[190] Yet, because I concur with Johnson's statement that any comprehensive treatment or defense of Barth's doctrine of the atonement would have to address the logical entailment of universalism that flows from his doctrine, I offer, nevertheless, the following comments.[191]

On the one hand, that Barth's doctrine of atonement and, on a larger note, his doctrine of reconciliation *tends towards* universalism is in my opinion undeniable. Two aspects of Barth's theology fix him on this trajectory. The first is his doctrine of election, which sets him apart from his Reformed predecessors. To repeat, Barth with his doctrine of election aims at the abolishment of the *decretum absolutum* as the secret hidden will of God in which some part of humanity is elected unto salvation while others are condemned to destruction. Instead, Christ himself now becomes the content of the decree. Barth seeks to assure us that there is no other God behind the "back of Jesus Christ" carrying out a secret election via the absolute decree. In the words of Greggs: "[T]here is no room for a prior decision of God to . . . elect and condemn before the decision to elect Jesus Christ."[192] We know Christ is the decree because he is the *electing God* and *elected man*.[193] The doctrine of election is therefore in Barth's hands rehoused from its customary dwellings under the doctrine of salvation to the doctrine of God. This is the God who is for *every* man.

I suggest that it is in this very specific notion of the election of God no longer being about a secret *decretum absolutum* spelling either the salvation or condemnation of all of humanity that establishes Barth's firm footing in the universalistic trajectory. That Jesus Christ is the decree means that he alone is both the elect one and the reprobate one, and that in turn signifies at least the possibility or even the actuality that nobody else needs to be counted among the ranks of the reprobate.[194]

---

190. See, however, Greggs, *Barth, Origen, and Universal Salvation*, a work dedicated to a full treatment of this theme in Barth's theology.

191. Johnson, *God's Being in Reconciliation*, 16.

192. Greggs, "'Jesus Is Victor,'" 200–201.

193. It is worth reminding ourselves that Barth was not being revisionist simply for the sake of doing so, but as he wrote in his preface to *CD* II/2, x: "I would have preferred to follow Calvin's doctrine of predestination much more closely, instead of departing from it so radically . . . . But I could not and cannot do so. As I let the Bible itself speak to me on these matters, as I meditated upon what I seemed to hear, I was driven irresistibly to reconstruction."

194. In *CD* II/2, 319, Barth states: "Their concern [i.e., the godless] is still to be aware of the threat of their rejection. But it cannot now be their concern to suffer the execution of this threat, to suffer the eternal damnation which their godlessness deserves . . . because it has already been taken away by the eternally decreed offering of the Son of God to suffer in place of the godless."

The second impetus toward universalism in Barth's theology has to do with his doctrine of the atonement. Barth has a view of the cross of Christ that entails the *actuality* of reconciliation and not merely its *potentiality*.[195] The work of Christ on the cross is not the first of a two-stage work that is reliant on something else to bring it to its effectual completion. In traditional Reformed understanding, this second stage is often accomplished by the Holy Spirit who wields faith and repentance on the part of the sinner. Rather, in Barth's account, the ontological transformation of the sinner is already instated in the work of Christ dying on the cross. As we have seen, the *aufgehoben* of sin and the sinner took place in Christ's own person in the suffering of his passion.[196] Since Jesus Christ is the primal elected man, and all of humanity finds their derivative election in him, the question for humankind is no longer an ontological one: "Am I among the elect or not?" (to which the answer is a resounding "Yes," because the decision has already been made through the decision of Jesus Christ to become the elected one). Instead, the question posed to humankind is now an epistemological one: "Do I know and understand what my relationship to God in Christ Jesus is?"[197]

In this regard, Williams draws a comparison between Barth and John Owen, highlighting that both men share a similar view of the atonement as actual and not merely potential.[198] This is not withstanding the deeper underlying difference between the two that results in them ending up on opposite sides of the shore in regard to the outcome and scope of God's reconciliation. This is a difference that comes down, once again, to the *decretum absolutum*. Owen actively espouses the notion of the divine decree, and he sees predestination and reprobation as having to do with the secret will of God (*voluntas arcana Dei*), while Barth repudiates the idea from the outset of his mature doctrine of election.[199] The actual versus the potential accomplishment of reconciliation brought about in Christ Jesus can also be underscored from a third perspective, that of Christ's descent into hell. If Christ suffered "hell" on behalf of all—if all of humanity were "in him"

---

195. A point similarly observed and highlighted by Crisp, "I Do Teach It," 315, and Williams, "Karl Barth and Atonement," 249.

196. Barth states in regard to the actuality and effectiveness of the atonement: "As [God's] act, it is the most actual thing in heaven or earth. Effective by Him, it is effective as nothing else is effective" (*CD* IV/1, 83). See also *CD* IV/1, 312 where he affirms that the alteration of "the world and every man" is "not dependent upon the way in which it is regarded, upon whether it is realised and fulfilled in faith or unbelief."

197. Crisp, "I Do Teach It," 317.

198. Williams, "Karl Barth and Atonement," 263–64.

199. See Tay, *Priesthood of Christ*, 29–30, for more on Owen's views of the divine decrees.

in his descent—in the words of McCormack, "'hell' ought to be an empty set. Zero inhabitants."[200]

Together, these two aspects of Barth's theology suggest that Barth is a universalist, and according to Crisp, not only a "contingent universalist" (I hope or believe God *will* save all human beings in this world) but a "necessary universalist" (God *must* save all human beings in the world).[201] Yet, famously, Barth stops short of an explicit endorsement of universalism. Indeed, he explicitly rejects the doctrine of *apokatastasis*. In my view, this explicit rejection accounts for why the key word "alleged" must be emphasized whenever the topic of Barth's universalism is discussed.[202]

Nonetheless, the question remains: how do we make sense and reconcile this tension, even aporia, within Barth's theology? Some have traded on the charge of logical inconsistency and pressed for Barth to choose between two alternatives. Either he admits to universalism, which appears to run against the grain of Scripture's teaching of the final judgment and condemnation of some portion of mankind (Matt 25:31–46; Rev 20:11–15; 21:6–8, to name but a few passages), or he admits to a conditional election. The latter option means in turn that Barth's doctrine of election, in the final analysis, fails to provide the assurance of our election in Christ.[203] Some, however, seek to absolve Barth of the charge of logical inconsistency by asserting his rejection of *apokatastasis* on a different ground than that commonly presupposed.[204] Others assert that there is actually no logical contradiction, but instead it is (logically) consistent for Barth to reject

---

200. McCormack, "So That He May Be Merciful," 228.

201. See Crisp, "I Do Teach It," 306–9, for a further explanation of the difference between the two species of universalism.

202. Barth writes: "It is [God's] concern what is to be the final extent of the circle [of salvation]. If we are to respect the freedom of divine grace, we cannot venture the statement that it must and will finally be coincident with the world of man as such (as in the doctrine of the so-called *apokatastasis*). No such right or necessity can legitimately be deduced" (*CD* II/2, 417). See also *CD* II/2, 477, and *CD* IV/3.1, 477. Yet Barth also states that while we cannot insist on *apokatastasis*, there is no reason why we cannot be open and hopeful to the possibility of it (*CD* IV/3.1, 478).

203. Williams, "Karl Barth and Atonement," 265–68, is especially emphatic on this point: "[I]t is on account of these undeclared deductions that we must reject the Barthian doctrine of the atonement" (268). To a much lesser degree, Crisp, "I Do Teach It," 320–323, adopts this position. He offers what he calls a "spirit-not-letter" account of Barth's doctrine of election that allows for some degree of conditionality.

204. In Greggs, "'Jesus Is Victor,'" Greggs argues that Barth's rejection of *apokatastasis* arises not because Barth sees any limitation on the salvific work of God, but rather because *apokatastasis* inevitably replaces the person of Jesus Christ with a principle in securing the reality of the final victory of Christ Jesus. Greggs affirms: "'[U]niversalism' itself can never be the victor: this victory is Jesus Christ's" (206).

universalism even though his theology is indeed logically universalistic!²⁰⁵ Still others find the point of inconsistency not in the disparity between Barth's doctrine of election with its universalistic tendency and his rejection of *apokatastasis*, but in Barth's doctrine of election in relation to his pneumatology.²⁰⁶ Finally, there are those who prefer to take the way of "reverent agnosticism"²⁰⁷ or "holy silence."²⁰⁸

My own sympathy lies with this last group. That is, I neither wish to say "too much" nor "too little" in relation to Barth's alleged universalism. On the one hand, to say "too much" by categorically conceiving Barth as a universalist and subsequently dismissing his doctrine of the atonement or—worse—the entirety of his theology on the grounds of his universalism. On the other hand, to say "too little" by conceding to some form of conditionality in Barth's doctrine of election that inevitably attenuates the reality that Barth intends with his doctrine of election: "Jesus is victor!"²⁰⁹

Rather, I believe that Barth genuinely held onto this reality, and saw *each and every human being* as placed ever anew in the constantly *open situation* of the proclamation concerning this very reality of Jesus as victor, a reality that has come to include them *de iure*. Therein lies the mission and witness of the church, the purpose of the elect: to bridge the chasm between the *knowing* in the church and the *not-knowing* in the world so that an increasing proportion of humanity might live *de facto* in correspondence to this reality.²¹⁰ For Barth, *apokatastasis* or universalism is not something one can dogmatically conclude or assert. It is at best something that we can—or better, we *should*—hope for.²¹¹ In other words, the glorious proclamation of

---

205. Responding to Oliver Crisp's essay on Barth's alleged universalism, for example, Congdon, "Apokatastasis and Apostolicity," 479, argues that Barth rejects *apokatastasis* because it "sets up a 'metaphysics of history' . . . that . . . runs roughshod over the historical contingencies related to each person's existential participation in the mission of God. . . . Universalism sets up a timeless picture of the world which entirely overlooks the particularity of each person's calling to become an apostolic witness."

206. See, for example, McDonald, "Evangelical Questioning," 267.

207. Hunsinger, *How to Read*, 134.

208. Hunsinger, "Hellfire and Damnation," 243.

209. *CD* IV/3.1, 173.

210. Berkouwer, *Triumph of Grace*, 120. The elaboration of the relationship between Barth's construal of the all-embracing reality of Jesus as victor and what he sees as the mission and witness of the church forms a topic worthy of further investigation. For an essay providing initiatory insights to this topic, not covering Barth's treatment on this topic but certainly in a direction Barth undertook, see Rae, "A Remnant People," 93–108.

211. The same point stated differently by McCormack, "So That He May Be Merciful," 248: "Universal salvation is something for which we ought to hope and pray but it is not something we can teach." I should at this point justify my choice of the stronger

the doctrine of election on Barth's account lies not in the notions of *apokatastasis* or universalism in themselves but in the reality "Jesus is victor!"

Conclusion

The preceding discussion has revealed that the novelty and genius of Barth's doctrine of the atonement lies in him locating the atonement through the divine election as an event in God's own divine being and perfect life. Because God is the God who from eternity has self-determined via the divine election to be the God who is *for us* in Christ Jesus, a "pattern of exchange" involving a substitutionary framework is already called into action, given that the "us" is humanity who has transgressed and broken the covenant. A "pattern of exchange" prevailing in the eternal divine life whose efficacy is in turn vouchsafed by the obedience of Jesus Christ in his incarnate life means that *that* obedience is lifted from its circumscription within the incarnation, and "stretched" backwards to bear on the immanent divine ontology and life. Notwithstanding the criticisms and the questions that remain of Barth's bold and revisionist reading of the doctrines of election and atonement, Barth certainly has through these two doctrines produced an endearing vision of the gospel that speaks of "the friendliness of God towards man which appeared in Jesus Christ."[212] On his reading, the being

---

term "should" in contrast to "can" in regard to the universalistic hope we cherish. As Crisp, "Augustinian Universalism," 127–45, demonstrates in his thought-experiment essay, there are no theoretical and logical reasons to preclude those who espouse traditional Augustinianism from maintaining what Crisp calls "Augustinian Universalism." Since election is entirely according to the divine decree of God and solely out of his grace and mercy and none of our own doing, it is highly plausible to construe an election that sees 1) God decreeing to create and elect all human beings, 2) God decreeing that the mechanism by which the sin of all human agents is atoned for is in the death of Christ, 3) that the sin and guilt accrued to all sinful human agents is transferred to Christ on the cross, and hence 4) all human agents are saved; none are lost or in hell. This model retains all the essential elements of traditional Augustinianism while affirming universal salvation for all human agents (134–37). Crisp proceeds to identify key affinities and differences between Augustinian universalism and Barth's own doctrine of election (137–39). In the final analysis, however, Crisp concedes that a traditional Augustinian might stop short of embracing Augustinian universalism on scriptural grounds: "[Universalism] simply does not reflect the teaching of the Bible. This is, seems to me, undeniable" (142). It is also on similar scriptural grounds that our universalistic hope be kept as a *hope* and not elevated to a dogma. Yet, if traditional Augustinianism could provide a logical justification for this universalistic hope, how much more could Barth's doctrine of election do the same?

212. Barth, "The Humanity of God," 62. In there, the word "friendliness" is actually translated as "loving-kindness." I have chosen to follow the translation of Greggs, "'Jesus Is Victor,'" 199, who likewise quotes that passage.

of God in his perfect triune life—and this must be said in a doxological tone—is really the being of the God who is obedient to save.

Part III

The "Forward" Movement of the Obedience of Jesus Christ

7

"The Obedient One, Obedient in Our Place"

An Alternate Account of Barth's Doctrine of the Atonement

WE ARE NOW VENTURING into the third part of this volume. Having drawn via a "backward" movement the obedience of Jesus Christ all the way to the eternal triune relationships within the Godhead in the first part, and having explored metaphysically and pneumatologically in the second part the obedience of Jesus Christ "as it is" in the incarnation, this third part explores the "forward" movement of the obedience of Jesus Christ.

In this current chapter, I show how Barth's unique understanding of the role and function of Jesus' obedience within his doctrine of reconciliation holds potential for an alternative and complementary way of envisaging the doctrine of the atonement; one where the motif of obedience provides material content. This is followed by our final chapter where I focus the exploration on how Jesus' obedience relates to our own obedience by centering on one parallel notion that surfaces whenever obedience is mentioned—freedom. But first, we will direct our attention to the alternative account of the atonement following after Barth's.

As seen in the previous chapter, the notion of God *pro nobis* and the substitutionary "pattern of exchange" concomitant with it form what Barth considers to be "the thing itself [*der Sache selber*]"[1] lying at the core of his doctrine of the atonement. A secondary argument transpiring from this core notion is that Barth remains munificently open to other means or frameworks expressing this particular *Sache*, notwithstanding that Barth settled for the judicial framework. It is this secondary argument that I develop in this chapter. Specifically, I contend that the motif of obedience provides an alternative way of beholding Barth's doctrine of the atonement. Similar to the judicial account, this alternate account is likewise guided by the structure of Barth's "fourfold 'for us' [*vierfachen 'Für uns'*],"[2] and is most

---

1. *DO*, 116 / *DG*, 137.
2. *CD* IV/1, 273 / *KD* IV/1, 300.

fittingly expressed under the central rubric "Jesus Christ the obedient one, obedient in our place." Stated differently, given that the previous chapter established the causative and instrumental functions of Jesus' obedience, this chapter posits that obedience itself could serve as the *material content* of a doctrine of the atonement.

The chief utility of approaching Barth's atonement doctrine this way is that such an approach is congruous with and supports what I term a "narrative of obedience." This narrative of obedience is one that emerges from a holistic reading of Scripture, and proffers itself as a fitting way of accounting for the divine purpose and intent of God in bringing to pass the divine economy of creation and salvation. In particular, the narrative presents a fecund ground for generating plausible answers to questions that confront us as we cogitate on the divine economy.

Generally, these questions fall into two broad categories. The primary category of questions is concerned with the correlation of the beginning consisting in creation to the end found in the eschatological kingdom, that is to say, the relationship between protology and eschatology. Examples of questions in this category include: "Why did God put the tree of the knowledge of good and evil in the garden knowing that humankind might eat of its fruit?" "Why didn't God create humankind perfect from the outset?" and "Is the new creation merely a return to its pristine state in Eden?" The second category of questions is directed toward a secondary theme that emerges from the primary category, namely, the interrelationship between divine sovereignty/action and human responsibility/action. A key point to be demonstrated in this chapter is that the narrative of obedience embodies an overall framework of understanding that arrives at a plausible explanation in response to both sets of questions. We will deal with the first category of questions in this chapter, and leave the second category to the next chapter.

The central argument of this chapter thus unfolds in two major sections. In the first section, I elaborate on the narrative of obedience propounded above, drawing largely from the work of the early second-century theologian Irenaeus of Lyons. Irenaeus, because of his overall understanding of the divine economy of creation and salvation, offers a reading of the entire Scriptural narrative that supports a reading of the narrative of obedience and presents its basic contours. In the second section, I turn to an exposition of the proposed alternative account of Barth's doctrine of the atonement. This, as mentioned, is an account that appropriates the theme of obedience and is couched under the rubric "Jesus Christ the obedient one, obedient in our place." Following Barth's format of the fourfold "for us," I show how i) Jesus is the truly obedient one ii) Jesus is counted as the disobedient one iii) Jesus is the disobedient one *in our place* and iv) Jesus acted in true obedience. Our exposition of this alternate account of Barth's atonement doctrine is steered by the aim of demonstrating how this alternative account not only corroborates the narrative of obedience, but also supplies its own unique perspective at various points in response to the two broad categories of questions highlighted above.

An Outline of the "Narrative of Obedience" Drawn from Irenaeus

I begin by providing, in conversation with Irenaeus, an orientation to the form and shape of the "narrative of obedience" propounded above.

The Developmental and Maturation Theory of Humankind in Irenaeus' Theology

Drawing upon Irenaeus' fundamental understanding of the divine economy that regards the history of humankind and the history of salvation as one and the same, Irenaeus posits the novel thought that humankind at the point of creation was not wrought in a state of perfection, but from the outset was set on a God-given path whose trajectory consists in a gradual growth to perfection.[3] Irenaeus' developmental or maturation theory of humankind is born out of two of his basic convictions. The first is a metaphysical consideration. That humankind is created means, for Irenaeus, a necessary lack of perfection. As Irenaeus states: "[C]reated things must be inferior to him who created them . . . for it was not possible for things recently created to have been uncreated. But since they are not uncreated, they come short of being perfect."[4] To be created entails a beginning of existence, and that in turn implies a necessary imperfection in the beginning.[5]

The second conviction is derived from a theological reading of the protological texts, and underpinning that reading is nestled Irenaeus' underlying Christology. Irenaean scholarship is largely agreed that Gen 1:26 "Then God said, 'Let us make man in our image, in our likeness,'" forms for

---

3. AH 4.38.3 states emphatically: "Now it was necessary that man should in the first instance be created; and having been created, should receive growth; and having received growth, should be strengthened; and having been strengthened, should abound; and having abounded, should recover [from the disease of sin]; and having recovered, should be glorified; and being glorified, should see his Lord."

4. AH 4.38.1. I have chosen to follow the translation of Payton, *Irenaeus*, 148. See also *AH* 4.11.1–2.

5. Minns, *Irenaeus*, 88.

Irenaeus a key scriptural text in his understanding of salvation history.[6] This verse indicates for Irenaeus the notion that Adam was not created perfect, but was intended to arrive at the fullness of the image and perfection of the likeness only after a process of development.[7] Irenaeus confirms this developmental view by maintaining that because "the Word after whose image humanity had been created remained invisible . . . humanity easily lost the similitude [likeness]."[8] For Irenaeus, humanity being created in the image and likeness of God is to be conceived neither in static nor completed categories. Instead, the reality is a dynamic one, taking on an eschatological orientation. Humanity undergoes "discipline for incorruptibility" as the image and likeness reaches its full perfection only in the incarnation of the Son and in the kingdom he inaugurates.[9]

Obedience within the Developmental Framework of Irenaeus

It is at this juncture that the "narrative of obedience" finds its entry point. In essence, Irenaeus' developmental and maturation theory of humankind opens up space for obedience to be posited as one of the main aspects of the *imago Dei*. Therefore, obedience—much like the *imago Dei* of which it forms a crucial part—requires *growth and "discipline" in order to be realized in full*.

Obedience as an Aspect of the Image and Likeness

That obedience forms an aspect of the image and likeness lies not too distant from Irenaeus' own thought is evidently displayed in the answer he gives to the following question: "Why could God not have made humankind perfect from the beginning?"

---

6. Minns, *Irenaeus*, 72; Steenberg, *Irenaeus on Creation*, 73.

7. It is admitted a tinge of inconsistency characterizes Irenaeus' use of "image" and "likeness"—sometimes he uses the two terms interchangeably and at other times he distinguishes between them. So, if distinguished, the term "image" is used to denote the mortal and glorified body of Christ, which serves not only as the model for humankind's own body at the initial point of first creation but also equally as the terminal benchmark for that body's final perfection (*AH* 4.33.4; 5.16.2 and *Dem* 22). Similarly, "likeness," if distinguished from "image," denotes for Irenaeus rationality and moral freedom (*AH* 4.4.3; 4.37.4; 4.38.4), or at other times the incorruptibility that human flesh will receive when the divine economy reaches its fulfilment (*AH* 5.6.1; 5.7.2; 5.8.1). See Minns, *Irenaeus*, 72–73, for a further elaboration of this point.

8. *AH* 5.16.2, following translation of Payton, *Irenaeus*, 169.

9. Steenberg, *Irenaeus on Creation*, 56; the idea of "discipline for incorruptibility" comes from *AH* 5.35.2.

Besides his earlier explanation that created things necessarily entail a lack of perfection, Irenaeus concurrently seeks recourse in the activity of human volition. He holds that it is only through God maintaining human wills free and under man's own control that the good would be comprehended and sought after for the beauty that it is, and communion with God valued as precious. Otherwise, if humankind did good and were good by nature, and hence necessarily, rather than by will and choice, the good would have been "implanted of its own accord and without their concern."[10] Underlying Irenaeus' argument lies the notion of obedience. In order for humankind to exercise their volition freely, it is required, as Irenaeus stated, that "humans [know] both the good of obedience and the evil of disobedience, that the eye of the mind, experiencing both, might use good judgment and choose the better things."[11] Based on the above statement, obedience—defined accordingly as the right exercise of human volition leading to the following of God's commands—is conceived by Irenaeus as constituting a key aspect of what it means for humankind to be created in the image and likeness of God.[12]

Irenaeus affirms the above statement despite granting the following two allowances. First, this obedience, much like other aspects of the image and likeness, is tentative and shaky, and easily lost at the point of humankind's creation. Second, and moreover, this obedience was already meant from the outset to embark on a journey of growth (and struggle) toward perfection, as opposed to an instant achievement or even bestowal of that perfection. Irenaeus deems that it is only via the route of growth and development that the rationality and the liberty of human volition can be effectively preserved. Anything other than that, such as an immediate instantiation of the perfection of obedience either at creation or even—for us now—at the immediate point of our Christian conversion, would seem to Irenaeus a violation of the core liberty of human volition.

---

10. *AH*. 4.37.5–6, following translation of Payton, *Irenaeus*, 147–48. This particular line of thought leads Minns, *Irenaeus*, 91, to assert: "If being a creature, being in process of Becoming, implies being undetermined to good or evil, if it implies initial immaturity and the need to grow to perfection, if it implies, for a rational creature, the necessity of learning by experience of contraries, then God cannot be blamed for creating us as he did. For it was this, or nothing. It would be difficult to prove that nothing would be better than this."

11. *AH* 4.39.1, following translation of Payton, *Irenaeus*, 150.

12. Irenaeus holds this to be true even for Adam and Eve. See Steenberg, *Irenaeus on Creation*, 161: "Despite their limited knowledge, Adam and Eve yet possessed a knowledge of 'their maker's law', that is, God's commandment, sufficient unto either obedience or disobedience." Steenberg hence maintains that Irenaeus considered Adam and Eve to be morally culpable for their act of disobedience.

Obedience as Portraying the Recapitulation Work of Jesus Christ

The "recapitulation" work of Jesus Christ is the other major strand of Irenaeus' theology that corroborates the idea of obedience being a quality requiring nurturing to perfection. "Recapitulation" summarizes for Irenaeus the incarnation of Jesus Christ and his undertaking of the economy of salvation in order to sum up all things in himself by going through the principal points or moments of their history.[13] Specifically, this involves Christ recapitulating Adam's life and history.[14] Given further that the first sin committed by Adam and Eve and perpetuated subsequently by future generations is a sin of disobedience, it is highly appropriate that obedience be displayed as an explicit repudiation and correction of that first sin. This explains why the chief rubric Irenaeus employs to portray the recapitulation brought about by Jesus Christ is that of Jesus' obedience that negates and cancels out the disobedience of humankind.

The recapitulating work of Christ in relation to the disobedience of Adam is, in turn, depicted at two levels. The first occurs at the broad definitional level. To reiterate, obedience on the part of humankind is characterized by a careful listening to our creator and a right exercising of our human volition leading to the following of God's commands.[15] Irenaeus concurrently identifies this obedience with the recognition that, as the created, "it is necessary . . . to hold the rank of a human being, and only afterwards to partake of the glory of God."[16] This points to obedience for Irenaeus having to do with a patient awaiting of the maker's hand who creates and glorifies everything in his "due time."[17] Irenaeus renders the point poetically as follows: "Offer your heart to him in a soft and pliable state, preserving the form in which the creator fashioned you, having moisture in yourself—so that you do not, by becoming hardened, lose the impressions of his fingers."[18] In fact, the first

---

13. Minns, *Irenaeus*, 107–9. The place of recapitulation in Irenaeus' theology has been a subject of discussion. See the first chapter of Holsinger-Friesen, *Irenaeus and Genesis*, 1–41, for a survey of the discussion. Holsinger-Friesen's conclusion is that recapitulation should be viewed equally, if not more, as a hermeneutical strategy for a theological reading and appropriation of protological texts (in Holsinger-Friesen's case, Gen 1–2) as Christian Scripture (26–27). While there is truth in Holsinger-Friesen's conclusion, I do not think it needs to come at the expense of negating the theme of recapitulation functioning as material content in Irenaeus' theology.

14. Minns, *Irenaeus*, 109.

15. *AH* 4.39.1.

16. *AH* 4.39.2, following translation of Payton, *Irenaeus*, 151.

17. *AH* 4.39.2.

18. Following the translation of Payton, *Irenaeus*, 151.

disobedience of Adam and Eve laid precisely in their refusal to accept their status and to wait patiently for "the time of [their] increase."[19]

Such obedience that failed to be displayed in Adam and Eve was displayed preeminently and supremely in the life of the human being Jesus of Nazareth. Jesus' life was characterized by a careful listening to his heavenly Father and a patient submitting to and awaiting of the Father's time (Matt 4:4 cf. Luke 4:4; John 5:30; 8:55; 14:24 and passages that bear reference to the ὥρα in John's gospel such as 2:4; 7:30; 8:20; 12:23, 27; 13:1; 17:1). In this way Jesus' obedience encapsulates perfectly this key aspect of the image and likeness of God. As Denis Minns, OP, aptly states: "Christ can be the image and likeness of God only because in his humanity, in his flesh, he is totally responsive to the creative touch of the creator's fingers, totally open to and receptive of the transforming Spirit."[20] Another biblical passage that Irenaeus could have referred to, but regrettably did not, is that of Heb 5:8: "Although he was a son, he learned obedience from what he suffered."[21] This verse speaks compellingly to the idea of Jesus Christ—"Son though he was"—nevertheless undergoing the process of learning to obey God in the face of suffering. This is a learning not due to any failing on Jesus' part, but one that is occasioned on the grounds of it forming a crucial and necessary element of his recapitulation work.[22]

The second level depicting the recapitulating work of Christ is found in the numerous parallelisms that Irenaeus detects in his reading of the Old and New Testament narratives. These parallelisms can be further divided into those that are explicit and those that are, in my view, implicit. Examples in the former category include the genealogical record in Luke's gospel beginning with Joseph and working backwards to Adam (Luke 3:23–38),[23] or Jesus' temptations in the wilderness by which he reverses through obedience the path of Adam's own temptation and disobedience in the paradisical garden.[24] The examples in the latter category include Jesus'

---

19. *AH* 4.38.4. See also *Dem* 12 and 15.

20. Minns, *Irenaeus*, 116.

21. Bingham, "Irenaeus and Hebrews," 52, highlights that the absence of Irenaeus' direct usage of Hebrews arose largely from his belief that the letter did not come from Paul's hand.

22. Attridge, *Hebrews*, 152–53, reminds us to be careful not to read the "learning" as implying any failing on Christ's part in any way. Peterson, *Hebrews and Perfection*, 95, states that if there is any hint of the "moral development" of Jesus, it must be remembered that it is the development of one who could be uniquely judged as without sin at every stage of his life.

23. *AH* 3.22.3.

24. *AH* 5.21.2.

human generation being in like manner to Adam's wherein there was no involvement of a human father,[25] Mary's undoing and destroying of Eve's "virginal disobedience" by her own "virginal obedience" (Luke 1:38),[26] and Christ's undoing of Adam's disobedience and transgression that he (Adam) committed through the tree, via his (Christ's) own obedience unto death on the tree.[27] With the last example, Irenaeus presses the parallelism to its finest details, including the coincidence of the day that Adam and the Lord suffered death, the former out of disobedience while the latter, obedience.[28] Regardless of whether one views Irenaeus' readings of the parallelisms as hermeneutically strained, it cannot be denied that in expressing the recapitulation work of Christ largely in obedience language, he is merely following an eminent biblical motif. As Rom 5:19 states: "For just as through the disobedience of the one man the many were made sinners, so also through the obedience of the one man the many will be made righteous."

The central contention advanced up to this point, namely, that Irenaeus views obedience as requiring nurturing and disciplining to reach perfection, is further bolstered when the effects of Jesus' recapitulation on us are considered. At one level, Irenaeus sees Christ's obedience as an example for us to follow. As seen, Jesus' attentive listening to the Father's word, his total openness and responsiveness to the Father, and his patient awaiting of the Father's time stands in sharp contrast to the disobedience of Adam and the rest of humanity. Moreover, it is only because of Jesus' obedience that humankind is given the hope of sharing in the glory of God.[29] However, to construe the effects of Jesus' obedience on us merely as an example is to severely underplay the significance of Jesus' incarnation in Irenaeus' conception of the divine economy. Rather, as Minns states: "Irenaeus understands [Jesus'] obedience to have had a physically therapeutic effect on the sinful flesh he shares with us."[30] By becoming the same flesh and blood as humankind who had perished, Irenaeus affirms that Jesus Christ "[recapitulated] in himself, not something else, but the original handiwork of the Father . . . .

---

25. *AH* 3.18.7; 3.21.10; 5.14.1–2; *Dem* 31; 32.

26. *AH* 3.22.4; 5.19.1; the terms "virginal obedience and disobedience" are from *Dem* 33.

27. *AH* 5.23.2; *Dem* 34.

28. For Adam, that day was the sixth day of creation while for the Lord, it was the (sixth) day preceding the Sabbath. In this way, Irenaeus deems Christ to be "[granting] humankind a second creation through his passion, which is the creation out of death" (*AH* 5.23.2, following translation of Payton, *Irenaeus*, 177).

29. Minns, *Irenaeus*, 115–16.

30. Minns, *Irenaeus*, 116.

[H]is righteous flesh has reconciled that flesh which was kept in bondage to sin and brought it into friendship with God."[31]

The Holy Spirit and Jesus' Recapitulation

Delving deeper, a key link in connecting the therapeutic—even perfecting—effect the recapitulation of Jesus Christ has on us is through Irenaeus' doctrine of the Holy Spirit. Irenaeus clearly identifies the work of the Spirit as "[remaking] humanity after the image and likeness of God."[32] And since the image and likeness of God is ultimately defined on Irenaeus' terms as the incarnate and glorified flesh of the Lord Jesus Christ, it would not be wrong to affirm that the Spirit's work on us is conforming us to the full image and likeness of Christ.[33]

An opening avails itself at this particular juncture to pursue a train of thought that Irenaeus provided preliminary indications of but stopped short of developing fully. That is, greater specificity could be given to the notion of *the Spirit's "first" work on the incarnate Christ*, who is the true image and likeness of God, even as the Spirit conforms us to that true image and likeness.

Irenaeus notably upholds the involvement of the Word and the Spirit—his famous "hands of God" axiom—in the creation of humanity.[34] Perhaps, less recognized is the fact that Irenaeus further distinguished between the Spirit as the "breath of life" and the "life-giving Spirit."[35] Irenaeus considers the Spirit at the point of creation to function in the capacity of the former in which the "breath of life . . . having been united to what had been fashioned, animated the man, and manifested him as a being endowed with reason."[36] Adam, as a rational being, hence had the freedom to choose between the

---

31. *AH* 5.14.2, following translation of Payton, *Irenaeus*, 166. A favourite passage of Irenaeus cited as evidence of the therapeutic effect Jesus' incarnation has on humanity is that of Jesus' miraculous healing of the man born blind in John 9 (*AH* 5.15.1–4). The blind man serves as symbol for Irenaeus of Adam and disobedient humanity. In the same way that the blind man came to see after washing his eyes and thus to "know him who had fashioned him . . . we might [also] learn to know him who has conferred life upon us" (*AH* 5.15.3, following translation of Payton, *Irenaeus*, 168).

32. *AH* 5.8.1, following translation of Payton, *Irenaeus*, 161. See also *AH* 5.12.4 where the Spirit is said to make the human flesh mature and capable of incorruption.

33. See *AH* 5.9.3 where Irenaeus states that the Spirit makes us "conformable to the Word of God."

34. *AH* 5.1.3.

35. *AH* 5.12.2.

36. *AH* 5.1.3.

Spirit and the flesh.³⁷ Familiar to us, by now, is the sequence of events that recount how it was through the misuse of this freedom that Adam likened himself to irrational animals and was given over to death.³⁸ Equally familiar, by now, is the narrative of Jesus subsequently appearing as the true image and likeness of God in his incarnation to recapitulate the life of Adam, righting the wrong of disobedience through his own obedience.

That which Irenaeus states but deserves heavier emphasis is the fact that the incarnate Lord is also the Spirit-anointed one. He receives not only the breath of life which all humanity receives, but is the one anointed with the life-giving Spirit.³⁹ Moreover, Irenaeus remains silent with respect to the Spirit's empowerment of the man Jesus of Nazareth, particularly in relation to his obedience. A plausible line of inquiry that Irenaeus could have embarked upon would be to focus on the Spirit being both the "breath of life" and the "life-giving Spirit." If the same Spirit who is the breath of life—granting humankind their rationality and freedom of choice—is also the life-giving Spirit, the Spirit could then be conceived as the one who so worked in the man Jesus of Nazareth that in him, the rational faculties reach their perfection. On this account and according to Minns, Jesus would still experience struggle and suffering, because although bettering Adam in his intellectual and volitional faculty, he nevertheless shared in Adam's mortal human flesh, and that is "where the battle really lay."⁴⁰ In this way, Jesus' obedience could be presented, as Minns states, "the victory of a human being as God intended human beings to be, and, indeed, the victory of the first such human being to have existed."⁴¹

Given that the above argument is an accurate depiction of the case with Irenaeus, he could be regarded as the progenitor of a key idea that

---

37. *AH* 5.9.1.

38. *AH* 5.8.2–3; 5.9.3.

39. See *AH* 3.9.3 where Irenaeus acknowledges: "Therefore did the Spirit of God descend on Him, [the Spirit] of Him who had promised by the prophets that He would anoint Him, so that *we, receiving from the abundance of His unction, might be saved*" (added emphasis). See also *AH* 3.17.3, another difficult passage that could arguably be interpreted as the Holy Spirit recreating God's image in the human nature of Jesus, hence serving as the pattern of the Spirit's work in us. In all of this, Irenaeus remains clear that it was only on account of Jesus being man that the anointing took place (*AH* 3.9.3). Based on the above, Spence, *Incarnation and Inspiration*, 9–11, posits Irenaeus as the very first theologian to maintain both an incarnational and inspirational Christology. See also Briggman, "Spirit-Christology in Irenaeus," 1–19, who argues that Irenaeus' Spirit-Christology does not compromise his Trinitarian logic.

40. Minns, *Irenaeus*, 106. On the importance and even necessity of Jesus suffering in the flesh, see *AH* 3.18.6.

41. Minns, *Irenaeus*, 106.

extends into the tradition—one that I will return to—namely, the idea of Jesus' obedience being carried out under the paradoxical conditions of, on the one hand, a pristine and perfect rational and volitional faculty, and on the other hand, genuine struggle.

Summary of the Irenaean Narrative of Obedience

Taken together, Irenaeus' doctrine of the creating, recapitulating and perfecting work of the Holy Spirit brings into full relief the contours of the "narrative of obedience" advanced in this chapter. The Spirit as the "breath of life" grants humankind their rational and volitional faculties and establishes in the process obedience. This obedience is defined in turn as the careful listening and right exercising of human volition leading to a tender-heartedness and responsiveness to the Creator's hands and his due timing.

That this obedience is in a state of growth and nurturing en route to perfection is to be expected, given that the Spirit as the "life-giving Spirit" was yet to anoint and empower humanity in the way he would with the conception of Jesus Christ (*conceptus de Spiritu sancto*). After all, on Irenaeus' account, Jesus Christ is the true image and likeness of God, and only in the incarnation occurring in the "fullness of time" (Gal 4:4) does the Lord recapitulate the life of Adam and undo through his obedience the disobedience of all who had gone before him.[42] Furthermore, the obedience of our Lord has a therapeutic, even perfecting, effect on our sinful flesh. Through the Holy Spirit whom "the Word borne by the Father grants . . . to all as the Father wills,"[43] the Spirit conforms humankind to be like the Son in perfect rationality and freedom, even as it is this same Spirit who first wrought in the man Jesus of Nazareth the perfection of his rationality and freedom. By this "certain portion of his Spirit" that we have now received, we are increasingly "[led] . . . towards perfection and [prepared] . . . for incorruption, as little by little we become accustomed to receive and bear God." This carries on till the day the "complete grace of the Spirit" accomplishes what it was set out for: "[rendering] us like him and [accomplishing] the will of the Father, for it will remake humanity after the image and likeness of God."[44] The perfection of obedience will truly be part of the incorruptibility and glorification that we shall come to inherit then.[45]

---

42. *AH* 3.16.7. The theme of the undoing of our disobedience is heavily emphasized in *Dem* 34.

43. *AH* 5.18.2.

44. *AH* 5.8.1, following translation of Payton, *Irenaeus*, 161.

45. *AH* 4.14.1; 4.16.4

Seen from the above, the Irenaean narrative of obedience offers a felicitous vantage point from which to comprehend the divine intent and purpose of God in bringing about the divine economy of creation and salvation. At the least, it provides this basic answer—God takes his time with the divine economy to wrought within us obedience, an attribute which calls for nurturing, growth and progress to perfection. This idea is one opposed to obedience being something that is immediately instantiated in its perfect state. The eschatological economy reveals time to be the display of the hospitality of God toward the creaturely other.[46]

Three Closing Comments on the Irenaean Narrative of Obedience

Three more comments that bear on our later discussion merit attention. First, although serving as a key premise, one would be mistaken in supposing that Irenaeus' emphasis on the development and maturation of humankind in itself constitutes the core of his theology. Instead, the crux lies in Irenaeus' emphasis on anthropology viewed in the light of Christ, that is, a kind of Christological anthropology, which in turn governs his conception of the divine economy spanning between protology and eschatology.[47] As Michael Reeves argues, to say that it is only in the perfecting and maturing of childish Adam that the true man is displayed would be a far cry from Irenaeus' vision of the divine economy.[48] He states: "Adam never was the Image of God and neither can his race be of themselves. But 'the image of God is the Son, according to whose image was man made'. Thus it was only with the visible appearance of the true Image in the incarnation that Adam, created to be like Christ, could be perfected after the Image and the Likeness."[49] In this sense, Reeves reads Irenaeus as holding out the complex and enigmatic idea that Jesus Christ, before the incarnation, was not simply *homo futurus* but *homo humanus*, "the first and true man who would come after the second (Adam) and so make visible what he eternally was."[50] Ar-

---

46. Knight, *Eschatological Economy*.

47. Steenberg, *Irenaeus on Creation*, 6, reaches a somewhat similar conclusion in his fine study of the doctrine of creation in Irenaeus' thought: "[I]t is not the cosmos that stands at the heart of [Irenaeus'] thought, but the human person, and this is among the first principles of Irenaean thought that must be identified and retained in a study of his cosmology." I am proposing the further step that Irenaeus' anthropology finds its crowning point in a Christological anthropology.

48. Reeves, "Glory of God," 19.

49. Reeves, "Glory of God," 20. The quote comes from *Dem* 22.

50. Reeves, "Glory of God," 39–40. A passage that could substantiate Reeves'

guably, within the theology of Irenaeus, at least as read by Reeves, lies the novel thought that Adam was consequent upon Jesus Christ—certainly not in a chronological sense but in a logical sense.[51] Applied to our enquiry, the position of Jesus being true humanity amounts to saying that the true definition of human obedience is to be found in Jesus Christ, as opposed to Jesus merely measuring up to some externally conceived standard of human obedience. As we shall soon see, this position was one that Barth similarly espoused, given the extensive congruence between his own Christological anthropology and that of Irenaeus.

Second, we must not underestimate the differences in perspectives between the Irenaean narrative of obedience and the alternate narrative built upon an Augustinian framework. Minns observes that both theologians share common viewpoints, the most crucial of which is free will being the hinge on which creation in the beginning could either incline toward the reality of its creator and hence be strengthened in its own existence, or incline toward non-being and thus begin its downward spiral into nothingness.[52] However, when it comes to their views of the history of mankind and the history of salvation, the common path bifurcates. For Augustine, the story of Adam's sin and his punishment and death forms the primal history of mankind, since all humanity descends from Adam and hence is inescapably embroiled in his tragic story. With this underlying premise, Augustine views the history of salvation culminating in the appearance of Jesus Christ as an intervention—notwithstanding, a *gracious* intervention—of God in the history of humankind, but this intervention, as Minns highlights, "does not form a single whole with human history."[53] It stands rather as an alternative history that a selected portion of humanity is able to be a part of through Christ and the grace he offers to them, thereby escaping from the otherwise primal history leading to punishment and death that the rest of humankind

---

particular viewpoint is found in *AH* 3.22.3: "The Word—the Creator of all—sketched out in advance in Adam *the future economy of the humanity of the Son of God*: God first gave definition to the first, ensouled, human being (ψυχικός), with a view to its being saved by the spiritual human being (πνευματικός) (cf. 1 Cor. 15.46). For, since the one who was going to save already existed, in order that he should not be a saviour to no purpose, there was need that what was to be saved should come into existence" (quoted in Minns, *Irenaeus*, 101 [added emphasis]). As Minns acknowledged, there are "problems about time, freedom and necessity bound up in all this, but they are not problems that Irenaeus addresses" (101).

51. It is admitted that Reeves' viewpoint is his own and not one universally adopted by Irenaean scholars.

52. Minns, *Irenaeus*, 83.

53. Minns, *Irenaeus*, 71.

is still inextricably bound up with.⁵⁴ In contrast to this Augustinian narrative, however, Minns notes of Irenaeus:

> [F]or him, *the history of humankind and the history of salvation are one and the same* . . . . Hence Irenaeus is unable to think of most of the action as having happened in the first chapter of the history of the race. Much did happen then, but it was symbolic of things that were still to happen in the future. The human race was predestined in Adam, but it was predestined to come to be in the image and likeness of God. This predestining did not interfere with the power of human beings to refuse to be part of human history, part of the history of salvation. However, for those who choose not to follow the path of salvation history there is no other path to follow, only a blind stumbling about in dead ends.⁵⁵

Reiterated differently: Augustine affirmed a finely tuned cosmos hinging on the free will of first humanity that tragically slid into a path toward disintegration and nothingness. Irenaeus, however, saw in the creatureliness of the creature the possibility of continual and ongoing progression and development toward its maker.⁵⁶ On Augustine's account, Adam fell from a state of original justice and righteousness, but on Irenaeus' account, Adam was created as a "little one," intended from the beginning to grow into the full stature of Christ.⁵⁷

The above point leads to the third comment. Concerning the interrelationship between divine and human action, I hope it has been sufficiently demonstrated the extent to which the Irenaean narrative of obedience places a heavy weightage on the idea of the (human) free will. That is to say, the exercise of human volition remains "free" in nature throughout all stages from its inception through its progress to its perfection. In terms of the inception of obedience (at the point of Adam's creation upon his reception of the breath of life), the Irenaean narrative hinges on the idea that

---

54. Minns, *Irenaeus*, 71–72.

55. Minns, *Irenaeus*, 72 (added emphasis).

56. Minns, *Irenaeus*, 83–84.

57. Minns, *Irenaeus*, 153. The idea of Adam as a "little one" comes from *Dem* 12. I consider it a misreading, however, to press this emphasis of development in Adam so far as to say that Adam's sin is "necessary" as part of his development or progress. The above reasoning forms the building blocks for the "Irenaean" type of theodicy proposed by Hick, *Evil and God of Love*, 211–15. It is preferable instead to adopt Irenaeus' viewpoint that the first sin was a grievous misdirection from the course of growth and perfection (Steenberg, *Irenaeus on Creation*, 153), altering the shape of the divine economy (Minns, *Irenaeus*, 153).

obedience must be voluntary and not coerced in any way.[58] In terms of the progress of obedience, the fact that the life-giving Spirit anoints and empowers the incarnate Christ such that his rational and volitional faculties reach a level of perfection neither negates nor vitiates Jesus Christ's exercising of his volition to be obedient to the Father. The same applies to the Spirit now granted by Jesus to those whom the Father wills.[59] Even at this point, the Father's "willing" is not enforced against our own wills, but Irenaeus maintains a premium place for freedom in volition, and along with that, the consequences of one's choice.[60] Moreover, that it is "a certain portion of the Spirit" that is now received rather than the full instalment points to the Father's patient and gentle manner of bringing to fulfilment the divine economy, not by overwhelming or overriding our wills, but by "[preparing] us for incorruption, as little by little we become accustomed to receive and bear God."[61] Finally, in terms of the perfection of obedience, those who are found in God will find their free wills so finely and perfectly tuned via the gentle and non-coercive work of the Spirit that they will choose to continue and remain permanently in God's service. That, according to Irenaeus, is their glorification and their incorruptibility.[62] At the slight risk of anachronism, it could be asserted that when it comes to relating divine-human action, Irenaeus leans more toward a framework of Arminianism than he does toward Augustinianism/Calvinism.[63]

An Alternative Account of Barth's Doctrine of the Atonement Using the Obedience Motif

The second major section of this chapter considers an alternative account of Barth's doctrine of the atonement that centers on the notion of

58. *AH* 4.37.1 states: "God made human beings free from the beginning, possessing their own power, even as they do their own souls, to obey the commands of God voluntarily, and not by divine compulsion. For there is no coercion with God . . . " (following translation of Payton, *Irenaeus*, 145). As Minns, *Irenaeus*, 77n14, reinforces: "God will not use force to make us obedient to him."

59. *AH* 5.18.2.

60. See the following passages: *AH* 4.4.3; 4.11.2; 4.37.1; 4.39.4.

61. *AH* 5.8.1, following translation of Payton, *Irenaeus*, 161.

62. *AH* 4.14.1.

63. A key passage substantiating this viewpoint would be *AH* 4.39.4: "But since God foreknows all things, he prepared fit habitations for both, kindly conferring the light which they desire on those who seek after [it] . . . but preparing darkness suitable to those who oppose the light." In fact, Stanglin and McCall, *Jacob Arminius*, 136, in referring to the antecedent roots of Arminius' doctrine of predestination, list Irenaeus as one of the antecedent theologians, quoting the above passage.

obedience. Following Barth's own format of the fourfold "for us," the central notion that "Jesus Christ is the obedient one, obedient in our place" is advanced. A key feature will be the consideration of how this account corroborates the Irenaean narrative of obedience, while offering its own unique perspective at key junctures.

Jesus Christ as the Truly Obedient One

Analogous to the first point where Barth affirmed Jesus Christ as the true judge under his judicial presentation of the doctrine of the atonement, I begin by showing how Jesus Christ is the truly obedient one within this account of Barth's atonement doctrine. Accomplishing this requires turning to Barth's theological, more precisely Christological, anthropology as found in *CD* III/2 §44 and §45.

Barth's Centering of Anthropology in Christology

CD III/1–4 contains Barth's expansive treatment of the doctrine of creation. Undoubtedly, the most striking feature of his treatment is the thorough re-alignment of the doctrine and its related sub-topics to Christology.[64] Of particular interest to us is Barth's grounding of anthropology in Christology.[65] Barth maintains that it is only in the person of Jesus Christ, the perfect union of true deity and true humanity, that the fullness of the relationship between God and humanity is revealed. He asserts: "*This man* [i.e., the man Jesus] is *man*. As certainly as God's relation to sinful man is properly and primarily His relation to this man alone, and a relation to the rest of mankind only in Him and through Him, *He alone is primarily and properly man.*"[66] Nimmo is right on this score: the Christological derivation

---

64. Webster, *Barth*, 97, cautions against conceiving Barth's re-orientation of the doctrine as an absorption of the doctrine of creation into Christology. Rather, the opposite effect happens. By providing a Christological ambience, Barth actually infuses into the doctrine of creation a teleological character: creation is only understood in light of God's purpose for it enacted in Jesus Christ. See Gabriel, *Barth's Doctrine of Creation*, for a brief introduction to Barth's doctrine of creation in interaction with certain criticisms mounted against it.

65. The steps leading to this point are carefully laid out by Barth: creation is oriented around the concept of covenant (*CD* III/1, 94–95), and this leads to an anthropological focus, given that humanity alone is God's covenantal partner (*CD* III/1, 18). Insofar as creation is grounded in theological anthropology, the latter is grounded in Christology. See Cortez, *Embodied Souls, Ensouled Bodies*, 19.

66. *CD* III/2, 43 (added emphasis).

of Barth's theological anthropology results from the eternal election of God to be for humanity in Christ Jesus.[67]

The centering of theological anthropology in Christology, in turn, means that humanity finds its ontological determination (*ontologische Bestimmung*) in Jesus Christ alone. All other starting points will lead only to the phenomena of the human.[68] The immediate basic notion that humanity's ontological determination is to be located in Jesus Christ leads Barth to describe theological anthropology using criteria and norms derived from Christology. Underlying this move is Barth's conviction that the starting point of anthropology is not based on fallen human nature that we see around us, but on the true humanity that is found in and originates from Christ Jesus. In this sense, Barth states that one must always look in the first instance at "the nature of man as it confronts us in the person of Jesus, and only secondarily . . . at the nature of man as that of every man and all other men."[69]

The Criterion for a Christological Anthropology —Humanity as a Being Obedient to God

Barth's methodology stated above is consistently applied towards the end of the first sub-section "Jesus, Man for God" and the beginning of the second sub-section "Phenomena of the Human" in §44. Here, Barth sketches the foundation of his Christological anthropology as derived from the *human nature and essence seen in the man Jesus Christ*, and applied to *humanity at large*.[70] Deserving special mention are Barth's fourth and fifth aspects converging on the concept of human freedom. In what comes to be a position that Barth consistently maintains, human freedom is propounded not as freedom of choice, but primarily as that freedom for God wherein our human actions correspond to the divine action. Hunsinger's comment is valuable on this score: "As in Jesus so also in us, substantive freedom is strictly the freedom to decide for God, and not otherwise. Freedom is therefore not something neutral. Nor is it something independent of grace or outside it."[71]

---

67. Nimmo, *Being in Action*, 88.

68. *CD* III/2, 132.

69. *CD* III/2, 46. It is in this sense that Mangina, *Karl Barth*, 95, speaks of Barth's understanding of what it means to be a human being as an "ek-centric" understanding. He explains: "ek-centric literally means being off-centre, having one's centre located outside a given boundary. Barth thinks about human identity in ek-centric terms, referring it to the particular life of the man Jesus."

70. *CD* III/2, 68–74. For a more detailed analysis, see McLean, *Humanity in Karl Barth*, 26–28, and Hunsinger, "What It Means to Be Human," 246–49.

71. Hunsinger, "What It Means to Be Human," 248.

Barth's conception of the human being could be summarized as *a being who is with God in the particular history that is the history of Jesus Christ.*

Having defined the being of humanity fundamentally and essentially as a being with God, Barth pushes on in the third subsection of §44 "Real Man" to develop the material content of what that being with God involves. He lays out his definition in four steps. First, the being of man is a being with Jesus, since the being of man rests upon the election of God and consists in his hearing of the Word of God.[72] Second, the being of man is best understood as "history," even as it is a being caught up in the particular history of Jesus Christ.[73] Third, the being of man is a being-in-gratitude.[74] Fourth, the being of real man is defined as responsibility—further understood in turn as knowledge, obedience, invocation, and freedom.[75]

Barth's classification of "obedience" as part of the responsibility of the being of man is of pressing interest to us. The following points summarize Barth's considerations. First, obedience translates the hearing of the Word into the action of the subject who hears the Word.[76] Barth construes this action as a fulfilment of the knowledge gained by the acting subject.[77] Second, obedience is the link bridging "I am" to "I will." Here, Barth offers a penetrating insight concerning human volition. In line with Barth's understanding of freedom, willing is not the choice of one option among many. Rather, "to will" is first and foremost "to obey," specifically, that which Barth terms as "the only one possibility . . . prescribed and offered me in my knowledge of God."[78] Third, more than just invoking an "I will," obedience leads further to an "I do." Action actualizes the activity of volition, bringing the individual into the new sphere of his or her future.[79] The significant point is that Barth's treatment of obedience, while seemingly abstract, is in fact lodged in the concrete. Congruent with Barth's overall methodology for his anthropological considerations where he consistently begins with the particular (Jesus Christ) before moving to the universal (humanity at large), Barth carries out his treatment of obedience at this point with the concrete backdrop of Jesus' own obedience presiding over his thoughts.

---

72. *CD* III/2, 142–50.
73. *CD* III/2, 157–63.
74. *CD* III/2, 164–74.
75. *CD* III/2, 174–98.
76. *CD* III/2, 179.
77. *CD* III/2, 180.
78. *CD* III/2, 180.
79. *CD* III/2, 181.

To summarize, Barth in *CD* III/2 presents his basic conviction governing his anthropology: *true* humanity can only be grasped by looking at *the true* humanity of Jesus Christ, the one who is truly *for* God and others. It is this history of Jesus Christ that vouchsafes the core of humanity's being, revealing it to be, formally, a being defined in relationship to God. Materially, the being of man consists in his election by God, his hearing of the Word of God, his responding in gratitude, and his being bound in responsibility, the last of which obedience forms a major component. In other words, *CD* III/2 discloses to us Barth's entire anthropological program as one that moves in a direction from the particular to the universal.[80] The upshot of our discussion as it is applied to the notion of obedience is nothing short of a paradigmatic shift. It means that Jesus' obedience resists being pressed into any definition derived from philosophy or pre-conceived notions of what obedience consists in. Instead, the opposite holds true: *Jesus' obedience serves as the benchmark that defines what it means to be the truly obedient human being.*

Irenaeus and Barth Compared

Already then, a strong resonance between Barth and Irenaeus is sounded. Both men via the congruence of their Christological anthropology maintain the idea of Jesus Christ being the truly obedient one, by whom all other human obedience is measured and defined. A further step is to assert that the resonance between their Christological anthropologies emerges from their similar conviction that *the humanity of Jesus Christ forms the image of God in which Adam was created.*[81] This statement, by itself, is already sufficient to ground the notion that Jesus Christ's obedience is the definitive measure of human obedience.

A deeper probe into the manner in which Jesus is the *praeexistierende* God-man, or stated alternatively, the way that Jesus' humanity serves as the archetypical man, however, reveals a fundamental difference between the two interlocutors.[82] For Irenaeus, it is the humanity that the Son of God assumes in the incarnation at a particular juncture in time and history that

---

80. Hunsinger uses the term "particularism" to describe Barth's characteristic of moving from the particular to the universal, and emphasizes the importance of this motif in reading Barth's theology. See Hunsinger, *How to Read*, 32–35.

81. *Dem* 22; *AH* 3.22.3; *CD* III/2, 219 where Barth states: "The humanity of Jesus is not merely the repetition and reflection of His divinity, or of God's controlling will; it is the repetition and reflection of God Himself, no more and no less. It is the image of God, the *imago Dei*."

82. A point highlighted by Reeves, "Glory of God," 119, 219.

serves as the image of God, the pivotal key in this case being that humanity is considered "in advance" and counted proleptically even before its actual occurrence in chronological time.[83] More illuminating is the fact that the *praeexistierende* God-man never comes to bear directly on the identity and being of the second mode of being of the triune God, the Son of God. Who the second mode of being of the triune God essentially is remains sealed off from any implications flowing from the humanity that he assumes in time.

Barth, on the other hand—as seen in the earlier chapters—is averse to any notion that could smuggle in the idea of a Christ "above and behind" that of Jesus of Nazareth. For him, the *praeexistierende* God-man is the second mode of being of the triune God, and to go with a terminology that we have been using consistently: the *logos-asarkos-and-incarnandus*, Jesus Christ.[84] Recall, as argued in chapter 1, that the immediate statement must not be conceived so as to suggest the eternal existence of humanity or human flesh. Rather, similar to Irenaeus, Barth maintains that it is by the humanity that the Son of God assumes at a particular juncture in time and history that Jesus Christ serves as the image of God. But where Barth stands in contrast to Irenaeus is that his actualism allows for Jesus' humanity—assumed in the *act* of the incarnation—to bear from the outset upon the *identity* and *being* of the second mode of being of the triune God in eternity.[85]

So, while Irenaeus appropriates a proleptic motif that facilitates him seeing Jesus as the archetypal man, it is clear that Barth's "actualistic ontology" runs deeper than Irenaeus' "proleptic ontology" does. With Barth, the *praeexistierende* God-man goes all the way down to bear on the second mode of being of the triune God, such that—repeating a key finding advocated throughout this thesis—the Son who is eternally begotten by the Father is at the same moment and within one and the same divine act the *praeexistierende* God-man Jesus Christ, whose obedience constitutes him as the *Logos incarnandus*, ready to save.

Springing from the above observation is another notable difference between Irenaeus and Barth, as Reeves highlights. Given the difference in

83. Reeves, "Glory of God," 119, states it the following way: "Creaturely man—and Adam in particular—[Irenaeus] saw as types of the divine Man who then became a creature in the incarnation."

84. Recall Barth's definitive assertion in this regard in *CD* IV/1, 66: "In this free act of the election of grace *the Son of the Father is no longer just the eternal Logos*, but as such, as *very God from all eternity* He is also *the very God and very man He will become in time*" (added emphasis).

85. As reiterated at various points throughout this volume, Barth's actualistic thought where an act or event in temporality is able to have an impact on eternity is substantiated largely by his view of eternity consisting in the simultaneity of pre-, supra-, and post-temporality.

the way they view the humanity of Jesus as the image of God, it follows that there will likewise be a divergence in the way they conceive the temporal alignment of reality under their respective theological schemata.[86] On the one hand, Barth, with his emphasis on the divine election of Jesus Christ, effectively aligns reality more to the past, to pre-temporality. Irenaeus, on the other hand, with his emphasis on the development of humankind, aligns reality more to the future, to post-temporality. In other words, resolution, for Barth, lies in the eternal decision of election in the "beginning"; for Irenaeus, it lies in the "end." It must not be supposed, however, that notions of development or the perfection of humanity are altogether absent from Barth. In the beginning of *CD* IV/1, where Barth summarizes the heart of the doctrine of reconciliation as the truth of "God with us," he states in language resonating with the theme of development so visibly present in Irenaeus:

> Salvation is the perfect being which is not proper to created being as such but is still future. Created being as such needs salvation, but does not have it: it can only look forward to it. To that extent salvation is its *eschaton*. Salvation, fulfilment, perfect being means—and this is what created being does not have in itself—being which has a part in the being of God . . . not a divinised being but a being which is hidden in God, and in that sense (distinct from God and secondary) eternal being.[87]

The theme of development or perfection and its corresponding emphasis on the *eschaton* might not be as pronounced in Barth as it is in Irenaeus, but it is certainly present, albeit second in emphasis to the primary theme of God's eternal election of Jesus Christ.

Jesus Christ Counted as the Disobedient One in Our Place

Under Barth's judicial account of his atonement doctrine, the second and third points (according to the fourfold "for us" pattern) posit Jesus as the true judge who nevertheless was judged, and one who was judged *in our place*. This alternative account of Barth's atonement doctrine centering on obedience similarly explores the manner in which, as part of his recapitulation, Jesus Christ is counted as the disobedient one, and considered as such *in our place*. This happens even though, as we have just seen, Jesus is the definitional embodiment of the truly obedient one (just as Jesus is the

---

86. Reeves, "Glory of God," 222–23.
87. *CD* IV/1, 8.

true judge). What follows are two points established in interaction with the Irenaean narrative of obedience.

The Place of Disobedience in Barth's Doctrine of Sin

It is undeniable that disobedience features centrally in the Irenaean narrative. Indeed, commentators have identified disobedience as the archetypal or paradigmatic sin in Irenaeus' thought.[88] Barth's hamartiology, however, reveals no such privileging of the sin of disobedience. One might be inclined to think, instead, that occupying that place are the trio sins of pride, sloth and falsehood.[89] Yet, to conclude as such would also be too hasty a move, given as always the intricacies of Barth's thought.

Adam Johnson has brought to our attention the relation between "nothingness" (*das Nichtige*) and the various expressions of sin on Barth's part, showing that the multiple forms of sin are best conceived as the "concrete form in which nothingness is active and revealed."[90] This particular thought of the "concrete form of nothingness" standing behind the diversity of the forms of sin, Johnson suggests, derives from Barth's fundamental understanding of what "nothingness" "is." Because creation has its basis only in the will and act of God, "nothingness" and its associated concrete manifestations of sin likewise also have their basis only in the will and act of God, although—one must hasten to emphasize—not God's creative and permissive will, but his negative or nullifying will that clearly rejects that which he does not will.[91] "Nothingness" is present only in connection with the negating will and activity of God,[92] and only ever as that which assails, opposes, resists and offends God,[93] a counter-movement to all that God does. Based on this, Johnson posits the diversity of sin as a derivative of and a counter-movement against the diversity of God's own proper perfections.[94] That Johnson's interpretive suggestion is on the right track is validated by Barth's own highlighting of sin as pride, sloth and falsehood. These three particular expressions of sin, upon closer examination, stand as man's counter-movement to God's own salvific movement of humility, exaltation, and true witnessing in Christ Jesus.

---

88. Minns, *Irenaeus*, 76, and Steenberg, *Irenaeus on Creation*, 160.
89. *CD* IV/1, 358–513; *CD* IV/2, 378–499, and *CD* IV/3.1, 368–478.
90. Johnson, *God's Being in Reconciliation*, 140. Johnson quotes from *CD* III/3, 305.
91. Johnson, *God's Being in Reconciliation*, 139.
92. *CD* III/3, 353.
93. *CD* III/3, 356.
94. Johnson, *God's Being in Reconciliation*, 140.

Leaving aside the appeal to *das Nichtige* as the primeval source for the diversity and multitude of the manifestations of sin, it could be argued that Barth has in mind a "master" form of sin under which the sins of pride, sloth and falsehood could be further subsumed. In speaking about pride as the sin of man, Barth introduces this larger, more embracing definition of sin: "The pride of man is a concrete form of what a more general definition rightly calls the disobedience of man and Christianity rightly and more precisely calls the unbelief of man."[95] From the above quotation, Barth could be seen as holding out both disobedience and unbelief as the "master" manifestations or expressions of sin. Barth's deliberate contrast between rebellious man and the person of Jesus Christ further advances this line of thinking. He states: "What [God] wills of man is that which corresponds in its human way to His own divine action in Jesus Christ. The sin of man is the human action which does not correspond to the divine action in Jesus Christ but contradicts it. To that extent it is the action of *unbelief* and therefore of *disobedience*."[96]

Barth carries on the same categorization when it comes to a description of sloth, stating that sloth "obviously fall[s] under the general definition of sin as disobedience," and a little further on, that it "obviously falls under the even more penetrating definition of sin as unbelief."[97] Interestingly, however, when it comes to sin as falsehood, Barth refers only to unbelief, making no mention of disobedience. Moreover, the reference to unbelief is made tangentially, and only within the wider triad of "unbelief, superstition and error."[98] Alongside the inconsistency, the apparent lack of a conscious effort on Barth's part in further developing the notion of unbelief and disobedience as "master" forms of sin leads Johnson to suggest that the two concepts function more as "a starting point for branching out than a rigid framework by which to comprehend and order Barth's ensuing exposition [of sin]."[99] Johnson returns to his fundamental thesis that the "ordering principle of the doctrine of sin is not immanent to that doctrine,

---

95. *CD* IV/1, 414.

96. *CD* IV/1, 415 (added emphasis). A page earlier, Barth takes the further step of relating disobedience to unbelief, stating that "[d]isobedience springs up necessarily and irresistibly from the bitter root of unbelief." On this account, Barth posits unbelief as the original form and source of all sins. Barth, in this particular move, follows Calvin, who likewise posited unfaithfulness arising from unbelief in the word of God as the source of Adam's disobedience and sin (*Inst.* II.1.4).

97. *CD* IV/2, 404–5.

98. *CD* IV/3.1, 450–51.

99. Johnson, *God's Being in Reconciliation*, 145.

but derivative from . . . the doctrine of the divine perfections."[100] Repeating an earlier conclusion, Johnson states: "The unity and diversity of evil and sin is a variation of and dependent upon the unity and diversity of God's perfections with which it is in conflict."[101]

It seems that Barth, in the final call, might be more interested in the diversity of the forms of sin than he is in locating the foundational sin.[102] That being the case, while Barth would not have followed Irenaeus in elevating disobedience to the status of the archetypal or paradigmatic sin, he would have retained an openness and amicableness to the idea of the narrative of obedience serving as a lens by which to conceive the atonement.

The Place of Israel in Barth's Account of the Recapitulating Work of Jesus

The second point to be raised under the notion of Jesus being counted as the disobedient one in our place strikes a contrast between Irenaeus and Barth in regard to the chief focus of the "object" of recapitulation under their respective accounts. To be precise, the contrast revolves around the question: "*Whose life and history* was Jesus Christ recapitulating in his obedience?" It is clearly evident by now that for Irenaeus the prime candidate is Adam.

Similarly, Barth does not fail to portray the recapitulative work of Christ Jesus in relation to Adam's life and history. The very fact that Scripture, specifically Rom 5:12–21, portrays Christ's salvific work and obedience as recapitulating Adam's trespass and disobedience would have served as impetus for Barth to maintain the notion of Jesus acting as a "second" Adam, who has come to recapitulate the latter's history.[103] However, in *CD* IV/1 under Barth's doctrine of reconciliation, the spotlight surprisingly falls on a different "object" of recapitulation, landing instead on Israel as the son of God.

In his opening section "The Obedience of the Son of God," Barth states that the section is titled thus because that is how Jesus Christ "was and is and will be very God"—willing as the eternal Son to be obedient to the Father, undergoing the incarnation and becoming man so as to fulfil in his death the reconciling will of God.[104] What comes across as particularly interesting

---

100. Johnson, *God's Being in Reconciliation*, 145.
101. Johnson, *God's Being in Reconciliation*, 146.
102. Johnson, *God's Being in Reconciliation*, 147.
103. See especially Barth, *Christ and Adam*, for Barth's emphasis of this theme. See also *CD* I/1, 152, and *CD* IV/1, 49–50 and 62.
104. *CD* IV/1, 159.

"THE OBEDIENT ONE, OBEDIENT IN OUR PLACE" 255

is Barth's subsequent assertion that the Word did not just become incarnate in any "flesh," but Jewish flesh.[105] He carries on to insist that this fact must not be regarded as "something accidental and incidental," otherwise "[t]he Church's whole doctrine of the incarnation and the atonement becomes abstract and valueless and meaningless."[106] Barth admits that New Testament Christology might have been shaped in a non-Jewish environment, but that must not be allowed to obscure the fact that Jesus comes as the conclusion and summation of "the history of God with the people of Israel," specifically by "[fulfilling] the covenant made by God with this people."[107]

Barth explains two further ideas under the main point of Jesus coming as an Israelite. The first has to do with the idea that "[u]nder the name of Son of God Jesus took the very place which in the Old Testament had often enough been allotted to the 'children' of Israel in their relation with God."[108] That which we find to be so in the Old Testament with Israel, we now find in the New Testament with the one Israelite Jesus. Jesus, Barth affirms, is "bound to the same obedience and service of God."[109] Yet, Barth is aware that Jesus' sonship is of a higher divine order, since this one man who is the Son of God is "one with God the Father and is himself God." In Jesus, we find not only the God who commands, but also the same God who "is called and pledged to obedience."[110] In this notion, we find the major constituents of the "narrative of obedience"—Israel, Jesus, and the concept of obedience that joins them.

Barth sharpens the narrative even further. That is, he asserts that the Old Testament attests the gratuitous nature of man's election by God—that man is in no way worthy of it—by attesting to Israel's history with God being a history of unfaithfulness, corruption, and rebellion.[111] Here lies the crux of

105. CD IV/1, 166.

106. CD IV/1, 166.

107. CD IV/1, 166.

108. CD IV/1, 169. Barth refers to this term "son/sons of God" being applied to the people of Israel (Exod 4:22; Hos 11:1; Jer 31:20; Isa 43:6ff.; and Mal 3:17), the priests (Mal 1:6), and the kings (2 Sam 7:14; Ps 89:26 and Ps 2:7).

109. CD IV/1, 170.

110. CD IV/1, 170.

111. CD IV/1, 171. Barth refers to Israel's unfaithfulness in the following passages: Isa 1:2, 4; 30:1, 9; Jer 3:21f. and Hos 11:2 (pp. 171–72). See Gignilliat, *Karl Barth and Fifth Gospel*, 68, where Gignilliat states: "Isaiah's canonical voice is called on by Barth as a witness to Israel's recalcitrant and unfaithful ways before her God." That Barth gives considerable weight to the Old Testament's attestation to election is seen in the following quote: "[T]he Old Testament alone attests the election of God, and it is only in the light of God's election that we see who and what is man—his unfaithfulness, his disobedience, his fall, his sin, his enmity against God" (CD IV/1, 171).

the argument: Jesus not only takes the place of Israel in being the Son called to obedience, but also takes Israel's place in being counted as the disobedient Son. The following quote from Barth captures the point pertinently:

> The Son of God in His unity with the Israelite Jesus exists in direct and unlimited solidarity with the representatively and manifestly sinful humanity of Israel. Everything which can be said against it, everything which is said against it, not by men, but by God speaking through His prophets—He allows to be said against Him. He accepts personal responsibility for all the unfaithfulness, the deceit, the rebellion of this people and its priests and kings.[112]

Barth is clear that Jesus taking the place of rebellious and disobedient Israel means Jesus fully identifying and locating himself in "the situation of Old Testament man," who, because he has "negated God," now finds himself under the wrath and sentence and judgment of God. In other words, Jesus finds himself as "the man negated by God."[113] By drawing Israel into the picture of sonship, Barth reveals the type of "place-taking" that is happening here: Jesus takes on both Israel's obedience and service, as well as her unfaithfulness.[114]

Barth's focus on Israel here, specifically, his insistence on Jesus' Jewishness, has led commentators like Mark Lindsay to question whether Barth regards Jewishness exclusively "as the archetypal form of sinful humanity,"[115] thus fueling anti-Semitism. Although Barth appears at times to convey this message, Lindsay's concluding comment upon this question is worth noting:

> The journey of the Son of God into the far country of sin and judgment is not, therefore, a journey undertaken purely on behalf of . . . an especially sinful Israel. On the contrary, the continuing election of the Jews as those chosen, loved and forgiven by God determines Israel to be the necessary and appropriate place in which God, in Christ, condescended to come—certainly in solidarity with Israel, its life and suffering, but on behalf of both Israel and the whole world.[116]

The ostensive focus in *CD* IV/1 on Jesus recapitulating the disobedience of Israel should be conceived on the basis of the category of election

---

112. *CD* IV/1, 172.
113. *CD* IV/1, 173.
114. Gignilliat, *Karl Barth and Fifth Gospel*, 68.
115. Lindsay, *Barth, Israel, and Jesus*, 94.
116. Lindsay, *Barth, Israel, and Jesus*, 96.

"THE OBEDIENT ONE, OBEDIENT IN OUR PLACE" 257

rather than sin. Just as the divine election of God to be God *pro nobis* is manifested wholly in the covenant between God and humankind, the indissolubility of that covenant extends equally to the covenant between God and Israel. In fact, from the perspective of Scripture's narrative and chronological flow, it is through the covenant with Israel that the covenant God has with the world is revealed.[117] Barth's presentation of Jesus' descent into the far country, his becoming man in Jewish flesh, conforms to the chronological and narrative shape of Scripture, in particular, Israel's Scriptures.[118] In this manner, Barth's presentation could be said to supplement what is latently present but overshadowed by a predominantly Adamic-centered theme in Irenaeus' account of recapitulation.[119]

Jesus Acted in True Obedience

LOCATING THE STRUGGLE IN THE OBEDIENCE OF JESUS CHRIST VIA THE PRAYER AT GETHSEMANE

Arriving at the final point of the alternative account of Barth's doctrine of the atonement that centers on the notion of obedience, we come to the litmus test of all that has been said so far. Jesus as the truly obedient one, his being counted as the disobedient one, and his undertaking in our place, would all fall apart if it were uncovered that Jesus failed at precisely this point. That is, either he did not act in obedience—a scenario ruled out of court by Scripture's attestation—or his obedience was facile and "docetic" in nature, requiring no struggle on Jesus' part. The problem with a "docetic"

---

117. CD IV/1, 31–34. One could argue, however, that from the perspective of the divine election, the order is reversed. Just as Jesus Christ is the electing God and elected man, he is both the covenant-Lord and faithful covenant partner of the covenant between God and humankind, out of which arises the covenant between God and Israel.

118. Gignilliat, *Karl Barth and Fifth Gospel*, 71.

119. One derives the sense in reading Irenaeus' *AH* that insofar as it pertains to the undoing of Adam's disobedience by the obedience of Jesus, Adam himself is the principal focus. The same could be said of *Dem*. Even as Irenaeus presents a succinct history of Israel in *Dem* 17–30, he switches the focus back to Adam in *Dem* 31–33, casting the obedience theme within the Adamic context. However, see Carter, *Race*, 31–33, who argues that Irenaeus' recapitulation motif involves him embarking on a "concentric feedback loop" that begins with creation, extends to Israel (the story of Israel serves as a compendium to the story of creation), whose story (Israel's) is suddenly "cut short" by the recapitulation Jesus undergoes in the incarnation, which in turn loops back to Adam (33). The upshot of Carter's argument is that "the recapitulation of creation in Christ's flesh . . . is at the same time a recapitulation of Israel, the Law, and the Prophets in Christ's flesh" (32). In my opinion, Carter's argument is possible, but at best lies implicit within Irenaeus' writings.

obedience is that it fails to comport with the biblical witness that Jesus is our merciful and faithful high priest who identifies with us totally in our suffering and struggle, even as he himself learned obedience from what he suffered (Heb 2:10-11, 14-18; 4:14-15; 5:7-9).

Our focus in this section is thus to explore the nature of Jesus' specific acts or actions that display his obedience to the Father, paying close attention to the source of Jesus' struggle in the process. For this purpose, there is no better passage than to return to the fateful prayer uttered in the Garden of Gethsemane (I say "return" because we did look at the prayer earlier in chapter 4 within the context of a discussion of dyothelitism). In that prayer, we perceive a struggle undeniably attested to by the scriptural narratives (Matt 26:36-46; Mark 14:32-42; Luke 22:39-46) and by Barth himself.[120] Even as chapter 4 has established that a dyothelite position provides a felicitous environment by which to conceive the prayer, the question remains as to how one should regard Jesus' utter agony and anguish.[121] At a deeper level, the difficulty is compounded by the conundrum of reconciling the portrayal of Christ as one who wrestles in his obedience to God's will with the confession that the one who so acts in this way is also divine.[122] The concern of this section, therefore, is to disclose Barth's own view of this matter by undertaking a close reading of his account of Gethsemane as recorded in *CD* IV/1.

Interestingly, Barth's reading of Gethsemane falls under the fourth point of his judicial account of the atonement, where he sought to show Jesus as the one who acted justly, or righteously, in our place. For Barth, Jesus' righteousness or his just manner of acting is established in his obedience.[123] The fourth point of both accounts of looking at Barth's atonement—be it the judicial or obedience account—coincide at this point.

---

120. *CD* I/2, 158.

121. I agree with Jones, *Humanity of Christ*, 46-47, that one cannot evade the turmoil of Gethsemane. Rather than explaining away the difficulties of the scriptural attestation by "recourse to idealized understandings of the human"—be they the God-consciousness program of Schleiermacher that insists upon the total absence of conflict of any kind in the development of Christ (*Christian Faith*, 382), or the particular reading of Emil Brunner, who sees in the Gethsemane account the picture "in which all the temptations of Satan glance off [Jesus] harmlessly like blunted arrows" (*Mediator*, 365)—it is preferable to allow the scriptural attestation to Jesus' struggle to "stimulate new texturings, even new expansions, of the Christological and dogmatic imagination" (Jones, *Humanity of Christ*, 47).

122. Davidson, "'Not My Will,'" 184.

123. *CD* IV/1, 258.

The Tradition in Terms of Locating the Struggle in the Gethsemane Prayer

First, however, it would be beneficial to hear the tradition on where it has commonly located the struggle in Jesus' Gethsemane prayer, so that Barth's own unique contribution can be captured more distinctively.

Our earlier section on Irenaeus revealed that he considered the Spirit as the breath of life who grants human beings their rationality and freedom of choice. The Spirit could then be envisaged as the one who so worked in the man Jesus of Nazareth that his rational faculties reached a level of perfection yet to be seen in humankind. On this reading, Jesus would still experience struggle by virtue of sharing in Adam's mortal flesh. Importantly, the conditions for an authentic display of obedience would have been met, one involving struggle—because of the natural characteristics of human flesh that Jesus assumed—yet guaranteed of its victory—because of Jesus' perfect rational and volitional faculty. More importantly, Irenaeus sets off a trajectory that extends into the tradition stating how Jesus' struggle in his obedience is to be conceived. Two salient points along this trajectory are found in the specifications given by Maximus the Confessor and Thomas Aquinas. We will turn briefly to these two interlocutors before returning to Barth.

Maximus' argument for dyothelitism has already been presented in chapter 4. Notwithstanding Christ's possession of an authentic human will, Maximus maintained that the *mode of willing* for this human will takes on a different expression when applied to the *sui generis* event of the incarnation.[124] Specifically, Christ is devoid of a "gnomic" will—otherwise plaguing the rest of fallen humankind—and instead only possesses a "natural" will. As the name suggests (*gnome* meaning "opinion," "idea" or "inclination"), a "gnomic" will refers to a will subjected to and disposed towards deliberation, which in turn presupposes ignorance and the following of deviant courses of action.[125] In fact, the "gnomic" will is the only way by which fallen humankind can will any decisions at all.

Because the human nature of Jesus is assumed by the distinct divine hypostasis that the Son of God is, the mode of willing for Jesus will necessarily be different. By virtue of the deification of his will, Christ's human will is one free of the slightest tinge of a "gnomic" will and instead consists wholly and solely in a "natural" will. That is, Christ wills only in such a manner that his human will is fixed on God and oriented entirely toward the will of God.[126]

---

124. Davidson, "'Not My Will,'" 191.

125. *Opusc.* 1, 20A, 24B, 28D–29B, as quoted by Bathrellos, *Byzantine Christ*, 149.

126. *Opusc.* 3, 56A–D, as found in Louth, *Maximus*, 197–98; *Opusc.* 7, 81C–D, as found in Louth, *Maximus*, 187.

A pivotal question arises at this point: does predicating a "natural" will to Jesus strip away any notions of a struggle that Jesus underwent? Maximus (and his interpreters) argue not.[127] The fact that Jesus' natural (human) will is not opposed to his true human nature means that when Jesus wills as a human, his human volition operates amidst the usual appetites, desires, fears and aversions common to a human nature. Specific to Gethsemane, Maximus *locates Jesus' struggle evinced in his prayer to his natural aversion and instinctive recoil from death.*[128] Yet, at the same time, because Jesus' willing is "natural" and not "gnomic," the way by which Jesus experiences these natural emotive responses necessarily *transcends ours.*[129] Jesus' aversion to death is therefore void of the ingredients of an inner state of double-mindedness, or turmoil arising from a human desire actively resisting and rebelling against a divine purpose.

Maximus goes so far, in fact, as to explicitly deny that Christ had to genuinely deliberate (and hence struggle?) with the prospect of refusing the cup.[130] McFarland questions the necessity of Maximus' move on the basis that elsewhere, Maximus had identified deliberation as an inherent part of the operation of the natural will.[131] In summary, Maximus' location of Jesus' struggle in the Gethsemane prayer could be aptly captured in the following statement from Davidson: "Christ actively chooses a fate from which his human will, with all its normal human aversions, instinctively shrinks."[132] There is real fear and real agony involved, but yet without sin.

What Maximus achieves, Thomas Aquinas similarly accomplishes via his distinction between a *voluntas ut natura* [an instinctive type of willing] and a *voluntas ut ratio* [a deliberative type of willing]. In the *Tertia Pars* of the *Summa*, Thomas deals with the question of Christ's unity of will, and it

---

127. Neither does "natural" willing take away human freedom. Similar to Barth's understanding of human freedom, in Jesus exercising his natural will, humanity is most "natural" and hence most free, because it is a willing that is oriented toward God. See Davidson, "'Not My Will,'" 195; McFarland, "'Willing Is Not Choosing,'" 3–23, and "'Naturally and by Grace,'" 410–33.

128. *Opusc.* 7, 80D, as found in Louth, *Maximus*, 186; see also McFarland, "'Willing Is Not Choosing,'" 13.

129. As Maximus affirmed in relation to Gethsemane: "[T]hough he was truly afraid, he did not fear as we do, but in a mode transcending us" (*Disputatio*, 297D–300A, as quoted in McFarland, "'Naturally and by Grace,'" 425). See also Davidson, "'Not My Will,'" 194.

130. *Disputatio*, 369A, as quoted in McFarland, "'Naturally and by Grace,'" 432–33.

131. McFarland, "'Naturally and by Grace,'" 433.

132. Davidson, "'Not My Will,'" 196.

is here that we find the major segment of his reflections on Jesus' agony in the Garden of Gethsemane.[133]

Following an affirmation of dyothelitism,[134] Thomas goes further to assert in Christ the presence of what he terms a "will of sensuality" arising from the sensitive appetite, which in itself forms part of a genuine human nature.[135] This means that Jesus had within his human will an affective type of willing, one intimately connected to the desire for bodily goods. But like all other humans, Jesus too enjoyed a higher rational type of willing.[136] The two classes of willing within the one human will of Christ led Thomas to distinguish between the will as nature (*voluntas ut natura*) and the will as reason (*voluntas ut ratio*).[137] It is important to note that for Thomas, he allows for deliberation in the *voluntas ut ratio*, hence distinguishing himself from Maximus the Confessor.[138]

It is the above distinction between the will as nature and the will as reason that Thomas profitably applies to Jesus' Gethsemane prayer. The first segment of Jesus' prayer—"Father, if you are willing, take this cup from me"— signifies his spontaneous, natural, and instinctive desire to preserve his life. Thomas assigns this segment of the prayer to an act of Jesus' willing *ut natura*. But in the second segment—"yet not my will, but yours be done" (Luke 22:42)—Jesus, in view of choosing something towards the procurement of a grander outcome (in this case, the redemption of the humanity), exercises his willing *ut ratio* and finally embraces the Father's cup.[139] By virtue of the

---

133. *ST* III, q. 18. The rest of his discourse on Gethsemane appears a few questions further on in q. 21 where he discusses the topic of Christ's prayer.

134. *ST* III, q. 18, a. 1.

135. *ST* III, q. 18, a. 2. Thomas states it as such: "[T]he Son of God assumed human nature together with everything pertaining to the perfection of human nature. Now in human nature is included animal nature . . . . Hence the Son of God must have assumed together with the human nature whatever belongs to animal nature; one of which things is the sensitive appetite, which is called the sensuality. Consequently it must be allowed that in Christ there was a sensual appetite, or sensuality." As Gondreau, "Humanity of Christ," 268, reminds us, the term "animal nature" for Thomas carries none of the pejorative sense it does for us moderns. In fact, this term, under Thomas' usage, supports his contention of Christ's genuine consubstantiality with our humanity.

136. Gondreau, "Thomas Aquinas and Suffering of Christ," 227.

137. In *ST* III, q. 18, a. 3, Thomas speaks of these two types of willing in operation with reference to the act of volition. But if the discussion is with reference to the power, or efficacy of the will, Thomas maintains that there is strictly only one will seen in its singular result and efficacy.

138. *ST* III, q. 18, a. 4, Thomas states: "[C]hoice is the same as the *will as reason*, and is the proper act of free-will."

139. *ST* III, q. 18, a. 5. Thomas offers a similar explanation of the Gethsemane prayer with exquisite clarity in another of his works, *Compendium theologiae*, ch. 233,

perfect harmony that Christ enjoys between his lower appetitive ordering and his higher appetitive ordering, Jesus' willing *ut natura* becomes "rational by participation" to become a willing *ut ratio*. Here is a will of reason in full conformity with the Father's will and Jesus' own divine will.[140]

Thomas' notion of fear and aversion of death evident in Jesus' willing *ut natura* is further reinforced by his commentary on the presence of real sorrow and fear in Christ.[141] Thomas locates the emotions of sorrow and fear within the sensitive appetite and states that these emotions are aroused whenever anything hurtful or evil is apprehended interiorly by the reason or imagination. This was the case for Christ. As Jesus apprehended his passion and death in Gethsemane, "fear was in Christ, even as sorrow [was]."[142] Yet, Thomas was cognizant that Christ could not possess any defects that would obstruct his mission of salvation (e.g., sin, the form of sin, or even ignorance). For this reason, Thomas resists escalating the sorrow and fear experienced by Jesus into full-blown passions, but limits them instead to the initial stirrings of *propassions*.[143] Jesus' emotions are ultimately subjected to his rationality. Whereas these passions when present in us lead to unlawfulness, are involuntary, and forestall our judgment of reason, they wield none of these effects in Christ. Instead, Thomas affirms that "by [Christ's] disposition they so remained in the sensitive appetite that the reason was nowise hindered in doing what was right."[144]

Already then, one can identify in Maximus and Thomas a common thread traced back to Irenaeus. Because both interlocutors affirm a genuine

---

as quoted in Gondreau, "Thomas Aquinas and Suffering of Christ," 233: "In saying, 'Remove this cup from me,' Christ indicates the natural movement of his lower appetite, whereby all naturally recoil from death and desire to preserve their life. In saying, 'not my will, but yours be done,' he expresses the movement of his higher reason, which considers all things in relation to the ordinances of divine wisdom." See, finally, also *ST* III, q. 21, a. 4.

140. The phrase "rational by participation" is one that Thomas borrowed from Aristotle. It refers to the situation where, as Gondreau, "Thomas Aquinas and Suffering of Christ," 230, states: "[T]hrough the work of moral virtue, reason and will penetrate into the very sensitive appetite and endow it with a real, albeit derived and partial, sharing in rationality and freedom." For more on this idea, see *ST* I-II, q. 56, a. 4. In *ST* III, q. 18, a. 2, Thomas also affirms this idea of the sensual appetite becoming "rational by participation."

141. *ST* III, q. 15, a. 6 and a. 7. On a large part, Thomas' positing of sorrow and fear in Christ is to demonstrate Christ's assumption of a genuine human nature and soul, which would have included various defects or weaknesses—sorrow and fear among them (*ST* III, q. 14, a. 1).

142. *ST* III, q. 15, a. 7.

143. *ST* III, q. 15, a. 6, ad. 1 and 2, and *ST* III, q. 15, a. 7, ad. 1.

144. *ST* III, q. 15, a. 4.

human will at work in Jesus' Gethsemane prayer, both locate Jesus' struggle in Gethsemane in the emotions of fear and apprehension arising from his natural aversion toward his impending death. However, because both interlocutors are also committed to the view that it is the divine *hypostasis* of the Word that has assumed true human nature, the mode of (human) willing for Jesus will necessarily be different. Be it Maximus' account of Jesus' "natural" willing versus a "gnomic" willing, or Thomas' positing of Jesus' human willing *ut natura* becoming a willing *ut ratio*, the way Jesus goes about experiencing sorrow and fear, and the effects these emotions have on his human willing are both quantitatively and qualitatively different in comparison to us. Inasmuch as Maximus and Thomas affirm the genuineness of the struggle Jesus faced, they also circumscribe or qualify the struggle on the basis of the peculiarity of the incarnation. With the above background in place, it is timely to turn to Barth, and consider the unique contribution he brings to the discussion.

Karl Barth's Reading of Jesus in the Garden of Gethsemane

Barth sites his Gethsemane excursus within *CD* IV/1 at a point where the obedience of Jesus Christ leading to his sinlessness is affirmed.[145] In particular, Barth avers that Jesus' obedience occurs in a context where the moments of "temptation to a renewal of sin" are ever-present to him.[146] That Barth begins the excursus by referring to a string of passages in Hebrews (Heb 2:11, 14, 17–18; 4:15; 5:7–9) vouchsafes his affirmation of Jesus' capacity to be tempted. As a matter of fact, Barth reads in the very last set of verses mentioned a specific reference to Jesus' conflict in the Garden of Gethsemane.[147] Just at the moment that one anticipates a discussion of the Gethsemane account, Barth averts our attention to the event of Jesus' temptations in the wilderness instead. This move clearly reveals his

---

145. Barth's remarks on the account of Jesus in the Garden of Gethsemane occur intermittently throughout the *Dogmatics*, but his most sustained commentary appears in this excursus. Barth's reading of Jesus' Gethsemane account has been elaborated in greater detail and over a wider range in Jones, "Karl Barth on Gethsemane," 148–71, largely reproduced in Jones, *Humanity of Christ*, 229–42. Of particular importance is Jones' delivered lecture at the 2015 Annual Karl Barth conference, now available as "Riddle of Gethsemane," 124–54. I wish to acknowledge the generosity of Prof. Jones for sharing with me the transcript of his lecture prior to its publication.

146. *CD* IV/1, 258.

147. *CD* IV/1, 260.

intention that the wilderness account be read as of a piece and, in fact, as a preamble to the Gethsemane account.¹⁴⁸

Over four pages, the three temptation episodes in the wilderness are briskly recounted and incisively commented upon.¹⁴⁹ For Barth, the stakes are high. Succumbing to any of the three temptations would have meant the breaking of Jesus' obedience that was crucially instrumental in achieving the reconciliatory aim of Jesus' life and being. Instead, by Jesus' obedience, he remained the sinless one who "remained faithful to the baptism of John" and who achieved the required righteousness for "the justification of us all and for the reconciliation of the world with God."¹⁵⁰

Barth's final comment on the last verse of the Lukan version of the wilderness temptation (Luke 4:13) segues into his commentary on the Garden of Gethsemane. Barth reads the devil's withdrawal from Jesus "until an opportune time" (ἄχρι καιροῦ) as a reference to the decisive moment at Gethsemane.¹⁵¹ According to Barth, the story of Gethsemane serves as a bridge and a turning point between "the two parts of the whole Gospel record."¹⁵² To recall: the first part presents Jesus as an active subject who acts and takes charge, while the second part reverses the role to present Jesus as a passive subject who is acted upon and whose life appears to come increasingly under the control of others.¹⁵³ The function of the Gethsemane account in this regard deliberately retards the narrative pace to enable us to linger in the transition between the two parts, whereby he who "won in the temptation in the wilderness" will now be led to his final end that, on an incongruous and ironic note, involves "the death of the victor." On Barth's count, the "reversal in which the Judge becomes the judged is now about to take place."¹⁵⁴ Barth heightens the tension by raising the question abounding in Jesus' mind as he prays to the Father: "Does all this have to happen?"¹⁵⁵ Barth even takes the further step in asserting that "[i]n this solemn moment

---

148. Barth might have received his impetus from John Calvin. In *Harmony*, 147, Calvin links the wilderness account to the Gethsemane account with the following words: "Though God had trained His Son in some preliminary bouts, now at the closer aspect of death He deals a heavier blow and strikes Him with unaccustomed terror."

149. *CD* IV/1, 261–64.

150. *CD* IV/1, 264.

151. *CD* IV/1, 264. In fact, the Greek ἄχρι καιροῦ is translated in German as "*bis zum entscheidenden Augenblick*" ("until the decisive moment") (*KD* IV/1, 290).

152. *CD* IV/1, 264.

153. *CD* IV/1, 224–27. See also Jones, "Riddle of Gethsemane," 124–25.

154. *CD* IV/1, 264.

155. *CD* IV/1, 264.

... there is a pause."¹⁵⁶ A pause and trembling (*Aufhalten und Zögern*), as he goes on to tell us, that is "not only on earth and in time, not only in the soul of Jesus which is 'sorrowful even unto death' (Matt 26:38), but in a sense in heaven, in the bosom of God Himself, in the relationship between the Father and the Son; a moment in which the question is raised of another possibility."¹⁵⁷ Barth queries what this "frightful thing" could be, given that the ominousness of what Jesus foresaw was enough to bring him to this "terrified and shaken halt," even to the point of Jesus questioning if it really had to be this way. This is surprising granted that none of such behavior was evident in Jesus' earlier temptations in the wilderness.¹⁵⁸

In seeking an answer to this "frightful thing," this problem or "riddle" (*Rätsel*) of Gethsemane,¹⁵⁹ Barth upholds the following three areas to be considered: i) the content of what Jesus says, ii) the fact that Jesus is quite alone in what he says, and iii) the truth that the answer of God will only be given in the language of facts.¹⁶⁰ In an unexplained switch of order, Barth addresses the second point first. On Barth's reading, the significant point not to be missed is that despite the timely need for companionship, this is a prayer Jesus makes alone. Yet, it is precisely in uttering this solitary prayer and bearing this unaccompanied burden, that, as Barth affirms, "Jesus does it for them, and 'for them' in the strictest sense, in their place."¹⁶¹ Here in the Gethsemane prayer is found the synoptic version of the "high priestly" prayer in John 17,¹⁶² a prayer spoken on behalf and in the place of the disciples and the church. For Barth, the representative and substitutionary import of the Gethsemane prayer cannot be overemphasized: "If there is anything which brings out clearly this simple 'for us' as the content of the Gospel, then it is this aspect of the event in Gethsemane . . . . He alone watched and prayed in their place."¹⁶³

Carrying on to the third area of Gethsemane to be considered, Barth offers a somewhat brief and terse explanation, stating unequivocally the absence of any answer or indication from God that Jesus' prayer was accepted.

---

156. *CD* IV/1, 264.

157. *CD* IV/1, 265 / *KD* IV/1, 291. Jones, *Humanity of Christ*, 237, states it pointedly: "Christ's disorientation is 'held over' in the divine life, marking the Son for all eternity."

158. *CD* IV/1, 265.

159. *CD* IV/1, 266.

160. *CD* IV/1, 267.

161. *CD* IV/1, 268.

162. *CD* IV/1, 268.

163. *CD* IV/1, 268.

If there was any answer, Barth asserts, it would only be given "in this inconceivable, this frightful event, and not otherwise."[164]

With that, Barth flows into a full elaboration of the first area of consideration for Gethsemane. The horrific riddle that Jesus encountered was "*the impending unity* between *the will of God* on the one hand . . . and, on the other hand, the *power of evil* which He had withstood . . . . What shook Him was *the coming concealment of the lordship of God under the lordship of evil and evil men.*"[165] As expressed by Jones, this "gruesome convergence of divine action and human sin" was what Jesus beseeched the Father to be spared from.[166] Barth writes impassionedly:

> [Jesus] prays . . . that the good will and the sacred work and the true word of God *should not coincide* with the evil will and the corrupt work and the deceitful word of the tempter and of the world controlled by him, the ἁμαρτωλοί . . . . He prays that for the sake of God's own cause and glory the evil determination of world-occurrence should not finally rage against Himself, the sent One of God and the divine Son. Surely this is something which God cannot will and allow. Such is the prayer of Jesus as prayed once in Luke, twice in Mark and as many as three times in Matthew.[167]

As Barth himself stated earlier: "The coincidence of the divine and the satanic will and work and word was the problem of this hour, the darkness in which Jesus addressed God in Gethsemane."[168]

Two further points may be noted in this portion of Barth's commentary. First, even as Barth affirms the genuine struggle of Jesus in accepting the divine order and will of the Father, he is equally quick to affirm that Jesus' prayer should not be seen as a struggle in obedience, but rather that *obedience prevailed throughout the struggle*. Speaking of the specific words uttered by Jesus "Yet not my will, but yours be done" (Luke 22:42), Barth sees this statement as "not a kind of return of willingness to obey, which was finally forced upon Jesus and fulfilled by Him in the last hour; it is rather a readiness for the act of obedience which *He had never compromised in His prayer.*"[169] The obedience begun at Jordan and maintained in the wilderness

---

164. CD IV/1, 268.
165. CD IV/1, 269 (added emphasis).
166. Jones, "Riddle of Gethsemane," 147.
167. CD IV/1, 269 (added emphasis).
168. CD IV/1, 268.
169. CD IV/1, 270 (added emphasis).

is here completed by Jesus at Gethsemane.[170] In this sense, Jesus' prayer at Gethsemane remains, as it is, a *prayer*. It is neither a demand nor a pressing of claims or conditions on God. Instead, as Barth states, Jesus "prays only as a child to the Father . . . knowing . . . that the Father disposes what is possible and will therefore be . . . the only thing that is possible and right."[171]

The second point flows from the first. That is, having affirmed that obedience prevailed amidst the struggle, Barth ultimately conceives the Gethsemane prayer in the affirmative: "It is a positive prayer and not a negative."[172] In saying "Thy will be done," Jesus rises from his prayer and—as articulated in the peculiar expression of Barth's—"stands upright in what we might almost call a supreme pride (*in höchstem Stolz*)."[173] With this sense of a renewed pride, Jesus not only faces the reality of that which he had earnestly desired the avoidance of, but in doing so, proceeds all the more determinedly along the way which he never veered from. Jones insightfully comments that this is not a pride consisting in self-aggrandizement and rebellion—common and characteristic of fallen mankind—but a pride that "accompanies a wholehearted response to God's command," a pride that is more basically exhibited as *freedom*.[174] Barth reads in the utterance of Jesus "Thy will be done" none of the overtones of forced acquiescence or oppressed submission.[175] Nor does he see it as signifying the grudging resignation and withdrawal on the part of Jesus. Instead, the prayer evinces "a great and irresistible advance."[176] In uttering the prayer, Jesus effects his freedom to finish his work and to execute the divine judgment upon himself; as Barth states: "[T]he sin of the world was now laid upon Him."[177]

Barth's Account of Gethsemane in Comparison with Maximus and Thomas

An evaluation of Barth's reading of Gethsemane vis-à-vis Maximus' and Thomas' is in order. On the one hand, the observation is made that like Maximus and Thomas, Barth shares a similar impetus in reading the account of

---

170. *CD* IV/1, 272.
171. *CD* IV/1, 270.
172. *CD* IV/1, 270.
173. *CD* IV/1, 270; *KD* IV/1, 297.
174. Jones, "Riddle of Gethsemane," 150.
175. Otherwise present in the reading of, for example, Moltmann, *Trinity and the Kingdom*, 76 onwards.
176. *CD* IV/1, 271.
177. *CD* IV/1, 271.

Gethsemane within a context of an affirmation of Jesus' obedience.[178] That Barth sees obedience as the foreground is further substantiated by an earlier comment of his: "The story of Gethsemane (like the story of the temptation at the beginning of the Gospels) shows two things: first, that *we have to do with His genuine human decision*; and second, that *it is a decision of obedience*. He chooses, but He chooses that apart from which, being who He is, He could not choose anything else."[179] To summarize, the following key ingredients are present in all three interlocutors.

First, it is a case of dyothelitism whereby Jesus acts to bring his *human will* into conformity with his *divine will* (which is the Father's will). Second, it is a *genuine* and *authentic* case of the human volition at work that involves *an act of obedience with all its attendant struggles*, including the full spectrum of the emotive feelings of distress (Mark 14:33), anguish (Luke 22:44) and sorrow (Matt 26:38). Third, it is an act of human volition whereby even though there is a struggle, *the obedience rendered is secured* and *guaranteed*. The agreements are made while acknowledging that Barth secures Jesus' obedience via a different route from his two counterparts. While Maximus and Thomas turn to subdivisions and subcategorizations of the human will in order to secure Jesus' obedience amidst his genuine willing, Barth retreats from such metaphysical intricacies. Instead, Barth turns to the doctrine of the *communicatio gratiarum*. Having his human origin effectively determined by the divine, Jesus carried out the human act of his life from this origin, consciously willing not to sin, and as a matter of fact, being unable to choose sin.[180] Barth is content to leave the securement of Jesus' obedience at this level of explanation, without delving further into the finer metaphysical details of the type of human volition involved. Fourth, all three interlocutors are agreed that even though the obedience is guaranteed, in no way does this guarantee *nullify the exercise of volition*, nor *negate the freedom Jesus had* in exercising his volition, nor *lessen the struggle Jesus felt*.

The above said, Barth's reading of Gethsemane juxtaposed with the accounts of Maximus and Thomas does reveal certain glaring variances. Two points in particular stand out. The first concerns the specific location

---

178. For Maximus, as recalled, his insistence on a dyothelite reading of the Gethsemane prayer is primarily to safeguard and accentuate the human obedience of Jesus Christ as a Son to the Father (Bathrellos, *Byzantine Christ*, 147, 173). For Thomas, the theme of Jesus' obedience is certainly not absent from his consideration of Gethsemane. But it could be said that the pronounced theme forming the background for his discussion of Jesus' sorrow and fear is perhaps more the notion of fittingness and the credibility of Jesus' human nature in the incarnation than it is obedience.

179. *CD* IV/1, 166 (added emphasis).

180. *CD* IV/2, 92–93.

attributed to the source of Jesus' struggle. Whereas Maximus and Thomas turn to the naturally occurring orderings of the lower sensitive appetite found in any authentic human nature—locating Jesus' struggle in his natural recoil and aversion to his impending death—Barth looks elsewhere. The following quote immediately draws out the difference between Barth and his counterparts on this point. In describing what it was that Jesus struggled with as he accepted the Father's cup, Barth says:

> It was not simply that He had to suffer and die, and that in contrast to others who have gone a similar way He accepted it rather painfully and tardily. . . . It was not a matter of His suffering and dying in itself and as such, but of the dreadful thing that He saw coming upon Him. . . . It was the coming of the night "in which no man can work" (Jn. 9:4), in which the good will of God will be indistinguishably one with the evil will of men and the world and Satan. It was a matter of the triumph of God being concealed under that of His adversary. . . . It was a matter of the divine judgment being taken out of the hands of Jesus and placed in those of His supremely unrighteous judges and executed by them upon Him. . . . It was a matter of the obedience and penitence in which Jesus had persisted coming to fruition in His own rejection and condemnation—not by chance, but according to the plan of God Himself. . . . That was what came upon Him in His suffering and dying, as God's answer to His appeal. Jesus saw this cup. He tasted its bitterness. . . . There was every reason to ask that it might pass from Him.[181]

The above quote represents faithfully what Gethsemane poses as the struggle faced by Jesus that fateful evening. To be precise, the struggle does not repose in the fact that Jesus had to come under the judgment and wrath of God in his role as the bearer of sin—here, we see Barth going even further than Calvin did.[182] The struggle lies, rather, in something far more unnerving and petrifying, namely, that the divine will executing the divine judgment should be conjoined to the evil schemes of men and the full unsparing fury of Satan's onslaught.

181. *CD* IV/1, 271.

182. In reading Calvin, *Harmony*, 145–52, this seems to be the sense of how Calvin locates the struggle in Jesus' prayer. He states: "It was not simple horror of death, the passing away from the world, but the sight of the dread tribunal of God that came to Him, the Judge himself armed with vengeance beyond understanding" (148). And again: "[W]e should bear in mind the cause of all the grief: death in itself would not have so agonised the Spirit of God's Son unless He realized that He had to deal with the judgment of God" (149). See also Jones, "Riddle of Gethsemane," 147, for a similar observation.

In this regard, I uphold Barth's insight at this point as particularly commendable. In my opinion, Barth has managed to retain somewhat better the sense of the true horror lying behind the Gethsemane *Rätsel*; one found not merely in a natural aversion to a torturous death, or even that the beloved Son of God should in his sin-bearing role take upon himself the full judgment and wrath of God. Rather, in drinking this cup down to its dregs, Jesus wills and allows that the time and space of his own person becomes the one nexus where the *worst* that God can do against sin—his crushing, annihilative "No"—and the *worst* that humanity can do against God—a vicious attack on God himself—come together in this twisted and uncanny merger. This explains why Barth treats the account of Jesus' wilderness temptations together with the Garden of Gethsemane. The two accounts side by side underscore the perplexity of Gethsemane: he who triumphed and was victor over Satan's temptations should now, in an almost sinister twist of deep irony, come to be the victor who dies in accordance with the divine will under the full assault of Satan's schemes. Barth's reading of Jesus' struggle in Gethsemane also translates well to Jesus' struggle on the cross. Jesus' prayer at Gethsemane—with all its angst, perplexity, dare we say, sense of abandonment in the silence of the Father—anticipates the cry at Golgotha.[183] Barth's exposition brings to the forefront, otherwise hidden, the horrendous cost that 2 Cor 5:21 speaks of: "God made him who had no sin to be sin for us, so that in him we might become the righteousness of God."[184]

The second striking variance in Barth's account is that he does not make any explicit or direct reference to dyothelitism, whereas for Maximus and Thomas, dyothelitism appears as a prominent feature of their comments upon the Gethsemane discourse, especially so for Maximus. As mentioned in chapter 4, while Barth maintains a position of dyothelitism, and while a dyothelite position is better able to achieve the desideratum Barth sought after in describing the incarnate obedience of the Son, Barth

---

183. *CD* IV/1, 264.

184. I am aware that Barth's reading of Jesus' struggle rests upon the following question—did Jesus know what would happen to him *after* the cross? This, however, is a question Barth does not seek to answer. While there are indications that Jesus was so engulfed by the sin he bore that he might not have known what laid ahead (*CD* IV/1, 458–59), how this postulation coheres with the Scriptural attestation that Jesus knew what was the final end for him (Mark 8:31) is not something Barth speaks about. See Jones, "Riddle of Gethsemane," 151–53, for a good commentary on this question. I agree with Jones' conclusion: "Whatever premonitions Jesus may or may not have had about his future, the Gethsemane prayer amounts to a decision that leads him to a time and place in which he beholds, *and is defined by*, nothing other than God's crushing judgment upon sin" (152–53, emphasis original). That, I suggest, in itself is already a reality horrific enough for anyone to grasp.

does not make much use of dyothelitism in expressing the obedience of Jesus Christ. Rather, the Gethsemane account teaches us that Barth's final means of expressing the obedience of Jesus Christ resides instead in the activity of *prayer*. In this way, Barth's conception of the embodiment and visualization of obedience as prayer brings a refreshing touch to any reading of Gethsemane offered so far. Deliberately shying away from talk of qualifying Christ's fear and sorrow by means of relegating them to the status of *propassions* or by seeking recourse in the intricate metaphysical distinctions of Christ's willing, Barth allows the full weight of the horrors of Gethsemane to press fully upon Christ, even as he presents Christ's obedience refreshingly and simply in the act of prayer. In other words, while the following maxim might be true for Maximus and Thomas: "Jesus submits his human will to the Father's will at Gethsemane, in this way displaying his obedience," I suspect Barth's preference might be for the following: "Jesus *prays*, in this way displaying his obedience."

More, in fact, can be said. Barth not only sees prayer as functioning within the Gethsemane episode to express the obedience of Christ, he also views prayer as coordinating between obedience and its parallel notion of freedom. In this manner, Barth perceives prayer to be a suitable coordinating nexus for divine action and human action. This notion forms the key idea that we will elaborate in the next and final chapter, as we continue our exploration of how the obedience of Jesus Christ can be carried in a "forward" direction to relate to our own obedience.

Conclusion

Our discussion in this chapter has traversed considerable ground. To reiterate, the third part of this volume explores how the motif of the obedience of Jesus Christ could be carried in a "forward" direction. As part of that task, this chapter highlights Jesus' obedience as not only serving a causative and instrumental role in Barth's doctrine of the atonement, but it holds potential to function in a material sense as well. To that end, I proffered an alternative account of Barth's doctrine of the atonement, retaining the structure of the fourfold "for us" but centering on the notion of obedience instead of the judicial motif. In this vein, the second major section of this chapter was directed towards presenting Jesus Christ as "the obedient one, obedient in our place." Barth's theology is capable of funding the following ideas: (i) Jesus as the truly obedient one (ii) who nonetheless was counted as the disobedient one (iii) who acted in in our place, and (iv) who went about all of the above in a truly obedient manner.

The above central notion when expanded reveal the following details. Specifically, Barth's Christological anthropology endorses Jesus as the true human being whose obedience constitutes the definitional embodiment of what human obedience looks like. Although Barth does not propose disobedience as the "foundational" or "master" sin, the basic foundation of Barth's hamartiology that posits sin in its multi-variant and diverse forms as counter-movements to the diverse divine perfections of God signifies an openness on Barth's part to conceive of sin as disobedience. Moreover, Barth's emphasis on Jesus taking the place of Israel and redressing her disobedience accounts for an immense theme of Scripture which has often been overshadowed by the Adamic motif. Finally, by focusing on the event of Gethsemane, Barth demonstrates Jesus to be one who acted in full and complete obedience, notwithstanding Gethsemane being a moment for Jesus where the temptation to disobedience was at its greatest. Most refreshing is Barth's pinpointing the source of Jesus' struggle: in drinking the cup, Jesus was acting in full obedience to the Father's will, where in an uncanny merger, the *worst* that God can do against sin and the *worst* that sinners can do against God converge in the event that is due to befall upon him.

The main reason for presenting this alternative account of Barth's atonement doctrine centered on obedience is to show its major coherence with what has been termed the "narrative of obedience." To that end, the first major section of this chapter presented a reading of this "narrative of obedience" built upon the theology of Irenaeus. In turn, I advocate this narrative of obedience because I am persuaded that it provides a good framework by which to grasp the divine purpose and intent of God in bringing to pass the divine economy of creation and salvation. Specifically, in our case, the realization that obedience is a trait in which God through his Spirit has—from the very outset of creation—been growing within us and nurturing us to perfection even as he conforms us to the true image and likeness of Christ the Son is one that engenders our own response of joyful obedience. Barth and Irenaeus, despite their differences, worked toward this grand vision. Both men envisage the perfection of our obedience as part of our participation in the being of God. Irenaeus would say: we are "[led] . . . towards perfection and [prepared] . . . for incorruption,"[185] and as Barth would say: the human creature is a "being which has a part in the being of God . . . not a divinised being but a being which is hidden in God, and in that sense . . . eternal being."[186]

---

185. *AH* 5.8.1, following translation of Payton, *Irenaeus*, 161.
186. *CD* IV/1, 8.

8

"Freedom to Obey"

Relating Divine Freedom and Divine Obedience, and Human Freedom and Human Obedience

As MENTIONED IN THE introduction to the previous chapter, the third major section of this volume explores how, on Barth's reckoning, the obedience of Jesus Christ can be carried in a "forward" direction. This final chapter considers how the obedience of Jesus Christ relates or flows to our own obedience as part of the reconciled, focusing on one parallel notion that surfaces whenever obedience is mentioned: freedom. In particular, I will not only delineate the way Barth conceives the relation between obedience and freedom in general, but will also include Barth's consideration of the relation between, on the one hand, *divine* freedom and obedience, and, on the other hand, *human* freedom and obedience.

The overall argument of the chapter is a culmination of smaller partial arguments derived from the five sections that comprise the chapter. First, I show that Barth was keen, from the outset of his writings, to align freedom and obedience together. This means that Barth views the two concepts as complementary notions in an amicable relationship. Such a conception of the freedom-obedience relation counters a certain strand of philosophical thought that conceives the two notions in an antithetical relation. As a starting point, it also locates Barth on the philosophical continuum at the end closer to the framework of compatibilism. Given this complementarian nature of the freedom-obedience relationship, it is not altogether surprising that Barth would utilize the notion of (divine) obedience as his entry point in *CD* IV/1, even though it could be claimed that between the two, the notion of divine freedom has been privileged thus far in *CD*.[1] At this point, I raise the idea that paying attention to the social and political background that *CD* IV/1 was written in offers a fecund suggestion to why Barth chose to capitalize on obedience as his entry point.

---

1. As seen in Barth's chief description of God as the "God who loves in freedom."

This is followed by closing in on the obedience-freedom relation in the second section, beginning with *divine* freedom and obedience. Reiterating the idea as seen in chapter 2 of divine freedom being a freedom-in-Godself that is simultaneously a freedom-for-creation-and-redemption-in-election, I contend that Barth's conception of divine freedom already draws divine obedience into the closest possible connection with it. Because divine freedom on Barth's terms involves the divine election, and since divine election in turn involves the divine obedience of the eternal Son, it could be said at the level of the divine ontology that divine freedom is intricately related to divine obedience; more specifically: that divine obedience is an expression of the divine freedom.

The third section devotes more detailed attention to how Barth coordinates *divine* and *human* action and agency. Here, I draw upon Barth's presentation of the theological basis for ethics as grounded in the divine election (*CD* II/2 §36) and his treatment of the *concursus Dei* (*CD* III/3). In both concepts, I contend that, once again, the key connecting link is the obedience of Jesus Christ, equated to the divine obedience of the eternal Son under Barth's actualistic construal. Barth clearly understood that the center from which both divine and human agency are to be comprehended is the obedience of Jesus Christ in the divine election, wherein Jesus Christ from eternity self-elects to be the God who is for us. A coordination of divine and human action and agency that orients as its starting point the person of the perfect God-man Jesus Christ would mean that while Barth could be said to subscribe to a basic version of philosophical compatibilism when it comes to the freedom-determinism issue, it is nevertheless a modified compatibilism.

In the fourth section, I argue that as it is with the relation between *divine* freedom and *divine* obedience as seen in the *God*-man Jesus Christ, so it is with the relation between *human* freedom and *human* obedience seen equally in the God-*man* Jesus Christ. In both relations, obedience serves as the full and perfect expression of freedom. I show further that this correlation between the divine and human aspects is grounded on Barth's understanding of the *analogia fidei* and *analogia relationis* that has as an essential feature the human component corresponding to the divine component; the center of the correspondence being located in the one true God-man Jesus Christ.

The fifth and final section returns to Gethsemane again. Jesus Christ at the garden of Gethsemane provides Barth the clearest picture of the coordination and connection between obedience and freedom, with that intimate connection expressed in the activity of prayer. For Barth, the human being who is obedient and free is the one deeply engaged in the exercise of prayer.

Barth's Basic Conception of the Freedom-Obedience Relation

I begin with what could be stated as Barth's basic amicable and complementary conception of the freedom-obedience relation. From the outset of his writings, in *Der Römerbrief* (1922 edition), Barth read Rom 6:12–23 and Rom 7 through the lens of an obedience-freedom relation.[2] The one constant refrain running through Barth's commentary in Rom 6:12–23 is "grace is the power of obedience."[3] His conception of the freedom-obedience relation within Rom 6 is captured especially in his comments on verses 15 and 16. Barth begins with the question: "Does grace then carry with it in any sense the freedom to sin?" carrying on to tease the further thought that "[i]f grace were a human possibility, it would be right and natural to let it run its course adjusting itself to other human possibilities as best it can. Grace would then involve a broad freedom to sin."[4] It is in view of this hypothetical question that the apostle Paul raised that Barth concludes similarly as the apostle did: "And so we conclude: God forbid that that should be grace!"[5]

Rejecting the idea of grace as a human possibility, Barth proceeds to define grace as "the impossible possibility of God which is beyond every possibility of our own: it is the freedom which God takes to Himself in us." This is a freedom which leads to us becoming "servants to God, existentially appointed unto obedience to the divine 'No', which is pronounced in us against sin."[6] Barth concludes by stating that "[t]he freedom of the man under grace is founded upon the good pleasure of God, and has no other foundation; it is *the freedom of the will of God* in men, and freedom of no other kind."[7] This is a concept that Barth repeats in his commentary on chapter 7: the freedom of God is our freedom.[8] It is precisely this freedom of God that debunks religion—represented by the law in Rom 7—and reveals it as a limited human possibility. Religion's ineffectiveness, in turn, points to the freedom of God to confer grace upon mankind.[9] This is a grace that enables

---

2. The chapter heading for Rom 6:12–23 is "The power of obedience," while that for Rom 7 is "Freedom."
3. Barth, *Romans*, 207, 210, 211–13, 218, 228.
4. Barth, *Romans*, 213–14.
5. Barth, *Romans*, 215.
6. Barth, *Romans*, 216.
7. Barth, *Romans*, 220 (added emphasis).
8. Barth, *Romans*, 246.
9. Barth, *Romans*, 229–30.

one to experience the power of Christ's resurrection, which functions as the power of obedience for that individual.[10]

The cursory survey of Rom 6–7 above suffices to reveal Barth's basic conception of the freedom-obedience relation as a complementary relationship. Human freedom locates its ground in the divine freedom of God to carry out the "impossible possibility" of bestowing grace upon mankind. Human freedom is thus situated in the realm of that grace and in the experience of the power of Christ's resurrection leading to a power to be obedient. In other words, *human freedom is grounded in divine freedom* and *expressed in human obedience*; conversely, *to be obedient is to show that one is free*. Barth carries this basic complementary relation between obedience and freedom into the rest of his writings.

That Barth's take on the obedience-freedom relation resists any shifts and remains essentially the same is vouchsafed in his essay "The Gift of Freedom: Foundation of Evangelical Ethics" written nearer the end of his career.[11] There, Barth maintains unequivocally the stand that "man's freedom is his as the gift of God."[12] The order of understanding the freedom given to mankind calls for a prior consideration of the divine freedom.[13] Just as the divine freedom is essentially not a freedom *from* but a freedom *to* and *for*,[14] so human freedom that is given to mankind should not be conceived as a freedom of alternatives or a freedom without limits, with the latter category including even the freedom to sin or to contradict the divine freedom.[15] The following quote captures felicitously what Barth means by human freedom:

> The gift of freedom . . . involves more than being offered one option among several. It involves more than being asked a question, being presented with an opportunity, and having a possibility opened up. . . . We are dealing with the gift of the free God. God does not put man into the situation of Hercules at the crossroads. The opposite is true. God frees man from this false situation. He lifts him from appearance to reality. It is true that man's freedom is choice, decision, act. But it is genuine choice; it is genuine decision and act in the right direction.[16]

10. Barth, *Romans*, 213, 219, 228, 234.

11. Found in Barth, "Gift of Freedom," 67–96. The address itself on which the essay is based was delivered in 1953.

12. Barth, "Gift of Freedom," 69, 75.

13. Barth, "Gift of Freedom," 71.

14. Barth, "Gift of Freedom," 72.

15. Barth, "Gift of Freedom," 77.

16. Barth, "Gift of Freedom," 76.

In line with Barth's thinking, man becomes free not so that he can neutrally or equally choose to act wrongly or rightly, rather he becomes free and is free by choosing and determining himself in conformity to the freedom of God. Human freedom is thus *not*, of all things, man becoming "Hercules at the crossroads"—a phrase Barth was particularly fond of using—able to choose between right or wrong by the brute power of his volition.[17] This immediate thought brings freedom into relation with obedience: freedom is "the venture of obedience whereby man reflects in his own life God's offer and his own response."[18] Human freedom is, on this final score, the God-given freedom to obey.[19] As Couenhoven remarks correctly, the above thoughts summarize Barth's central commitments about human freedom, consistently revealed in his works that span from 1929 to the end of his writing career in 1960.[20]

Barth's Obedience-Freedom Relation within Contemporary Philosophical Discussion

When framed within contemporary philosophical discussion, Barth's manner of specifying the obedience-freedom relation carries with it two implications.

Autonomy, Heteronomy, Theonomy

First, Barth's depiction of the obedience-freedom relation runs counter to popular contemporary thought that the exercise of human freedom is incompatible with any form of submission to religious law, that is, human freedom and obedience are seen in antithetical rather than amicable terms.[21] Such thinking has gained momentum since Immanuel Kant, whose contrast between autonomy and heteronomy has resulted in an association of, on the one hand, human freedom with autonomy, and on the other hand, obedience with heteronomy.

According to Kant, autonomy in the field of moral thinking means that a good will is the only thing in the world that is good without limitation; good in itself, or the highest good. A good will such as this acts from

---

17. See *CD* II/1, 627; *CD* II/2, 517; *CD* III/1, 264; *CD* III/2, 235; *CD* IV/1, 616, 746; *CD* IV/2, 494 and *CD* IV/4, 162.
18. Barth, "Gift of Freedom," 80.
19. Barth, "Gift of Freedom," 82.
20. Couenhoven, "Karl Barth's Conception(s)," 247.
21. In the discussion to follow, I am assisted by Roy, "Does Christian Faith?," 606–23.

duty, and one is said to be doing just that whenever one's volitional activity is determined by universal maxims processed rationally that are in turn considered as being binding in all situations for all rationale beings; that is to say, when one's volitional activity is determined according to Kant's famous nomenclature, the "categorical imperatives."[22] Only when one is acting this way is one autonomous and free. Louis Roy, OP, captures the issue succinctly when he states that for Kant, "[p]ractical reason must be its own sovereign and legislative authority. It is autonomous provided it finds within itself the whole binding power and all the principles of the good will; by contrast, it is heteronomous whenever it finds its principles externally, be it in ends, objects, ideas, values, or even God."[23] Moral reasoning, from the time of Kant onwards, is divorced from classical theology and takes on a "moral space" of its own, as Alexis-Baker puts it.[24]

Drawing from Thomas Aquinas for its wider theological background and Paul Tillich for the specific application of the concept, Roy posits a third position "theonomy" (= God's law) in contrast to the two positions of heteronomy (= another's law) and autonomy (= one's own law).[25] Theonomy, Roy contends, has the advantage of drawing from the best of the ideas of personal liberty and openness to the mystery from the positions of autonomy and heteronomy respectively.[26] Theonomy is also participatory in nature in identifying a human ethics that partakes of divine wisdom, expressed in the Thomasian categories of a fourfold participation of natural, positive, revealed, and new law in divine law.[27] Roy recognizes that there is still a

---

22. Kant states it as such: "*Autonomy (Autonomie)* of the will is the sole principle of all moral laws and of the duties in keeping with them; *heteronomy (Heteronomie)* of choice, on the other hand, not only does not ground any obligation at all but is instead opposed to the principle of obligation and to the morality of the will. That is to say, the sole principle of morality consists in independence from all matter of the law (namely, from a desired object) and at the same time in the determination of choice through the mere form of giving universal law that a maxim must be capable of. That *independence*, however, is freedom (*Freiheit*) in the *negative* sense, whereas this *lawgiving of its own* on the part of pure and, as such, practical reason is freedom in the *positive* sense. Thus the moral law expresses nothing other than the *autonomy* of pure practical reason, that is, freedom" (Kant, *Critique of Practical Reason*, as quoted in Roy, "Does Christian Faith?," 608).

23. Roy, "Does Christian Faith?," 608.

24. Alexis-Baker, "Theology Is Ethics," 425–38.

25. Roy, "Does Christian Faith?," 615.

26. Roy, "Does Christian Faith?," 617.

27. Roy, "Does Christian Faith?," 617–18. Roy defines the various laws as follows: "Eternal law consists in the general design over history, as found in the divine mind. Natural law is man's incomplete and yet valid understanding of eternal law. Revealed law is the one written in the Bible and interpreted by the Church. Positive law is the

definite exteriority to the law that comes with theonomy that leads inevitably to a sense of dependency, but he contends that Kant would be willing to concede this exteriority, given that it is one coming from the Creator while being discovered in us via our practical reasoning.[28] More importantly, this dependency is one couched within the terms of a theonomy that makes autonomy possible in the first place.[29]

On this issue, Barth would go a certain distance in agreeing with the analysis of Roy above. Barth's theological vocabulary abounds in the terms bandied around—"autonomy,"[30] "categorical imperative,"[31] even "theonomy"[32]—although it must be emphasized that Barth does not appropriate these terms uncritically but in a transformative sense. But the significant point is that Barth would agree with the basic assertion that obedience is a response grouped under theonomy, not heteronomy, and it is in this "theonomic" response that autonomy is founded. For Barth, the main "theonomic" activity would be the divine election:

> [T]he fulfilment of the election involves the affirmation of the existence of elected man and its counterpart in man's election, in which God's election evokes and awakens faith, and meets and answers that faith as human decision. . . . [T]his means that for his part man can and actually does elect God . . . . There is, then, a simple but comprehensive autonomy of the creature which is constituted originally by the act of eternal divine election and which has in this act its ultimate reality.[33]

Barth, however, would not adopt the approach taken by Roy in seeking recourse to a participatory theonomy through the means of the four laws participating in the divine/eternal law. The approach bears too much the overtones of natural theology. Instead, Barth's approach takes a christocentric route. Via Jesus Christ showing us what it means to be truly human specifically by his obedience, Jesus reclaims the lost ground such that now, as stated by Alexis-Baker, "[t]he 'moral space' within which we all move is the

---

corpus of regulations fashioned by a society. And the law of the Gospel [or new law] is the inner grace, instilled in us by the Holy Spirit, that enables us to act out of love" (614).

28. Roy, "Does Christian Faith?," 618.
29. Roy, "Does Christian Faith?," 619.
30. E.g. *CD* II/2, 177.
31. The usage of the term appears as early as Barth, *Romans*, 207, 220, and 234, with the first two references referring to the "categorical imperative" of God's grace. Barth deals with the term again in *Ethics*, 76–78, and *CD* II/2, 666–67.
32. E.g. *CD* I/2, 815–16, 858–59; *CD* II/2, 177–80; *CD* III/2, 123, *CD* IV/2, 17.
33. *CD* II/2, 177.

obedient Son of God."[34] If Kant shifted the "moral space" in which one maneuvers ethically to the realm of one's autonomous will, then in Jesus Christ, an ontological (re)shift has happened such that Jesus' followers now exist in a moral space which Jesus defines and constitutes. As Alexis-Baker puts it succinctly: "Jesus' faithful obedience . . . establishes and defines humanity as a life of faithful obedience."[35] This is why for Barth, "[t]he categorical imperative as such will never be a command. It can become this only when we receive, not this formula, but a real imperative"—[36] the real imperative being that which has addressed us in the theonomic event of Jesus Christ the electing God and elected man.

Compatibilism, (Hard) Determinism, Libertarianism

The second implication flowing from Barth's specification of the obedience-freedom relation has to do with contemporary philosophical discussions on freedom. Philosophical debate about human freedom is currently preoccupied with the philosophical knot of freedom and causal determinism, with the issue often expressed through a discussion of the topic of "free will." In this regard, it would be a fair to locate Barth's view within the general position of compatibilism on the philosophical continuum. The following paragraphs outline the key positions within philosophical discussions on freedom and free will, showing in the process why Barth's notion of freedom is best located within the compatibilist pole in the spectrum of thought.[37]

In broad terms, compatibilists see the idea of freedom as coherent with determinism; incompatibilists see the situation as one of either freedom or determinism. Incompatibilism can be further divided into Libertarianism or Hard Determinism. The first sub-group (the libertarians) may hold onto a "softer" position, which while not denying other definitions of a free will permitted under compatibilism, go beyond those definitions to affirm that it is possible to have and to make sense of a free will that is totally undetermined in any way. The libertarian may also choose to adopt a "harder" position which states that the only true freedom and consequently truly free

---

34. Alexis-Baker, "Theology Is Ethics," 433.
35. Alexis-Baker, "Theology Is Ethics," 427.
36. CD II/2, 666–67.
37. I say the above recognizing the tinge of anachronism involved. Barth's theology not only antedates the philosophical terminology used, but Barth was disinterested in offering a philosophical treatment of the notion of freedom. Yet, it is my belief that a philosophical consideration clarifies and renders more precise Barth's notion of human freedom via the distinctions of analytic philosophy on this subject matter. See Couenhoven, "Karl Barth's Conception(s)," 254.

"free will" must be one that excludes all forms of determinism. The second sub-group (the hard determinist) denies the compatibility or coherence of free will and determinism, hence distinguishing themselves from the compatibilists (sometimes also termed "soft determinists"). However, they also deny the possibility of a libertarian free will, in that way distinguishing themselves from libertarianism. In other words, hard determinists deny the possibility of free will at all, or at best they allow for the "illusion" of the free will to remain. Philosopher Robert Kane clarifies this very complex and difficult discussion by proposing five ways to think about what we mean by freedom. This is important as his clarification illuminates what Barth means by freedom.[38] I repeat the five forms of freedom provided by Kane:

1. *The Freedom of Self-realization.* This is the power or ability to do what we want or will to do. In order to exercise this freedom, there must be no external constraints or impediments (such as physical restraints, coercion, and compulsion) that would prevent us from realizing our wants and purposes in action. Sometimes, this freedom is referred to as "freedom of choice or decision."

2. *The Freedom of (Reflective) Self-control.* This is the power to reflect upon and evaluate the reasons and motives one wants to act on, or should act on, and to control one's behavior in accordance with such reflectively considered reasons. It is an instance where the agent's second-order desires are aligned with their first-order desires, that is, the agent owns or identifies with her particular first-order desire. The pointed question moves from "Can I get what I want?" (the previous form of freedom) to "What should I want?" (this current form of freedom). It is also at this level that issues concerning responsibility enter the picture.

3. *The Freedom of Self-perfection.* This level of freedom goes beyond the ownership of one's first-order desires to a power to understand and appreciate the right reasons for action and to guide one's behavior in accordance with these right reasons. This definition of freedom requires, for true freedom and responsibility, not just the ability to undergo reflective self-evaluation and control (as stated above) but the further ability to do so in accordance with "the True and the Good."

With the first three definitions, each definition deepens in coverage of what is required for freedom: from the most basic requirement of self-realization to self-control and "ownership" of what we want to do, to self-perfection

---

38. Kane, *Free Will*, 163–74.

of that self-control and "ownership" in accordance to a higher measure of truth and goodness. Yet, all three conceptions of freedom are still compatible with determinism. The picture changes, however, with the fourth and fifth forms of freedom.

> 4. *The Freedom of Self-determination.* This is the power or ability to act *of your own free will* in the sense that this is a will that you yourself, to some degree, were *ultimately responsible* for forming. This conception of freedom in turn presupposes the fifth form of freedom stated below.
>
> 5. *The Freedom of Self-formation.* This is the power to form one's own will in a manner that is undetermined by one's past by virtue of *will-setting* or *self-forming* actions (SFAs) over which one has plural voluntary control, that is, one is able to will and act on *alternative possibilities* voluntarily, intentionally, and rationally.

The fourth and fifth conceptions of freedom are incompatible with determinism. Kane explains why: "[W]e have the following chain of inferences: (1) *free will* entails (2) *ultimate responsibility* [UR] for our wills as well as for our actions, which entails (3) *will-setting* actions at some points in our lives, which in turn entail that some of our actions must satisfy (4) the *plurality conditions* . . . which in turn entails that (5) the agents *could have done otherwise* or had alternative possibilities."[39] The very presence of alternative possibilities which can be willed and acted upon in a voluntary, intentional, and rational manner is what rules out determinism.

Couched within the above philosophical discussion, it is evident that Barth sees human freedom essentially as compatibilist freedom, a freedom compatible with determinism. Human freedom, according to Barth, does not require alternative possibilities in which the human agent could have otherwise willed and acted upon in a voluntary, intentional and rational manner (according to the plural voluntary control conditions). The free human agent is not, as Barth reiterated constantly, "Hercules at the crossroads," able to choose equally between good and evil,[40] obedience and disobedience,[41] or faith and unbelief.[42]

The strong element of determinism is detected—put across in a negative way—in Barth's maintenance of the impossibility of human freedom to be either a freedom to sin or a freedom to contradict the divine freedom, and—stated in a positive way—that human freedom is given or

39. Kane, *Free Will*, 129 (emphasis original).
40. *CD* II/2, 517.
41. *CD* III/1, 264.
42. *CD* IV/1, 746.

determined to man via the divine election. Man's self-determination in his electing or choosing of God (i.e., his freedom) is always premised upon and corresponding to God's prior and antecedent determination of man. Colin Gunton was on the mark when he stated: "[A]ccording to Barth one must be determined in order to be free. But unless it is God who determines us, we are under the power of a demon, not the truth. His determination, because it is the work of the personal God, is a determination that liberates for true self-determination."[43]

Yet, in saying that Barth's understanding of human freedom remains essentially a compatibilist or a determinism-related freedom, Barth's notion of freedom is able to encompass all three conceptions of freedom stated above that fall within the compatibilist range. The human agent, although she has a determined and derived freedom, is nevertheless able to carry out what she wills (freedom of self-realization), "owns" that desire in wanting to do whatever she has willed (freedom of reflective self-control), and could even be said to be able to check and self-evaluate her "ownership" of that desire (freedom of self-perfection). After all, on Barth's count, "man's God-given freedom is choice, decision, act," albeit a "genuine decision and act in the right direction."[44]

"Obedience" as the Entry-Point in CD IV/1: A Further Suggestion Why

Given Barth's basic amicable and complementary relation between the two notions of freedom and obedience, it is not altogether surprising that Barth would appropriate the motif of obedience as the entry point into his doctrine of reconciliation in *CD* IV/1. Since reconciliation ultimately concerns a liberation or determination of freedom to mankind, and since the human freedom gifted to mankind is a *determined freedom to obedience*, obedience functions as a suitable and prime conceptual tool to capture the reconciliatory reality of freedom that is involved. Because of the close connection, Barth recognizes that to have obedience function as the entry point for his doctrine of reconciliation leads eventually to the theme of freedom anyway. This explains partially why even though it could plausibly be argued that freedom has functioned as a uniting motif that threads the *Dogmatics* thus far—just think of Barth's favorite expression to capture the essence of who the triune God is: "the One who loves in freedom"—[45] he formally

43. Gunton, "Triune God and Freedom," 52.
44. Barth, "Gift of Freedom," 76.
45. The title of *CD* II/1 §28. In fact, Gorringe, *Hegemony*, 271, suggests that Gal

chose obedience over freedom as the entry-point in *CD* IV/1. On Barth's reckoning, freedom and obedience are two sides of the same coin of salvation, and regardless of the doorway of freedom or obedience that is used, one enters the same hallway where the two intermingle and where one is never mentioned in isolation of the other.[46]

True as the above is, I venture to suggest one other reason for Barth's preference to employ the theme of obedience as his entry point. This possible reason arises when consideration is given to the social and political background that *CD* IV/1 to IV/3 were written in during the years 1951 to 1959. Socially and economically, this decade was the period of European industrial and economic recovery. Standards of living rose dramatically across almost all the European countries so far as to lead to what Gorringe calls the "emergence in both Europe and North America of . . . the victory of pragmatic welfare reformism, committed to a mix of free market and limited state regulation."[47] The result was that freedom became the popular and dominant concept of the day, with the concept gradually being defined as a freedom of choice. Politically, this decade was dominated by the three major issues of the Cold War, nuclear weapons and decolonization, in which Barth intervened publicly on the first two issues.[48] In terms of the mood, the anti-communism vibe and rhetoric was palpable in the political atmosphere, and Barth drew much criticism and flak for his apparently "soft" stance on communism.[49]

The above said, the reader reading *CD* IV/1–3 could be excused for being oblivious to the whole host of issues stated above, for Barth succeeded in rendering invisible the social and political background of what lay behind the *Dogmatics*. In part, this was deliberate. As Barth stated in the beginning of his brochure "*Theologische Existenz heute!*" addressing the rise of Nazi fascism that was confronting the German Church in the 1930s, he always

---

5:1, "For freedom Christ has set us free," serves as a suitable epigraph to the entire *Dogmatics*.

46. For a feel of how it is like to enter the hallway of Barth's doctrine of reconciliation via the doorway of freedom, see Gorringe, *Hegemony*, 217–67. Gorringe sees the doctrine of reconciliation as a "massive exposition of the claim that 'Jesus means freedom'" (225). At every stage in the doctrine of reconciliation, Gorringe depicts Barth as one whose concern for human freedom functions as a critical response to the Enlightenment's own preoccupation with this subject matter (267).

47. Gorringe, *Hegemony*, 218.

48. Gorringe, *Hegemony*, 219. Barth gave a cursory treatment to the question of nuclear weapons in the section dealing with war in *CD* III/4, and he later drew up the ten theses on nuclear weapons produced by the German Evangelical Church in 1958. The ten theses can be found in Williams, "Barth, War and the State," 171–72.

49. See Jehle, *Ever Against the Stream*, 87–99, for a fuller account of this issue.

endeavored to "carry on theology, and only theology . . . as if nothing had happened."⁵⁰ Barth was guided by his principal belief that the role of theology, especially dogmatic theology, was always to summon the teaching church to the voice of Jesus Christ alone.⁵¹ Dogmatics hence became not a matter of inquiring about the voices of the day, but about the voice of God for the day; the direction of speech is always from the church to the world, and not from the world to the church.⁵² As such, Barth was intentional and careful in not explicitly mentioning any of the social or political events surrounding the time of writing, though pressing these events may be, lest the voice of God be diluted by these external voices.

A deeper reading into the *Dogmatics*, however, reveals that Barth's theological overtures are never as contextually void as his methodological principle might imply—Barth was no theologian "doing theology in antiseptic isolation from his surroundings," as Gorringe states.⁵³ Lying hidden beneath the text are Barth's occasional comments to what was happening around him; at times, the way a particular doctrine is explicated gestures towards Barth's response to specific events, implicit though these responses remain.⁵⁴

I suggest that this is what is happening with Barth's choice of the notion of obedience rather than freedom as the entry point into his doctrine of reconciliation. Even as Barth perceived the complementary relationship between obedience and freedom would bring the two ideas into discussion eventually regardless of their starting point, Barth's preference for obedience serves as a pointed address to what he saw was happening in the West and the East from where he was located.⁵⁵ America in the west was witnessing a rise in popularity in terms of conceiving an individualistic freedom that came with little or no restrictions, while the Communist Soviet Bloc in the east was emphasizing a kind of obedience to the command of the State. In this context, Barth's preference to begin with obedience functions as an implicit but pointed challenge to both movements on the western and eastern fronts. The challenge appears in the form of what Mark Lindsay calls "'discursive resistance'—resistance that deliberately

50. Barth, *Theological Existence To-Day!*, 9.
51. *CD* I/2, 812.
52. *CD* I/2, 843.
53. Gorringe, *Hegemony*, 219.
54. As an example, see Lindsay, "Evolution of Election," 107–28, who takes Barth's doctrine of election in *CD* II/2 and brings it into conversation with the Nazi anti-Semitism of Barth's day at the time of writing.
55. I owe the following insight to a conversation I had with Professor Willie Jennings at the 2015 Karl Barth Conference at Princeton Theological Seminary.

*en*counters, and then *counters*, the prevailing ideology."[56] So toward the West, by starting with obedience instead of freedom, Barth was encountering the popular notion that true freedom is the freedom of choice and countering it instead with the idea that *true freedom comes from true obedience*.[57] And toward the East, by relating freedom to obedience, Barth was encountering the demand for an absolute obedience from the State and countering it instead with the notion that even as the Christian serves God within the strictures of Marxism or Communism, her *true obedience to God is what leads to true freedom*.[58] For those prepared to grant to Barth a robust albeit implicit contextual element to his theology, Barth's deliberate move in appropriating obedience as the entry point to his doctrine of reconciliation carries the overtones of a "discursive resistance" to the prevalent ideologies of both West and East then.

Barth's Specification of the Relation between Divine Freedom and Divine Obedience

Having outlined above Barth's basic amicable manner of ordering the relationship between freedom and obedience, I turn now to his specification of the relation between *divine* freedom and *divine* obedience in particular.

56. Lindsay, "Evolution of Election," 121 (emphasis original).

57. Barth's "discursive resistance" towards the Western conception of individualistic freedom often comes through his comments on the Statue of Liberty. In Barth, *Table Talk*, 37, he renders the following comment: "We are confused by the political idea of freedom. What is the light in the Statue of Liberty? Freedom to choose good and evil? What light that would be! Light is light and not darkness. If it shines, *darkness is done away with*, not proposed for choice! Being a slave of Christ means being free" (original emphasis). See also Barth, *How I Changed My Mind*, 79, where on his trip to America in 1962, Barth mentioned that the Statue of Liberty in terms of the conception of freedom it holds out for many needed to be demythologized—a true theology of freedom is the one which the Son frees us to and which is gifted to us.

58. The above implicit and silent challenge that Barth offers to the eastern front with his appropriation of the motif of obedience is consistent with the message conveyed in two of his other writings concerning Marxism or Communism. The two writings are Barth, "The Church between East and West," and "Letter to a Pastor in the German Democratic Republic" found in Barth and Hamel, *How to Serve God*, 45–80. In both writings, Barth did not actively oppose Marxism or Communism. Rather, Barth maintained that the Church's real task was to call all men back to true humanity held out in the Word of God ("Church between East and West," 76–77) and to "resist" the "roaring lion" mentioned in 1 Pet 5:8–9, without simplistically equating the "roaring lion" with communism or the "resisting" with being anti-communist ("Letter to a Pastor," 49–50). As mentioned earlier, Barth has been heavily censured for failing to respond with a stronger stand towards communism. For a fair evaluation, see the introductory essay by Robert McAfee Brown in Barth and Hamel, *How to Serve God*, 11–44.

To begin with, I direct our attention to Barth's core understanding of human freedom as gleaned from the previous section: it consists not in a freedom of choice of alternatives, but in the freedom to be what one has been *determined* for. Here, I wish to underscore the point that Barth's conception of human freedom is as it is because such is also the case for Barth when it comes to divine freedom. To recall what was stated in chapter 2, Barth sees the divine freedom that consists of being free from external constraint and conditioning, or internal lack and deficiency, as only a secondary definition of freedom. His primary definition of divine freedom lies in the freedom to be Godself, to be God in *this* particular way. Divine freedom is primarily to be, as Barth said, "grounded in one's own being, to be determined and moved by oneself."[59] Fundamentally, divine freedom for Barth is the *freedom of God in his lordship to be the triune God*. Barth states in the first volume of *CD*: "[T]he lordship . . . consists in the freedom of God to differentiate Himself from Himself, to become unlike Himself and yet to remain the same, . . . to exist as the one sole God in the fact that in this way that is so inconceivably profound He differentiates Himself from Himself, being not only God the Father but also . . . God the Son."[60] Towards the end of his academic career, Barth reiterated the same fundamental formula of divine freedom in equally stark and clear terms:

> God's freedom is not merely unlimited possibility or formal majesty and omnipotence, that is to say empty, naked sovereignty. Nor is this true of the God-given freedom of man. If we so misinterpret human freedom, it irreconcilably clashes with divine freedom and becomes the false freedom of sin, reducing man to a prisoner. God Himself, if conceived of as unconditioned power, would be a demon and as such His own prisoner. . . . In his own freedom, as the source of human freedom, *God above all willed and determined Himself to be the Father and the Son in the unity of the Spirit*. This is not abstract freedom. Nor is it the freedom of aloof isolation.[61]

As Gunton remarked: "God's freedom is not that of an arbitrary willing machine, but that of the triune God, and takes shape in the mysterious life of Father, Son and Spirit."[62]

---

59. *CD* II/1, 301.
60. *CD* I/1, 320.
61. Barth, "Gift of Freedom," 71 (added emphasis).
62. Gunton, "Triune God and Freedom," 49. Couenhoven, "Karl Barth's Conception(s)," 252–54, interestingly advocates that God's freedom in his divine self-determination should be construed within a philosophical compatibilist framework,

Yet—as argued at length throughout this volume—God's freedom that he has in himself is essentially at one and same instance a freedom for us. The singular eternal act of self-determination where God is the triune God is the one concurrent and coterminous act of self-determination where God is also the God who elects in Jesus Christ. In other words, God's freedom-in-Godself is simultaneously his freedom-for-creation-and-redemption-in-election. Barth articulates this clearly again: "God's freedom is essentially not freedom *from*, but freedom *to* and *for*. . . . God is free for *man*, free to coexist with man and, as the Lord of the covenant, to participate in his *history*. The concept of God without man is indeed as anomalous as wooden iron."[63] This explains why a little earlier in the same essay, Barth stated that "[w]e may not speak of God's own freedom apart from the history of God's dealings with man."[64]

It is admitted that Barth's language could be read as dangerously poised in a position that somehow or another suggests the necessity of creation for the being of God. Such a position, however, is far from Barth's intent. This explains why, although Barth relegates the idea of freedom from external constraint and conditioning or internal deficiency to a secondary role, he never did away with this idea altogether. "Through His revelation God is known in His loving-kindness to us as the God of *man*," Barth states, "[h]owever, God was not and is not bound to choose and to decide Himself for man alone and to show His loving-kindness to him alone."[65] God's aseity grounds his divine freedom, and therefore it is right and proper to exclude any conceptual notions of "necessity"—even divine "necessity"—in discussing

---

that is, Barth does not present God's "choosing" to be the triune being in love as a choice among alternatives. It is "not a matter of a pre-existing will selecting among possible divine perfections, but rather the triune God's wholehearted good pleasure in and affirmation of the life in love that God is" (253). On my part, I am not sure if the *divine* freedom can or should be subject to such philosophical consideration. The philosophical frameworks of compatibilism or incompatibilism presuppose the existence of a being and the exercise of her volition. Divine self-determination, however as we have seen, is concerned with the "willing-into-being" of a (divine) subject. Given already the complexity of the discussion of divine self-determination (or constitution) as seen in chapter 2, I neither think that the philosophical language of compatibilism/incompatibilism is the right language to appropriate for the phenomenon of divine self-determination nor is it "transferrable" over to this new context.

63. Barth, "Gift of Freedom," 72 (emphasis original).

64. Barth, "Gift of Freedom," 70. On p. 72, Barth repeats this idea in the strongest terms possible: "The well-known definitions of the essence of God and in particular of His freedom, containing such terms as 'Wholly other,' 'transcendence,' or 'non-wordly,' stand in need of thorough clarification . . . . The above definitions might just as well fit a dead idol."

65. Barth, "Gift of Freedom," 73 (emphasis original).

the divine freedom. The fact that God's divine freedom is fundamentally a freedom in his lordship to be the triune God means that between triunity and election, the former should have the logical priority and precedence, and that is the position I have maintained throughout this volume.[66]

Continuing along the line of thought of God's aseity, however, even though the divine aseity does preclude any constraint or deficiency or necessity when speaking about the freedom of God, the preclusions do not exhaust the meaning of divine aseity for Barth. Rather, as Barth stated earlier in *CD* I/1: "God's aseity is not empty freedom. In God all potentiality is included in His actuality and therefore all freedom in His decision. Decision means choice, exercised freedom."[67] In this case, God has exercised the divine freedom in his son Jesus Christ, loving him (and therefore Godself) from all eternity, and loving the world in him.[68] The divine freedom is a freedom for the world. As appropriately captured in the axiom by Kevin Hector: "God is free-*from* the world in order to be free-*for* it."[69]

The above string of arguments leads to the conclusion that when it comes to the specification of the relationship between divine freedom and divine obedience, Barth's understanding of divine freedom already draws in and includes divine obedience in the closest connection possible. Given that divine freedom involves the divine election (God's freedom-in-Godself is a freedom-for-election), and given that—as established in the earlier chapters—the divine election is conceived within an actualistic ontological framework that supports Barth's tendentious notion of the divine obedience of the eternal Son, it could be said that *divine freedom involves divine obedience from the outset* on Barth's reckoning. Insofar as we have seen in the previous section that Barth says the human freedom is a "freedom to obey,"

---

66. One who argues adopting an approach of divine "necessity" for a logical priority and precedence of triunity over election within the Trinity-election debate is Hector, "Immutability, Necessity and Triunity," 64–81. Hector affirms that both "triunity" and "election" are "necessary" to God, albeit in a differentiated sense, whereby triunity is an "absolute" necessity whereas election is a "volitional" necessity (71–73). God could have been the triune God he is without us, because election to the covenant of grace is not an absolute necessity to him in the way his triunity is (69). Yet God has, in election, so bound himself to the covenant that he has rendered it as a "volitional" necessity to himself, and "necessary" in a way that God has no being-in-Godself apart from the covenant (74–75). Despite arguing for the same outcome, my main reservation with Hector's proposal is that it depends on the language of "necessity" to carry the weight of the argument, and I am not altogether confident that Barth's preference would have been to use the same language Hector employs.

67. *CD* I/1, 157.
68. *CD* II/1, 320–21.
69. Hector, "God's Triunity," 256.

the same could be posited of Barth's take on divine freedom: divine freedom is likewise a "freedom to obey."

The above manner of stating the relationship, however, reverses the order and borders on a principle like the *analogia entis*; an approach Barth disavowed. Barth's preference would lie more with the argument that because the divine freedom is a freedom to obey, human freedom is likewise a freedom to obedience, with the key connecting link being the *analogia fidei* and *analogia relationis* centered on the singular person of the perfect God-man Jesus Christ. The task of the fourth section is to elaborate the immediate mentioned statements. But before that, Barth's specification of the relation or coordination between divine action and human action warrants a closer look.

Barth's Specification of the Coordination between Divine Action and Human Action

Before detailing Barth's coordination between divine and human action, one must first defend Barth against the charge that his pronounced emphasis on the dominance—even hegemony as so claimed by his detractors—of divine action has crowded out space for human action. This charge tended to prevail in earlier scholarship especially in the area of Barth's ethics.[70] Nimmo, however, remarks that this specific charge has been mitigated and even reversed by more recent scholarship, with the result that it is now recognized that while "the theological ontology of Barth yields a very particular concept of the context of ethical agency, it is a context in which there is nonetheless created a clearly defined space for meaningful theological ethics and being in action."[71] One clear space created for human action is located under Barth's concept of mankind's election to the command of God, found in *CD* II/2 §36, and the other in the *concursus Dei*.

---

70. For example, Werpehowski, "Command and History," 298–320, examines and defends Barth against two criticisms leveled at his "ethics of divine command": i) that Barth's account is basically an "intuitionist" account that short-circuits the rational processes of moral agents, and ii) that Barth's account excludes the component of growth-in-continuity. Lying at the core of the two criticisms is Barth's view of the person as a "free self undetermined by its phenomenal history" (300). Werpehowski defends Barth against the first criticism by drawing in the notion of a theonomous understanding and judgment that comes with the divine command (307–10). He responds to the second criticism by highlighting areas where Barth allows for the development of the theme of "character" (314–16).

71. Nimmo, *Being in Action*, 3.

Our Election to the Command of God—Space for Human Action

In this paragraph, Barth contends that insofar as the covenant of God with man has the doctrine of the divine election of grace as its first element, it has the doctrine of the divine command as the second element.[72] Within the eternal covenant established between God and man, the divine election of man in Jesus Christ is an election unto obedience to the command of God. Barth states: "As election is ultimately the determination of man, the question arises as to the human self-determination which corresponds to this determination.... How is he going to exist under this determination? As the one who is determined in this way, what sort of a man will he be and what will he do?"[73]

The answer to the above question, Barth affirms, inevitably draws out the notion of obedience: "That God wills to rule over him clearly means that He wants his obedience, and the question of obedience is therefore put to him."[74] God's determining of man in the event of God's divine election calls for a correspondent human self-determining on man's part in terms of his responsibility and decision, his obedience and action. Stated differently: God's "being-in-action" calls forth a particular and corresponding "being-in-action" of the ethical agent, and as Nimmo puts it, this leads to the emergence of "a clearly defined space ... within which meaningful human action can take place."[75] Election, then, is understood as the sanctifying claim of the electing God upon the elected man that comes through the command of God directed to him. As Barth states it pithily: "[W]hen God turns to [man] and gives Himself to him He becomes his Commander."[76]

Two points illuminate this space carved out for human action under Barth's doctrine of the divine command, and they deserve mentioning. First, we should take note of the centrality and weight that Barth devotes to the notion of obedience as the overall rubric by which to capture man's ethical response, his human action and even his human existence as a moral agent. Barth is adamant that the universally experienced ethical question of human action and existence—as he phrases it: "What is the right choice? What ought I to do? What ought we to do?"—when it comes under the theological banner of the divine lordship, becomes at once a question of

---

72. *CD* II/2, 509.
73. *CD* II/2, 510–11.
74. *CD* II/2, 511.
75. Nimmo, *Being in Action*, 11.
76. *CD* II/2, 512.

human obedience.⁷⁷ Barth states: "Starting out from the knowledge of the divine election of man, we can know of no human action which does not stand under God's command, of no human existence which does not respond in one way or another to God's command, which has not the character of obedience or disobedience to God's command."⁷⁸ Clearly, obedience forms the central feature within the contours that shape Barth's description of the space given to human action.⁷⁹

The second point of significance is that even as obedience answers the ethical question of human existence, by virtue of the fact that this ethical question is not posed in a vacuum but within the event of the grace of God, Barth affirms that the question is "already answered by the grace of God."⁸⁰ The result is that "[w]e cannot act as if the command of God, issued by God's grace to the elect man Jesus Christ, and again by God's grace already fulfilled by this man, were not already known to us as the sum total of the good."⁸¹ In other words, for Barth, if obedience counts as the definitive human action and response to the electing grace of God, then Jesus' action further defines the shape and outlook of that obedience. Barth reinforces this thought a few pages further on:

> When we say: What ought we to do? we are asking about Him [i.e., Jesus], for it is in Him that this question of ours is answered. In Him the obedience demanded of us men has already been rendered. *In Him the realisation of the good corresponding to divine election has already taken place*—and so completely that we, for our part, have *actually nothing to add*, but have only to *endorse this event by our action*. The ethical problem of Church dogmatics can consist only in the question whether

---

77. *CD* II/2, 535. Barth states that this universal ethical problem is not only one belonging to the church, but extends to "philosophy, politics, and pedagogy."

78. *CD* II/2, 535

79. It is precisely this point that Fout, *Fully Alive*, takes issue with. Beginning with his basic premise that the glory of God is such that it "overflows" from the triune God into the creation, Fout contends that the "overflowing" of God's glory need not bracket out human agency. Instead, the fullness of the overflow of the glory of God leads to an analogous "overflow" in human agency. Fout considers that Barth (and Balthasar) have captured the essence of this "overflow" of God's glory, but thinks that by anchoring the human response, including its "overflow," in the notion of obedience to the divine command, they have unwittingly failed to carry through their basic intuition about the overflow of God's glory to the very end. In Fout's words: "[H]eteronomy [in the sense of a commandment-obedience relation] . . . does not comport with 'overflow'" (1).

80. *CD* II/2, 518.

81. *CD* II/2, 518.

and to what extent human action is a glorification of the grace of Jesus Christ.[82]

It is evident that Barth's christocentric anthropological considerations reverberate all the way down to the response of obedience that encapsulates the meaningful human action that arises whenever the human agent is confronted by the divine command.

The concursus Dei—Divine and Human Action Coordinated

The preceding discussion established Barth as clearing a space within his theology for genuine and meaningful human action to occur, but the question remains as to how divine and human action are coordinated or ordered within that "common" space. To gain an insight into that question, we turn to Barth's doctrine of the *concursus Dei* which he defines as the doctrinal attempt to specify "the lordship of God in relation to the free and autonomous activity of the creature."[83] The key to grasping how the *concursus Dei* coordinates divine and human action lies in recognizing two aspects of the doctrine.

On the one hand, the *concursus Dei* specifies the divine and human action as a singular action in unity. This unity is founded upon the *concursus Dei* conceived as a divine accompaniment of the act of the creature from first to last.[84] God precedes, accompanies, and follows human action so that, as Barth states, "all the activity of the creature is primarily and simultaneously and subsequently His [i.e., God's] own activity, and therefore a part of the actualization of His own will revealed and triumphant in Jesus Christ."[85] On Barth's reckoning, the activity of God and that of the creature is to be understood as a single action,[86] an action in whose singularity and unity the will of God is accomplished. Yet, the sovereignty of God is not compromised through Barth's careful maintenance of asymmetry between the divine and human action. That is to say, even as divine and human action are brought together in their singularity and unity, the will of God is neither limited nor conditioned by the determination and act of the creature. Instead, the reverse is true: the will of God conditions these human acts. In this sense, strictly speaking, as Barth affirms, "[t]he

82. *CD* II/2, 540 (added emphasis).
83. *CD* III/3, 90.
84. Nimmo, *Being in Action*, 119.
85. *CD* III/3, 105.
86. *CD* III/3, 132.

concept of *concursus* is itself irreversible. God 'concurs' with the creature, but the creature does not 'concur' with God."[87]

On the other hand, the *concursus Dei* also specifies the divine and human action as an action in distinction. This move offers a clear affirmation of the genuine activity of the human creature and so quells any suspicions that the unity of divine and human action leads effectively to a dissolution of human action.[88] As we have seen, Barth affirms human action by speaking of the creaturely human action as possessing its own autonomy. He maintains that the operation of the Word and Spirit in the *concursus Dei* "does not prejudice the autonomy, the freedom, the responsibility, the individual being and life and activity of the creature, or the genuineness of its own activity, but confirms and indeed establishes them."[89]

The key to grasping Barth's perplexing move in conceding autonomy to human action lies in the following twofold recognition. First, Barth's conception of "autonomy" differs thoroughly from that of its rival construal derived from the Enlightenment, wherein the autonomy of the human agent is cast in an unqualified and autocratic manner.[90] Second, this autonomy is itself constituted and actualized only in the prior and antecedent event of the free and eternal election of humanity in Jesus Christ.[91] The autonomy of the creature is thus one that is theocentrically circumscribed. As Barth puts it, "the theonomy of God . . . wills and decrees as such the autonomy of man."[92] Under these conditions, the autonomy works itself out in such a manner that the human agent "in its autonomy . . . recognises and acknowledges that it is wholly and utterly responsible to God."[93]

Barth's two specifications—action in unity and action in distinction—coalesce to uncover the root theological principle undergirding the *concursus Dei*. That is, inasmuch as there is true unity of divine and human action within the *concursus Dei*, there is also genuine distinction. This translates to

---

87. *CD* III/3, 112–13. As Nimmo, *Being in Action*, 119–20, notes, the divine conditioning of human action such that "nothing can be done except the will of God" (*CD* III/3, 113) raises the question of theodicy. For this, Nimmo posits that Barth seeks recourse in the standard Reformed distinction between the *efficiens* and the *permittens* will of God.

88. Nimmo, *Being in Action*, 120.

89. *CD* III/3, 144.

90. Nimmo, *Being in Action*, 122. Barth speaks of this autonomy as one that is "over against God" and "is simply the theological form of human enmity against God's grace, the theological actualisation of a repetition of the fall" (*CD* II/1, 586).

91. Nimmo, *Being in Action*, 121.

92. *CD* II/2, 180.

93. *CD* II/2, 121.

the fact that divine and human actions, while each remains true to its nature, do not unite in their singularity on equal terms. Rather, as Barth asserts: "Even in the union of the divine activity and creaturely occurrence there remains a genuine antithesis which is not obscured or resolved either by admixture or transference, either by divine influence or infusion."[94] Divine and human actions, on the final count, do not stand as two species of the same genus.[95] While Barth maintains freedom and autonomy in the actions of the human creature, he concurrently affirms that "God controls the activity in its freedom no less than its necessity. . . . Between the sovereignty of God and the freedom of the creature there is no contradiction. The freedom of its activity does not exclude but includes the fact that it is controlled by God."[96] In the final analysis, Barth asserts that any understanding of the *concursus Dei* has to be derived more from faith than intellect.[97] As a case *sui generis*, the *concursus Dei* concerning "[t]he true God and His activity can never be perceived within the framework of a general philosophy."[98]

The above said, however, Barth does offer a particular viewpoint from which to comprehend the *concursus Dei*. Consistent with his theological methodology, he again approaches the topic christocentrically. Barth affirms that the actuality of God's operation is revealed and seen fully in the covenant of grace effected in and through Jesus Christ. This specific event, in turn, "forms the centre and meaning and goal of all creaturely occurrence."[99] In this event, we see "actualised in Jesus Christ both the lordship of God and also the subordination of the creature";[100] in other words, the outworking of the *concursus Dei*. Recalling our earlier finding in the third chapter where Barth posited Jesus as the first human being to be involved in the "divine activity in the form of the history, encounter and decision between God and man,"[101] we find the operation of the *concursus Dei first premised and worked out in that divine activity between God and the man Jesus, and only then applied to us in an analogous and correspondent manner*. In this way, the apparent paradox within the doctrine of the *concursus Dei*—the ethical agent is set free by the grace of God only to respond with obedience and to come under the authority of the divine

---

94. *CD* III/3, 136.
95. *CD* III/3, 102.
96. *CD* III/3, 165–66.
97. *CD* III/3, 146.
98. Nimmo, *Being in Action*, 123 (quote is from *CD* III/3, 140).
99. *CD* III/3, 142.
100. *CD* III/3, 241.
101. *CD* II/2, 175.

command of God—is somewhat reduced by the preeminent example of the first encounter between divine and human activity in Jesus Christ and in the confession of our election as humanity in the same Christ.[102] In apprehending our election in Jesus Christ, we apprehend not so much by pure intellect as by faith the final goal and outworking of the *concursus Dei*: that we might come to be "freed by God for God."[103] The upshot of the discussion pertinent to our thesis is that it is in Jesus Christ that we find the full display of this freedom spoken of and intended by the *concursus Dei*: a freedom-in-obedience and an obedience-in-freedom.[104]

A Closer Examination of Barth's Coordination of Divine and Human Action

While the *concursus Dei* provides us a framework by which to coordinate divine and human action on Barth's account, the question has been asked whether Barth's insistence on considering human action only in relation to divine action—and not human action in and by itself—leaves Barth's account of human agency finally incomplete. Specifically, Gerald McKenny has asked and in turn addressed three questions: (i) can human action be rendered intelligible as the agent's own action if it is considered only in conjunction with divine action? (ii) is not human action left in a persistently unstable condition in Barth's account, given the absence of any notions of virtue and moral or spiritual growth? And (iii) how does the full range of the ethical agent's moral capacities participate in this freedom prescribed to him in the divine encounter between God and man?[105] Garnering mainly from *Evangelical Theology: An Introduction* and *The Christian Life*, McKenny offers plausible responses from Barth's later writings to each of these questions. As McKenny's responses pertain to an in-depth treatment of Barth's coordination of divine and human action, we will examine them in closer detail.

Addressing the first question, McKenny outlines the basic contours of Barth's conception of human freedom, and his findings are similar to our earlier treatment. Human freedom is a miraculous gift given by God and rendered effectual by the Holy Spirit.[106] This gift of freedom is bestowed

---

102. Nimmo, *Being in Action*, 125.
103. The expression comes from *ChrL*, 88.
104. Nimmo, *Being in Action*, 130.
105. McKenny, "'Freed by God for God,'" 121–24.
106. McKenny, "'Freed by God for God,'" 130. McKenny states that the theme of our freedom for God being linked to the gift of the Holy Spirit is one that gains prominence in *ET*.

and actualized only in the encounter mankind has with God in Jesus Christ. In lucid terms, McKenny states that, for Barth, the freedom that "is given to us is not the capability to decide either for or against God but rather the capability, which we otherwise lack, to decide *for* God";[107] it is a freedom to do *this*—decide for God—and not anything else. Understood on these terms, freedom is not human action that is undertaken by itself and on its own without the superintending intervention of divine action, because there is no such capability on its own on the part of the human agent. Yet, the gift of freedom for God does become genuinely our human action when the bestowed capability to choose—or better, to obey—God is exercised through our endowed creaturely capacities.[108] The following statement from McKenny summarizes the issue well: "Freedom for God is therefore not a matter of a natural capacity perfected and elevated by grace; it is itself a gift of God in which we participate by activating it through the exercise of our natural capacities."[109]

As for the second question, McKenny maintains that Barth views our freedom for God as a gift of the grace of God that is not simply imparted to us but rather is given to us anew. This constant giving (on God's part) and receiving (on our part) of the gift of freedom reflects the personal covenant relationship in which God and humanity have entered and which has been fulfilled in Jesus Christ. McKenny states: "The freedom of God for humanity and humanity for God has already been realized in Christ, and the work of the Holy Spirit is to make this realization of freedom effectual, to actualize it in our concrete lives."[110] Hence, a suspicion and worry that our human action is left in an unstable condition is to fail to comprehend the basis of our freedom already founded in the covenant relationship fulfilled in Christ. Given this background, as McKenny states, one can understand why Barth shies away from virtue or moral progress theories. Our freedom for God is not dependent on whatever growth—monumental or insignificant—that is experienced in our creaturely capacities. In fact, a full-orbed virtue theory might lead us down the misguided path of thinking our freedom is commensurate to our growth in virtue or habits.[111] Instead, the Christian is to

---

107. McKenny, "'Freed by God for God,'" 128 (emphasis original).

108. McKenny, "'Freed by God for God,'" 128–30.

109. McKenny, "'Freed by God for God,'" 130.

110. McKenny, "'Freed by God for God,'" 132.

111. McKenny's comments at this point must be balanced by those of Werpehowski, "Command and History," 314–16, who highlights aspects where Barth seems to allow for the idea of a "growth-in-continuity" of the human ethical agent. More importantly, Werpehowski outlines the theological context in which the "growth" statements are made by Barth, and that wider theological context coheres with what McKenny is saying here.

be ready through constant prayer for the Spirit's coming, since it is the Spirit who effectuates that gift of freedom. This is why, as McKenny pointed out correctly, Barth considers prayer as the human activity that most definitively corresponds to the gift of freedom—and might I add—obedience.[112] This is an idea that I will elaborate in the final section of this chapter.

In relation to the third question, McKenny states that while the human activation of the capability of the freedom for God is understood "along the lines of Kantian spontaneity rather than Aristotelian habituation, that is, as an act that is not conditioned by prior states,"[113] there is no reason to suppose that the full range of human capacities is not engaged when human agents "activate" the God-given capability for freedom. Highlighting *Evangelical Theology*, McKenny states that the "affirmation, trust, and obedience that comprise the human action of faith involve understanding, will and feeling."[114] Notwithstanding the above, McKenny admits that the deeper question remains: granted that all of the human agent's capacities are engaged in the activation of the gift of freedom, how does one know what these capacities are or that one is in full possession of these capacities in the first place, since on Barth's terms, human action is never considered by itself in isolation and in abstraction from the divine action?[115] McKenny, however, leaves the answering of this question to another occasion.

Karl Barth's Conception of Freedom: A Christocentrically Modified Philosophical Compatibilism

Our consideration above reveals that despite claims to the contrary, Barth does have space for genuine human action. He locates that space in mankind's election to the divine command, which forms the other side of an election to grace. Consequently, mankind's response of obedience to the divine command is also at the same time his freedom. This is a freedom gifted by God and made effectual through the Holy Spirt. The capability to choose (and obey God)—otherwise termed a capability of the freedom *for* God—is one that is bestowed by God through the Holy Spirit, whose work in us, rather than being conceived as a mere "push" which sets human action in motion, is more accurately envisaged as the liberation of man into the new direction

---

112. McKenny, "'Freed by God for God,'" 132.
113. McKenny, "'Freed by God for God,'" 133.
114. McKenny, "'Freed by God for God,'" 133. McKenny refers to *ET*, 101.
115. McKenny, "'Freed by God for God,'" 134.

given to him which has become his reality.¹¹⁶ In the process of doing so, all of man's creaturely capacities are engaged and activated.

As seen, the above is a specific outworking of Barth's larger doctrine of the *concursus Dei*, which coordinates divine action and human action in their unity and distinction while ordering divine action into an asymmetrical relationship of priority and precedence over human action. The above description dovetails with the specification of compatibilist freedom outlined in the first section and confirms our initial pass at grouping Barth's conception of human freedom under that category. The following quote from Couenhoven summarizes what I read as Barth's position succinctly:

> [Human freedom] does not leave us with free will in the incompatibilist sense: we do not determine our wills in a manner that is solely up to us, such that we are the originators of our choices and actions. No, God moves in our wills, such that we choose him. But Barth's view is that our choosing God is nevertheless free and in some sense autonomous, because we really do that, of our own wills and with our own minds. The fact that in doing so we cannot do otherwise than ratify what the Spirit is working in us is not a fact that Barth sees as detracting from our freedom; rather, he sees it as the basis of . . . normative Christian freedom . . . .¹¹⁷

At this juncture, it is worthwhile recalling our major interlocutor from the previous chapter, Irenaeus. Clearly, a noticeable difference between Irenaeus and Barth is surfaced when it comes to the specification of the relationship between divine and human action. As presented earlier, the Irenaean narrative of obedience rests upon the notion that the exercise of human volition remains free throughout its inception to its perfection. Relating back to Robert Kane's illuminating taxonomy of freedom, at the most basic level, "free" here connotes a willing not done under coercion or force (level 1 freedom). In this regard, Barth would certainly agree: the exercise of human volition all throughout its inception to its perfection may be *determined* but it is neither *forced* nor *coerced*. In fact, as argued earlier, Barth's conception of human freedom can possibly be stretched to accommodate the third level of freedom as defined by Kane: the human agent "owns" the desire to want to do what she has willed, and is even able to evaluate that "ownership" of the desire according to a higher measure of goodness and truth.

---

116. *CD* IV/2, 531 / *KD* IV/2, 601: "What He [the Holy Spirit] imparts to man when He gives him His direction is not a possibility [*Möglichkeit*] but the new actuality [*Wirklichkeit*] in which he is really free in face of that bondage [of sin]."

117. Couenhoven, "Karl Barth's Conception(s)," 249.

In reading Irenaeus, however, one derives the sense that Irenaeus' conception of the free will ventures into the fourth and fifth levels of Kane's categorization of freedom. At its inception—at the point of Adam's creation upon his reception of the breath of life—all the way to its renewal and perfection, Irenaeus leans towards a view of the free will in which the human agent possesses the power or ability to undertake *self-forming actions* (SFAs) in choosing between alternative possibilities voluntarily, intentionally, and rationally, hence forming or shaping her own will in such a manner that she can assume *ultimate responsibility* (UR) for *that* will.[118] I believe it is on the mark to say that Irenaeus draws the notion of human freedom and free will towards a philosophical framework of incompatibilist-libertarian freedom and a theological framework of Arminianism.[119] Barth, on the other hand, is aligned with a compatibilist freedom and in that way, as Couenhoven remarks, is placed "in continuity with a venerable host of theologians who defend related views, including Augustine, Aquinas, and Calvin."[120]

Those who espouse a notion of human freedom as compatibilist freedom generally maintain that mankind possesses a will post-fall that is determined but "free" (in a level 1–3 kind of freedom as defined by Kane). John Calvin, for example, held that there were four classifications of the will: the coerced, self-determined, bound and free will. The first of the cluster he sees as an antinomy; the second as the will which directs itself in the direction in which it is led (not by force or coercion though); the third as the corrupt will held captive under the authority of evil desires such that it can choose nothing but evil, and the fourth as the will not determined in any way. The post-lapsarian will, according to Calvin, consists in the second and third categories.[121] It is at the definition of the pre-lapsarian will, though, that the

---

118. See *AH* 4.37.1; 4.4.3; 4.39.1–4; 4.14.1, for a sampling of passages. The terms "self-forming actions" and "ultimate responsibility" come from Kane.

119. On the side, I continue to remain intrigued by how a libertarian free will can be maintained under the theological framework of Arminianism. Granted that, let us say, this is a will that has been "restored" to a level of libertarian freedom (corresponding to levels 4 and 5 of Kane's definition of freedom) by God's divine prevenient grace, and given that God divinely foreknows the choice of the human agent in exercising her free will, the Arminian will still have to argue and show how i) the agent's choosing of God in temporality and history is neither determined by the events of her past and history, or her inner state of being including desires and intentions, nor reduced to mere arbitrariness, and ii) how the divine foreknowledge itself is not be conceived as a form of determinism. The proving of the above two conditions would take us beyond the scope of this volume though.

120. Couenhoven, "Karl Barth's Conception(s)," 255.

121. Calvin, *Bondage and Liberation*, 69. Calvin's classification of the "self-determined" will translates to the second level freedom of Kane's taxonomy, and it is at this second-level definition of human freedom that Helm, *John Calvin's Ideas*, 174–76, bases

interlocutors stated above are prepared to concede to Adam a free will that ventures into and straddles the fourth and fifth levels of Kane's taxonomy, although it is debatable even then whether a full-fledged libertarian pre-lapsarian free will is posited.[122] But clearly, the pre-lapsarian free will is one that is not bound in a way that the post-lapsarian free will is.

In this regard, Barth bears a nuanced view of the pre-lapsarian free will. Even at that point, a case can be made that Barth read the free will that Adam had within a compatibilist rather than an incompatibilist-libertarian framework. In discussing the tree of the knowledge of good and evil, Barth conceives the willing involved in heeding the prohibition not to eat of the fruit less as "a freedom of choice between obedience and disobedience" and more as "a confirmation and actualisation of his obedience."[123] For Barth, the existence of the tree of the knowledge of good and evil with its attached prohibition means that God has not created man in such a way that either God compels his obedience or brings about his obedience in a mechanistic manner, but rather that man in his own decision (to obey) confirms and actualizes "the obedience proposed in and with [God's] creation."[124] As Barth states:

> This certainly does not consist in his standing between good and evil and being able to choose between the two. But it does consist in the fact that the man who stands thus before the God

---

his argument of Calvin's maintenance of the free and voluntary nature of the actions of the agent who is under bondage to sin. The agent is not considered to be under external coercion because the agent owns and identifies with her desire to serve and worship the creature rather than the Creator, and whose actions express her desire.

122. For example, Calvin states in *Inst.* I.15.8 that Adam "by [his] free will had the power, if he so willed, to attain eternal life." The difficulty comes in when at the same time Calvin presents that pre-lapsarian free will as unstable, and "if not given the constancy to persevere" would fall. See also Calvin, *Secret Providence*, 76. The key question is: should that sustenance and giving of the constancy to persevere be counted as a form of determinism? The difficulty is further compounded by Calvin's notion of God's predestining of the Fall. As for Augustine's understanding of the free will, a good article to begin with would be Stump, "Augustine on Free Will," 124–47. Stump's argument is that it is possible to construe Augustine as espousing a "modified" libertarian *post-lapsarian* will which ceases to actively refuse grace and is "quiescent" instead. This is the point that God then acts on the will in such a way that it is moved to the acceptance of grace. Stump states that on this account, "the will of faith is a gift of God, but a human person's will is still ultimately in the control of that person, because it is up to her either to refuse grace or to fail to refuse grace, and God's giving of grace depends on what the will of a human person does" (141). Stump's proposal has been debated among Augustinian scholars, but my point in highlighting it is that if her proposal holds for the *post-lapsarian* will, all the more it should hold for the *pre-lapsarian* will.

123. *CD* III/1, 263 and 264.

124. *CD* III/1, 264.

who in his creation has determined him for good is not only subject to this divine decision but can respect it in the form of his own decision. This is the freedom which God gave him at his creation. It is in this and no other way that [God] has determined him in [God's] own decision for good. He expects and has made him capable of confirmation, of the obedience of his own free will and act.[125]

As seen from the above, rather than reading the exercising of prelapsarian free will on the part of Adam as a choosing between the alternative possibilities of good and evil or obedience and disobedience, Barth was more inclined to read *the working of Adam's volition as a confirmation and actualization of the freedom which God gave to him at creation*, that is, a freedom to obey. "[T]he freedom to obey," Barth states, "is obviously the true *tertium comparationis* [basis of comparison], and therefore the sign of the fellowship already established between God and man at his creation."[126]

The above treatment signals an important aspect of Barth's conception of human freedom not to be missed. That is, even as I have grouped his conception of freedom under the wider philosophical category of compatibilist freedom, it is nonetheless a modified compatibilist freedom. The modification, I propose, lies in the center and point of origin from which human freedom and consequently the "free will" is to be considered. The theological interlocutors stated above, let alone philosophical interlocutors, begin their considerations from an anthropological perspective or at best a theological-anthropology, but Barth, in alignment with his overall theological methodology, grounds his consideration of human freedom in a *christocentric-anthropology*. If Jesus Christ is true man and "[h]e alone is primarily and properly man,"[127] if humanity finds her ontological determination only in Jesus Christ,[128] all consideration of the human nature—in this case our consideration of human freedom and the free will—must begin from the true humanity that is founded and originated in Jesus Christ.

A consideration of human freedom and free will that begins with Jesus Christ reveals a consistent conception of human freedom: it is a compatibilist freedom from first to last. Because the human nature of Jesus receives a determination of grace from the divine within the hypostatic union via the *communicatio gratiarum*, Jesus *would not* and *could not* choose to sin.[129]

---

125. *CD* III/1, 265.
126. *CD* III/1, 265.
127. *CD* III/2, 43.
128. *CD* III/2, 132.
129. *CD* IV/2, 92–93.

This means that Jesus' volition (in this area of doing good and obedience) was *determined* in that no alternative possibility was open to him by which he could choose and act upon in a voluntary, intentional, and rational manner (according to the "plural voluntary control conditions" as depicted by Kane). Yet, Jesus' volition remained *free* within the compatibilist framework. Jesus' "inability" to choose sin, as mentioned earlier in chapter 4, should not be perceived as debilitating the human freedom he had; instead it confirms Barth's conception of human freedom, challenging and changing in turn our existing paradigm for how we think about human freedom. What constitutes true human freedom for Barth is when one is living and acting in a way following and corresponding to the decisions and the determination of God, and *this*, Jesus shows us through his freedom that consists wholesale in his obedience.[130] Human freedom—as envisaged (christocentrically) in Jesus Christ the true man—is from the outset (theologically) a determined freedom for obedience that locates itself (philosophically) on the compatibilist end of the continuum. My conjecture is that it is this pivotal paradigm governing Barth's conception of human freedom that led him to speak on the pre-lapsarian free will in a way nuanced from his predecessors within the compatibilist tradition.

The *Analogia Fidei* and *Analogia Relationis* as the Way of Relating Divine Freedom/Obedience and Human Freedom/Obedience

It is timely to summarize the arguments that have preceded us so far, with a view of showing how they contribute to the overall argument this chapter advances. In the first section, I showed that human freedom for Barth is conceived essentially as a freedom for God, a freedom to obey. Such a conception, if it should be pegged to the autonomy-heteronomy discussion, situates Barth's understanding within a "middle-ground" position that allows for a form of autonomy conceived under a wider "theonomy." Likewise, Barth's conception of human freedom also locates him on the philosophical continuum nearer to the compatibilist-freedom position. The second section carried on to argue how it came to be that human freedom is conceived in this manner by Barth; it is because that is how he similarly understood divine freedom. Divine freedom, more than being a freedom *from*, is to be conceived as a freedom *for*; specifically, a freedom for humankind. Since the divine freedom for humanity is expressed in the divine election from

130. *CD* IV/2, 93.

eternity wherein God determines Godself in Jesus Christ to be both electing God and elected man, the obedience of Jesus Christ is translated under the framework of Barth's actualistic ontology to be the divine obedience of the eternal Son—that has been the main argument advanced in this volume. It is in this manner that Barth can posit the divine freedom as a freedom to obey. The third section explored the nature of the coordination between divine and human action and agency, locating the link to lie in Barth's doctrine of the *concursus Dei*. While the divine action and agency superintends over human action and agency, the latter is nonetheless maintained to be a free response within the bounds of a compatibilist freedom. Although a mysterious doctrine in itself, Barth deems that the outworking of the *concursus Dei* is best envisaged in the person of Jesus Christ. Having his (human) origin divinely determined from the outset via the *communication gratiarum*, Jesus reveals human freedom to be a determined and compatibilist freedom from first to last; it is a freedom to obey.

I intend, in this section, to crystallize the above arguments by making just one further statement. That is: as it is with the relation between *divine* freedom and *divine* obedience seen in the *God*-man Jesus Christ, so it is by an *analogia relationis* (analogy of relation) the relation between *human* freedom and *human* obedience seen equally in the God-*man* Jesus Christ. In both relations, obedience serves as the full and perfect expression of freedom, while freedom is seen as the freedom for obedience.

The significant point not to be missed, though, is the way Barth draws the analogy between *divine* freedom and obedience, and *human* freedom and obedience.[131] Certainly, it is not based on an *analogia entis* (analogy of being) that proceeds from "below to above." That is to say, it is not by philosophizing about human freedom, and then utilizing a principle like the *analogia attributionis* to attribute similar properties or predicates to the divine freedom. To clarify: the *analogia attributionis* is the aspect of the *analogia entis* that captures the pole of similarity. It is the analogy that is used whenever a comparison is made between two things of commonality, and the direction of the analogy proceeds from "below" (the human) to the "above" (the divine). Like the entire *analogia entis* that it is a part of, the *analogia attributionis* is premised upon a participation in being (*participatio entis*). Keith Johnson states concerning the *participatio entis*: "[T]he human stands even now in a real relation to God simply by virtue of the fact that he exists, because this existence indicates that God has created the human and that the human, as a result, exists by participation in God's being."[132]

---

131. For the discussion to follow, I am indebted to Johnson, *Analogia Entis*.

132. Johnson, *Analogia Entis*, 137. Johnson's statement is made in the context of him describing the *analogia entis* of the Roman Catholic theologian Erich Przywara.

Barth would definitely demur against this way of drawing the analogy that operates from "below to above," given that this approach resonates much with natural theology which Barth firmly rejected.

It should be concurrently noted that Barth's analogy between divine freedom and obedience and human freedom and obedience is also not based on an *analogia entis* that is from "above to below" or an *analogia entis* that is within the *analogia fidei* (analogy of faith). The two proposals just mentioned hail from the soil of Roman Catholic theology, with the former proposed by Erich Przywara and the latter by Gottlieb Söhngen.[133]

Przywara maintains that it is valid to draw an *analogia attributionis* between God's being and human being, provided the analogy is bracketed or prefixed by an even greater *analogia proportionis*. The converse of the *analogia attributionis*, the *analogia proportionis* represents the pole of dissimilarity and is used when the two things in comparison are essentially distinct from one another, resulting in the only way of bringing these two items together being through the notion of proportionality. Framed within the relation between the divine being and human being, the *analogia proportionis* captures the otherness of God within the *analogia entis*. For Przywara, the *analogia attributionis* and the *analogia proportionis* together constitute the *analogia entis*, which functions with a certain tension that comes from straddling the similarity and dissimilarity between the being of God and that of the human. Przywara maintains the viability of the *analogia entis* though, convinced that because there is a commonality between the being of God and that of humanity, the relationship between the divine being and creaturely being can be described by an *analogia attributionis*. This, however, is an analogy that is bracketed throughout by the doctrine of creation *ex nihilo*, which preserves the aspect of the *analogia proportionis* and the ontological distinction between God and humanity.[134] As Johnson states of Przywara's *analogia entis*: "[W]hen viewed together, the *analogia attributionis* and the *analogia proportionis* appropriately describe and define the nature of the human's 'open upwards' relationship to God, and through this relationship, the knower can recognize God's transcendence by means of a reflection *first* upon God's immanence."[135] Przywara calls this a "descending *analogia attributionis*," one that works from "above to below" in contrast to the earlier *analogia entis* cited that operates in the opposite direction.[136]

---

133. Przywara's proposal is covered in detail in Johnson, *Analogia Entis*, 127–50, and Söhngen's on pp. 170–78.

134. Johnson, *Analogia Entis*, 136–38.

135. Johnson, *Analogia Entis*, 138–39 (emphasis original).

136. Johnson, *Analogia Entis*, 140.

Gottlieb Söhngen's assertion of his central claim consisting in "an *analogia entis* within the *analogia fidei*" can be understood in its full intention only when the background is taken into regard. Söhngen's claim was made in response to Barth's famous umbrageous remark of Przywara's *analogia entis* being "the invention of Antichrist"[137] and Barth's own counter proposal of the *analogia fidei* in *CD* I/1. For Barth, the *analogia fidei* is meant to stand in contrast to the *analogia entis* (at least as conceived by Przywara). As analyzed by Johnson, the *analogia* fidei comes to refer to the "'point of contact' between God and the human that takes place solely because of and within the ongoing event of God's self-revelation to the human."[138] Söhngen's claim essentially contends against Barth's depiction of the contrasting relationship between the *analogia entis* and the *analogia fidei*, arguing instead for a complementary relationship. After all, as Söhngen perceives it, the *analogia fidei* is unable to account for participation in the divine life without referencing to the notion of "being," and the *analogia entis* is unable to operate in isolation because any participation in "being" is the result of faith alone.[139] For Söhngen, to reject the *analogia entis* on the grounds of an *analogia fidei* is to fail to realize that an understanding of "participation by faith" necessarily includes within itself an account of a "participation of being,"[140] and Söhngen's worry is that Barth runs the danger of portraying the *analogia fidei* as merely "an *analogia attributionis mere extrinsecae*, a correspondence relationship of purely external allocation" that fails to speak about the actual "being" of the human at all.[141]

For all the theological safeguards of Przywara and Söhngen, Barth's usage of analogy neither draws near to an *analogia entis* from "above to below" nor "an *analogia entis* within the *analogia fidei*." Barth does recognize that talk of the *analogia fidei*, which at its core involves God's act of grace, will involve a *participatio entis*. So, as Johnson asserts, "by talking about the human in faith who has her true, reconciled being by participation in Christ, [Barth] is, in fact, *talking about being*."[142] But the key point of distinction that makes all the difference between Barth and his Roman Catholic counterparts is *where* he situates the participation of being: Barth's *participatio entis* is grounded in *the doctrine of election, not creation*. As Johnson observes, for Barth's Roman Catholic interlocutors, "the human as created stands in continuity with the

---

137. *CD* I/1, xiii.
138. Johnson, *Analogia Entis*, 168.
139. Johnson, *Analogia Entis*, 173.
140. Johnson, *Analogia Entis*, 177.
141. Johnson, *Analogia Entis*, 172.
142. Johnson, *Analogia Entis*, 180 (emphasis original).

human in grace as a function of God's act of creation," whereas for Barth, "what humans *are* intrinsically is not a function of their creation by God; it is a function of God's election of them in Jesus Christ."[143]

The above immediate statement resonates with tremendous significance for Barth. It means that what the human being *internally* is, is at every moment defined *externally* by their relation to God in Jesus Christ. This idea brings Barth into direct contrast with Söhngen, who rejects such an extrinsic analogy of attribution because it sets "faith against being," and whose own account posits instead a strong line of continuity between the grace available through Jesus Christ and the grace found in nature by dint of God's act of creation.[144] This, Barth will not accept. As Johnson iterates, if there is any analogy that can be drawn between God and the human—and there is because Barth maintained the *analogia fidei* involves the *participatio entis*—"the human in analogy with God is the human *in Christ*, and the being of this human is *objectively distinct* from the being of the human as such."[145] On Barth's account, the being of the human graced by the event of the divine election in Jesus Christ, far from being a mere fulfilment in continuation with the being of the human found in creation, is more accurately perceived as a disruptive determination of the original definition of human "being" in the first place. It is this being determined in election that forms the ground and starting point for any analogy drawn between the being of God and that of the human.[146] As we have seen, this notion of Barth's is well supported by his treatment of creation, especially how he relates creation and the covenant—"creation is the external basis of the covenant, and covenant is the internal basis of creation,"[147] and his grounding of anthropology in Christology.[148]

The above discussion brings us to the main point of this section—Barth's own specific use of analogy by which he draws into relation divine freedom and obedience and human freedom and obedience. That analogy is

143. Johnson, *Analogia Entis*, 160 (emphasis original).
144. Johnson, *Analogia Entis*, 181.
145. Johnson, *Analogia Entis*, 187 (emphasis original).
146. It is this central conviction of Barth's that forms also the counter-argument against Von Balthasar's remark that Barth had misunderstood Przywara's *analogia entis* in Balthasar, *Theology of Karl Barth*. Balthasar reads God's act in creation and God's act in Jesus Christ as taking place within "one interlocking order" (165) that effectively prioritizes the being of the human at the point of creation and sees the aspects that are in correspondence in the analogy between divine being and creaturely being as intrinsic to human being itself. See Johnson, *Analogia Entis*, 193–201, for a detailed account of Balthasar's interpretation of Barth.
147. *CD* III/1 §41.
148. *CD* III/2 §43.

the *analogia relationis* (analogy of relations), which at its core maintains that if there is any point of similarity between God and humanity, that similarity occurs in and through *the humanity of Jesus* directly at the relational level. Barth states regarding the *analogia relationis*:

> *This is not a correspondence and similarity of being,* an *analogia entis*. The being of God cannot be compared with that of man. . . . It is a question of the relationship within the being of God on the one side and between the being of God and that of man on the other. *Between these two relationships* as such—and it is in this sense that the second is the image of the first—*there is correspondence and similarity.* There is an *analogia relationis*.[149]

From the above quote and Barth's larger treatment, one can detail the logic of Barth's *analogia relationis* according to three levels, each of which translates into the other. At the first level, the relation between God and the human Jesus corresponds to the relations between the eternal Father and the eternal Son; at the second level, the relationship between the human Jesus and God translates to the corresponding relation between the human Jesus and humanity in general, and finally, at the third level, the relation between humans to other humans correspond to the relationship between the human Jesus and humanity. In this way through these various levels of translation and correspondence, the relation between humans to other humans could be said to correspond to the relations within the Trinity.[150] Nonetheless, it must be noted that this is an analogy that occurs directly at the level of *relationship*, not *being*, with Jesus Christ as the nexus. Johnson captures the essence of Barth's *analogia relationis* succinctly: "Jesus Christ, fully God and fully human, is the connecting point between the various analogies, and through him, the human who exists *for* others in the same way that Jesus did stands in analogy to the triune God who eternally determined to be God-*for*-us by relating to humanity in Jesus."[151]

Notwithstanding the above, the fact that the analogy happens directly at the level of the relationship does not preclude there being a *participatio entis*. As seen earlier, Barth knew that the *analogia fidei* involves a *participatio entis*; a participation in the salvific benefits of Christ is nothing less than a participation in Christ himself. To participate in the being of Christ, in turn, is to allow who we are intrinsically as a human "being" to be solely determined extrinsically by God's free and eternal decision to enter into human

---

149. *CD* III/2, 220 (added emphasis).
150. Johnson, *Analogia Entis*, 197.
151. Johnson, *Analogia Entis*, 216 (emphasis original).

history in Jesus Christ; it is to respond in our existence and actions to be *for* others in a way that corresponds to the being of God who is *for* us.

It is here at this point that one could say an "analogy of being" happens for Barth, but to be precise, it is an analogy of *being-in-action*. The "human action in human freedom when we speak of the being and life of the Christian," that is, *the (Christian) human's being-in-action*, corresponds to the "divine-human action in divine-human sovereignty when we speak of the being and life of Christ," that is, *the divine being-in-action*.[152] This correspondence in action is what serves as the point of contact for the analogy between God and the human. Barth is very specific here: when he talks about the *participatio entis* or even an analogy of being(-in-action), he has in mind the being of Jesus Christ, and as Johnson captures it, the analogy drawn between the divine and human "being" is "not based upon an intrinsic capacity given to the human by God in the act of creation . . . but upon the always-extrinsic relationship between the human and Jesus Christ that takes place in and through Christ's fulfilment of God's eternal decision to exist in relationship to the human in the covenant of grace."[153]

To sum up, it would be fair to say that Barth's *analogia relationis* seals on the one hand the relation between divine freedom and obedience and on the other hand human freedom and obedience. Just as the divine being-in-action is seen in the divine freedom for Godself-election leading to the divine obedience of the eternal Son, so it is with the human being-in-action, when the human being in her God-given freedom responds by obeying. That is to say, the *human* freedom-for-obedience corresponds and is analogous to the *divine* freedom-for-obedience.

Prayer as the Expression of Freedom and Obedience for Barth

The above section set forth Barth's conception of human freedom as a freedom-for-obedience that corresponds and is analogous to the divine freedom-for-obedience by way of an *analogia relationis* or an analogy of "being-in-action." This section takes the argument one final step and shows how, for Barth, human freedom and obedience are best coordinated and expressed through the spiritual exercise of prayer. A full consideration of Barth's treatment on prayer, however, would neither be realistic nor

---

152. *CD* IV/3.2, 597.
153. Johnson, *Analogia Entis*, 225.

necessary at this point; instead it will suffice to highlight two aspects of Barth's treatment that are pertinent to our argument.[154]

The first point has to do with the intimate connection that Barth draws between prayer and obedience. Prayer, for Barth, is the preeminent act of obedience. In a section within *CD* III/3, Barth identifies the appropriate response of the Christian to the doctrine of God's providence as one of faith, obedience and prayer. Barth establishes prayer as the "most intimate and effective form of Christian action," in fact describing prayer as "Christian obedience *in nuce*." Barth asserts that any activity of willing and doing, if it proceeds from faith and is carried out in obedience, "must pass over into . . . prayer, ending and also beginning afresh in prayer." As the "primitive" movement, prayer is itself "the act of obedience *par excellence*, the act of obedience from which all other acts must spring."[155] This fundamental idea carries on with Barth even as he enters into the later stage of his thinking on prayer, where he shifts from capitalizing on the notion of prayer as petition to settle for the idea of prayer as invocation.[156] There, Barth upholds the very vocative "Father!" as "the primal form of the thinking, the primal sound of the speaking and the primal act of the obedience demanded of Christians . . . . [I]t is the primal act of the freedom Christians are given, the primal form of the faithfulness with which they may correspond to his faithfulness."[157]

Flowing from the above, prayer as invocation functions further to coordinate two other key concepts related to obedience, namely, the interaction between divine and human agency, and freedom. In regard to the former, the notion of invocation facilitates the articulation of a key concept

---

154. Barth's treatment of prayer is spread across his writings, but is more pronounced in the following sections listed in chronological order: his comments on Romans 7 and 8 in *Romans*; in the third "sphere" of redemption within his Münster lectures on ethics, captured in *Ethics*; *Holy Spirit and Christian Life*, 59–68; in the three major segments within the doctrine of creation in *CD* III/2, 186–92, *CD* III/3, 265–88, and *CD* III/4, 87–115; in the seminars on the Lord's Prayer (roughly contemporaneous with the segment on prayer in *CD* III/3) captured and reprinted in *Prayer: 50th Anniversary*; and within his treatment of ethics in the doctrine of reconciliation, albeit incomplete, found in *ChrL*. Finally, one must not forget Barth's mention of prayer in his lectures delivered in America, published in English as *ET*, 159–70. The task of outlining and evaluating Barth's theology of prayer has been undertaken recently by Cocksworth, *Prayer*. See, in particular, his fine overview and introduction on pp. 1–21.

155. *CD* III/3, 264–65. See also Hesselink, "Prayer," 83, who makes a similar point between obedience and prayer.

156. Cocksworth, *Prayer*, 77–82, raises some difficulties with Barth's conception of prayer as petition, and on pp. 97–116 shows how invocation builds upon and improves much of what Barth had written on prayer earlier.

157. *ChrL*, 51.

of Barth's, especially profitable when it comes to describing the interrelation between divine and human agency—the concept of "correspondence" or "analogy" (*Entsprechung*). Correspondence provides a felicitous way to capture the distinctively participative shape of the human ethical agent. Responding to the prior divine initiative, human agents find that in and through their responses, the Holy Spirit brings their human agency—more than that, the human agents themselves—into the closest possible correspondence with divine agency and the divine agent himself. In fact, as seen in the previous section, "correspondence" is the main way by which Barth portrays the *participatio entis*: through the human agent's actions, the being-in-action of the human corresponds to the divine being-in-action. According to Jüngel, human agents in the process of their correspondence are brought into "the immediacy of the intercourse of the human person with God."[158] In the act of invoking God, the human person is already pictured as an agent who corresponds to the God who acts.[159] I submit that the obedience of the reconciled people of God is best conceived as a correspondence, an analogous response, an *Entsprechung* to the obedience first rendered by the incarnate Christ himself.

In regard to the latter concept—freedom—there is a passage in *CD* III/2 that resounds of the intimate connection between prayer (as invocation) and true human freedom. Speaking of the limitations of our creatureliness, Barth at the same time states that this limitation can be "transcended" in the very act of invocation, even as he deftly adds the qualification that our very act of calling upon the name of God and our going to God is predicated upon God's summoning of us and his coming to us in the first place.[160] Yet, in that invocation, God truly establishes and posits man as a human subject: "Offering and disposing himself to go to God and to be obedient to the divine call: 'Come,' he pushes open the gate and steps out into freedom. As he does so, he is a creature which transcends the limits of the creature."[161] The last quote is strikingly reminiscent of Barth's description of the final scene in Gethsemane, whereby having spoken the words "Thy will be done" and having accepted the Father's cup, Jesus rises, stands upright "in a supreme pride

---

158. Jüngel, "Invocation," 159. See also Cocksworth, *Prayer*, 107–16. In my view, Jüngel and Cocksworth should be credited for taking up the concept of *Entsprechung* as the chief way of describing the interrelation between divine and human agency in prayer. In this way, they have taken the discussion further than some of the other essayists, who mainly relied on a kind of Chalcedonian-patterned concept of "double agency," for example, Hesselink, "Prayer," 84–88, and Migliore, "Freedom to Pray," 105–9.

159. Jüngel, "Invocation," 161.

160. *CD* III/2, 187–88.

161. *CD* III/2, 189.

(*in höchstem Stolz*)," and steps out of the garden into the deathly silence of God's divine judgment. An ominous moment, no doubt; yet, it is in this moment that true human freedom is ushered in and established.[162]

The above connection, far from being an accidental link, actually leads to the second point I wish to make regarding Barth's consideration on prayer. That is, even as Barth is keen to link obedience with the act of prayer, he is equally desirous to present Jesus as the *pray-er* and the *prayer*. This point receives its most sustained attention in a segment of CD III/3 where Barth describes prayer as being chiefly petitionary in nature. There, Barth designates Jesus as the supreme pray-er, stating: "The first and proper suppliant is none other than Jesus Christ Himself."[163] Not only is Jesus the pray-er, he himself is the prayer, in the sense that if prayer at this point is conceived as petition, it follows that prayer (or petition) is "simply the taking and receiving of the divine gift and answer as it is already present and near to hand in Jesus Christ."[164] Barth issues a short pithy statement that captures these two dimensions: "As the Son of God, He was the divine gift and answer [i.e., the prayer], but as the Son of Man He was human asking [i.e., the pray-er]."[165]

The point not to be overlooked in the certainty of Jesus being the pray-er is the vicarious nature of Jesus' petitionary prayer. Barth emphasizes that in Jesus' praying and petitioning, he was not doing it for himself, since Jesus "did not need to confess either the glory of God or the transgression of man." Rather, Jesus "did it for others, and first of all for his own people," in that way becoming their "representative" and "substitute."[166] This explains why Barth can finally assert Christian prayer as "participation in Jesus Christ; participation, basically, in the grace which is revealed and active in Him, in the Son of God; and then only, and on this basis, participation in the asking of the Son of Man."[167]

Much remains the same even as Barth shifts from his depiction of prayer as petition to prayer as invocation in his later theology. He continues to hold out the Christological basis of invocation, asserting that man's calling upon God becomes an event and is determined to be so only by virtue of "the basic event between God and man in Jesus Christ."[168] Invocation is

162. CD IV/1, 270; cf. Jones, *Humanity of Christ*, 236.
163. CD III/3, 274.
164. CD III/3, 274.
165. CD III/3, 274–75.
166. CD III/3, 276.
167. CD III/3, 282.
168. ChrL, 45.

predicated solely upon Jesus Christ who, as the representative of all men before God, prayed the Lord's Prayer to the Father,[169] and who similarly invoked God as his Father in Gethsemane.[170] By taking his own people up into the movement of his own prayer, Jesus Christ "enables, invites, and summons them to invoke [God] as such."[171] It is clear for Barth: what grounds our freedom to call upon God as Father is the way Jesus Christ first called upon him in a similar manner.[172]

Jesus' solitary prayer in the Garden of Gethsemane—and Barth reminds us it had to be *this* way—captures the vicarious nature of the prayer, in that it was a prayer for us and in our place. In uttering that prayer, Jesus carries out his high-priestly and kingly office and in doing so, mysteriously opens the way for us to "participate" in his prayer.[173] In petitioning God for the cup to be removed, Jesus, as our representative and substitute, "passed through the narrow archway of asking" and received the "divine gift and answer"—[174] an answer reposing in the surprising truth that Jesus himself is to be that "divine gift and answer" for all who would now follow him in likewise petitioning the Father. Invoking the name of God as "Father," Jesus takes his people into the movement of his invocation and enjoins them to do the same.[175] This act of petitioning and invocation in the prayer of Gethsemane, fully accompanied by its attendant travail and agony, expresses, for Barth, the obedience of the incarnate Christ.[176] By enjoining us to do the same, Jesus leads us and, more important, enables us to respond to this divine call. To pray is to display fully the invocational existence we have found ourselves in. This is an existence abounding in obedience and true human freedom, in correspondence (*Entsprechung*) to our Lord's own obedience and freedom. It is for this reason that Barth asserts of the children of

169. *ChrL*, 44.
170. *ChrL*, 64.
171. *ChrL*, 63–64 (quote is from p. 63).
172. *ChrL*, 65.
173. For some suggestions on how this is so, see Cocksworth, *Prayer*, 67–73.
174. *CD* III/3, 276.
175. *ChrL*, 63.
176. The importance of the fact that the invocation comes in the midst of struggle and agony cannot be overemphasized. It means that rather than explaining Jesus' prayer by the framework of Christian prayer, it is better and more proper, as Jones reminds us, to recognize that "Christian prayer—that is, the freedom to unburden oneself before God, to struggle with what God asks, to view torment and disorientation as not alien but native to one's humanity—has as its anterior condition Jesus' prayer in Gethsemane" (*Humanity of Christ*, 238). This insight counterbalances the point made by Migliore, "Freedom to Pray," 109–13, that Barth has not given enough attention to lament as an essential form of biblical prayer.

God: "How could they ever forget that this cry activates the freedom they are given and therefore the obedience required of them, the epitome of all Christian ethos?"[177] For Barth, contained in this very prayer of invocation is the freedom of their faith and the obedience of their corresponding action, and together, these two components constitute the Christian life.[178]

---

177. *ChrL*, 52.

178. Smit, "'(T)His Cry,'" 56.

Conclusion

OUR INQUIRY INTO THE role and function occupied by the obedience of Jesus Christ in Karl Barth's doctrine of reconciliation has taken us on a journey spanning eight chapters, uncovering exciting discoveries and insights. We considered Barth's treatment of Jesus' obedience from three major perspectives, which together form the three major parts constituting this volume.

To recap, we first looked at the perspective consisting in a "backward" movement where Barth draws Jesus' incarnate obedience into the triune Godhead to relate to the obedience of the eternal Son. A relation such as this certainly bears on the divine trinitarian ontology, and the implications were considered along the way. Second, we navigated the perspective constituted by a present orientation of Jesus' obedience "as it is" in the incarnation. A wide range of issues—albeit all related to Jesus' obedience—was addressed. They included the function of Jesus' obedience in Barth's Christological descriptors; the type of human nature assumed by Jesus and the account of how Jesus remained without sin; the monothelite or dyothelite nature of Jesus' volition; the Spirit's role in Jesus' obedience, and the place occupied by Jesus' obedience in Barth's judicial account of the atonement. Finally, we examined the perspective formed by the "forward" movement of Jesus' obedience as it relates to our own obedience. This involved exploring an alternative account of the atonement centered on the obedience of Christ, and relating obedience with a parallel concept that is often surfaced together with it—freedom. This conclusion draws all that has been said so far across broad themes and ideas into a cohesive whole with the aim of providing a final statement of the distinct contribution that Barth brings to our dogmatic understanding of Jesus' obedience.

At the most basic consideration, Barth can be said to assert a twofold affirmation when it comes to the obedience of Jesus Christ. The first affirmation is: at its most basic level, *Barth affirms the obedience of Jesus Christ as a genuine and authentic human obedience, involving an act of human volition in response to a higher calling or command.*

From the very outset in *CD* I/1, Barth's description of Jesus Christ as "*vere Deus, vere homo*" already grounds the obedience of Christ as genuine human action (arising from the "*vere homo*") that nonetheless bears the effects of divine action (arising from the "*vere Deus*"). As seen in chapter 3, Barth considers that the divine subject assuming human nature in the incarnation is no hindrance to the reality and authenticity of the humanity assumed. On the contrary, Barth sees the divine initiative and action to be the engendering source of true human action: it is because God is the subject of the incarnation that the being and acting found in Jesus Christ is a genuine and true *human* being and acting.[1] That Jesus Christ, as the elected man, is the first and primal human being to be caught up in the "history [*Geschichte*], encounter [*Begegnung*] and decision [*Entscheidung*] between God and man,"[2] speaks categorically of Jesus' human obedience. Although being the Son of God, Jesus Christ humanly participates in God's reconciliatory program, including its most painful and intense moment, by being obedient to death—even death on a cross (Phil 2:8). Barth's chief Christological descriptors found in *CD* IV/1, namely (i) Jesus is both covenant-Lord and covenant-partner (ii) his history is the nexus of the history of God and the history of man, and (iii) he is eternally and simultaneously the humbled and exalted one, all involve one way or another the human obedience of Jesus Christ.

The topics explored in chapters 4 and 5 further attest to the nature of Jesus' true human obedience. For Barth, Jesus' assumption of a "fallen" human nature, as opposed to an "unfallen" human nature, grounds the entire event of the incarnation within the concrete situation of the very humanity he came to save. It also identifies Jesus as the "man of sin" who has incurred the wrath of God and is liable to his judgment and verdict, although Jesus voluntarily takes upon himself this position rather than one that is his by nature.[3] Because Barth excises the notion of inherited or imputed *hereditary* corruption from his understanding of original sin, replacing it instead with the idea of *natural* corruption which humanity inevitably brings upon and owns for herself through her sin, Barth is able to attribute to Jesus a fallen human nature without concomitantly attributing sin to that (fallen) nature in itself. After all, in the *sui generis* instance of the incarnation and unlike the rest of humanity, fallenness does not need to be equated with sinfulness. This explains the importance of obedience for Barth's maintenance of Jesus' assumption of a fallen human nature: it is

---

1. *CD* I/2, 151.
2. *CD* II/2, 175 / *KD* II/2, 192.
3. *CD* I/2, 151.

through his obedience and sinlessness that Jesus is freed from any form of corruption in his human nature.

In regard to Jesus being without sin, Barth presents a paradigmatic shift in the discussion. Rather than sourcing and grounding the impeccability of Jesus guaranteeing his obedience in Jesus' divine nature—true as that is—Barth, especially in the later writings of the *Dogmatics*, chooses to present the impeccability of Jesus in "functional" rather than "essential" terms. That is, Barth presents the impeccability of Jesus not on the basis of his metaphysical make-up but by virtue of his actions of obedience: Jesus *would not* and *could not* choose sin.[4] The next topic explored reveals that Barth's endorsement of dyothelitism not only reinforces the account of Jesus' human obedience (Jesus renders his human will subject to his divine will), but also coheres best with Barth's understanding of divine agency and intentionality (this divine will internally resides within Jesus Christ rather than externally acts upon him). Finally, Barth's pneumatology discloses a generous working of the Holy Spirit in the human being Jesus of Nazareth, to the extent that Barth could be said to maintain both a Logos and Spirit Christology. Inasmuch as Jesus Christ is the Word made flesh and the Son of God, he is also the Son of Man who is the Spirit-filled one. The Spirit, on this account, is the power that empowers Jesus for his human acts of obedience.

Chapter 6 carries on the picture of Jesus' authentic obedience, vouchsafing a causal and instrumental role to that obedience in Barth's doctrine of the atonement: it is *because* of Jesus' obedience and *by* that obedience that atonement is made and reconciliation achieved. Chapter 7 brings a refreshing dimension to Jesus' unwavering obedience. Even as Jesus' obedience is rendered in the midst of struggle, Barth's pinpointing the source of that struggle to the gruesome apprehension that the divine reconciliatory plan of God is to be conjoined with the full onslaught of Satan accentuates Jesus' human obedience. This is so especially when Barth's account is contrasted with the traditional account that tend to locate Jesus' struggle in the (natural) human emotions or *propassions* of fear and aversion to death. Chapter 8 reveals that Jesus' human obedience goes hand in hand with his human freedom. Barth's conception of human freedom is best conceived philosophically as a compatibilist freedom; determinism does not mean that Jesus' actions cannot be counted as free. In fact, Barth's consistent picture of human freedom is that it is a (determined) freedom to obey.

Together, the key findings summarized above reveal a compelling picture of the genuine nature of Jesus' human obedience at work. That, in turn, forms the first affirmation that Barth asserts with regard to Jesus' incarnate

---

4. *CD* IV/2, 93.

obedience. This affirmation, in many ways, does not deviate from what the Tradition has consistently upheld.

It is in Barth's second affirmation, however, that takes the notion of Jesus' incarnate obedience in a novel and unprecedented direction. While affirming the human obedience of Jesus Christ in the incarnation, *Barth equally affirms a divine obedience of the eternal Son within the triune Godhead*, going so far as to tether the command-obedience relationship between the Father and the Son in eternity to the eternally begetting-and-being-begotten relations of origin that characterize the Father and the Son within the divine processions.[5] This move, as detailed in chapter 1, creates a major difficulty for Barth. It conflicts with his basic doctrine of the Trinity: the triune God is one divine subject with one mind, one will and one center of volition.[6] Going by the conventional understanding of obedience, positing a command-obedience relation within the triune Godhead presupposes two wills or two centers of volitional activity.

The way out of the conundrum, as shown in chapter 1, is to leverage on the theological context in which Barth posits the divine obedience of the eternal Son. That context is Barth's doctrine of election and, specifically, the actualistic ontology concomitant with it.[7] It is within this context of election and the actualistic effects flowing from it that occasion Barth to conceive of the identity of the second divine person of the triune God in relation to the incarnation: the *perfect God-man the eternal Son becomes in time bears indelibly from the very start on his own being and identity as the second mode of being of the triune God*. In other words, for Barth, the eternal Son in every "moment" of his being as the one "eternally begotten of the Father" is identified as Jesus Christ.

It is in this basic move that Barth finds an open door to equate the obedience that Jesus Christ shows in his incarnate life with the obedience displayed by the eternal Son to the Father, bearing in mind that this is an obedience rendered by the *human* will Jesus comes to possess in virtue of the human nature assumed.[8] It is on this "actualistically foreseen" note that the obedience of Jesus Christ becomes identified as the obedience of the

---

5. *CD* IV/1, 208–9.

6. *CD* I/1, 357–58; *CD* IV/1, 205.

7. As mentioned at various points, by using the term "actualistic ontology," I am not suggesting Barth held to some form of a preconceived and pre-existing metaphysical or philosophical schema that actively controlled his theology. Rather, I am using the term as a catchword to describe the implications and effects that Barth's doctrine of election has on the divine ontology.

8. This explains, as I sought to demonstrate in chapter 4, the importance of dyothelitism for Barth.

eternal Son. In the final analysis, I argue that the notion of the divine obedience of the eternal Son only makes sense when read against the backdrop of Barth's actualistic ontology.[9]

Having said the above, the other side of the equation holds true as well. That is, not only does Barth's actualistic ontology enable him to identify Jesus' obedience as the obedience of the eternal Son, that move also has the reverse effect of corroborating Barth's actualistic ontology. In this regard, chapter 2 was devoted to establishing the parameters within which Barth's actualistic ontology is to be read, a much-contested issue within Barth scholarship itself. The conclusion reached was that God's self-determination to be the triune God—Father, Son, and Holy Spirit—is at the one and same "moment," in a coincident and coterminous fashion, his self-election to be the God-who-is-for-us-in-Christ Jesus. That is to say, both triunity and election happen in the same "constitutive" divine act of self-determination and election. Stated another way—in classical terminology—the divine processions and the divine missions are both contained in the same divine act.

At the same time, however, I contend that while it is not possible to assign a chronological or temporal ranking or precedence to either triunity or election—or even to ontologically prioritize between the God who is triune and the God who is the electing God—Barth's presentation does lean toward a logical precedence of triunity over election. That is, when we conceive God's triunity and election, we should think of triunity first. I am convinced that this reading of Barth's actualistic ontology most fittingly demonstrates and preserves Barth's famous confession of God as "the One who *loves in freedom*";[10] who, in his election, "does not will to be God without us."[11]

Barth's two assertions in relation to the obedience of Christ—first, this obedience is a genuine human act, and second, this obedience when read in the light of Barth's actualistic ontology is equated with the divine obedience of the eternal Son—combine to form what I consider to be Barth's distinct and unique contribution to our dogmatic understanding of Christ's obedience. That is, under Barth's account, *the obedience of Jesus Christ as a cause and instrument in our salvation and reconciliation is lifted from its usual*

---

9. As highlighted in chapter 1, it seems that Barth intends the divine obedience of the eternal Son to be the antecedent ground for the obedience Christ comes to show in the incarnation. As argued in the chapter, such an antecedent obedience sought is not possible without contravening Barth's basic Trinitarianism of a single divine subject. At best, the antecedent ground can be located in the filial-paternity relation that characterizes the divine procession between Father and Son, without in any way turning that filial-paternity relation into an antecedent obedience.

10. The title of *CD* II/1 §28.

11. *CD* IV/1, 7.

domain within the economy of salvation to extend to the domain of the divine will, purpose, and even divine ontology. Never before in the Tradition has the incarnate obedience of Jesus Christ borne such ramifications within the inner triune life of God. Once again, that Barth is able to make such a bold and unprecedented move arises from his doctrine of election which spills over to form an actualistic ontology. Short of this actualistic undertaking, attempts to speak of a divine obedience eventually hobble and stumble over the point of not contravening Barth's basic Trinitarian affirmation of one divine subject with one will and one volition.

The main consequence arising from our discussion above is that *the human obedience of Jesus Christ is given a significant and co-participatory role and function in the determination of the divine ontology itself arising from the divine election.* A claim as tendentious sounding as this requires immediate substantiation.

The three primary Christological descriptors found in CD IV/1, that Jesus is covenant-Lord and covenant-partner, that his history is the history of God and of man, and that he is simultaneously the eternally humbled and exalted one, carry in one form or another ontological implications arising from Barth's doctrine of election. Underscoring these key Christological descriptions, in turn, is the obedience of Jesus Christ, lifted from its circumscription in the economy of salvation to obtain in the immanent divine life. Jesus Christ is the one who by his obedience brings about the divine and human fulfilment of the covenant;[12] it is by his obedience that Jesus embraces his history of suffering even as that history serves as the primal history of God with man,[13] and it is by the obedience of Jesus Christ that the Son of Man is eternally exalted. As seen in chapter 3, the accentuation of the obedience of Jesus Christ reaches its crescendo in Barth's revised understanding of the *communicatio operationum*. There, the obedience of Jesus Christ comes to play a *co-participatory* role in the "common actualization" of the human and divine essences united in the one person and existence of Jesus Christ.[14] One must not forget: this is an actualization of the very being God has eternally determined for himself qua Son via election.

A vital qualifier is in place though. It is true that Barth, under his particular account of actualistic ontology, gives pride of place to the human obedience of Jesus Christ in a way exceeding the Tradition. Yet, in all this, Barth is very careful to maintain the primacy of the divine initiative and not turn salvation into a work that is dependent on the human initiative,

---

12. CD III/2, 214.
13. CD II/2, 7–9.
14. CD IV/2, 113.

even if it is the work of the human person Jesus of Nazareth that is on view. This explains why, for Barth, the concept of *asymmetry* is so important in negotiating the divine-human interrelationship. Even as Jesus Christ is "the electing God and the elected man," the emphasis always lies in the first half of the clause.[15] That Jesus Christ is the electing God adverts the whole divine activity of election as one grounded and carried out solely and entirely in divine grace.[16] Inasmuch as the human obedience of Jesus Christ underscores the three chief Christological descriptors in *CD* IV/1, the human response of obedience is still ordered to the divine initiative. It is *God* who wills to be covenant-Lord, who "allows" his *Geschichte* to be conditioned by the *Geschichte* of the man Jesus of Nazareth, and who, as the Son of God, first stoops low in humility and humiliation.

The same priority applies to the *communicatio operationum*, where we find the pinnacle of Barth's description of Christ's human obedience within the divine ontology. Barth is intransigent that the divine essence as "the eternal essence of Father, Son and Holy Ghost . . . does not, *of course*, need any actualisation."[17] This similarly extends to the divine essence of the Son, which did not need the incarnation to become actual. Rather, it is only on account of God's eternal election and self-determination to be the God-man he will become in time that this special common actualization is called for. Even then, the prepositions used clearly reveal Barth's emphasis: "[T]he divine [essence] acquires a determination *to* the human [essence], and the human [essence] a determination *from* the divine [essence]."[18] At no point in Barth's specification does the divine essence receive a determination *from* the human essence.

The same principle of asymmetry is clearly observed in the coordination of the divine-human relation within Barth's doctrine of the *concursus Dei*. That is, despite divine and human action being brought together in a singularity and unity in the *concursus Dei*, they do not unite on equal terms, but the genuine human response is ordered to the divine initiative. Throughout, Barth sees no contradiction between the sovereignty of God and the freedom of the creature.[19] In fact, it could be asserted that Barth's entire outworking of the *concursus Dei* is premised upon its first occurrence in Jesus Christ in the divine election. As Barth would say: "Actualised in Jesus Christ [is] both the lordship of God and also the subordination of

15. *CD* II/2, 116.
16. *CD* II/2, 177.
17. *CD* IV/2, 113 (added emphasis).
18. *CD* IV/2, 70 (added emphasis).
19. *CD* III/3, 165–66.

the creature."[20] Delving deeper, the parallel and analogy extends further. In the same manner that the Holy Spirit empowers the man Jesus of Nazareth to obedience (under the *communicatio gratiarum*), the same Holy Spirit renders effectual and "sustains" our human freedom and human volition, even as that freedom and volition is one bestowed and actualized only in an encounter with God in the Lord Jesus Christ.

To sum up for the final time: besides affirming the incarnate obedience of Jesus as a genuine and authentic act of human volition (something affirmed all along in the Tradition), the distinct and unique contribution Barth brings to our understanding of Christ's obedience is seen in his equating of that human obedience to the divine obedience of the eternal Son within the triune Godhead. This effectively results in Jesus' genuine human response of obedience being given nothing less than a co-participatory role in the determination of the divine ontology arising from the eternal self-election of God. This, however, is a co-participation that is asymmetrically related to the divine initiative, with the precedence always located in the divine action. Nonetheless, even with this qualification, the idea of the obedience of Jesus Christ extending to the eternal being of God's own perfect divine life is something unseen and unheard thus far in the Tradition. In this way, Barth's account enables one to say: inasmuch as our God is the one who loves in freedom, he is also the one who in the depths of his being is characterized by an obedience that is from first to last.

---

20. *CD* III/3, 241.

Bibliography

Ahn, Ho-Jin. "The Humanity of Christ: John Calvin's Understanding of Christ's Vicarious Humanity." *Scottish Journal of Theology* 65/2 (2012) 145–58.
Alexis-Baker, Andy. "Theology Is Ethics: How Karl Barth Sees the Good Life." *Scottish Journal of Theology* 64/4 (2011) 425–38.
Allen, R. Michael. "Calvin's Christ: A Dogmatic Matrix for Discussion of Christ's Human Nature." *International Journal of Systematic Theology* 9/4 (2007) 382–97.
———. *Karl Barth's Church Dogmatics: An Introduction and Reader*. London: T. & T. Clark, 2012.
Aquinas, Thomas. *Summa Theologica*. Translated by the Fathers of the English Dominican Province. 22 vols. London: Burns, Oates & Washbourne, 1912–36.
Athanasius. *Four Discourses Against the Arians*. Edited by Archibald Robertson. Vol. 4. NPNF 2. Peabody, MA: Hendrickson, 1994.
———. *On the Incarnation of the Word*. Edited by Archibald Robertson. Vol. 4. NPNF 2. Peabody, MA: Hendrickson, 1994.
Attridge, Harold W. *The Epistle to the Hebrews*. Philadelphia: Fortress, 1989.
Ayres, Lewis. *Augustine and the Trinity*. Cambridge: Cambridge University Press, 2010.
Baillie, D. M. *God Was in Christ: An Essay on Incarnation and Atonement*. New York: Scribner's, 1948.
Balthasar, Hans Urs von. *The Theology of Karl Barth: Exposition and Interpretation*. Translated by Edward T. Oakes. San Francisco: Communio/Ignatius, 1992.
Barth, Karl. *Christ and Adam: Man and Humanity in Romans 5*. Translated by T. A. Smail. 1956. Reprint, Eugene, OR: Wipf & Stock, 2004.
———. *The Christian Life: Church Dogmatics, Volume IV, Part 4; Lecture Fragments*. Translated by G. W. Bromiley. Edinburgh: T. & T. Clark, 1981.
———. "The Church between East and West." *Cross Currents* 2 (1951) 64–77.
———. *Church Dogmatics*. Edited and translated by G. W. Bromiley and T. F. Torrance. 14 vols. Edinburgh: T. & T. Clark, 1956–75.
———. "Concluding Unscientific Postscript on Schleiermacher." In *The Theology of Schleiermacher: Lectures at Göttingen, Winter Semester of 1923/24*, edited by Dietrich Ritschl, translated by Geoffrey W. Bromiley, 261–79. Grand Rapids: Eerdmans, 1982.
———. *Die Kirchliche Dogmatik*. 13 part vols. 5th ed. Zurich: Evangelischer, 1947–67.
———. *Dogmatics in Outline*. Translated by G. T. Thomson. New York: Harper, 1959.
———. *Dogmatik im Grundriss*. Zurich: Evangelischer, 1947.
———. *The Epistle to the Romans*. Translated by Edwyn C. Hoskyns. Oxford: Oxford University Press, 1933.

———. *Ethics*. Edited by Dietrich Braun. Translated by G. W. Bromiley. 1981. Reprint, Eugene, OR: Wipf & Stock, 2013.

———. *Evangelical Theology: An Introduction*. Translated by Grover Foley. Grand Rapids: Eerdmans, 1963.

———. "The Gift of Freedom: Foundation of Evangelical Ethics." In *The Humanity of God*, 67–96. Translated by Thomas Wieser. London: Collins, 1961.

———. *The Göttingen Dogmatics: Instruction in the Christian Religion*. Vol. 1. Edited by Hannelotte Reiffen. Translated by G. W. Bromiley. Grand Rapids: Eerdmans, 1991.

———. *The Holy Spirit and the Christian Life: The Theological Basis of Ethics*. Translated by R. Birch Hoyle. Louisville: Westminster John Knox, 1993.

———. *How I Changed My Mind*. Edinburgh: Saint Andrew, 1969.

———. "The Humanity of God." In *The Humanity of God*, 37–65. Translated by John Newton Thomas. London: Collins, 1961.

———. *Karl Barth's Table Talk*. Edited by John D. Godsey. Richmond: John Knox, 1963.

———. *Prayer: 50th Anniversary Edition*. Edited by Don E. Saliers. Translated by Sara F. Terrien. Louisville: Westminster John Knox, 2002.

———. *Theological Existence To-Day! (A Plea for Theological Freedom)*. Translated by R. Birch Hoyle. 1933. Reprint, Eugene, OR: Wipf & Stock, 2011.

———. *The Theology of the Reformed Confessions*. Translated by Darrell L. Guder and Judith J. Guder. Louisville: Westminster John Knox, 2002.

———. *Witness to the Word: A Commentary on John 1*. Edited by Walter Fürst. Translated by Geoffrey W. Bromiley. Grand Rapids: Eerdmans, 1986.

Barth, Karl, and Johannes Hamel. *How to Serve God in a Marxist Land*. Translated by Thomas Wieser. New York: Association Press, 1959.

Bathrellos, Demetrios. *The Byzantine Christ: Person, Nature, and Will in the Christology of Saint Maximus the Confessor*. Oxford Early Christian Studies. Oxford: Oxford University Press, 2004.

Berkouwer, G. C. *The Triumph of Grace in the Theology of Karl Barth*. Translated by Harry R. Boer. Grand Rapids: Eerdmans, 1956.

Bingham, D. Jeffrey. "Irenaeus and Hebrews." In *Christology, Hermeneutics, and Hebrews: Profiles from the History of Interpretation*, edited by Jon C. Laansma and Daniel J. Treier, 48–73. London: Bloomsbury, 2012.

Blocher, Henri. "Karl Barth's Christocentric Method." In *Engaging with Barth: Contemporary Evangelical Critiques*, edited by David Gibson and Daniel Strange, 21–54. Nottingham: Apollos, 2008.

Bloesch, Donald G. *Jesus Is Victor! Karl Barth's Doctrine of Salvation*. Nashville: Abingdon, 1976.

Briggman, Anthony. "Spirit-Christology in Irenaeus: A Closer Look." *Vigiliae Christianae* 66 (2012) 1–19.

Bromiley, Geoffrey W. *An Introduction to the Theology of Karl Barth*. Grand Rapids: Eerdmans, 1979.

Brown, Robert McAfee. "Scripture and Tradition in the Theology of Karl Barth." In *Thy Word Is Truth: Barth on Scripture*, edited by George Hunsinger, 3–19. Grand Rapids: Eerdmans, 2012.

Brunner, Emil. *The Mediator: A Study of the Central Doctrine of the Christian Faith*. Translated by Olive Wyon. Philadelphia: Westminster, 1942.

Burgess, Andrew. *The Ascension in Karl Barth*. Burlington, VT: Ashgate, 2004.

Burnett, Richard E., ed. *The Westminster Handbook to Karl Barth*. Louisville: Westminster John Knox, 2013.
Busch, Eberhard. *Meine Zeit Mit Karl Barth: Tagebuch 1965–1968*. Göttingen: Vandenhoeck & Ruprecht, 2011.
Calvin, John. *The Bondage and Liberation of the Will: A Defence of the Orthodox Doctrine of Human Choice against Pighius*. Edited by Anthony N. S. Lane. Translated by Graham I. Davies. Grand Rapids: Baker, 1996.
———. *A Harmony of the Gospels: Matthew, Mark and Luke Volume III and The Epistles of James and Jude*. Edited by David W. Torrance and Thomas F. Torrance. Translated by A. W. Morrison. Edinburgh: Saint Andrew, 1972.
———. *Institutes of the Christian Religion*. Edited by John T. McNeill. Translated by Ford Lewis Battles. 2 vols. Philadelphia: Westminster, 1960.
———. *The Secret Providence of God*. Edited by Paul Helm. Translated by Keith Goad. Wheaton, IL: Crossway, 2010.
Carter, J. Kameron. *Race: A Theological Account*. Oxford: Oxford University Press, 2008.
Cocksworth, Ashley. *Karl Barth on Prayer*. London: Bloomsbury T. & T. Clark, 2015.
Congdon, David W. "Afterword: The Future of Conversing with Barth." In *Karl Barth in Conversation*, edited by Travis W. McMaken and David W. Congdon, 255–78. Eugene, OR: Pickwick, 2014.
———. "Apokatastasis and Apostolicity: A Response to Oliver Crisp on the Question of Barth's Universalism." *Scottish Journal of Theology* 67/4 (2014) 464–80.
Cortez, Marc. "Body, Soul, and (Holy) Spirit: Karl Barth's Theological Framework for Understanding Human Ontology." *International Journal of Systematic Theology* 10/3 (2008) 328–45.
———. *Embodied Souls, Ensouled Bodies: An Exercise in Christological Anthropology and Its Significance for the Mind/Body Debate*. London: T. & T. Clark, 2008.
Couenhoven, Jesse. "Karl Barth's Conception(s) of Human and Divine Freedom(s)." In *Commanding Grace: Studies in Karl Barth's Ethics*, edited by Daniel L. Migliore, 239–55. Grand Rapids: Eerdmans, 2010.
Crisp, Oliver D. "Augustinian Universalism." *International Journal for Philosophy of Religion* 53 (2003) 127–45.
———. "Did Christ Have a Fallen Human Nature?" *International Journal of Systematic Theology* 6/3 (2004) 270–88.
———. *Divinity and Humanity: The Incarnation Reconsidered*. Cambridge: Cambridge University Press, 2007.
———. "The Election of Jesus Christ." In *God Incarnate: Explorations in Christology*, 34–55. London: T. & T. Clark, 2009.
———. *God Incarnate: Explorations in Christology*. London: T. & T. Clark, 2009.
———. "I Do Teach It, but I also Do Not Teach It: The Universalism of Karl Barth (1868–1968)." In *"All Shall Be Well": Explorations in Universalism and Christian Theology from Origen to Moltmann*, edited by Gregory MacDonald, 305–24. Eugene, OR: Cascade, 2011.
———. "John Owen on Spirit Christology." *Journal of Reformed Theology* 5/1 (2011) 5–25.
———. "On Original Sin." *International Journal of Systematic Theology* 17/3 (2015) 252–66.
———. "Was Christ Sinless or Impeccable?" *Irish Theological Quarterly* 72 (2007) 168–86.

Davidson, Ivor J. "'Not My Will but Yours Be Done': The Ontological Dynamics of Incarnational Intention." *International Journal of Systematic Theology* 7/2 (2005) 178–204.

———. "Pondering the Sinlessness of Jesus Christ: Moral Christologies and the Witness of Scripture." *International Journal of Systematic Theology* 10/4 (2008) 372–98.

Dawson, R. Dale. *The Resurrection in Karl Barth*. Burlington, VT: Ashgate, 2007.

Dempsey, Michael T., ed. *Trinity and Election in Contemporary Theology*. Grand Rapids: Eerdmans, 2011.

Dorrien, Gary. *Kantian Reason and Hegelian Spirit: The Idealistic Logic of Modern Theology*. Chichester: Wiley-Blackwell, 2012.

Dorries, D. "Nineteenth Century British Christological Controversy, Centering Upon Edward Irving's Doctrine of Christ's Human Nature." PhD diss., University of Edinburgh, 1987.

Drury, John L. "The Priest Sacrificed in Our Place: Barth's Use of the Cultic Imagery of Hebrews in Church Dogmatics IV/1, §59.2." In *1st Annual Barth Conference*. Center for Barth Studies, Princeton Theological Seminary, 2006. http://www.drurywriting.com/john/The_Priest_Sacrificed_in_Our_Place.pdf.

Edwards, Jonathan. "Economy of the Trinity and Covenant of Redemption." In *The "Miscellanies" 883–1152*, edited by Amy Plantinga Pauw, 430–43. Works of Jonathan Edwards 20. New Haven: Yale University Press, 2002.

Elwell, Walter A., ed. *Baker Theological Dictionary of the Bible*. Grand Rapids: Baker, 1996.

Emery, Gilles. "Essentialism or Personalism in the Treatise on God in Saint Thomas Aquinas." *The Thomist* 64 (2000) 521–63.

———. *The Trinitarian Theology of Saint Thomas Aquinas*. Translated by Francesca Aran Murphy. Oxford: Oxford University Press, 2007.

Erickson, Millard J. *Christian Theology*. 3rd ed. Grand Rapids: Baker Academic, 2013.

Fiddes, Paul S. "Salvation." In *The Oxford Handbook of Systematic Theology*, edited by John B. Webster, Kathryn Tanner, and Iain Torrance, 176–96. Oxford: Oxford University Press, 2007.

Fong, Edmund. "'The One and the Many': Pondering the Hermeneutics of the Doctrine of the Atonement from the 'Reception of Doctrine' Approach." *Journal of Theological Interpretation* 12/1 (2018) 127–46.

Fout, Jason A. *Fully Alive: The Glory of God and the Human Creature in Karl Barth, Hans Urs von Balthasar and Theological Exegesis of Scripture*. London: Bloomsbury T. & T. Clark, 2015.

Freedman, David Noel, ed. *Eerdmans Dictionary of the Bible*. Grand Rapids: Eerdmans, 2000.

Frei, Hans W. *The Identity of Jesus Christ: The Hermeneutical Bases of Dogmatic Theology*. Philadelphia: Fortress, 1975.

Gabriel, Andrew. *Barth's Doctrine of Creation: Creation, Nature, Jesus, and the Trinity*. Eugene, OR: Cascade, 2013.

Gibson, David. *Reading the Decree: Exegesis, Election and Christology in Calvin and Barth*. London: T. & T. Clark, 2009.

Gignilliat, Mark S. *Karl Barth and the Fifth Gospel: Barth's Theological Exegesis of Isaiah*. Burlington, VT: Ashgate, 2009.

Giles, Kevin. "Barth and Subordinationism." *Scottish Journal of Theology* 64/3 (2011) 327–46.
Gockel, Matthias. *Barth and Schleiermacher on the Doctrine of Election: A Systematic-Theological Comparison.* Oxford: Oxford University Press, 2006.
Goebel, Hans Theodore. "Trinitätslehre und Erwählungslehre bei Karl Barth." In *Wahrheit und Versöhnung: Theologische und philosophische Beiträge zur Gotteslehre*, edited by D. Korsch and H. Ruddies, 147–66. Gütersloh: Gütersloher Verlagshaus Gerd Mohn, 1989.
———. *Vom freien Wählen Gottes und des Menschen. Interpretationsübungen zur "Analogie" nach Karl Barths Lehre von der Erwählung und Bedenken ihrer Folgen für die Kirchliche Dogmatik.* Frankfurt: Peter Lang, 1990.
Gondreau, Paul. "The Humanity of Christ, the Incarnate Word." In *The Theology of Thomas Aquinas*, edited by Rik Van Nieuwenhove and Joseph Wawrykow, 252–76. Notre Dame: University of Notre Dame Press, 2005.
———. "St. Thomas Aquinas, the Communication of Idioms, and the Suffering of Christ in the Garden of Gethsemane." In *Divine Impassibility and the Mystery of Human Suffering*, edited by James F. Keating and Thomas Joseph White, 214–45. Grand Rapids: Eerdmans, 2009.
Gorringe, Timothy. *Karl Barth against Hegemony.* Oxford: Oxford University Press, 1999.
Grebe, Matthias. *Election, Atonement, and the Holy Spirit: Through and Beyond Barth's Theological Interpretation of Scripture.* Eugene, OR: Pickwick, 2014.
Greggs, Tom. *Barth, Origen, and Universal Salvation: Restoring Particularity.* Oxford: Oxford University Press, 2009.
———. "'Jesus Is Victor': Passing the Impasse of Barth on Universalism." *Scottish Journal of Theology* 60/2 (2007) 196–212.
Grenz, Stanley J., David Guretzki, and Cherith Fee Nordling, eds. *Pocket Dictionary of Theological Terms.* Downers Grove, IL: InterVarsity, 1999.
Griswold, Daniel M. *Triune Eternality: God's Relationship to Time in the Theology of Karl Barth.* Minneapolis: Fortress, 2015.
Gunton, Colin E. *Act and Being: Towards a Theology of the Divine Attributes.* London: SCM, 2002.
———. *The Barth Lectures.* Edited by Paul Brazier. London: T. & T. Clark, 2007.
———. *The Christian Faith: An Introduction to Christian Doctrine.* Malden, MA: Blackwell, 2002.
———. "The Doctrine of God: Karl Barth's Doctrine of Election as Part of His Doctrine of God." In *Theology through the Theologians*, 88–104. Edinburgh: T. & T. Clark, 1996.
———. "God the Holy Spirit: Augustine and His Successors." In *Theology through the Theologians*, 105–28. Edinburgh: T. & T. Clark, 1996.
———. "Salvation." In *The Cambridge Companion to Karl Barth*, edited by John B. Webster, 143–58. Cambridge: Cambridge University Press, 2000.
———. "The Triune God and the Freedom of the Creature." In *Karl Barth: Centenary Essays*, edited by S. W. Sykes, 46–68. Cambridge: Cambridge University Press, 1989.
Guretzki, David. *Karl Barth on the Filioque.* Burlington, VT: Ashgate, 2009.
Habets, Myk. *The Anointed Son: A Trinitarian Spirit Christology.* Eugene, OR: Pickwick, 2010.

Härle, Wilfried. *Sein und Gnade. Die Ontologie in Karl Barths "Kirchliche Dogmatik."* Berlin: de Gruyter, 1975.

Hartwell, Herbert. *The Theology of Karl Barth: An Introduction.* London: Gerald Duckworth, 1964.

Hattrell, Simon, ed. and trans. *Election, Barth and the French Connection: How Pierre Maury Gave a "Decisive Impetus" to Karl Barth's Doctrine of Election.* Eugene, OR: Pickwick, 2016.

Hector, Kevin W. "God's Triunity and Self-Determination: A Conversation with Karl Barth, Bruce McCormack and Paul Molnar." *International Journal of Systematic Theology* 7/3 (2005) 246–61.

———. "Immutability, Necessity and Triunity: Towards a Resolution of the Trinity and Election Controversy." *Scottish Journal of Theology* 65/1 (2012) 64–81.

Helm, Paul. *John Calvin's Ideas.* Oxford: Oxford University Press, 2004.

Heppe, Heinrich. *Reformed Dogmatics.* Edited by Ernst Bizer. Translated by G. T. Thomson. Grand Rapids: Baker, 1978.

Hesselink, I. John. "Karl Barth on Prayer." In *Prayer: 50th Anniversary Edition*, edited by Don E. Saliers, 74–94. Louisville: Westminster John Knox, 2002.

Hick, John. *Evil and the God of Love.* 2nd ed. San Francisco: Harper, 1977.

Holmes, Christopher R. J. "The Church and the Presence of Christ: Defending Actualist Ecclesiology." *Pro Ecclesia* 21/3 (2012) 268–80.

———. *The Holy Spirit.* Grand Rapids: Zondervan, 2015.

———. "The Person and Work of Christ Revisited: In Conversation with Karl Barth." *Anglican Theological Review* 95/1 (2013) 37–55.

———. *Revisiting the Doctrine of the Divine Attributes: In Dialogue with Karl Barth, Eberhard Jüngel, and Wolf Krötke.* New York: Peter Lang, 2007.

Holmes, Stephen R. "A Simple Salvation? Soteriology and the Perfections of God." In *God of Salvation: Soteriology in Theological Perspective*, edited by Ivor J. Davidson and Murray A. Rae, 35–46. Burlington, VT: Ashgate, 2011.

Holsinger-Friesen, Thomas. *Irenaeus and Genesis: A Study of Competition in Early Christian Hermeneutics.* Journal of Theological Interpretation Supplements 1. Winona Lake, IN: Eisenbrauns, 2009.

Horton, Michael S. "Covenant, Election, and Incarnation: Evaluating Barth's Actualistic Christology." In *Karl Barth and American Evangelicalism*, edited by Bruce L. McCormack and Clifford B. Anderson, 112–47. Grand Rapids: Eerdmans, 2011.

———. *Lord and Servant: A Covenant Christology.* Louisville: Westminster John Knox, 2005.

Hunsinger, George. "Barth on What It Means to Be Human: A Christian Scholar Confronts the Options." In *Evangelical, Catholic, and Reformed*, 245–59. Grand Rapids: Eerdmans, 2015.

———. "Election and the Trinity: Twenty-Five Theses on the Theology of Karl Barth." *Modern Theology* 24/2 (2008) 179–98.

———. "Hellfire and Damnation: Four Ancient and Modern Views." In *Disruptive Grace: Studies in the Theology of Karl Barth*, 226–49. Grand Rapids: Eerdmans, 2000.

———. *How to Read Karl Barth: The Shape of His Theology.* Oxford: Oxford University Press, 1991.

———. "Karl Barth's Christology: Its Basic Chalcedonian Character." In *The Cambridge Companion to Karl Barth*, edited by John B. Webster, 127–42. Cambridge: Cambridge University Press, 2000.

———. "Karl Barth's Doctrine of the Trinity, and Some Protestant Doctrines after Barth." In *The Oxford Handbook of the Trinity*, edited by Gilles Emery and Matthew Levering, 294–313. Oxford: Oxford University Press, 2011.

———. "The Mediator of Communion: Karl Barth's Doctrine of the Holy Spirit." In *Disruptive Grace: Studies in the Theology of Karl Barth*, 148–85. Grand Rapids: Eerdmans, 2000.

———. "*Mysterium Trinitatis*: Karl Barth's Conception of Eternity." In *Disruptive Grace: Studies in the Theology of Karl Barth*, 186–209. Grand Rapids: Eerdmans, 2000.

———. "The Politics of the Nonviolent God: Reflections on René Girard and Karl Barth." In *Disruptive Grace: Studies in the Theology of Karl Barth*, 21–41. Grand Rapids: Eerdmans, 2000.

———. *Reading Barth with Charity: A Hermeneutical Proposal*. Grand Rapids: Baker Academic, 2015.

Irenaeus of Lyons. *Against Heresies*. Translated by A. Roberts and W. H. Rambaut. *The Ante-Nicene Fathers Down to A.D. 325*. 2 vols. Edinburgh: T. & T. Clark, 1868–69. Reprint, Grand Rapids: Eerdmans, 1979.

———. *Proof of the Apostolic Preaching*. Translated and annotated by Joseph P. Smith. Ancient Christian Writers 16. Mahwah, NJ: Paulist, 1952.

Jeffery, Steve, Mike Ovey, and Andrew Sach. *Pierced for Our Transgressions: Rediscovering the Glory of Penal Substitution*. Nottingham: InterVarsity, 2007.

Jehle, Frank. *Ever Against the Stream: The Politics of Karl Barth, 1906–1968*. Translated by Richard and Martha Burnett. Grand Rapids: Eerdmans, 2002.

Jenson, Robert W. "Once More the *Logos Asarkos*." *International Journal of Systematic Theology* 13/2 (2011) 130–33.

———. "You Wonder Where the Spirit Went." *Pro Ecclesia* 2/3 (1993) 296–304.

Johnson, Adam J. *God's Being in Reconciliation: The Theological Basis of the Unity and Diversity of the Atonement in the Theology of Karl Barth*. London: T. & T. Clark, 2012.

———. "The Servant Lord: A Word of Caution Regarding the Munus Triplex in Karl Barth's Theology and the Church Today." *Scottish Journal of Theology* 65/2 (2012) 159–73.

Johnson, Keith L. *Karl Barth and the Analogia Entis*. London: T. & T. Clark, 2010.

Jones, Paul D. "The Atonement: God's Love in Action." In *New Perspectives for Evangelical Theology: Engaging with God, Scripture, and the World*, edited by Tom Greggs, 44–62. London: Routledge, 2010.

———. "Barth and Anselm: God, Christ and the Atonement." *International Journal of Systematic Theology* 12/3 (2010) 257–82.

———. *The Humanity of Christ: Christology in Karl Barth's Church Dogmatics*. London: T. & T. Clark, 2008.

———. "Karl Barth on Gethsemane." *International Journal of Systematic Theology* 9/2 (2007) 148–71.

———. "Obedience, Trinity, and Election: Thinking With and Beyond the *Church Dogmatics*." In *Trinity and Election in Contemporary Theology*, edited by Michael T. Dempsey, 138–61. Grand Rapids: Eerdmans, 2011.

———. "On Patience: Thinking With and Beyond Karl Barth." *Scottish Journal of Theology* 68/3 (2015) 273–98.

———. "The Riddle of Gethsemane: Barth on Jesus's Agony in the Garden." In *Reading the Gospels with Karl Barth*, edited by Daniel L. Migliore, 124–54. Grand Rapids: Eerdmans, 2017.

Jowers, Dennis W. "The Reproach of Modalism: A Difficulty for Karl Barth's Doctrine of the Trinity." *Scottish Journal of Theology* 56/2 (2003) 231–46.

Jüngel, Eberhard. *God's Being Is in Becoming: The Trinitarian Being of God in the Theology of Karl Barth; A Paraphrase*. Translated by John B. Webster. Edinburgh: T. & T. Clark, 2001.

———. *Gottes Sein ist im Werden: Verantwortliche Reden vom Sein Gottes bei Karl Barth; Eine Paraphrase*. 2nd ed. Tübingen: J. C. B. Mohr (Paul Siebeck), 1967.

———. "Invocation of God as the Ethical Ground of Christian Action: Introductory Remarks on the Posthumous Fragments of Karl Barth's Ethics of the Doctrine of Reconciliation." In *Theological Essays*, translated by John B. Webster, 154–72. Reprint, London: Bloomsbury T. & T. Clark, 2014.

———. *Karl Barth: A Theological Legacy*. Translated by Garrett E. Paul. Philadelphia: Westminster, 1986.

Kane, Robert. *A Contemporary Introduction to Free Will*. Fundamentals of Philosophy. Oxford: Oxford University Press, 2005.

Kapic, Kelly M. "The Son's Assumption of a Human Nature: A Call for Clarity." *International Journal of Systematic Theology* 3/2 (2001) 154–66.

Knight, Douglas H. *The Eschatological Economy: Time and the Hospitality of God*. Grand Rapids: Eerdmans, 2006.

Lang, U. M. "Anhypostatos-Enhypostatos: Church Fathers, Protestant Orthodoxy, and Karl Barth." *Journal of Theological Studies* 49/2 (1998) 630–57.

Langdon, Adrian. *God the Eternal Contemporary: Triunity, Eternity and Time in Karl Barth*. Eugene, OR: Wipf & Stock, 2012.

Lauber, David. *Barth on the Descent into Hell: God, Atonement and the Christian Life*. Burlington, VT: Ashgate, 2004.

Leftow, Brian. "Anti Social Trinitarianism." In *The Trinity: An Interdisciplinary Symposium on the Trinity*, edited by Stephen T. Davis, Daniel Kendall, and Gerald O'Collins, 203–49. Oxford: Oxford University Press, 1999.

———. "A Timeless God Incarnate." In *The Incarnation: An Interdisciplinary Symposium on the Incarnation of the Son of God*, edited by Stephen T. Davis, Daniel Kendall, and Gerald O'Collins, 273–99. Oxford: Oxford University Press, 2002.

Leigh, Robert. *Freedom and Flourishing: Being, Act and Knowledge in Karl Barth's Church Dogmatics*. Eugene, OR: Cascade, 2017.

Letham, Robert. *The Holy Trinity: In Scripture, History, Theology and Worship*. Phillipsburg, NJ: P&R, 2004.

Levering, Matthew. "Christ, the Trinity, and Predestination: McCormack and Aquinas." In *Trinity and Election in Contemporary Theology*, edited by Michael T. Dempsey, 244–73. Grand Rapids: Eerdmans, 2011.

Lindsay, Mark R. *Barth, Israel, and Jesus: Karl Barth's Theology of Israel*. Burlington, VT: Ashgate, 2007.

———. "Pierre Maury, Karl Barth, and the Evolution of Election." In *Election, Barth and the French Connection: How Pierre Maury Gave a "Decisive Impetus" to Karl Barth's Doctrine of Election*, edited and translated by Simon Hattrell, 107–28. Eugene, OR: Pickwick, 2016.

Loke, Andrew Ter Ern. *A Kryptic Model of the Incarnation*. Burlington, VT: Ashgate, 2014.

———. "On Dyothelitism versus Monothelitism: The Divine Preconscious Model." *The Heythrop Journal* (2013) 1–7. https://doi.org/10.1111/heyj.12073.

Louth, Andrew. *Maximus the Confessor*. London: Routledge, 1996.

Macchia, Frank D. "The Spirit of God and the Spirit of Life: An Evangelical Response to Karl Barth's Pneumatology." In *Karl Barth and Evangelical Theology: Convergences and Divergences*, edited by Sung Wook Chung, 149–71. Grand Rapids: Baker Academic, 2006.

MacDonald, Neil B. "Karl Barth's Narrative Doctrine of Substitutionary Atonement." In *Calvin, Barth, and Reformed Theology*, edited by Neil B. MacDonald and Carl Trueman, 91–117. Milton Keynes: Paternoster, 2008.

Macquarrie, John. *Jesus Christ in Modern Thought*. London: SCM, 1990.

Mangina, Joseph L. *Karl Barth: Theologian of Christian Witness*. Louisville: Westminster John Knox, 2004.

Mansini, Guy. "Can Humility and Obedience Be Trinitarian Realities?" In *Thomas Aquinas and Karl Barth: An Unofficial Catholic-Protestant Dialogue*, edited by Bruce L. McCormack and Thomas Joseph White, 71–98. Grand Rapids: Eerdmans, 2013.

Martin, Shirley. "Freedom to Obey: The Obedience of Christ as the Reflection of the Obedience of the Son in Karl Barth's *Church Dogmatics*." PhD diss., University of St. Andrews, 2008.

Maximus, Confessor, Saint. *On the Cosmic Mystery of Jesus Christ: Selected Writings from St. Maximus the Confessor*. Translated by Paul M. Blowers and Robert Louis Wilken. Popular Patristics 25. Crestwood, NY: St. Vladimir's Seminary Press, 2003.

McCormack, Bruce L. "The Actuality of God: Karl Barth in Conversation with Open Theism." In *Engaging the Doctrine of God: Contemporary Protestant Perspectives*, edited by Bruce L. McCormack, 185–242. Grand Rapids: Baker Academic, 2008.

———. "Divine Impassibility or Simply Divine Constancy? Implications of Karl Barth's Later Christology for Debates over Impassibility." In *Divine Impassibility and the Mystery of Human Suffering*, edited by James F. Keating and Thomas Joseph White, 150–86. Grand Rapids: Eerdmans, 2009.

———. "The Doctrine of the Trinity after Barth: An Attempt to Reconstruct Barth's Doctrine in the Light of His Later Christology." In *Trinitarian Theology after Barth*, edited by Myk Habets and Phillip Tolliday, 87–117. Eugene, OR: Wipf & Stock, 2011.

———. "Election and the Trinity: Theses in Response to George Hunsinger." *Scottish Journal of Theology* 63/2 (2010) 203–24.

———. "For Us and Our Salvation: Incarnation and Atonement in the Reformed Tradition." *The Greek Orthodox Theological Review* 43/1–4 (1998) 281–316.

———. "Foreword to the German Edition of *Karl Barth's Critically Realistic Dialectical Theology*." In *Orthodox and Modern: Studies in the Theology of Karl Barth*, 291–304. Grand Rapids: Baker Academic, 2008.

———. "God Is His Decision: The Jüngel-Gollwitzer 'Debate' Revisited." In *Theology as Conversation: The Significance of Dialogue in Historical and Contemporary Theology*, edited by Bruce L. McCormack and Kimlyn J. Bender, 48–66. Grand Rapids: Eerdmans, 2009.

———. "The God Who Graciously Elects: Seven Lectures on the Doctrine of God." The 2011 Kantzer Lectures in Revealed Theology, given at Trinity Evangelical Divinity School, Deerfield, Illinois, 2011. https://henrycenter.tiu.edu/kantzer-lectures-in-revealed-theology/past-lectures-publications/bruce-mccormack/.

———. "Grace and Being: The Role of God's Gracious Election in Karl Barth's Theological Ontology." In *The Cambridge Companion to Karl Barth*, edited by John B. Webster, 92–110. Cambridge: Cambridge University Press, 2000.

———. "The Identity of the Son: Karl Barth's Exegesis of Hebrews 1.1–4 (and Similar Passages)." In *Christology, Hermeneutics, and Hebrews: Profiles from the History of Interpretation*, edited by Jon C. Laansma and Daniel J. Treier, 155–72. London: Bloomsbury, 2012.

———. "*Justitia Aliena*: Karl Barth in Conversation with the Evangelical Doctrine of Imputed Righteousness." In *Justification in Perspective: Historical Developments and Contemporary Challenges*, edited by Bruce L. McCormack, 167–96. Grand Rapids: Baker Academic, 2006.

———. "Karl Barth's Christology as a Resource for a Reformed Version of Kenoticism." *International Journal of Systematic Theology* 8/3 (2006) 243–51.

———. *Karl Barth's Critically Realistic Dialectical Theology: Its Genesis and Development 1909–1936*. Oxford: Oxford University Press, 1997.

———. "Karl Barth's Historicized Christology: Just How 'Chalcedonian' Is It?" In *Orthodox and Modern: Studies in the Theology of Karl Barth*, 201–34. Grand Rapids: Baker Academic, 2008.

———. "Karl Barth's Version of an 'Analogy of Being': A Dialectical No and Yes to Roman Catholicism." In *The Analogy of Being: Invention of the Antichrist or the Wisdom of God?*, edited by Thomas Joseph White, 88–144. Grand Rapids: Eerdmans, 2011.

———. "Let's Speak Plainly: A Response to Paul Molnar." *Theology Today* 67/1 (2010) 57–65.

———. "The Lord and Giver of Life: A 'Barthian' Defense of the Filioque." In *Rethinking Trinitarian Theology: Disputed Questions and Contemporary Issues in Trinitarian Theology*, edited by Robert J. Wozniak and Giulio Maspero, 230–53. London: T. & T. Clark, 2012.

———. "The Ontological Presuppositions of Barth's Doctrine of the Atonement." In *The Glory of the Atonement: Biblical, Historical and Practical Perspectives*, edited by Charles E. Hill and Frank A. James, 346–66. Downers Grove, IL: InterVarsity, 2004.

———. "Processions and Missions: A Point of Convergence between Thomas Aquinas and Karl Barth." In *Thomas Aquinas and Karl Barth: An Unofficial Catholic-Protestant Dialogue*, edited by Bruce L. McCormack and Thomas Joseph White, 99–126. Grand Rapids: Eerdmans, 2013.

———. "Seek God Where He May Be Found: A Response to Edwin Chr. van Driel." *Scottish Journal of Theology* 60/1 (2007) 62–79.

———. "So That He May Be Merciful to All: Karl Barth and the Problem of Universalism." In *Karl Barth and American Evangelicalism*, edited by Bruce L. McCormack and Clifford B. Anderson, 227–49. Grand Rapids: Eerdmans, 2011.

———. "'We Have "Actualized" the Doctrine of the Incarnation . . .': Musings on Karl Barth's Actualistic Theological Ontology." *Zeitschrift für dialektische Theologie* 32/1 (2016) 179–98.

———. "'With Loud Cries and Tears': The Humanity of the Son in the Epistle to the Hebrews." In *The Epistle to the Hebrews and Christian Theology*, edited by Richard J. Bauckham et al., 37–68. Grand Rapids: Eerdmans, 2009.

McDonald, Suzanne. "Evangelical Questioning of Election in Barth: A Pneumatological Perspective from the Reformed Heritage." In *Karl Barth and American Evangelicalism*, edited by Bruce L. McCormack and Clifford B. Anderson, 250–70. Grand Rapids: Eerdmans, 2011.

McFarland, Ian A. "Fallen or Unfallen? Christ's Human Nature and the Ontology of Human Sinfulness." *International Journal of Systematic Theology* 10/4 (2008) 399–415.

———. "'Naturally and by Grace': Maximus the Confessor on the Operation of the Will." *Scottish Journal of Theology* 58/4 (2005) 410–33.

———. "'Willing Is Not Choosing': Some Anthropological Implications of Dyothelite Christology." *International Journal of Systematic Theology* 9/1 (2007) 3–23.

McGowan, A. T. B. "Karl Barth and Covenant Theology." In *Engaging with Barth: Contemporary Evangelical Critiques*, edited by David Gibson and Daniel Strange, 113–35. Nottingham: Apollos, 2008.

McGrath, Alister E. *The Making of Modern German Christology: From the Enlightenment to Pannenberg*. Oxford: Blackwell, 1986.

McIntyre, John. *The Shape of Pneumatology: Studies in the Doctrine of the Holy Spirit*. Edinburgh: T. & T. Clark, 1997.

McKenny, Gerald. "'Freed by God for God': Divine Action and Human Action in Karl Barth's Evangelical Theology and Other Late Works." In *Karl Barth and the Making of Evangelical Theology: A Fifty-Year Perspective*, edited by Clifford B. Anderson and Bruce L. McCormack, 119–38. Grand Rapids: Eerdmans, 2015.

McLean, Stuart D. *Humanity in the Thought of Karl Barth*. Edinburgh: T. & T. Clark, 1981.

McMaken, Travis W. "Election and the Pattern of Exchange in Karl Barth's Doctrine of the Atonement." *Journal of Reformed Theology* 3/2 (2009) 202–18.

Migliore, Daniel L. "Freedom to Pray: Karl Barth's Theology of Prayer." In *Prayer: 50th Anniversary Edition*, edited by Don E. Saliers, 95–113. Louisville: Westminster John Knox, 2002.

———. "*Veni Creator Spiritus*: The Work of the Spirit in the Theologies of B. B. Warfield and Karl Barth." In *Karl Barth and the Making of Evangelical Theology: A Fifty-Year Perspective*, edited by Clifford B. Anderson and Bruce L. McCormack, 157–77. Grand Rapids: Eerdmans, 2015.

Mikkelsen, Hans Vium. *Reconciled Humanity: Karl Barth in Dialogue*. Grand Rapids: Eerdmans, 2010.

Minns, Denis. *Irenaeus: An Introduction*. London: T. & T. Clark, 2010.

Molnar, Paul. "Can Jesus' Divinity Be Recognized as 'Definitive, Authentic and Essential' if It Is Grounded in Election? Just How Far Did the Later Barth Historicize Christology?" *Neue Zeitschrift für Systematische Theologie und Religionsphilosophie* 52 (2010) 40–81.

———. "Can the Electing God Be God without Us? Some Implications of Bruce McCormack's Understanding of Barth's Doctrine of Election for the Doctrine of the Trinity." *Neue Zeitschrift für Systematische Theologie und Religionsphilosophie* 49/2 (2007) 199–222.

———. *Divine Freedom and the Doctrine of the Immanent Trinity*. London: T. & T. Clark, 2002.

———. *Faith, Freedom and the Spirit: The Economic Trinity in Barth, Torrance and Contemporary Theology*. Downers Grove, IL: InterVarsity, 2015.

———. "The Obedience of the Son in the Theology of Karl Barth and of Thomas F. Torrance." *Scottish Journal of Theology* 67/1 (2014) 50–69.

———. "The Perils of Embracing a 'Historicized Christology.'" *Modern Theology* 30/4 (2014) 454–80.

———. "The Trinity, Election and God's Ontological Freedom: A Response to Kevin W. Hector." *International Journal of Systematic Theology* 8/3 (2006) 294–306.

Moltmann, Jürgen. *The Trinity and the Kingdom of God: The Doctrine of God*. Translated by Margaret Kohl. London: SCM, 1981.

Morris, Thomas. *The Logic of God Incarnate*. 1986. Reprint, Eugene, OR: Wipf & Stock, 2001.

Muller, Richard A. *Dictionary of Latin and Greek Theological Terms*. Grand Rapids: Baker, 1985.

Neder, Adam. "History in Harmony: Karl Barth on the Hypostatic Union." In *Karl Barth and American Evangelicalism*, edited by Bruce L. McCormack and Clifford B. Anderson, 148–76. Grand Rapids: Eerdmans, 2011.

Nimmo, Paul T. "Barth and the Election-Trinity Debate: A Pneumatological View." In *Trinity and Election in Contemporary Theology*, edited by Michael T. Dempsey, 162–81. Grand Rapids: Eerdmans, 2011.

———. *Being in Action: The Theological Shape of Barth's Ethical Vision*. London: T. & T. Clark, 2011.

Ovey, Michael J. "A Private Love? Karl Barth and the Triune God." In *Engaging with Barth: Contemporary Evangelical Critiques*, edited by David Gibson and Daniel Strange, 198–231. Nottingham: Apollos, 2008.

Owen, John. *The Works of John Owen*. Edited by William Goold. 16 vols. Edinburgh: Banner of Truth Trust, 1965.

Payton, James R., Jr. *Irenaeus on the Christian Faith: A Condensation of Against Heresies*. Eugene, OR: Pickwick, 2011.

Peterson, David. *Hebrews and Perfection: An Examination of the Concept of Perfection in the "Epistle to the Hebrews."* Cambridge: Cambridge University Press, 1982.

Peterson, Robert A., Sr. *Calvin and the Atonement*. Fearn, Ross-shire: Mentor, 1999.

Price, Robert B. *Letters of the Divine Word: The Perfections of God in Karl Barth's Church Dogmatics*. London: T. & T. Clark, 2011.

Rae, Murray A. "A Remnant People: The Ecclesia as Sign of Reconciliation." In *The Theology of Reconciliation*, edited by Colin E. Gunton, 93–108. London: T. & T. Clark, 2003.

———. "The Spatiality of God." In *Trinitarian Theology after Barth*, edited by Myk Habets and Phillip Tolliday, 70–86. Eugene, OR: Wipf & Stock, 2011.

Reeves, Michael. "The Glory of God: The Christological Anthropology of Irenaeus of Lyons and Karl Barth." PhD diss., University of London, King's College, 2005.

Resch, Dustin. *Barth's Interpretation of the Virgin Birth: A Sign of Mystery*. Burlington, VT: Ashgate, 2012.

Rogers, Eugene F., Jr. "The Eclipse of the Spirit in Karl Barth." In *Conversing with Barth*, edited by John C. McDowell and Mike Higton, 173–90. Burlington, VT: Ashgate, 2004.

Rosato, Philip. *The Spirit as Lord: The Pneumatology of Karl Barth*. Edinburgh: T. & T. Clark, 1981.

Roy, Louis. "Does Christian Faith Rule Out Human Autonomy?" *Heythrop Journal* 53/4 (2012) 606–23.

Schleiermacher, Friedrich. *The Christian Faith*. Edited by H. R. Mackintosh and J. S. Stewart. Edinburgh: T. & T. Clark, 1928.

Shults, F. LeRon. "A Dubious Christological Formula: From Leontius of Byzantium to Karl Barth." *Theological Studies* 57/3 (1996) 431–46.

Smit, Dirk Jacobus. "'(T)His Cry Activates the Freedom Given and Therefore the Obedience Required': The Work of the Spirit from 'Calvin' to 'Barth'?" *Zeitschrift für Dialektische Theologie* 30/1 (2014) 51–87.

Smith, Aaron T. "God's Self-Specification: His Being Is His Electing." *Scottish Journal of Theology* 62/1 (2009) 1–25.

———. *A Theology of the Third Article: Karl Barth and the Spirit of the Word*. Minneapolis: Fortress, 2014.

Sonderegger, Katherine. "The Sinlessness of Christ." In *Theological Theology: Essays in Honour of John Webster*, edited by R. David Nelson, Darren Sarisky, and Justin Stratis, 267–75. London: Bloomsbury T. & T. Clark, 2015.

Spence, Alan. *Incarnation and Inspiration: John Owen and the Coherence of Christology*. London: T. & T. Clark, 2007.

———. "The Person as Willing Agent: Classifying Gunton's Christology." In *The Theology of Colin Gunton*, edited by Lincoln Harvey, 49–64. London: T. & T. Clark, 2010.

Stanglin, Keith D., and Thomas H. McCall. *Jacob Arminius: Theologian of Grace*. Oxford: Oxford University Press, 2012.

Steenberg, M. C. *Irenaeus on Creation: The Cosmic Christ and the Saga of Redemption*. Supplements to Vigiliae Christianae 91. Leiden: Brill, 2008.

Stratis, Justin. "Speculating about Divinity? God's Immanent Life and Actualistic Ontology." *International Journal of Systematic Theology* 12/1 (2010) 20–32.

Stump, Eleonore. "Augustine on Free Will." In *The Cambridge Companion to Augustine*, edited by Eleonore Stump and Norman Kretzmann, 124–47. Cambridge: Cambridge University Press, 2001.

Sumner, Darren O. *Karl Barth and the Incarnation: Christology and the Humility of God*. London: Bloomsbury, 2014.

———. "Fallenness and *anhypostasis*: A Way Forward in the Debate over Christ's Humanity." *Scottish Journal of Theology* 67/2 (2014) 195–212.

———. "Obedience and Subordination in Karl Barth's Trinitarian Theology." In *Advancing Trinitarian Theology: Explorations in Constructive Dogmatics*, edited by Oliver D. Crisp and Fred Sanders, 130–46. Grand Rapids: Zondervan, 2014.

———. "Some Observations on the 'Eternal Functional Subordination' Debate." *Out of Bounds: Theology in the Far Country* (blog), June 10, 2016. https://theologyoutofbounds.wordpress.com/2016/06/10/some-observations-on-the-eternal-functional-subordination-debate/.

Swain, Scott, and Michael Allen. "The Obedience of the Eternal Son." *International Journal of Systematic Theology* 15/2 (2013) 114–34.

Tanner, Kathryn. "Beyond the East/West Divide." In *Ecumenical Perspectives on the Filioque for the Twenty-First Century*, edited by Myk Habets, 198–210. London: Bloomsbury T. & T. Clark, 2014.

Tay, Edwin. *The Priesthood of Christ: Atonement in the Theology of John Owen (1616–1683)*. Milton Keynes: Paternoster, 2014.
Taylor, Iain. "In Defence of Karl Barth's Doctrine of the Trinity." *International Journal of Systematic Theology* 5/1 (2003) 33–46.
Terry, Justyn. *The Justifying Judgment of God: A Reassessment of the Place of Judgment in the Saving Work of Christ*. Milton Keynes: Paternoster, 2007.
Thomas, Günter. "Creation." In *The Westminster Handbook to Karl Barth*, edited by Richard E Burnett, kindle loc. 1907–2015. Louisville: Westminster John Knox, 2013.
Thompson, John. "The Humanity of God in the Theology of Karl Barth." *Scottish Journal of Theology* 29/3 (1976) 249–69.
Tolliday, Phillip. "Obedience and Subordination in Barth's Trinity." In *Trinitarian Theology after Barth*, edited by Myk Habets and Phillip Tolliday, 138–60. Eugene, OR: Wipf & Stock, 2011.
Torrance, Alan J. "The Trinity." In *The Cambridge Companion to Karl Barth*, edited by John B. Webster, 72–89. Cambridge: Cambridge University Press, 2000.
Torrance, T. F. *Atonement: The Person and Work of Christ*. Edited by Robert T. Walker. Downers Grove, IL: InterVarsity, 2009.
———. *The Christian Doctrine of God, One Being Three Persons*. Edinburgh: T. & T. Clark, 1996.
———. *Incarnation: The Person and Life of Christ*. Edited by Robert T. Walker. Downers Grove, IL: InterVarsity, 2008.
———. *The Trinitarian Faith*. London: T. & T. Clark, 1991.
Treat, Jeremy R. "Exaltation in and through Humiliation: Rethinking the States of Christ." In *Christology, Ancient and Modern: Explorations in Constructive Dogmatics*, edited by Oliver D. Crisp and Fred Sanders, 96–114. Grand Rapids: Zondervan, 2013.
Tseng, Shao Kai. *Karl Barth's Infralapsarian Theology: Origins and Development 1920–1953*. Downers Grove, IL: IVP Academic, 2016.
Turretin, Francis. *Institutes of Elenctic Theology*. Vol. 2. Phillipsburg, NJ: P&R, 1994.
Vanhoozer, Kevin J. "Atonement." In *Mapping Modern Theology: A Thematic and Historical Introduction*, edited by Kelly M. Kapic and Bruce L. McCormack, 175–202. Grand Rapids: Baker Academic, 2012.
Vorster, Nico. "The Augustinian Type of Theodicy: Is It Outdated?" *Journal of Reformed Theology* 5 (2011) 26–48.
Waldrop, Charles T. *Karl Barth's Christology: Its Basic Alexandrian Character*. Berlin: de Gruyter, 1984.
Ware, Bruce. *Father, Son, and Holy Spirit: Relationships, Roles, and Relevance*. Wheaton, IL: Crossway, 2005.
Webster, John B. *Barth*. London: Continuum, 2000.
———. *Barth's Moral Theology: Human Action in Barth's Thought*. Edinburgh: T. & T. Clark, 1998.
———. *Confessing God: Essays in Christian Dogmatics II*. London: T. & T. Clark, 2005.
———. "Gunton and Barth." In *The Theology of Colin Gunton*, edited by Lincoln Harvey, 17–31. London: T. & T. Clark, 2010.
———. "'It Was the Will of the Lord to Bruise Him': Soteriology and the Doctrine of God." In *God of Salvation: Soteriology in Theological Perspective*, edited by Ivor J. Davidson and Murray A. Rae, 15–34. Burlington, VT: Ashgate, 2011.

———. "The Theology of the Reformed Confessions." In *Barth's Earlier Theology*, 41–65. London: T. & T. Clark, 2005.

———. "Witness to the Word: Karl Barth's Lectures on the Gospel of John." In *The Domain of the Word: Scripture and Theological Reason*, 65–85. London: T. & T. Clark, 2012.

Weinandy, Thomas G. *The Father's Spirit of Sonship: Reconceiving the Trinity*. Edinburgh: T. & T. Clark, 1995.

———. *In the Likeness of Sinful Flesh: An Essay on the Humanity of Christ*. Edinburgh: T. & T. Clark, 1993.

Werpehowski, William. "Command and History in the Ethics of Karl Barth." *The Journal of Religious Ethics* 9/2 (1981) 298–320.

White, Thomas Joseph. "Divine Simplicity and the Holy Trinity." *International Journal of Systematic Theology* 18/1 (2016) 66–93.

———. *The Incarnate Lord: A Thomistic Study in Christology*. Washington, DC: Catholic University of America Press, 2015.

———. "Intra-Trinitarian Obedience and Nicene-Chalcedonian Christology." *Nova et Vetera* 6/2 (2008) 377–402.

———. "Introduction: Thomas Aquinas and Karl Barth—an Unofficial Catholic-Protestant Dialogue." In *Thomas Aquinas and Karl Barth: An Unofficial Catholic-Protestant Dialogue*, edited by Bruce L. McCormack and Thomas Joseph White, 1–39. Grand Rapids: Eerdmans, 2013.

Williams, Garry J. "Karl Barth and the Doctrine of the Atonement." In *Engaging with Barth: Contemporary Evangelical Critiques*, edited by David Gibson and Daniel Strange, 232–72. Nottingham: Apollos, 2008.

Williams, Rowan. "Barth on the Triune God." In *Wrestling with Angels: Conversations in Modern Theology*, edited by Mike Higton, 106–49. London: SCM, 2007.

———. "Barth, War and the State." In *Reckoning with Barth*, edited by Nigel Biggar, 170–90. Oxford: Mowbray, 1988.

Williams, Stephen N. "Appendix: Karl Barth on Election." In *The Election of Grace: A Riddle without a Resolution?*, 179–210. Grand Rapids: Eerdmans, 2015.

Wu, Kuo-An. "The Concept of History in the Theology of Karl Barth." PhD diss., University of Edinburgh, 2011.

Index

absoluteness (primary and secondary), 66
actualism, 20, 62, 103, 250
actualistic ontology, vii, ix, 2–5, 12–13, 20, 34–37, 38–41, 45–46, 48–49, 52–56, 60–66, 70–72, 74–75, 77–80, 83, 87, 90, 94–95, 98, 99n49, 103–4, 108–9, 117, 120n142, 121, 123–24, 126–27, 136, 143, 156n4, 172–73, 175, 181–82, 213–15, 222, 250, 304, 318–20
Adam, 92, 98, 129n10, 132,137n50, 138, 140, 154, 212, 234, 235n12, 236–44, 249, 250n83, 253n96, 254, 257, 259, 272, 300–302
ad extra 20, 52, 70, 73, 78–79, 99, 165, 167, 174n86, 175, 178, 213, 215
ad intra 30, 52, 70, 73, 78–79, 175, 177–78, 181, 213, 215
agency
  divine, 152–53, 155, 166–68, 174, 222, 274, 304, 310–11, 317
  human, 35, 93, 95, 102, 121–22, 141, 145, 274, 290, 292, 296, 304, 310–11
Alexis-Baker, Andy, 278–80
analogia attributionis, 304–6
analogia entis, 65, 290, 304–6, 307n146, 308
analogia fidei, 274, 290, 303, 305–8
analogia proportionis, 305
analogia relationis, 6, 274, 290, 303, 308–9
anhypostasis, 22–23, 90–91, 97
anti-Semitism, 256

Aquinas, Thomas, xiii, 3, 32n97, 39, 56–62, 67, 176n93, 259–63, 278, 300
Arminianism, 245, 300
ascension, 163, 220–21
aseity, 64n108, 288–89
atonement
  Aufgehoben/Annihilation of sin and the sinner, 198–99, 200, 203–4, 224
  actuality, 5, 183, 189, 191–92, 208
  cultic framework, 191n44, 204n101, 208–10
  event within the triune being, 184
  Judge judged in our place, 4, 97n41, 182n3, 184, 193–99, 206–7, 251, 264
  judicial framework 4–5, 182–83, 192–95, 197, 203, 204n101, 206–10, 231, 246, 251, 258, 271, 315
  obedience, vii, 5, 109, 182–84, 207, 211–15, 227, 231–33, 245–46, 251, 254, 257–58, 271–72, 315, 317
  "one and the many," 182, 207
  "pattern of exchange," 5, 183, 191–95, 199, 209–11, 227, 231
  penal substitutionary atonement, 200–3, 206
  plurality of approaches, 182
  Sache of the atonement, 207–9, 231
  theories, 207–8
Augustine, 56n78, 128, 130n16, 168–70, 175, 180, 243–44, 300, 301n122
autonomy, 227–79, 294–95, 303

being-in-act, being-in-becoming, being-in-eternal decision (God), 46–47, 49–52, 62–65, 66, 70–74, 82–83
being-in-action (human), 247–49, 291, 304, 308–9, 311
Berkouwer, G. C., 11, 218, 220n171, 226n210
Brunner, Emil, 81, 258n121

Calvin, John, 110n95, 111n103, 130n11, 138n53, 185, 187, 211, 212, 213, 223n193, 264n148, 269, 300, 301n121,122
categorical imperatives, 278–80
Chalcedon, 88n2,5, 102n65, 146n84, 151–52, 164, 311n158
Christology
    Alexandrian or Antiochian, 93–95
    Barth's "early" and "later" Christology, 87–88, 91, 97, 98, 103–4, 122, 125, 126, 143
    Cur Deus homo, 184, 195, 207
    "Jesus is victor," 193n48, 223n192, 225n204, 226, 227
    Logos and/or Spirit Christology, 152, 162–66, 317
    Quo iure Deus homo, 26, 184
church, 15n15, 54, 80n174, 90, 91n14, 102n65, 105, 128, 139n55, 147, 157, 161, 166n47, 172, 173, 177, 178, 182, 188, 226, 255, 265, 278n27, 284, 285, 286n58, 292
command (divine), 38, 290n70, 291–93, 298
command-obedience, 25, 38, 51–52, 54, 157n7, 171, 318
common actualization of the human and divine essences, 4, 46, 112, 115, 119–21, 124, 320, 321
communicatio gratiarum (the communication of graces), 92, 105, 112, 115, 116–19, 124, 135, 137, 161, 163, 268, 302, 304, 322
communicatio idiomatum (communication of idioms), 112, 113, 115
communicatio operationum (communication of operations), 3, 92, 101, 105, 112, 115, 119–21, 124, 320, 321
communio naturarum (the communion of natures), 105, 112–14
concursus Dei, 6, 274, 290, 293–96, 299, 304, 321
conversion, 111, 220, 235
correspondence (*Entsprechung*), 92, 112, 311, 313
Couenhoven, Jesse, 277, 287n62, 299, 300
covenant, 14, 16, 22, 50, 51, 60, 104–9, 123, 171, 187, 188, 190, 192, 199, 213, 221, 222, 227, 246n65, 255, 257, 288, 289n66, 291, 295, 297, 307, 309, 320
covenant-Lord, 105–8, 123–24, 257n117, 320
covenant-partner, 105–7, 109, 112, 123–24, 160, 163, 316, 320
Covenant Theology, 14–17
creation, 5, 6, 14, 19, 22, 37, 56, 57, 59, 66, 67, 75, 88, 99, 104, 105, 106, 149, 174, 199, 219, 220, 221, 222, 232, 233, 234n7, 235, 238n28, 239, 242, 243, 244, 246, 252, 257n119, 272, 274, 288, 292n79, 300, 301, 302, 305, 306, 307, 309, 310n154
Crisp, Oliver, 96n38, 129–31, 137, 138, 140, 143, 144n77, 145, 164n39, 166, 167, 187n24, 189n30, 224n195, 225, 226n205, 227n211
cross, 26, 123, 163, 184–86, 191n44, 199, 200–1, 211, 213, 214, 220, 222, 224, 227n211, 270, 316

decree (*decretum absolutum*), 19, 21, 53, 103, 186, 188–89, 223–24, 227n211
depravity, 130, 139
determinism, 274, 280–83, 300n119, 301n122, 317
discursive resistance, 285–86
disobedience, x, 5, 139n59, 154n104, 212, 232, 235–38, 239n31, 240, 241n42, 251–54, 255n111, 256–57, 271–72, 282, 292, 302

divine decision (*Entscheidung*), 20, 22n48, 23, 24, 44n29, 46, 48, 52, 62–65, 67, 70n135, 71–72, 81, 99, 102, 109, 121, 123, 145, 154, 172, 187, 188, 189, 218, 219n167, 223, 251, 289, 302, 308, 309, 316
divine freedom, viii, 3, 6, 62, 66–67, 69, 82, 90, 120n142, 215, 217, 273–74, 276, 282, 286–90, 393–9
divine knowing, 3, 62, 67–70
divine missions, 2, 3, 38, 39, 56, 59–62, 64, 77, 79, 181, 213, 215, 319
divine obedience, 273–74, 286–90, 303–9
divine perfections, 39, 202, 209, 210, 215–17, 254, 272, 288n62
divine processions, 2, 3, 31, 34, 36–39, 40, 47, 54, 56–57, 59–62, 64, 65, 76, 77, 79, 175, 177, 179, 181, 213–15, 221
divine willing, 69
"double structure" (God's being or God's extra-temporal eternity), 72, 73, 78, 79
dyothelitism, 4, 95, 127, 146–54, 174, 258, 259, 261, 268, 270, 271, 315, 317

economy of salvation, 5, 15, 27, 40, 42, 47, 56, 61, 87n1, 126, 175, 181, 213, 214, 232, 233, 234n7, 236, 238, 242, 243n50, 244n57, 245, 272, 320
election
    electing God, 3, 6, 13, 18, 19, 24, 48, 60, 70n134, 77, 98–100, 101, 102n58, 104, 106, 113, 121, 123, 124, 126, 172, 183, 186–88, 189, 190, 191n44, 192, 193n48, 194, 196, 197, 223, 257n117, 280, 291, 304, 319, 321
    elected man, 3, 18, 22n48, 100–1, 102n58, 103, 106, 113, 116, 121, 123, 124, 126, 183, 186, 188–89, 190, 191n44, 192, 193n48, 194, 204, 224, 257n117, 279, 280, 291, 304, 316, 321
    electing man who elects God, 3, 101, 102n58
    the elected and reprobate one, 186, 189, 190, 191n44, 223
Emery, Gilles, O.P., 56, 57n79, 58, 59, 60n94, 61n102
encounter (*Begegnung*), 102, 109n90, 123, 296–97, 316
enhypostasis, 22n53, 23, 90–91, 97
epistemology, 17, 135, 169n62, 180n112, 217, 224
essence (divine), 12, 26, 50, 56, 58, 61, 65, 113–15, 116, 119, 120, 159, 187, 216n155, 321
eternal "beginning," 14, 20–22, 37, 76, 79, 171, 187, 221, 251
eternal generation of the Son, 2, 24, 30–34, 51, 57
eternality, 3, 32n101, 41n15, 44, 46, 74, 75, 218, 250
eternity ("historicization" of), 218
ethics, 2, 6, 13n9, 27n78, 274, 276, 278, 279n31, 280n34, 290, 310n154

falsehood, 110n95, 252, 253
fellowship, 100, 120, 196, 302
fellowship (triune), 29, 76, 77n163, 99, 169, 171, 181
filial-paternity, 214, 319n9
filial receptivity, love, relation, 34, 35, 36, 176
filioque, 159n16, 177, 179
fittingness, 128, 132, 142, 158, 185n10, 232, 268n178
freedom (human)
    as gift, 277n18, n19, 283n44, 287n61, 288n63, n64, n65, 296–98
    compatibilist, 273, 274, 280–83, 287n62, 288n62, 298–303, 304, 317
    libertarian, 280, 281, 300, 301
    relation to human obedience, 273–74, 276, 277, 289, 290, 304, 305, 307, 313, 317

Garden of Gethsemane, 6, 146, 149, 207, 258, 261, 263, 264, 270, 274, 312, 313

Geschichte, 41, 102, 107–9, 123, 184, 316, 321
Gibson, David, 187
Giles, Kevin, 12, 28n83, 33n102
God *pro nobis*, 1, 5, 62, 80, 185, 186, 192, 193, 207, 209, 231, 257
gospel, x, 19, 227, 265, 279n27
grace, 14, 16, 19, 21, 41, 42, 49, 50, 51, 52n69, 60, 81n176, 97, 99, 100, 101, 105n76, 106, 107n83, 111, 113, 116–18, 123, 135–37, 161, 171, 185, 188n26, 189, 195, 214, 217, 219, 220n171, 222, 225n202, 226n210, 227n211, 241, 243, 247, 250n84, 275, 276, 279n27, 279n31, 289n66, 291, 292, 293, 294n90, 295, 297, 298, 300n119, 301n122, 302, 306, 307, 309, 312
Griswold, Daniel M., 74, 76, 77n167
guilt
  alien, 137, 142, 227n211
  original, 128–30, 137–38, 142, 154
Gunton, Colin, 1, 12, 19, 24, 78n168, 152n99, 153n103, 156, 157n6, 170n67, 283, 287

hamartiology, 25, 110n95, 137, 210, 252, 272
Hector, Kevin, 40n9, 289
heteronomy, 277–79, 303
history
"eternalization" of history, 218–19
evangelical history, 194
historia salutis, 219
"historicality" (of God), 73
Holmes, Christopher, xi, 24n63, 173nn76–78, 209n125, 216
Holy Spirit
  as "love," "charity," and "gift," 31, 57, 151n98, 157, 169–71, 175–78, 180–81
  as power of Jesus Christ, 117, 161–62, 163, 173, 317
  conceptus de Spiritu sancto, 158, 161, 163, 241
  "immanent" pneumatology, 157, 158, 168, 170, 172, 174
  in relation to Jesus' work of recapitulation, 237, 239–41
  pneuma anecclesion, 54, 172
  pneuma inecclesiandus, 54, 172
  "resolve" of the Spirit, 14, 171
  Spirit-Christ relation. See Christology, *Logos* and/or Spirit Christology.
  "Spirit of the Son," 165, 169, 173, 178
Horton, Michael, 213n142, 219–20
human nature (fallen), ix, 4, 92–93, 126, 127, 128–30, 132–34, 136, 137–38, 140–43, 154, 204, 247, 259, 316
human nature (corrupt)
  original corruption, 129, 139–40, 142, 316
  hereditary/inherited corruption, 129, 139–40, 142, 316
human nature (unfallen), 4, 126, 128–30, 316
humanity, x, 1, 13, 20, 41, 83, 91, 92, 96, 98, 103n66, 105, 111, 114n112, 128, 129n10, 132, 133, 138n51, 140, 141, 148n89, 154n104, 183, 186, 189, 191n44, 192, 203, 210, 211, 212, 215, 223, 224, 226, 227, 234, 238–41, 243–44, 246–51, 256, 260, 261, 270, 280, 286n58, 294, 296, 297, 302, 303, 308, 313n176, 316
humanity (of God), 92, 109n90, 115n122, 143
humility (God), 29, 33, 110, 112, 252
Hunsinger, George, 15n14, 20, 41–45, 55, 71n138, 76, 80n175, 81n175, 88n2, 94, 163n33, 164n35, 166n48, 169n62, 210n132, 218, 221, 226n207, 247n70, 249n80
hypostasis, 32n97, 90, 91, 140, 141, 143, 146n84, 150, 152, 157, 158, 163, 168, 170, 259, 263
hypostatic union, 36n114, 44, 112–15, 135, 164, 167, 302

imago Dei, 234, 249n81
immanence, 153n103, 305
immutability, 26, 49, 50, 289n66

impassibility, 49, 109n93
imputation, 138, 191n44, 194
incarnation, 2–4, 13, 22, 23, 26, 35, 38, 41, 47, 48, 50–52, 54, 75, 81, 87, 89, 90, 92–95, 97–99, 102, 111–14, 118–21, 127, 128, 133, 140, 141, 150, 152–55, 158, 159, 162n31, 163–68, 172–74, 181, 184n7, 204, 205n106, 212, 214, 220, 227, 231, 234, 236, 238, 239n31, 240–42, 249, 250, 254, 255, 257n119, 263, 268n178, 315, 316, 318, 319n9, 321
Irenaeus of Lyons, 5, 165, 232–45, 249–52, 254, 257, 259, 262, 272, 299, 300
Israel, 25, 26, 92, 132, 192, 254–57, 272

Jenson, Robert, 80n171, 156n1, 157n7, 181n117, 218
Jesus Christ
    as second Adam, 97, 142, 158n10, 212n135
    as the true human being, 243, 247, 249, 272, 316
    humanity, 22, 41, 47, 50, 80, 90–93, 95, 96, 106, 107, 112, 113, 117, 118, 121, 123, 124, 135–37, 149, 150, 153n103, 156, 161, 164, 178, 188, 201, 237, 249, 251, 308
    humility (Jesus Christ), 11, 25, 29, 31, 47, 50–52, 112, 118, 123, 173–74
    impeccability, 94, 126, 127, 130–32, 133–35, 137, 143–46, 154, 317
    sinlessness, 92–94, 97, 98, 117, 118, 129, 133–37, 140, 143–45, 154, 163, 207, 212, 263, 264, 317
    vere Deus, vere homo, 3, 88, 125, 316
Johnson, Adam, 110n95, 182, 206, 209, 210, 216n155, 223, 252–54
Johnson, Keith, 304–9
Jones, Paul D., xi, 18n22, 24, 33n102, 45, 47, 48, 54, 75, 88n5, 90n14, 91, 92, 93n27, 94, 95, 98, 99, 101n58, 102, 104n72, 108, 115, 116n123, 119, 121, 122, 145, 148n88, 171, 172n71, 174n85, 185, 186, 199n82, 210n131,

258n121, 263n145, 264n153, 265n157, 266, 267, 269n182, 270n184, 312n162, 313n176
judgment, Judge, 4, 26, 92, 97, 101, 103n67, 139n59, 141, 142, 154, 184, 190, 191n44, 193–200, 203, 206, 207, 209n123, 211, 212, 221, 225, 235, 237n22, 246, 251, 252, 256, 262, 264, 267, 269, 270, 290n70, 312, 316
justification, 220, 264
Jüngel, Eberhard, 3, 22, 23, 25n64, 39, 49n48, 70–74, 78, 79n169, 83, 91, 122n150, 311

Kane, Robert, 281, 282, 299–301, 303
Kant, Immanuel, 277–80
kenosis
    "Reformed Kenoticism," 49, 173

Langdon, Adrian, 74n152, 75, 76n157, 77
Lindsay, Mark, 256, 285, 286n56
Logos
    asarkos, 21, 37, 39, 40, 47, 51, 79–83, 94, 104, 172, 187, 250
    incarnatus, 11, 44n29
    incarnandus, 21, 37, 44n29, 51, 79, 80n171, 82, 83, 94, 187, 250
    ensarkos, 48, 81
Lord as servant, 3, 33, 104, 107, 110n95, 112, 150n96, 161, 184n7, 192, 193n48, 212, 213n142
love (divine), x, 14, 26, 31, 47, 57, 66, 71, 90, 98, 99, 105–7, 122, 151n98, 185, 204–6, 288

Maury, Pierre, 63
Maximus the Confessor, 4, 148–53, 259–63, 267–71
McCormack, Bruce, 12, 29n91, 45, 49–53, 60, 61, 63n106, 64n111, 67, 70n134, 71, 72n142, n143, 74, 79n171, 80, 81, 88n2, 91n15, 101n58, 112n104, 115n119, 116n123, 118n135, 120n142, 164n33, 168n57, 170n65, 173, 174, 188, 193, 194, 205, 206n108, 222n189, 225, 226n211

McFarland, Ian, 128, 129n5, n6, 132n25, 141, 142, 143n68, 260
McKenny, Gerald, 296–98
McMaken, Travis, 191–93, 194n54, 211
mediator, 21, 110n95, 117, 119n139, 166n48, 174, 187, 258n121
mercy (divine), 190, 200–2, 205, 215–17, 220n171, 227n212
metaphysics, 20, 33, 35n110, 48, 55, 61, 65, 80, 81, 87, 116n123, 120n142, 125, 126, 127, 135, 144, 147, 153, 155, 167, 193n48, 213, 220, 226n205, 231, 233, 268, 271, 317, 318n7
Migliore, Daniel, 163, 164n34, 311n158, 313n176
Minns, O.P., Denis, 234n6, 235n10, 236n13, n14, 237, 238, 240, 243, 244, 245n58, 252n88
modalism, 12n7, 15n14, 27, 28, 40
mode/s of being, 2, 15, 16, 23, 28–33, 35, 36, 42, 45, 49, 50–53, 70, 71, 75, 89, 90, 95, 97, 140, 168n57, 169–74, 178–81, 187, 214, 250, 318
Molnar, Paul, 39–41, 74
Moltmann, Jürgen, 151n98, 267n175
monothelitism, 4, 127, 146–55, 174, 315
munus triplex / threefold office, 110n95

nature (divine), 11, 26, 27, 31, 32, 34, 58n88, 89, 116, 130, 131, 143, 146, 152, 154, 174, 187, 317
necessity, 66, 74, 81, 82, 89, 120n142, 128, 132, 142, 184n7, 205n106, 216, 217, 225n202, 235n10, 240n40, 243n50, 260, 288, 289n66, 295
Neder, Adam, 36n114, 219
Nestorianism, 97, 152
New Testament, 11, 25, 27n78, 89, 92, 107, 131, 132, 141, 160, 162, 175, 203, 237, 255
Nimmo, Paul, 13n9, 20, 45, 53, 54n73, n74, 172, 173, 246, 290, 291, 294n87, n88, n90, n91, 295n98
non posse peccare. *See* Jesus Christ, impeccability.

"nothingness" (*das Nichtige*), 198, 199, 220n171, 244, 252, 253

obedience
  "antecedent obedience," 36, 41–45, 319
  as a causative and instrumental role in atonement, 211–13, 232, 271
  as providing material content for doctrine of the atonement, 5, 231, 232
  divine obedience, 2, 3, 6, 11–13, 14n10, 18n22, 24, 29, 30, 33, 34, 35n110, 36, 37, 38, 45, 46, 47, 49, 51, 52, 56, 87n1, 101, 214, 273, 274, 286, 289, 304, 309, 318–20, 322
  human obedience, 4, 6, 36n114, 93, 100, 118, 122, 124, 125, 150, 243, 249, 268n178, 272–74, 276, 304, 315–18, 320–22
  in relation to development theory of humankind, 233–35
  in relation to the eternal Son, 3, 11, 13, 14n10, 18, 24, 35n110, 37, 38, 39, 41, 44, 45, 49, 52, 87, 150, 168, 274, 289, 304, 309, 315, 318, 319, 322
  in relation to the Son of God, ix, 155, 254
  intra-Trinitarian obedience, 2, 4, 11, 12, 17, 31n95, 33, 34, 37–39, 41, 42, 44, 45, 156, 157, 168, 170, 171
  "Jesus Christ, the obedient one, obedient in our place," 210, 231, 232, 246, 271
  "narrative of obedience," 5, 232–34, 241–44, 246, 252, 254, 255, 272, 299
Old Testament, 105, 212, 255, 256
omnipotence, 32–34, 49n55, 68, 70n134, 120, 153n102, 174, 198, 287
opus internum ad extra, 20
"order of being," 13, 177
"order of knowing," 13
ordo salutis, 219–20

original sin, 128–30, 137–39, 316
Owen, John, 157, 164–68, 174, 213n144, 224

"pattern of exchange," 5, 183, 191–93, 194n54, 195, 199, 209–11, 227, 231
pactum salutis, 14–17, 213
parousia, 220
personality, 15, 43, 96n37
posse peccare et non pecarre. See Jesus Christ, sinlessness.
postlapsarian, 126, 132, 154
post-Reformation orthodoxy, 128, 187n24
prayer
    as petition, 310, 312
    as invocation, 310–14
    in relation to obedience, x, 6, 7, 147, 151n98, 257, 258, 266–71, 274, 298, 309–14
    Jesus as prayer and pray-er, 312
predestination, 60n97, 101n56, 223n193, 225n63
predestination (double), 190, 191, 224
"pre-existent" God-man, 2, 34–37
prelapsarian, 126, 142
prelapsarian (will), 301–3
pride, 110n95, 138, 139n55, 252, 253
primal decision (*Urentscheidung*), 71, 218, 219n167
primal history (*Urgeschichte*), 22, 108, 123, 124, 218, 221, 243, 320
prolepsis, proleptic, 2, 24, 34, 44–46, 53, 54, 75, 87, 123, 156n4, 173, 250
Przywara, Erich, 304n132, 305, 306, 307n146
punishment, 200, 201, 203, 204, 206, 243

Rae, Murray, ix–x, 79n170, 226n210
recapitulation, 97, 132, 236–39, 254, 257
receptivity (eternal), 34, 35, 50, 51, 173, 174
reconciliation, ix, 1, 24–26, 28, 80, 103, 105, 107, 110, 121, 157, 160n22, 161, 166n48, 182–84, 206–9, 212, 220n171, 223, 224, 251, 254, 264, 283, 284n46, 285, 286, 310n154, 315, 317, 319
Reeves, Michael, 242, 243, 249n82, 250, 251n86
Reformation, 128
Reformed Theology, 190, 205, 220
relations of origin, 32, 58, 177, 179, 180, 318
representation, 201n91, 204n101
Resch, Dustin, 141, 159
resurrection, 48, 103n67, 121, 191n44, 212, 220–22, 276
righteousness, 69, 101, 200–2, 204, 205, 207, 211, 215–17, 244, 258, 264, 270
Rosato, Philip J., 156, 161n22, 165, 166n47
Roy, O.P., Louis, 277n21, 278, 279
royal man, 112, 122, 161, 162

sanctification, 92, 159, 220
satisfaction, 74n150, 99n49, 200, 203–6, 212
Schleiermacher, Friedrich, 63n106, 166n48, 190n36, 258n121
"self-determination (divine)," 1, 3–5, 12, 19, 20, 24, 47, 48, 53, 54, 61, 66, 67, 71–73, 75, 78, 83, 95, 98, 100, 101, 109, 112, 121, 123–26, 152, 173, 186, 189, 191, 218, 287, 288, 319, 321
"self-forming actions," 282, 300
Servant as Lord, 3, 112, 192
sin, 4, 47, 93, 94, 97, 110, 112, 126–45, 154, 159, 185, 191, 196–201, 203–6, 210, 212, 220, 224, 227n211, 233n3, 236, 237n22, 239, 243, 244n57, 252–57, 260, 262, 263, 266–70, 272, 275, 276, 282, 287, 299n116, 301n121, 303, 315–17
sloth, 110, 252, 253
Söhngen, Gottlieb, 305–7
sovereignty (divine), 99, 232, 293, 295, 309, 321
status duplex, 110, 111, 123
subject of incarnation, 89, 92–95, 97, 98, 113, 114, 163, 166, 167, 174, 316

346 INDEX

subordinationism, 12, 27n83, 28, 29, 33n102, 40
substitution, 4, 5, 142, 154, 183, 189n31, 191, 195n62, 200–4, 206–11, 212n135, 219, 227, 231, 265, 312, 313
Sumner, Darren, 18n22, 29n91, 45, 46, 75, 82, 88n2, n3, 89n6, 91n14, 102n65, 103n69, 104n72, 107, 109n93, 114n112, 116n123, 137, 142n67, 144
supralapsarianism, 105

temporality (pre-, supra-, post-), 34, 44, 52, 60, 74–79, 83, 108, 109, 146, 169n64, 173, 185, 188, 221, 250n85, 251
temptation/s, 94, 131, 133, 134, 144, 147, 207, 237, 258n121, 263–65, 268, 270, 272
theonomy, 277–79, 294, 303
Thompson, John, 22
time, 2, 3, 5, 14, 20–23, 30, 32n101, 39, 41–44, 51, 53, 54, 74–81, 83, 103n66, 106, 107, 111, 118, 120, 125, 153n103, 169, 172–74, 183, 185–87, 191, 192, 194, 198, 199n82, 210, 211, 215, 218–22, 236–38, 241, 242, 243n50, 249, 250, 264, 265, 270, 318, 321
Torrance, Thomas F., 15n14, 39, 40, 128n5, 176n93, 212, 213
Trinity
  Opera Trinitatis ad extra sunt indivisa, 165, 167, 174n86
  perichoresis, perichoretic, 75–78, 176–80, 221
Trinity-election debate, 3, 55, 74, 219, 289n66

ultimate responsibility, 282, 300
union (personal). *See* hypostatic union.
universalism, 222–27

Vanhoozer, Kevin, 186, 200n83
Virgin birth, 158, 159
virtue, 134, 262n140, 296, 297
volition, 2, 16n19, 17, 18, 23, 24, 35n109, n110, 36, 37, 42–44, 103, 127, 144–47, 150, 151, 154, 155, 198, 235, 236, 241, 244, 245, 248, 260, 261n137, 268, 288n62, 299, 302, 303, 315, 320, 322
voluntas ut natura / voluntas ut ratio, 260, 261
von Balthasar, Hans Urs, 89n8, 164n33, 292n79, 307n146

Waldrop, Charles, 93–96
Webster, John, 15n12, 16n18, 19, 22n53, 24n63, 78n168, 88n2, 89n6, 139n59, 153n103, 189, 213, 246n64
Weinandy, Thomas, 129n5, 175–81
White, Thomas Joseph, O.P., 31–36, 43n24, 55n77, 60
will (divine), x, 4, 23, 31, 33, 35, 43, 46, 82, 118, 127, 136, 148–53, 174, 187, 268–70, 317, 320
will (human), 4, 23, 46, 87, 95, 118, 120, 127, 141, 147–53, 259, 261, 263, 268, 271, 317, 318
Williams, Garry, 200, 215–17, 220n172, 224, 225n203
Williams, Rowan, 11, 12n4, 33n102, 168n57, 284n48
Williams, Stephen, 64, 65n113, n114
Word, The, 11, 21, 57, 81, 82, 89, 90, 92, 93, 96n37, 102, 104, 115, 130, 132, 148, 153n103, 158, 163, 169, 184n7, 234, 239, 241, 243n50, 248, 249, 255, 263, 286, 294, 317
wrath, 26, 100n52, 141, 142, 189, 195n61, 201–6, 256, 269, 270, 316